AMERICAN PISTOL & REVOLVER DESIGN AND PERFORMANCE

L. R. Wallack

Winchester Press

Library of Congress Cataloging in Publication Data

Wallack, Louis Robert, 1919–
    American pistol & revolver design and performance.
    Includes index.
    1. Pistols, American. I. Title.
TS537.W34   683'.43'0973   77-20219
ISBN 0-87691-255-2

Winchester Press
1421 South Sheridan Road
P. O. Box 1260
Tulsa, Oklahoma 74101

  2 3 4 5 6 7 8 9 88 87 86 85 84 83 82 81

Printed in the United States of America

DEDICATION

To the Bill of Rights

The first ten amendments to the Constitution, known as "A Bill of Rights," were adopted by the first Congress, called to meet in New York City, March 4, 1789. They were later ratified by the various States, and on December 15, 1791, were made a part of the Constitution.

Amendment I

Freedom of Religion, Speech, and the Press;
Right of Assembly and Petition

CONGRESS shall make no law respecting an establishment of religion, or prohibiting the free exercise thereof; or abridging the freedom of speech, or of the press, or the right of the people peaceably to assemble, and to petition the government for a redress of grievances.

Amendment II

Right to Keep and Bear Arms

A well regulated militia, being necessary to the security of a free state, the right of the people to keep and bear arms shall not be infringed.

Amendment III

Quartering of Soldiers

No soldier shall in time of peace be quartered in any house without the consent of the owner, nor in time of war, but in a manner to be prescribed by law.

Amendment IV

Regulation of Right of Search and Seizure

The right of the people to be secure in their persons, houses, papers, and effects, against unreasonable searches and seizures, shall not be violated, and no warrants shall issue but upon probable cause, supported by oath or affirmation, and particularly describing the place to be searched and the persons or things to be seized.

Amendment V

Protection for Persons and Their Property

No person shall be held to answer for a capital or otherwise infamous crime, unless on a presentment or indictment of a grand jury, except in cases arising in the land or naval forces, or in the militia, when in actual service in time of war or public danger; nor shall any person be subject for the same offense to be twice put in jeopardy of life or limb; nor shall be compelled in any criminal case to be a witness against himself, nor be deprived of life, liberty, or property, without due process of law; nor shall private property be taken for public use, without just compensation.

Amendment VI

Rights of Persons Accused of Crime

In all criminal prosecutions, the accused shall enjoy the right to a speedy and public trial by an impartial jury of the State and district wherein the crime shall have been committed, which district shall have been previously ascertained by law, and to be informed of the nature and cause of the accusation; to be confronted with the witnesses against him; to have compulsory process for obtaining witnesses in his favor, and to have the assistance of counsel for his defense.

Amendment VII

Right of Trial by Jury in Suits at Common Law

In suits at common law, where the value in controversy shall exceed twenty dollars, the right of trial by jury shall be preserved, and no fact tried by a jury shall be otherwise re-examined in any court of the United States, than according to the rules of the common law.

Amendment VIII

Protection Against Excessive Bail and Punishments

Excessive bail shall not be required, nor excessive fines imposed, nor cruel and unusual punishments inflicted.

Amendment IX

Constitution Does Not List All Individual Rights

The enumeration in the Constitution of certain rights shall not be construed to deny or disparage others retained by the people.

Amendment X

Powers Reserved to the States and the People

The powers not delegated to the United States by the Constitution, nor prohibited by it to the States, are reserved to the States respectively, or to the people.

CONTENTS

Part I—The Handgun   1

ONE   Basic Handguns   3

TWO   Manually operated Breech
            Actions   11

THREE   Semiautomatic Breech Actions   31

FOUR   Breech-Action Locking Systems   43

FIVE   Feeding Systems   49

SIX   Extraction and Ejection   55

SEVEN   Firing Systems   61

EIGHT   The Gun Barrel   71

NINE   Handgun Grips   81

TEN   Sights   87

ELEVEN   Blackpowder Guns and
            Other Miscellany   97

Part II—Ammunition and Ballistics   103

TWELVE   Ammunition   105

THIRTEEN   Calibers   111

FOURTEEN   Cases and Primers   127

FIFTEEN   Propellants   133

SIXTEEN   Bullet Design, Construction,
                and Behavior   141

SEVENTEEN   The Bullet's Flight   149

EIGHTEEN   Barrel Length and
                Velocity   169

NINETEEN   Handloading   177

TWENTY   Whims, Engraving, and
                Accessories   181

TWENTY-ONE   Accuracy   191

TWENTY-TWO   Uses   203

TWENTY-THREE Experiences and
                Opinions   211

TWENTY-FOUR   Law Enforcement   219

Index   229

INTRODUCTION

M ost people tend to think of firearms as simple objects, something you simply stuff with ammunition and then bang away with at a target. Guns, however, are enormously more complicated than that; indeed, an amazing amount of work has gone into their design and development—work by many of the best engineering minds in the world over many long years of study. And this applies to any firearm from giant naval artillery to pistols and revolvers. These last terms refer to firearms that can be easily carried and are designed to be fired with one hand, thus the term "handgun," which includes them both.

The most important book covering handguns is *Textbook of Pistols and Revolvers* by J. S. Hatcher (Small Arms Technical Publishing Co., 1935). The late Julian Hatcher was a graduate of Annapolis, became a Major General in the U.S. Army Ordnance Department, and served as Chief of Field Service during World War II. He later was technical editor of *The American Rifleman* at a time when I was on the technical staff of that magazine. Hatcher was one of the foremost firearms authorities of his time. But although his book is a classic, it is also out of date. Many of the principles governing handgun design and performance remain the same, but there has been vast progress since 1935 in the arms industry. Methods have changed; tools have changed; and there have been a number of inventive geniuses at work.

This book seeks to update those principles and also to explain, in simple langauge, how today's guns work—why they operate as they do and how the various action systems function. This information should help the reader become a better shooter. By knowing what happens and why, if something goes wrong the informed shooter will be better able to understand and cope with the problem.

Today's revolver principles may not have changed much from the original Colt of 1836, yet they have been improved and modernized substantially. Many of these changes are recent and there are more changes coming. This book is intended to be a basic book that will tell the story of those changes. It is intended to last for a long time. There will be new developments after it is printed because men will continue to seek new solutions to old problems. And they will find them. And the impact of such men will have a profound impact on the gun world. In less than 30 years—a relatively short time span in the gun business—Bill Ruger, who cofounded Sturm, Ruger & Co., Inc. in 1949, has made a stunning impact on the handgun world—and has also become an important producer of rifles and shotguns. He will have more impact, and there will be others.

L. R. Wallack
November 1977

PART ONE

THE HANDGUN

CHAPTER ONE

BASIC HANDGUNS

Firearms were widely used in Europe for two centuries or more before the invention of printing. The records of early gun developments are confused or lost, and a good deal of conjecture must be applied to the early history of firearms development. The story of this development is the story of man's development, augmented by the inventions or discoveries of propellants, ignition systems, metals, projectiles, and mechanics.

The first guns were very crude affairs, and the early one-hand gun was simply a smaller gun made for greater portability. The same is true of today's sophisticated handguns. Handgun operational systems followed those used for shoulder guns of the day, from the muzzleloading types ignited by a match, to flint ignition, to percussion ignition, and finally to the modern cartridge as we know it today.

It is most unfortunate that, even today, so many publications are so loose with gun "facts"; many readers are led astray. While this applies primarily to errors in newspapers and "general" magazines (which really ought to know better), it is even more regrettable that it also applies to publications dealing chiefly with guns and outdoor sports (which have no business at all making such mistakes). The result is that one tends to place little faith in the "history of firearms" as it is written. Some history, however, is of both interest and importance.

Cylinder revolvers were first made in America by Colt in 1836 and are still used. Early revolvers were muzzleloaders, often with a bullet-seating ram fastened to and slung underneath the barrel. The shooter held the gun muzzle up, poured a charge of powder into each of the charge holes in the cylinder, slipped a bullet into place, and seated it firmly by the ram. The same operation was performed for each charge hole in turn. Then a percussion cap was placed over each of the percussion nipples located at the rear end of the charge holes and connected to the powder charge by a tiny hole called a flash hole. The cylinder revolver was then ready to fire six times without reloading.

Colt's invention was a good one. The rotating cylinder is still a foolproof method of operation. The gun's mechanism rotates the cylinder a sixth of a turn and locks it in place each time the hammer is cocked to bring a fresh cartridge under the firing pin (or a fifth of a turn for a five-shot revolver, etc.).

Breechloading firearms were developed and perfected over a span of years extending from about the 1830s to the present. The development of "fixed" ammunition—that is, a cartridge case containing its own primer, powder, and bullet in a single unit—could not proceed without guns in which to fire them. As a result, these improvements had to be parallel developments.

Next to Colt's invention of the revolver, probably the most important single advance in the world of handguns was an invention by Rollin White in the early 1850s. He bored cylinder

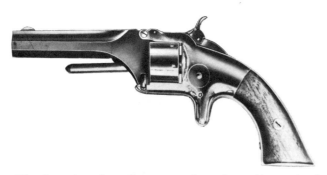

The first American firearm made to fire self-contained ammunition, the Smith & Wesson Number One model introduced in 1856 for the .22 Short. The company purchased the Rollin White patent for cylinder holes bored clear through, a necessity for self-contained cartridges. During the 17-year life of the patent, Smith & Wesson was able to achieve a dominant market position.

charge holes clear through the cylinder so that metallic cartridges could be seated from the rear just as we do today. White patented his invention and sold it to the new firm of Smith & Wesson. These two partners had just developed the .22 Short rimfire cartridge, the first really successful metallic cartridge. Interestingly, the .22 Short today is practically identical with the original, except for some changes in technology as the years have gone by.

With possession of the Rollin White patent, Smith & Wesson manufactured the majority of the handguns sold. During the seventeen-year life of this patent, Smith & Wesson established its reputation as the leading handgun producer.

Further development and perfection of the revolver has continued, but there have been no significant changes in the basic design. The single remaining major development was the double-action revolver in the mid-1800s, so called because the gun can be fired either by simply pulling the trigger for each shot or by cocking the hammer each time in the familiar "single-action" style.

Over the years there have been many other operational systems, such as the Deringer, a tiny one- or two-shot gun meant for quick action across the card table, and the "pepperbox," a strange-looking gun indeed. The pepperbox resembles a small revolver which appears to have no barrel but, rather, a long cylinder. In this gun, the cylinder is also the barrel—as many as six or nine or more of them. Some pepperboxes had rotating cylinders, others had a rotating firing pin which moved from barrel to barrel as the hammer cocked and the gun fired. The world of handguns has seen thousands of strange designs, but not many of them have been successful and only a few have lasted.

The firearms industry during the U.S. industrial revolution was one of the basic forces motivating industrial progress. The other basic industry at this time was the textile-machinery industry. These two spurred development of machine tools and production systems. For example, Eli Whitney, who, as every schoolboy knows, invented the cotton gin, was primarily an arms manufacturer. Though credited today with the cotton gin and not much else, Whitney was the first to develop, manufacture, and produce devices with part interchangeability, certainly a far more important contribution than the gin, important as it was.

Autoloading guns are usually called "automatics." The term is inaccurate, because only a machine gun is truly automatic: It continues to fire as long as the trigger is depressed and ammunition is kept supplied. An autoloading gun is one that performs every operation, except firing, by utilizing energy the gun develops. Put another way, you merely pull the trigger to fire each shot. However, the word "automatic" is in such general use that it has become acceptable for describing autoloading guns.

The story of early multifiring guns extends surprisingly far back in history. One design—the inventor is unknown—supposedly dates from 1664. However, the first commercially successful autoloading pistol was developed by a Connecticut Yankee named Hugo Borchardt, who had to go to Germany to provoke interest in his invention. It is better known today as the German Luger (or Parabellum) pistol. Another of the great early autos was the Mauser, perfected and made in Germany; according to DWM (Deutsche Waffen und Munitionsfabriken), much of the engineering credit belongs to the same Hugo Borchardt.

Auto pistols operate on either *recoil* or *blowback* principles. I will discuss a little later how and why these work. John Browning, an American, acknowledged by almost all serious arms students to be the greatest gun inventor who ever lived, introduced his first pistol in 1895. Browning's pistols were first manufactured by the FN (Fabrique Nationale) plant in Liège, Belgium. Some still are. John Browning also developed every auto pistol made by Colt, in addition to nearly every successful gun and rifle made by Winchester during that period and many made by Remington. The long list of successful Browning inventions includes machine guns, machine cannon, and machine rifles such as the famous BAR, which stands for Browning Automatic Rifle. Perhaps the most famous pistol ever made was the 1911 Browning or, as it's more commonly called, the Colt .45 Auto. It was adopted in 1911 by the U.S. Army and is still used. This has probably been the best pistol ever made, considering the purposes for which it was designed

and its long and excellent service record since 1911.

The history of firearms is an exciting study. Many gun collectors take an avid interest in older guns, their use and history. Collecting old guns can also be financially rewarding, since many guns appreciate in value over the years. Some individual handguns—and this is especially true of early Colt revolvers—are worth more than $10,000. On the other hand, many old guns are worth little; arms collecting requires quite a bit of knowledge. But if you know your guns and invest wisely, collecting can be financially rewarding as well as an interesting hobby.

Wars have always stimulated small-arms development, which has usually also benefited the civilian shooter, although we appear to have now reached the point where further military developments in small arms will be of little value in sporting gundom. For example, in World War II the basic infantrymen of all major armies employed semiautomatic rifles almost exclusively, and semiautomatic sporting guns are very popular today. But current millitary-arms development is concentrated on rapid-fire automatic weapons and does not appear to have much sporting application. The American Civil War resulted in a tremendous breakthrough, because it began with muzzleloaders and ended with breechloading rifles. That statement is somewhat oversimplified, as Civil War buffs will understand, but it is basically true.

DESIGN ACCORDING TO USE

A simple example will help explain how the use of firearms dictates their design. This is a very old example, but the same principle is as true today as it was in colonial days. The German and Palatine Swiss gunsmiths settled in two colonial areas; one was in Pennsylvania, near Lancaster, and the other was near Palatine Bridge, New York. These gunsmiths brought their Jaeger rifles to the colonies, but the Jaeger was a heavy rifle, too cumbersome for use on the American frontier. Over a period of time, the Jaeger underwent drastic changes, doubtless as frontiersmen came back from such places as Kentucky and complained about excess weight and so forth. What eventually emerged was the long, slim, and handsome small-caliber Kentucky rifle. Some people still think it should be called the Pennsylvania rifle because it was made there. But it's called the Kentucky because that's where it was used; the use dictated not only the design but also the name.

Some years later, when the frontier moved west of the Mississippi and St. Louis was the jumping-off place, other gunsmiths moved to St. Louis. Game in the West was different from game in the East. Instead of deer, black bears, an occasional panther, and Indians, the Western explorer had to contend with buffalo, grizzly bears, elk, and, some said, even more hostile Indians. Moreover, the Western hunter, or "mountain man," used a horse. The Kentucky rifle wasn't the gun for the West, and again there began a gradual evolution dictated by use. The rifle became much shorter so it would be handier on horseback, the stock much thicker so it wouldn't break in a fall with a horse, and the caliber much heavier because the game was meaner, bigger, and tougher. Thus was developed the plains rifle. Some think it uglier than the Kentucky, but I've always felt it was just as handsome. It was developed to do a job, and it filled an important niche in our Western history from the early 1800s until the breech loaders replaced it in the years after the Civil War.

The same kind of evolution took place with handguns. Early American sailors carried monstrous "horse pistols"; they used them in boarding parties (and in preventing boarding parties on their own ships) and on shore leave on occasion. On the other hand, the traveler of colonial days often carried a small pistol which could be concealed in his coat or cloak and was much handier for self-defense.

Military use also dictated the development of handgun types and calibers too. The handgun is primarily a defensive weapon (I use the word "weapon" only in the law-enforcement and military context) and, as such, is meant to be employed at close range. It is also meant to *stop* an assailant bent on killing you. As warfare has changed, so has the handgun, although the handgun is not a primary weapon and consequently has not required the developmental attention that has been lavished on such offensive weaponry as rifles, machine guns, and submachine guns.

THE SEVEN STEPS OF OPERATION

Every gun, no matter what its type or method of operation, goes through seven steps of operation for every shot that it fires. This is true with everything from a single-shot firearm to the most modern machine gun. And a thorough understanding of these basics is essential to an understanding of how and why any gun works—or doesn't work. The steps do not necessarily come in the same order, and in some cases two or more of them occur at the same time. But in every gun they all must be performed.

In a single-shot, for example, these steps work in the exact order given and each step is performed manually. In an autoloading system, every one of the steps is performed by the gun's energy except pulling the trigger. And in a true automatic system such as that of a machine gun, even that is done automatically. In a revolver, the order changes significantly; we'll get into these changes when we come to a thorough explanation of revolvers.

Again, the important thing to remember is that every single one of the following steps *must be performed for every shot fired* with any firearm using self-contained cartridges.

1. Firing: Pulling the trigger releases a mechanism, either a hammer or firing pin under spring tension, that strikes the primer of the cartridge in the barrel's chamber. The primer is activated by the blow and ignites the powder charge, which, in turn, generates propellant gas to drive the bullet or shot charge down the barrel.

2. Unlocking: The breech pressure required to drive a bullet must be contained until that bullet has left the bore. It is obvious that the magnitude of gas pressure we're talking about must move only the bullet, and it should be equally obvious that to open the breech prematurely would allow gas under pressure to flow into the action, with disastrous results. Consequently, the breech must be locked securely against this high pressure. Before any of the following steps can take place, the action must be unlocked. Unlocking is always performed by the very first part of the movement of the operating parts.

During unlocking, another event, completely automatic in modern handguns, occurs which is called "primary extraction." In firing, the high pressure developed forces the cartridge case tightly against the chamber walls. The precise amount of loosening required depends upon several factors, including the amount of pressure, the smoothness of chamber walls, and the condition of the cartridge case. Before this empty case can be withdrawn it must be loosened from the chamber. This is accomplished by mechanical leverage during the very first part of the unlocking process.

3. **Extraction:** The withdrawal of the fired, or empty, cartridge from the chamber is called extraction. It is usually performed by a hook on the breech bolt which pulls the empty out as the bolt is withdrawn from the barrel.

4. **Ejection:** This is the removal of the empty case from the gun. Note the difference between extraction and ejection; the words are often confused, but the distinction is important to an understanding of operating systems. Ejection is generally performed at the end of the rearward stroke of the breechbolt when the empty is flipped out of the gun.

5. **Cocking:** The firing-mechanism spring is cocked to store energy; it is drawn back and holds back either the hammer or the firing pin. It is held back itself by the trigger or by a small part connected with the trigger.

6. **Feeding:** A fresh, unfired cartridge is moved from the magazine into the chamber of the barrel ready for firing. In a single-shot firearm, feeding is manually performed by simply placing the new cartridge directly into the chamber with the fingers.

7. **Locking:** The reverse of unlocking, locking holds the breech block securely against the gas pressure generated during firing. Firearms are locked in many ways, as we shall see. As a safety feature, most guns will not fire until they are fully and securely locked.

That's what every firearm must do to shoot— and shoot again. A successful gun must perform every one of these steps logically, simply, and with as few parts as possible, and it must be able to perform every one of them thousands of times without failure.

TYPES OF HANDGUNS

We can now break down the guns we're going to talk about into two groups: those that are manually operated and those that are semiautomatic (or autoloading).

The principal manually operated handgun types in common use today are single-shots and revolvers. Those of semiautomatic types are operated either by short recoil or blowback.

Subsequent chapters cover each type of action in detail. Keep in mind the seven steps as you note how the different systems handle each of the steps.

Handguns can also be categorized by their use, and this is a natural and convenient way to discuss them. The major types are target, service, sport, defense, and military.

Target guns come in many varieties, all the way from simple, relatively inexpensive revolvers and auto pistols with precise adjustable sights to the fine free pistols used in Olympic and International Shooting Union (ISU) events, which can cost close to $1,000. These latter guns are single-shot masterpieces of perfection with set triggers and a lock time so fast as to be almost unimaginable.

Basically, a target gun is often defined as simply any gun that is fitted with adjustable sights. There are specific rules and regulations that apply to guns used in most American target events, which include those for .22, .38, and .45 caliber.

Handguns for "service" use are those commonly used by law-enforcement officers. The best-known example is the Smith & Wesson "military and police" Model 10—a .38 Special revolver with fixed sights and 4-inch barrel. Another is the .45 Colt autoloading pistol that has been the U.S. military sidearm since 1911. And there's a trend today toward the 9mm pistol as a popular service sidearm. Any gun for service use should meet certain qualifications; these are discussed later on, because the subject gets quite complicated and is not without emotion, as occasional flaps about expanding bullets suggest.

Any pistol or revolver in the "sport" category

is much more difficult to classify, simply because sporting use covers a wide range of subjects—some real, some imagined, and some pretty unique. Big-game hunting is one sporting use for the handgun that has a few devotees, but ought not to be encouraged except by the genuine expert shot. Varmint shooting is another sporting use that would appeal only to the excellent marksman, usually using a scope. Aside from these uses, most so-called sporting use is more or less confined to target shooting, either the formal kind or plinking. Plinking can best be defined as shooting at any object that's not a live target. Target shooting itself is also in the sport category by simple definition.

Many fishermen and campers like to carry a sidearm to deal with snakes. At the same time it can offer added recreation by providing some target shooting while in camp. The sidearms usually used for this purpose are in .22 or .38 caliber. Recently developed shot cartridges are ideal for snakes, which are a difficult target for the handgunner; solid bullets can ricochet, especially if the handgunner is a fisherman on a river. Needless to add, there are legal complications to this use, and you should thoroughly explore these before toting a gun on your hip no matter how innocent your plans.

Defense use of the handgun actually covers the whole range of handguns, because you can defend yourself with an Olympic pistol just as you can with a short-barreled belly gun. The usual gun for home defense is more apt to be a .22 or .38 Special than anything else, and nothing much is required in the way of fancy sighting equipment. Nor is a great amount of power required, since the range is generally short; a .22 Long Rifle is perfectly adequate.

The best choice of a gun for defense is probably the same as one for service use, since such a gun is handy and powerful. Undercover law-enforcement officers have a different defense requirement, in that their sidearm must be as small as possible while maintaining its potency. Hiding a powerful .44 Magnum revolver under a summer-weight suit is out of the question, so considerable compromise is necessary. The usual undercover choice is made by the individual officer, and considerable latitude is found.

The current popularity of black-powder guns, chiefly of muzzleloading types, points up another type of gun in wide use for sport and target shooting. Aside from the method of loading and the propellant (black powder), these guns fit under the broad heading of sporting handguns.

Sporting handguns have been given broader application in recent years because of the introduction of such guns as the single-shot Thompson/Center pistol, which is made in a seemingly limitless range of chamberings. A highly accurate gun, the T/C when suitably fitted with a scope has the power in several chamberings to bang a deer for the pot—or a grouse for that matter—by the simple expedient of changing barrels.

Despite the widening of sporting-handgun uses, it is important to note that only the skilled should use a handgun for difficult shots. Considerable discretion and common sense—not to mention practice—are necessary.

HANDGUN MAKERS

Changes in the pistol and revolver scene have been very dramatic over the past few years, chiefly in terms of the number of firms manufacturing guns. Before World War II, the market was dominated entirely by Colt, Smith & Wesson, Harrington & Richardson, Iver Johnson, and Hi-Standard (now "High Standard"). It is generally acknowledged that Colt and Smith & Wesson in those days were at the high-quality end of the scene while H&R and Iver Johnson were producers of lower-priced guns. The Hi-Standard was an out-and-out copy of the Colt Woodsman .22 auto pistol. However, Harrington & Richardson also manufactured a fine target .22 single-shot pistol known as the USRA model (for United States Revolver Association). This gun was widely used and highly regarded.

My favorite pre-World War II reference book is a 1940 Stoeger catalog which also lists the old Stevens Off-Hand single-shot pistol and the Marbles Game Getter, an 18-inch-barreled combination of .22 and .410 shot barrels with a folding skeleton stock. These guns are now off the market.

In the imported-gun section of this old Stoeger catalog, guns bearing the names of

Walther, Luger, Mauser, Webley, and Stoeger are listed. The Webley is a British revolver and includes the Webley-Fosbery automatic revolver, a unique piece indeed. The Stoeger guns are all single-shot target models of the type known as free pistols, used in International and Olympic matches.

The expansion of the handgun industry began very slowly. The first to break loose was Hi-Standard when A. W. "Gus" Swebilius formed that company. Swebilius had formerly worked for Marlin, where he redesigned the Marlin-Rockwell machine gun during World War I.

Consider too, when you think about the proliferation of today's pistols and revolvers, that shortly after World War II Colt stopped production of its Single Action Army revolver. That was the famous Model P, which first appeared in 1873, but sales did not warrant keeping it in the line any longer.

Today it is impossible to keep track of the U.S. makers of handguns, let alone the foreign makers that import guns. Just when you think you have them all located, a couple of new ones pop up. But it didn't come about quite so easily. Some fine guns appeared only to die a quick death in the market. Today these are collectors' items.

At some times over the past hundred years the lion's share of the market has been held by Colt, at other times by Smith & Wesson. Various changes in management, philosophy, and market conditions dictated most of those changes in market share. The major market for handguns has long been law-enforcement agencies and offices (and the military, but that's a separate type of market); they buy thousands upon thousands of revolvers every year. When you consider the number of cities and towns in America and begin to realize the vast number of police, to say nothing of guards and other security occupations that require the use of a sidearm, you begin to get an appreciation for this market. As a spokesman at Smith & Wesson said to me some years ago, "I don't know what retiring cops do with their revolvers, but they take them with them." (Many forces issue only a badge and make the officers buy their own equipment, including the revolver.)

I think the big break in the handgun business came when Bill Ruger first started production in the old railroad station in Southport, Conn. Bill Ruger's first gun was the "standard" model .22 auto which is still in the line. It was a fine gun, competitively priced, and it deserved a place in the market. But Ruger's timing was the thing that really got him going. Whether that was luck or whether he had some sense of what was about to happen, we don't know. But succeed he did with a fine business that's built on fine products.

The newcomers are showing the older companies a thing or two in terms of gun design, production techniques, and marketing. One of the problems that the older giants have which is not shared by their fresh, new competition is that they are part of conglomerates. Smith & Wesson is owned by Bangor Punta, a conglomerate based on old Cuban sugar holdings, and Colt is owned by a group now called Colt Industries but known as Fairbanks Morse at one time; the parent company raided the old Colt holdings in Hartford when the gun company was first purchased. Today Smith & Wesson has gotten itself into a political hassle, which is unfortunate. Colt is staggering, and the best-known name in the world of handguns is a long way from the company it once was.

The new companies—Sturm, Ruger is a shining example—have none of the old traditions to circumvent. They don't do things a certain way because they've always done them that way. Instead, they can innovate and create and churn up new ground that nobody has before. As a result, the world of handguns is changing, and changing fast. I have deep respect for the old makers like Colt and Smith & Wesson, but I have some advice for them too: They d better take a new look at the old ways of doing things, because the competition is surpassing them in design and marketing.

CHAPTER TWO

MANUALLY OPERATED BREECH ACTIONS

Manually operated breech-action pistols and revolvers are of several designs, the most notable and important of which is the revolver. We will examine this interesting action in detail because of its importance and because of its significant departures from any other gun design.

There is at least one bolt-action pistol, the Remington Fire Ball (sometimes spelled "Fireball"; Remington has spelled it both ways). Interestingly (and confusingly), federal law permits manufacture of this pistol but will not allow anyone to *remanufacture* a pistol from a rifle originally made with the same action. Remington has made several models of rifle with this action.

Then there are a variety of single-shot pistols, such as the popular Thompson/Center and the current Navy Arms replica of the old Remington rolling-block.

Despite the progress in gun design there are a few derringers and pepperboxes being manufactured today. The term "derringer" needs some clarification, for there was a man named Henry Deringer (with one *r*), a Philadelphia gunsmith who made excellent pocket pistols employing a "back-action" lock which made the gun more compact than his competition because the part of the action holding the spring was in back—hence the name.

Deringer operated shortly after the invention of the percussion cap and was among the first to employ this ignition system. A fine workman, Deringer turned out exceptionally well-made products and had many competitors who copied his designs. For one reason or another those who copied called their product a derringer, which became the generic word for any similar product not made by Henry Deringer. A few years ago I had the opportunity of meeting an army colonel named Deringer, a direct descendant of the Henry Deringer from Philadelphia. Henry Deringer's chief claims to fame were that he produced a well-made pistol and that one of his pistols was used one night in the old Ford Theater in Washington by John Wilkes Booth.

One of the more famous derringers was the Remington, a small over/under-barreled, two-shot affair in .41 rimfire caliber. According to the curator of Remington's museum, Mr. L. K. Goodstal, it was spelled "Deringer" in the 1877 catalog and "Derringer" in 1908. This gun was quite popular; it remained in the line from 1866

Open and closed positions of Remington's .41-caliber rimfire derringer. This was a very popular sidearm for many years but is now off the market.

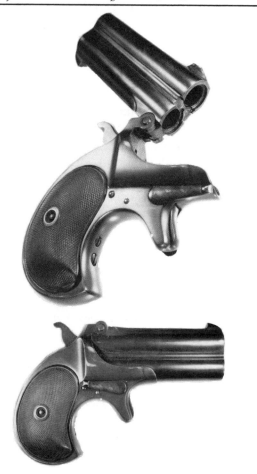

to 1935, which is a long period. There have been several replicas of this old gun that came out in recent years.

Pepperboxes are the reverse of a revolver: The cylinder is actually the barrel. Put another way, if you eliminated the revolver barrel and extended the cylinder to barrel length, you would have a pepperbox. That's oversimplified but essentially accurate. Pepperboxes had from two to four or more barrels. Sometimes the barrels were stationary and an arrangement was made to rotate the firing pin from barrel to barrel. The pepperbox remains a curio, one of the older, less efficient ways to produce a multifiring gun, but some are again being made.

THE DEVELOPMENT OF THE REVOLVER

In the early 1830s, so the story goes, a young cabin boy named Sam Colt got the idea for a revolving cylinder while watching the ship's wheel. During the remainder of that voyage, he whittled his idea into wood and, in 1836, started the Colt's Patent Fire Arms Co. in Paterson, N. J.

That was the beginning of the revolver, much as we know it today, although there were many multifiring devices built around a system of revolving barrels as early as the 1500s. The word "revolver" refers to a revolving cylinder, usually holding from five to nine cartridges in separate chambers (called "charge holes"). One charge hole at a time is lined up with the barrel. After firing, the cylinder is revolved one-sixth of a turn (in the case of a six-shooter) and another charge hole is brought into alignment.

Today's revolver is remarkably similar to Sam Colt's original. Colt's original was what we now call a "single-action" revolver, which means that the hammer must be cocked by hand each time the gun is to be fired. Colt's first gun, of course, was a muzzleloader; it fired by the percussion-cap ignition which had recently been invented.

The first cartridge revolver was the Smith & Wesson No. 1, a small revolver made for a cartridge virtually identical with today's .22 Short. We'll discuss the ammunition development later in this book; it was S&W that introduced it in America. At the same time, Smith & Wesson also bought out the Rollin White patent, which covered boring the charge holes in a cylinder clear through. That wasn't necessary for muzzle-loaders—it was undesirable, in fact—but it was an absolute necessity for cartridge revolvers. As a result of this patent, which was jealously guarded in continual patent-infringement actions, Smith & Wesson had a stranglehold on the market and vaulted into a strong market position. As soon as the patent expired in 1869, dozens of manufacturers began making cartridge revolvers similar to the popular S&W types.

The double-action revolver can be fired either by pulling the hammer back like a single-action, or simply by pulling the trigger each time it is to be fired. When the gun is fired single-action-style, the trigger moves back as the hammer is cocked and the resultant trigger pull is usually very short and crisp. When fired double-action, however, the trigger pull is very long, since it must push the hammer back all the way, rotate the cylinder, and finally allow the hammer to fall. In use, the double-action is usually fired single-action-style for target shooting and double-action-style for fast shooting.

While the double-action is considered much more modern and up to date, it was actually invented by Joseph Rider in 1859 while in the employ of Remington. This is the same J. Rider who invented the Remington-Rider rolling-block action. So the double-action, today's most modern revolver, is only twenty-three years younger than the single-action!

The revolver principle was sound, in both single- and double-action styles, which is why it has lasted so many years.

Colt's famous Model 1873, or Peacemaker, which has always been called the Model P at the Colt factory, was first produced in 1873. Because of lack of orders, it was dropped in 1940. That was before World War II, when Colt was still making firearms for the civilian market. There simply was almost no call for the old Model P, so it was quietly retired.

Following the war, however, Bill Ruger came along and formed Sturm, Ruger & Co. with a unique, popular .22 auto pistol. When he had that model off and running, Ruger turned his attention to the single-action revolver, because he had a hunch it would become a best seller. At

The first double-action revolver. A Remington, invented by Joseph Rider in 1859, the gun was marketed from 1860 to 1888. These were used during the Civil War as pocket revolvers, and about 100,000 were manufactured. The caliber was .31.

about the same time, TV became popular, the TV Western rode into American living rooms, and that old masculine symbol the single-action revolver was there as big as life. Ruger met that demand and the rest is history. Colt got the old Model P back in production again, and a couple of dozen other manufacturers have climbed on the wagon.

Another interesting modern phenomenon is the interest in black-powder guns, revolvers as well as rifles. Colt (having learned its lesson with the Model P) produced replicas of certain famous relics from its past glory days of percussion revolvers (but dropped them again in 1977), and a host of other makers are producing handguns for black-powder shooters. The gun world is moving forward, it's true, but in many respects it's going backward as well.

For many years the biggest demand for the double-action revolver was in law enforcement. There are a lot of cops in America, and they all carry a revolver. So do guards at industrial plants, various private detectives, bank messengers, and others in the business of moving valuable goods. That's a whopping market. In addition there has always been a vast export market for American revolvers (usually for police forces in other countries) and a military market.

And there has always been a civilian demand for revolvers—for defense and for sport, both thoroughly legal and constitutional purposes. The civilian market for handguns of all types has grown by leaps and bounds in the years since World War II.

Top: The famous old Colt Single Action Army Peace-maker or Model P as it has always been known at the Colt plant. Introduced in 1873, this is the oldest fire-arm still in production, although it was out of produc-tion for several years in the '40s and '50s. Center: His-tory tells us that Ned Buntline, the originator of the dime novel, ordered a small number of extra-long-bar-reled Colt revolvers, which he gave to certain Western friends, including Wyatt Earp and others. This has led to the manufacture of such as this contemporary Colt Buntline Special. Bottom: Known as a "top break" re-volver, this little Harrington & Richardson opens by lifting the little piece you see with lines just above the hammer. Raising this unlocks the gun, and the bar-rel then tips down as do a double shotgun's. The lower-ing extracts and ejects the cartridges. The system was widely used on a vast number of heavy-calibered Smith & Wesson revolvers during the latter 1800s. Harrington & Richardson has been making guns since 1871, and today's line includes a wide variety of inexpensive small revolvers like this.

At right is a starter's pistol, used at track meets to fire blank cartridges and constructed so that a live car-tridge cannot be chambered or fired. As you see, the barrel is solid, the cylinder is very short, and the pencil-pointed piece extending from the rear of the barrel simply ensures that the blank blast will be diverted harmlessly. This particular model is made by Harring-ton & Richardson.

Until very recently, the double-action market was pretty much controlled by Smith & Wesson and Colt. That was especially true with the law-enforcement market. Harrington & Richardson has been making revolvers since 1871 and has always been a factor in this market, though far smaller than the big two. But today others are challenging the position of S&W and Colt in law enforcement.

Dan Wesson, who toiled for Smith & Wesson (he's one of *those* Wessons) for thirty years, left to start his own company. Charter Arms started manufacture in Bridgeport, Conn. High Standard departed from its ".22s only" tradition. And now Sturm, Ruger has entered the same field with a fine double-action service revolver. Add a few interesting imports and you have a vastly different ball game than what we had a few years ago. These companies are all after that law-enforcement and defense market.

STAINLESS-STEEL HANDGUNS

In the 1960s, Smith & Wesson startled the gun world by manufacturing and marketing a stainless-steel revolver. Their first was the little 2-inch-barreled Chief's Special, Model 60. As far as I know, I was the first outsider to have one of these to shoot and test. After I shot it awhile I buried the little gun, uncleaned, in our rose garden in the fall. Next spring I dug it up, washing it off with the garden hose, and shot it some more. I never did clean that gun.

Ever since, the proliferation of stainless handguns has been something to see. The advantages are many, but the chief one is that they won't rust appreciably, and that means you don't have to clean them; you can get them soaking wet, even in salt water, with no worries, and they'll take all the abuse you can give them.

When I say stainless-steel revolvers, I mean just that. The only parts of these guns that aren't stainless steel are the wood grips, and sometimes the sights, which are blackened steel just because they provide better sighting.

Stainless is a very difficult steel to machine. To use an oversimplification, stainless is "stringy tough," and the more stainless it is (by addition of certain alloys) the harder it is to machine. Depending on the exact alloy, there are as many kinds of stainless steel as there are kinds of plants or insects. Stainless also costs more to buy in raw material form, so you'll pay a little more for the ST handgun. The big disadvantage to ST is that it's hard to blue; bluing is a process of controlled rusting, so you can't blue it by any conventional means. There are ways to "blue" a stainless-steel rifle barrel, and this is performed with most such barrels. But the handgun makers have chosen to apply a brushed finish, which dulls the surface considerably. As far as I can see, there's no reason to do it any other way. A handgun is not a game gun except in an emergency; otherwise, it's generally kept holstered until ready to use, so there's little reason to worry about alerting game when the sun hits the shiny metal.

For the record, the Germans were using a type of stainless, or rustless, steel way back in the '30s on sporting rifles, and they were bluing them. At that time there wasn't a great deal of interest in the material, because it really wasn't needed. But today, with the hot magnum cartridges like the .264 Winchester and 7mm Remington, stainless adds greatly to barrel life. For many years, Winchester used stainless in its .220 Swift varmint barrels, and these were extremely good-shooting rifles.

THE SEVEN STEPS

Our seven steps of operation go every which way in a revolver, and there is some difference between single- and double-action guns. But let's see how these work, in principle, which will help us understand what follows.

First, we must establish slightly different meanings for our terms. So let's keep that in mind too as we go along and we'll cover both single- and double-actions at the same time.

1. Firing is the same, simple step as it is in any other gun.

2. Unlocking in a revolver is caused by the very first movement of the hammer (single-action) or trigger (double-action) when it draws down the small cylinder bolt from engagement in one of the cylinder notches. There is a notch for each charge hole in the cylinder; this small lock holds the cylinder in place lined up with the barrel. (Of course, the revolver is also "locked" when the cylinder is swung into place in a double-action and pinned in place in the single-action gun. Thus the term "lock" is differently used for revolvers than it is for most other guns.)

3 & 4. Extraction and ejection are accomplished by poking each empty out of its charge hole by the ejector rod through the loading gate in a single action. All the cartridges in a double-action are extracted and ejected at once by swinging the cylinder out and pushing the ejector rod. This is usually done after the entire cylinder has been fired.

5. Cocking in the single-action is performed by pulling back the hammer. In the double-action, it's accomplished either by pulling back the hammer or by pulling the trigger.

6. Feeding is accomplished by rotating the cylinder one notch, and that action is performed during cocking by means of a part called the "hand," which engages a ratchet on the cylinder's rear surface that simply shoves the cylinder around a sixth of a turn (in a six-shot revolver).

7. Locking is accomplished by that small lock-

Closeup view of a Colt revolver cylinder showing the notches which the lock engages to align each charge hole with the barrel. The lock is located directly above the trigger.

ing bolt that snaps up into the notch when the new charge hold is lined up.

As you can see, the definitions are different. The workings of a revolver are somewhat complicated, largely because of refinements developed over nearly 150 years of manufacturing handguns with revolving cylinders. Just the same, improvements are still being made.

There has to be a great degree of precision in a fine revolver. The whole world is made up of tolerances, and no part can be made absolutely perfectly; there must be some tolerance in every part. Manufacture must be held within those tolerances. If you have a string of five parts all of which interact and all of which have a tolerance of, let's say, plus or minus .005 inch, it's possible for all five parts to be made to either the maximum — or the minimum — tolerance, which means a difference of nearly $\frac{1}{32}$ inch. This could clearly be too much in many cases.

With that example in mind, let's look at some of the things that must be done to a revolver to get every charge hole in alignment with the barrel. You can visualize how important that is, because the bullet has to jump from the cylinder into the barrel under high pressure. The barrel had better be there when the bullet jumps. That alignment depends upon the barrel; the threaded hole in the frame into which the barrel is screwed; the cylinder's axis pin and the holes in the frame and the cylinder for this pin; the charge holes and their placement in the cylinder; the cylinder stop (the little lock that holds the cylinder in place) and its seating in the frame plus its timing so it engages properly during rotation; the notches in the cylinder; and the hand that rotates the cylinder.

Thinking about that for a moment will give you a lot of respect for the manufacturers that can make such parts to close enough tolerances for everything to work. You can also now appreciate why, in a cheap revolver, it's rare that more than one charge hole delivers good accuracy. In a fine revolver, on the other hand, you usually find that all six charge holes deliver the same accuracy. This is an excellent way to test a revolver's quality (assuming you are a good enough shot to make a fair test).

Formerly, such manufacturing precision was a credit to individual workmanship. Today, it's a

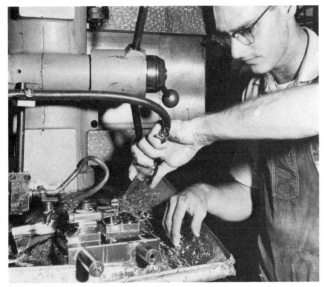 

Two views of machining operations at Smith & Wesson. A milling machine is "profiling" the complete outside edge of a K-size frame, and two cylinder blanks (visible in the two chucks) are being "faced" and also getting their center holes bored. This operation ensures proper alignment of center hole and face, the dimensions from which all other operations will be located.

credit to the sophistication of machine tools and other refinements in manufacturing.

SINGLE-ACTION DESIGN

In the latter 1800s there were two popular methods of making single-action revolvers. Smith & Wesson's system was a top-breaking revolver which was locked closed by a small latch where the frame and cylinder met (the piece running along the top of a revolver's cylinder is called the top strap). To open the revolver it was merely necessary to lift this latch and push the barrel down in a motion very like opening a double shotgun. When the barrel was moved down the extractor-ejector was activated and all empty cartridges were removed at once. Fresh cartridges were dropped into the charge holes and the gun was snapped shut.

The Colt system was different, and since that's the one that has survived, it's more familiar. Colt's barrel remains in position; loading and unloading are accomplished by means of a loading gate on the right side of the frame. Opening the gate gives access to a charge hole when it is lined up, and placing the hammer at half-cock allows the cylinder to rotate freely. To eject you simply rotate the cylinder till an empty cartridge is in alignment, then poke it out by means of the ejector rod lying alongside the barrel in its tube. You do this for each of the six charge holes, then reload by dropping new cartridges in, one at a time, as the holes are lined up with the loading gate. Then the gate is snapped shut.

Extensive trials of both systems were made by the U.S. Cavalry during the days of Indian warfare in the West. Each system had its devotees, but from reading history it's my opinion that Colt sold harder because he cared more—and needed the orders more. Smith & Wesson had curried the Russians and was filling huge orders for the Czar for a top-break revolver such as we have just described, chambered for a big, fat cartridge called the .44 Russian. The .44 American was virtually a duplicate of the Russian model, but lost out to the Colt for the U.S. Army. Both were superb revolvers for their time and both actually were quite popular.

The proper way to use a single-action revolver is to cock the hammer deliberately and squeeze

 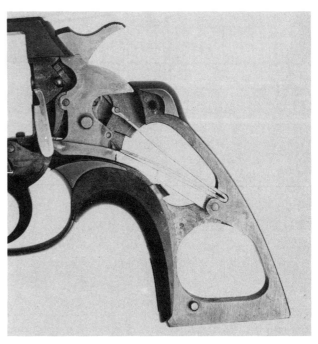

A rather ancient Colt revolver (rimfire) in my collection shown cocked and with hammer down. In the cocked position, note that the tip of the trigger (barely visible behind the "hand," which rotates the cylinder) is in contact with the hammer. In the hammer-down position, note that the same trigger tip rests under the "strut" and, if fired double-action, the trigger will lift the hammer via its strut until the strut slips off the trigger. Note too that a rubber grip adaptor is fitted and that it's held in place by the grips.

the trigger when you fire it. A single-action revolver may be "fanned," which is certainly more popular in old movies and on TV shows than it ever was for real. Fanning consists of holding the trigger back, then rapidly driving the hammer back with the heel of your left hand. This will fire the gun very rapidly—just as fast as you can hit the hammer. But the method is at once unsafe, inaccurate, and pretty stupid.

When the hammer falls on a single-action, the cylinder has been locked in position. That prevents turning of the cylinder, but since the gun has been fired the cylinder cannot turn for another reason (in Colt and some other brands, but not in all makes): the nose of the firing pin is buried in the primer of the fired cartridge. The very first part of the hammer retraction pulls the firing pin's nose out of the primer, and it also moves the cylinder stop out of its position in the notch. Once these two movements have taken place, the cylinder is free to rotate, which is caused by the "hand" coming in contact with the ratchet. When the hammer is nearly at full-cock

position, all the way back, it releases the cylinder stop, which is now free to snap up under spring tension into place in one of the cylinder notches. Now the new cartridge is in alignment with the barrel and the gun is ready to be fired once again.

If a single-action has any real advantages over the double-action, I'm at a loss to say what they might be. It is a little less costly to make, and I suspect that might be the only real point in its favor. Single-actions point better, some say, but that's a matter of opinion. Basically single- and double-actions are chambered for the same cartridges, so that's a wash. Single-actions are much slower to unload and reload. Older single-action models also had a great tendency to shake their screws loose and you had to constantly tighten them. This has been rectified in modern production by using screws with small filter plugs or one of the popular sealants (like Loctite). When you get right down to basics, there isn't any real reason for the single-action to have survived this long. But there s a lot more to guns than solid objectivity; the single-action revolver is a masculine symbol and it's bound to be around for a long time to come.

DOUBLE-ACTION DESIGN

Some say the hump at the top of the grip on a double-action revolver helps them get a better grip. That's not why it's there, though; its purpose is to house the more complicated mechanism, because a double-action fires with either single or double action, and an awful lot happens inside those sideplates. Actually, that hump does help. I've got a pair of Ruger single-action .44 Magnums—the early Blackhawk (now no longer made in .44) and the Super Blackhawk. I've also got the big .44 Smith & Wesson double-action. While I'm not going to tell you it's any fun to fire any of these with full loads, it is more pleasant to shoot the S&W, and I think one of the reasons is that hump. The Rugers tend to slip down in your hand a little more, and the back of the hammer can hit the web in your hand between your thumb and forefinger. That hurts. Another advantage in the S&W is that the grip is checkered, which helps greatly in preventing the gun from slipping during recoil.

One of the major differences between a double- and a single-action gun is that the double-action contains a part called the hammer strut. This strut functions only during double-action firing. A rather long tail on the rear end of the trigger engages the hammer strut, and it pushes the hammer back as you make the long trigger pull. After cylinder rotation (basically the same as on a single-action) and relocking, the trigger slips out from under the strut, allowing the hammer to fly forward and fire the gun.

If you hand-cock a double-action revolver, as you would a single-action, this strut is completely inoperative; it simply gets bypassed. And that is the major departure in the internal working of the two systems, vastly oversimplified.

Loading the double-action is, of course, also quite different. In the first place, only an idiot (or movie actor) snaps the cylinder in and out. To open the cylinder, you push, pull, or press (depending on the make) the cylinder thumb latch, which frees the cylinder to swing out. Now you push the cylinder out with the hand, very

gently. After reloading you push it back in very gently. Snapping the cylinder in or out invites serious damage, since it rotates on an axis with a very small stop. The mechanical advantage here is most powerful, and if you flip out the cylinder TV-style you'll surely spring the yoke and crane and soon ruin a perfectly good revolver.

DOUBLE-ACTION MAKERS

As we mentioned earlier, there are now a number of double-action revolvers on the market. We're going to examine some of them in more detail because some of the newer guns are quite interesting. For at least the past twenty-five or thirty years, Smith & Wesson double-action revolvers have held the dominant position in the market, so we'll first look at this old favorite.

SMITH & WESSON
This fine old company—it's been in business since 1852—catalogs more models of revolvers than anyone else in the world, and it manufactures more than anyone else. But this hasn't always been so. At one period between the wars, S&W couldn't have bought a bag of beans at a local store without paying cash. Then a man named Carl Hellstrom took over as president, and he turned the company around. Hellstrom built a new plant, bought new machinery, and made the old company an efficient producer. When he died, management fell to Bill Gunn, who expanded the company's business. S&W has been in the enviable position of being back-ordered ever since World War II!

One of the reasons is that S&W has been the most innovative of the handgun manufacturers, and the company has always produced products that were second to none in the industry. It pioneered new cartridges such as the .357, .44, and .41 Magnums (the word "Magnum" is a Smith & Wesson copyright for handgun use). And they fiddled temporarily with a couple of losers like the .22 Jet and .256 Magnum.

The basic S&W revolver hasn't changed much; it is made on three basic frames depending on the size and power of the cartridges. The big N frame belongs to the Magnum group: .44, .41, and some .357 models plus the .45 target revolver. The medium-sized frame is known as the

Smith & Wesson revolver in cocked position and with hammer down. Note that when the hammer is uncocked a hammer block is in its upper position and prevents the hammer from making contact with the cartridge. In the cocked position, this block is lowered, allowing the gun to fire. This is one of the older designs but one of the finest in the whole world of gundom. Note that the hammer spring employs a stirrup, which tends to accelerate the hammer blow as it moves forward.

K and is found on a variety of models from .22 through .357 Magnum calibers. The J frame is the smallest and is used from .22 through .38 Special in smaller guns.

COLT

The Colt double-action revolver closely resembles the S&W with some exceptions. The heaviest chambering in today's line is the .357 Magnum (.45 Colt in single-action). Colt cylinders revolve to the right, S&W cylinders to the left. The Colt cylinder latch is pulled back, the S&W latch is pushed forward. Colt rifling is to the left, S&W rifling to the right. These are all minor differences that don't mean a thing.

For years the Colt ejector rod hung out in midair, while the S&W has been shrouded for as long as I can remember. But today the Colt line is also equipped with shrouds to protect the ejector rod on all but two models.

DAN WESSON

As reported elsewhere in this book, Dan Wesson is a descendant of one of the founders of Smith & Wesson. He left to form his own company a few years ago and is currently producing a revolver in .357 Magnum caliber (all .357 guns shoot .38 Special cartridges too) that is remarkably different from the conventional guns that Dan grew up with.

This is unquestionably the most versatile revolver on today's market, for it comes with a choice of barrel length (2½, 4, 6, or 8 inches), in heavy and standard-weight barrel styles, and with plain or ventilated rib. The barrel interchange feature is quite simple and is worth exploring.

The barrels themselves are very small in diameter and fit inside a housing which is what resembles the whole barrel on a conventional revolver. Each Dan Wesson barrel is threaded at both ends and is of a length to fit the desired outer shroud. To install a barrel you screw the thin barrel directly into the frame, placing a shim between the barrel and cylinder to provide the correct clearance between these parts. Then you slip the shroud into place and install the front nut on the barrel and tighten it. Remove the

One of the most interesting features of the Dan Wesson revolver is its barrel-change system. Note that the barrel is screwed in place and that the shroud can be slipped over the barrel and ejector rod. Then the little nut you see at the right is screwed home tightly with the special wrench provided and you are ready to shoot. You can replace this 2-inch barrel with an 8-inch barrel in the time it took you to read this caption. It's hard to see in the photo, but there is a feeler gauge between the cylinder and barrel in place to maintain the proper gap.

shim and you're in business. This shim measures .006 inch, which is the correct spacing between these two parts for reliable functioning. The whole job is done in just about the length of time it takes you to read this.

Wesson also supplies several different grips, and a grip blank which fits the revolver but which you can shape as you want. This is quite a package, and one of its best features is that the buyer, whether sportsman or police officer, can have several guns in one with the interchangeable features.

Some criticism has been leveled at the Dan Wesson revolver because of the location of its cylinder latch at the forward end of the cylinder. To the normal shooter this does appear unhandy and awkward, but there's a lot more to the story, and this modern system has a whopping advantage: It provides a much stronger lockup.

Cylinders are locked into the frame by a small pin, usually at the rear end of the cylinder in conventional revolvers. Smith & Wesson has, for years, also locked the front end at the very tip of the ejector rod with a similar smaller button that snaps into the rod. Colt, until recently, has simply locked its cylinders with a rear button.

At one time Smith & Wesson produced a fine revolver which was called the "triple lock." It had an extra lock at the front end of the cylinder. It was later determined that this third lock was unnecessary and it was dropped; models with this feature are now valuable collector pieces.

But—and this is interesting—you can take al-most any revolver and move the front of the cylinder slightly back and forth. Not very much, but it doesn't have to move much to be a factor. The Dan Wesson is locked more tightly by virtue of its latch at the front, right where the charge hole and barrel align.

As to the charge that the Dan Wesson latch location is awkward, Fred Hills, who works for the Dan Wesson company, is a combat shooter and he described his method of reloading (which must be done in an instant) to me. He grabs the gun by its top in his right hand, uses the middle finger to open the latch, and pushes the cylinder open with his thumb. The ejector rod can then be pushed back to extract and eject all the fired cartridges, and the left hand, which meantime has extracted a speed loader from the belt, slips in the six fresh cartridges. The action is closed and he's back shooting. I suspect this takes a little practice, but it sounds logical, and I'm sure Fred Hills can reload as fast or faster than his competitors. Since the opening of a cylinder is a two-hand operation with most other shooters, I fail to see the latch position as a detriment and suspect the stronger lockup more than makes up for any awkwardness an individual shooter feels it causes.

RUGER

The Ruger Security Six, Speed-Six, and Police Service-Six revolvers are of quite conservative design, especially when compared with the Dan Wesson. While the Ruger models outwardly re-

One of Ruger's biggest contributions to double-action revolvers has been ease of disassembly. You can take this revolver down, just as you see it here, with only one tool: a small screwdriver to remove the grips! Formerly, one had to remove the sideplate to have access to other parts, and most people never did know how to properly remove a sideplate without damaging it, or the screws, or both.

semble both S&W and Colt models, the resemblance doesn't go much beyond that, for Ruger, in his customary way, has totally redesigned these guns.

In my opinion Ruger's simple takedown is the outstanding single feature of his design. It's been traditional that a revolver has been one of the toughest guns of all to take apart and get back together without messing things up by burring screw heads, damaging sideplates or their fit to the frame, and any one of a dozen other things once you get inside. But Ruger has uncomplicated this. The only tool you need is a screwdriver to remove the grips, and then everything comes apart neatly and in compact units so it is virtually impossible to screw anything up. There also is no sideplate to contend with, and the whole trigger and trigger guard come out as a unit. Simple and quite wonderful. Moreover, the instruction sheet is easy to follow.

HIGH STANDARD
This old firm has gone through several changes in the past few years. It has moved from Hamden, Conn., to East Hartford, and it has completely dropped long-gun production and developed an interesting new revolver for heavy calibers. According to the company, the new revolver will be made in two frame sizes, one for .357 and a larger one for .44 Magnum and .45 Colt. The gun has not been issued as this book is written, but it appears likely it will be manufactured on schedule (late 1977 introduction).

There are a number of innovations this re-

volver design can boast. One of the interesting features, though by no means among the most significant, is the square shank (like the Dan Wesson) to which grips are attached. These two guns deserve high praise for this design, which does not restrict grip shape in any way and allows any conceivable configuration of grip.

The most unusual thing about the new High Standard, however, is that the internal mechanism works on a gear segment system in which the teeth are always in contact. There is no transfer bar or other method of blocking the hammer as is now found in many other modern revolvers. Instead, the High Standard accomplishes the safety feature by using an eccentric. It works this way: when not operative, the hammer is allowed to rise approximately $1/8$ inch, which effectively prevents the firing pin from contacting the cartridge. When the trigger is engaged, the hammer drops this $1/8$ inch and assumes a new arc which will permit firing. And during double-action firing, the cocking leverages are ever changing, producing an easier trigger pull.

The company claims elimination of a transfer bar maximizes the hammer blow because it is a direct blow. This is technically correct, although I have no way of measuring how much of the hammer's blow is wasted by first impacting the transfer bar (which, in turn, hits the firing pin). There's no question it is a factor and that a direct blow is a superior method. However, this is not the only modern revolver that does not use a transfer bar; others employ designs that accomplish the same end but by means different from the new High Standard method.

High Standard also has incorporated an optional safety in the cylinder latch which requires two fingers to put in the ON position but can be instantly released by a sweep of the thumb. This is not the first safety on a revolver but will be the only one on a modern revolver to my knowledge. Its value, however, is debatable and I'm glad it's optional. There is no need for a mechanical safety on a revolver as there is on an auto pistol.

As this book is written, High Standard is contemplating the manufacture of a new revolver called the Crusader which has a number of interesting, different features. Chief among these is that hammer and trigger are connected by a gear arrangement. Another significant feature is that when you begin the trigger pull, the hammer is lowered ⅛ inch by an eccentric which then aligns its face with the firing pin. When the trigger is at rest, as shown, the hammer nose is too high to strike the pin, but rests against the frame. High Standard claims this feature delivers a more positive blow, and they are technically correct.

ADVANTAGES AND DISADVANTAGES OF REVOLVERS

One of the most important things to remember about a fine revolver is that it's a very difficult gun to take apart (with the exceptions already noted). You should not attempt to disassemble a fine double-action revolver unless it has been manufactured so that it can be. A gun of the S&W or Colt type, with a removable sideplate, ought to be left alone unless you know exactly what you're doing. The way to remove a sideplate properly is, after first removing the screws, to softly tap the frame next to the sideplate with a wooden or plastic screwdriver handle. Under no circumstances should it be pried off.

Remember too that screwdrivers have ruined more guns than shooting, neglect, rusting, or whatever else. You can destroy a $10,000 shotgun in half a second with a screwdriver, and you should never forget that.

Handguns cannot handle cartridges as powerful as those used in rifles. The .44 Magnum certainly is as heavy as most anyone wants to go in a handgun cartridge, and it's also amply powerful for any use to which a handgun should be put. There's nothing but your hand to absorb the recoil, and that's the limiting factor. While a few people have had handguns custom-made for such cartridges as the .45/70, this serves to prove only that there are some strange folks around who want to be different.

Another reason you can't use rifle-type cartridges is that there are definite limits to the cylinder's ability to hold pressures. You cut six holes in a cylinder and there isn't much wall thickness left.

Location of the small notch for the cylinder bolt is something that has had recent attention. Several revolver manufacturers place this notch in the center of a charge hole. This greatly reduces the wall thickness at that particular spot, and one sometimes sees a tiny dimple here when examining the charge holes. A recent trend is to place this notch off to the side enough so it doesn't weaken the sidewall of the cylinder. This is a wise move.

A revolver is normally considered safer than an autoloading pistol. I think this is arguable, but it is widely accepted as true. You can get a revolver into action faster than most autos (but not the relatively recent "double-action" autoloaders). The revolver is also less prone to jam than an auto. A failure to fire in a double-action revolver only means you must pull the trigger again.

You can use more loading flexibility in a revolver than in an auto. Autos are made to function with cartridges that develop a certain power or pressure. One for the .22 Long Rifle, for instance, won't work with the .22 Short. The revolver has no such restrictions. For example, you can fire .38 Specials in the .357 Magnum revolver (but not the other way around). Some .22 revolvers are sold with an extra cylinder for the .22 WMR (Winchester Magnum Rimfire), and you can shoot either standard .22 Long Rifle or .22 WMR cartridges as long as the correct cylinder is in place.

There are some who claim the revolver is outmoded and that it ought to be dropped in favor of the autoloading pistol. Their chief reason for making that statement seems to be only that the revolver has been around a long, long time. This is an argument that can't be supported, and one of the reasons is that revolvers handle far more powerful cartridges than the autoloader. The .41 and .44 Magnum revolver is a case in point. Either can flatten any North American game animal—and that firepower can't be built into an auto gun.

On the other hand, once your six shots are fired it's a long, cold period while you reload. With an auto you can simply insert a new magazine and away you go. A case could be made for the fact that you deserve to be in trouble if it takes more than six shots.

Either way, this argument will never be settled—but I very much doubt the modern double-action revolver is going to be phased out at any time in the foreseeable future.

A NEW SAFETY FEATURE FOR REVOLVERS

What's new about this one is that it's now being employed on just about every decent revolver made. But the original idea goes way back to the 1890s when Iver Johnson introduced it, and it has been employed in many double-action revolvers ever since.

The single-action revolver was another thing entirely, though, and it was always considered by anyone in the know that the only really safe way to carry any single-action handgun was with the hammer all the way down on an empty charge hole. This meant making a five-shot revolver out of a sixgun, but that was much better than boring a hole in your own leg, which happened quite a few times.

Bill Ruger went to work on the single-action revolver and, in 1973, introduced his new model single-action with essentially the same sort of safety device.

Briefly, it works like this. The firing pin cannot be contacted by the hammer unless the trigger is pulled all the way to the rear. This motion pushes a piece of steel called the transfer bar up into position behind the firing pin. Now, when the trigger is pulled to fire the gun, the hammer hits the transfer bar, which, in turn, drives the firing pin forward. If the transfer bar is down, as it is when the trigger is in its normal relaxed position, the hammer can't rest against the firing pin and there is no way the gun can be fired by dropping it so that it will fall on the hammer—nor can you fire the gun even by hitting the hammer with a tool such as a hammer.

A similar transfer bar is employed by other makers of both single-action and double-action revolvers. Ruger uses it in both double- and single-action guns, and Dan Wesson uses the system in his double-action. Smith & Wesson uses something which is a little different but has the same net effect in its double-action revolvers (S&W makes no single-action handguns).

The difference in the S&W system is that it employs a hammer with the firing pin mounted directly on the hammer. The counterpart of the transfer bar works the opposite way; it rises to block the hammer, lowers to allow firing. The idea is essentially similar; both methods prevent the firing pin from contacting the cartridge primer unless the shooter means to fire the gun. Accidental discharges from dropping a handgun or from having the hammer slip out from under your thumb in cocking are virtually impossible.

The "transfer bar," used by most modern revolvers, prevents ignition if the gun is dropped on the hammer. Seen here on a Ruger single-action, the bar is in position for firing; you see it behind the firing pin. Unless the gun is deliberately cocked, the bar remains below the firing pin and the lip on top of the hammer's front face contacts the frame. The hammer cannot reach the firing pin. The view of the parts involved shows how the transfer bar is pinned to the trigger; unless the trigger is deliberately pulled (which raises the transfer bar) the gun cannot fire.

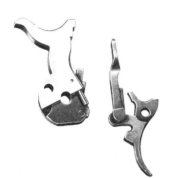

Another method of providing this added safety margin is seen in the new High Standard heavy double-action revolver. In this gun the hammer is on an eccentric pivot; only when the trigger is pulled can the hammer be moved into position to fire the gun. Otherwise it is out of position and won't strike the primer.

In the Ruger New Model single-action, the hammer has only one notch—the full-cock notch. Older single-action revolvers, including the early Rugers, had the familiar three-notch systems which could be heard a country mile on a dark, quiet night. The purpose of the second notch was so you could half-cock the revolver, and this position held the cylinder bolt down so the cylinder could be rotated for loading and unloading. With the new system, something else was called for.

So Ruger designed a new loading gate which, when open, withdraws the cylinder bolt and the cylinder can be rotated. The loading gate also prevents cocking. When the gate is open the gun cannot be cocked. And when the gun is cocked the gate cannot be opened.

THE SINGLE-SHOT PISTOL

There are a number of interesting single-shots on the market today, and they are becoming quite popular. Over the years there have been many such pistols, but most of the currently popular single-shots are relatively new.

Back in the dim days of my youth, Colt made a fine single-shot target pistol named the Camp Perry Model after the Ohio National Guard camp that's been the site of the National Matches for many years. It looked like a revolver and was, in fact, a basic revolver except that instead of having a conventional cylinder, it had a solid block containing only one charge hole. The block swung out like a cylinder and was loaded the same way. Viewed from the side, it resembled a revolver, because Colt fluted the block to look like a regular cylinder. The Camp Perry was a fine target gun, well accepted and highly regarded by target shooters. Its eventual demise, I suspect, came from the small market segment that target shooters constitute and the gradual improvement of the autoloader.

The unique locking arrangement of Ruger's single-shot Hawkeye model for the .256 Winchester cartridge. This was the first practical pistol made for the cartridge but is now off the market. As you see, the cartridge was loaded directly into the barrel and the "cylinder" rotated to lock the action.

Sometime during the 1960s Winchester, in a startling development, announced a new cartridge that had no gun in which to fire it. This was the .256 Winchester, a cartridge made by necking the .357 Magnum case down to .25 caliber. It was a very hot cartridge, and I understand that both Colt and Smith & Wesson tried to tame it for revolver use. But it was too hot to be broken. It remained for Bill Ruger to come up with a rather unusual single-shot which he called the Hawkeye. This, like the old Colt Camp Perry, was made on a revolver frame. This Ruger had a solid breech block which rotated and exposed the chamber, which was in the barrel itself. I have no idea how many of these Hawkeyes were made before the model was dropped, but they're now bringing choice prices

on the collectors' market and tears to the eyes of the rest of us who were not smart enough to buy one as an investment. The .256 lives on today, to a degree, in the Thompson/Center. Marlin also tried to market a rifle in this caliber, but it too died on the vine. There was never any excuse to introduce this cartridge in the first place and it never should have happened.

Another single-shot that I'd have to term an oddball is the Remington Fire Ball XP-100. This gun has a rather interesting development history; the action used is the same identical rifle action once used by Remington in Models 660 and 600, which were chambered for a pair of now obsolete rifle cartridges, the 6.5mm and .350 Remington Magnum. However, Remington still uses the action in a very popular rifle which it markets as the Mohawk Model 600, available in .243 Winchester, 6mm Remington, and .308 Winchester.

The only difference in the XP-100's action is that it's a single-shot and has no magazine cut in the bottom of the receiver. This has led some Remington executives to believe more of these guns are bought for the action—meaning that the buyers custom-build a rifle on the basic action—than as pistols. The advantage is that this is a genuine single-shot rifle action, somewhat stiffer because of the solid receiver bottom. Such a rifle would be used for target shooting in some special events. This procedure is legal according to federal law, although the same laws would not permit you to make a pistol out of any of the rifle models using the same action.

Remington's XP-100 shoots a red-hot cartridge called the .221 Fire Ball which is very similar to the .222 rifle cartridge. The combination spurts a 50-grain softpoint bullet out of the

Looking like something from outer space, the Remington Fire Ball is a bolt-action pistol made on a rifle bolt action. The cartridge is a rifle cartridge too, a slightly shorter .222 called the .221 Fire Ball. Equipped with a scope, this pistol is used for long-range varmint shooting.

10½-inch barrel at a muzzle velocity of 2650 fps — which is damned fast. The .222 drives the same bullet out of a 24-inch *rifle* barrel at just 3140 fps, for comparison.

The Remington pistol is ugly, to my way of thinking. It has a stock made of DuPont nylon and, I'm told by Remington officials, sells like hot cakes.

This pistol operates just like a bolt-action rifle. Raising the bolt handle 90° unlocks the bolt, cocks the firing pin within the bolt by means of a camming action, and performs primary extraction by backing the bolt slightly rearward, which breaks the seal of the cartridge in the chamber (this is a high-pressure cartridge). Retracting the bolt to its rear position completes extraction, ejects the cartridge, and leaves the breech open to hand-feed a new cartridge directly into the chamber. Pushing the bolt forward and down chambers the fresh cartridge and relocks the bolt when the locking lugs re-engage their recesses in the receiver.

Like the various Remington rifles made on the same action, a scope can be easily installed on this pistol, using the same bases intended for rifles.

Years ago there was a very interesting little .22 Long Rifle pistol marketed by Sheridan, the airgun and pellet-gun people. This was a single-shot with a barrel that tipped up automatically when you pressed a release. It was largely riveted together and sold for something under $20. It was the ideal kind of little gun that you could toss in an emergency pack because it could be used to bag small game if you needed to. It could save your life, and if you lost it over the side of a canoe or in some other mishap you weren't out enough to matter. Alas, Sheridan decided real guns were not their bag and took it off the market. But I suspect today some bureaucrat would label it a Saturday-night special because of its cost. Far from it. This was a fine little pistol and I'm glad I bought one when they were around.

There are a few very special single-shot target pistols on the market for Olympic and International Shooting Union (ISU) shooting that deserve special mention because they are so unusual. All of these that I know of today are imports, either the Swiss Hammerli imported by Gil Hebard or the Walther imported from Ger-

Today some boob would call this little gun a Saturday-night special. Regrettably it's off the market, but this was once a very handy single-shot pistol, because it was good, accurate, and cheap. I think I paid $11 for it wholesale more than twenty years ago. It's a .22 Long Rifle and just the thing to toss in your pack. There should be a demand for such a neat little gun today among hunters, trappers, fishermen, and other outdoorsmen. My daughter, at an earlier age, is shown firing this little gun. The barrel is simply pushed down to close the action, and the hammer is pulled back by hand. The little pin in front of the trigger guard is pulled to open the action.

many by Interarms. These are usually chambered for either the .22 Short or .22 Long Rifle cartridge and are marvels of perfection. Some of them cost over $800.

THE THOMPSON/CENTER

The T/C Contender has to rate as one of the unique guns of the times. It must also be said that many people thought it would never make the grade, but it has done handsomely and the company has prospered.

Some years ago, Warren Center worked for

Harrington & Richardson, and he came up with an idea for a single-shot pistol of pretty unusual design. H&R's president, C. Edward Rowe, Jr., wasn't interested, and so Center got together with a man named Ken Thompson in Rochester, N.H., who was in the business of making precision investment castings. The two began to produce pistols. They later expanded their line to the Hawken plains rifle for black powder, and who knows where they'll go from there.

The Contender is a break-open single-shot which operates somewhat like a double shotgun. You unlatch the barrel, which moves down to open the action. The extractor raises the fired cartridge enough so you can grasp it and pull it out of the chamber by hand. Then you slip in a fresh cartridge and close the breech. You have to hand-cock the hammer to fire. T/C pistols have a fine trigger that can be easily adjusted to an excellent pull.

One of the greatest features of the T/C is that you can interchange barrels easily and freely. You remove the wooden forearm (the pistol looks like an old-time dueling arm), push out the hinge pin, then remove and replace the barrel. It's just that easy, and the only tool needed is a screwdriver to remove the forearm.

Interchangeable barrels are available in the widest range of calibers on the handgun market — from .22 Long Rifle to .44 Magnum, with nearly twenty stops in between. Some of these chamberings include the .30/30 and .25/35 rifle cartridges, plus two of the hottest rip-snorting wildcats ever designed for handgun use: the .30 and .357 Herrett, both of which are made on reformed .30/30 brass cases.

Included with the Contender line is an unusual shot cartridge called the Hot Shot in .357 and .44 Magnum (for use exclusively in Contender guns). These loads contain essentially the same charges as a .410 shotgun cartridge and produce effective patterns at 20 yards.

It must be said that the Thompson/Center Contender concept provides the most versatility on the pistol/revolver market today. Its action has enormous strength — more than that of any other commercial one-hand gun. It has the capability of easily downing deer-sized game if that's your game and the capability of precision target

shooting or bagging a grouse for the pot. I have a sample Contender with a .22 Hornet barrel and a .25/35 barrel, both of which are delivering excellent 100-yard accuracy with the T/C Insta-Sight, and a .44 Magnum barrel with special choke device for the Hot Shot cartridges. One additional feature is an instantly changeable firing pin from rimfire to centerfire. This is truly a versatile concept.

ROLLING-BLOCKS

In the area of replicas or reproductions is the Navy Arms Rolling Block single-shot pistol. This is the old Remington Rider patent (first patent was in 1864) commonly called the rolling-block. The name comes from the breech block, which "rolls" back and forth to open or close much like the hammer. Located just in front of the hammer and with a hammer-type thumbpiece, the block can be moved only when the hammer is in cocked position. Pulling back the block opens the breech, and the extractor retracts the cartridge far enough so that it can be grasped and withdrawn. Then a fresh cartridge is inserted by hand and the block is closed. When the gun is fired, the hammer comes to rest inside the block, helping to hold it closed and locked.

This action was in the Remington line for years; at least one model lasted until 1933. It was made as a military rifle for several foreign nations, including Egypt, and a number were produced in 7mm Mauser caliber. As you can see, the basic action is simple and strong. Navy Arms has these pistols available in .22 Long Rifle, .22 WMR, .357 Magnum, and .22 Hornet.

HANDGUN TESTING

In what must be labeled one of the silliest tests the government ever undertook, it attempted to destroy 150 new handguns by shooting tests. These tests, reportedly, were to determine how many shots could be fired from an ordinary handgun — both costly and cheap, and at varying prices in between.

This boondoggle took place in 1971, cost the American taxpayers a couple of hundred thousand dollars, and was inconclusive. While actual

Gun manufacture in America includes proof testing, which is done in a sealed box, and function testing. Most manufacturers also target their guns, as you see here at the Smith & Wesson plant, where shooters are targeting .44 Magnum revolvers.

test results have never been released, some information has filtered down. The tests were performed by the H. P. White Laboratory in Bel Air, Maryland. This lab was formed by the late Henry P. White, a wealthy industrialist who had a yen for guns and ballistics and spared nothing in the development of his facility. Moreover, White was always objective, and I understand that the Laboratory has remained truly objective since his death.

The stated purpose of these tests was to assist in determining "standards" under which guns should be manufactured, thus assuring the public of better value in the form of safer handguns. Most gun folk felt it was a transparent attempt to categorize something they might label the Saturday-night special and thus be able to legislate these off the market.

They got fooled. The feds found that the cheap guns held up pretty darned well indeed.

Very briefly, this test procedure consisted of purchasing two identical handguns of the same make and caliber — 116 guns in total, and said to be a fair cross section of guns on the market based on availability and popularity. Apparently,

one of each model was to be given a real torture test, while the second gun was simply to be fired to a maximum of 5,000 shots.

The real "torture test" consisted of firing proof loads after each 100 rounds of highest-velocity regular commercial ammunition. A proof load is used in the industry to test guns in manufacture and is customarily loaded to about a third more pressure than the highest-pressure regular commercial cartridge. You can see that these guns were getting a healthy dose of torture — far beyond anything they were either designed or manufactured to withstand.

As might have been expected, the guns put through the wringing torture test with an abnormal number of proof loads did not stand up as well as those subjected only to repeated firing tests. Most American-made centerfire handguns showed up very well in the tests, while a number of foreign-made guns revealed some defects. As one example, an American-made .357 Magnum revolver (brand unidentified) stopped after it fired no fewer than 16,000 rounds — 96 of which were proof loads.

It must be said that the tests were of some use,

for they proved the superiority of well-made products, regardless of their cost (some of the low-priced revolvers compared favorably to the more costly ones).

Since another phase of the testing procedure was a "drop test," in which the revolver was dropped on its cocked hammer from a predeter- mined distance to see if the gun would fire. So many of them did fire that the industry got to work fast to prevent such accidental discharges, and revolvers of current manufacture contain a positive block that won't allow the firing pin to hit the primer unless the shooter takes positive action to see that the trigger is pulled.

CHAPTER THREE

SEMI-AUTOMATIC BREECH ACTIONS

A semiautomatic action is one in which the gun's firing energy is utilized to perform all the steps except firing. There are several ways to harness that energy, as we shall see in a few moments. Semiautos are sometimes called autoloaders, and the term is correct. They also are very often called automatics, especially when it comes to pistols. The term is dead wrong but is in such common usage that there is little point in trying to correct it. For the record, an automatic is any mechanism that fires and continues to fire until either the trigger is released or it runs out of ammunition. A machine gun (or a submachine gun) is the most common form of automatic action.

Auto pistols are generally quite different from auto shoulder arms in their operational systems, primarily because the latter have more room and more weight for designers to work with. The big, popular gas-gun actions seen in both shotgun and rifle designs can't be conveniently worked into an auto pistol because there isn't space. While most high-power auto pistols are operated by the short-recoil system, there are no rifles on today's market employing this system, and the popular long-recoil system used since 1900 by Browning on the Auto-5 is also not applicable to a pistol. We will explore recoil operation in depth in a moment. Virtually all the .22 autoloading rifles on the market today are operated the same as autoloading .22 pistols. This system is known as the blowback system.

Blowback is regarded by many as a form of

recoil operation. In the strict sense of the word this is essentially true. But blowback is sufficiently different that I prefer to keep it entirely separate, and I think you will understand it better if you also consider it separate.

In explaining recoil operation, the simplest approach is to remind you that a gun, any gun, kicks when fired. You fire a .30/30 Winchester lever-action rifle from the shoulder, and the rifle responds with a kick. You then work the action by whipping the lever down and up to ready the rifle to fire again.

Now imagine that you have fastened the end of the finger lever in a vise before you fire the rifle. You know that the gun's kick, or recoil, will force it back, and since the lever is held fast the rifle will kick so as to open the lever. This will extract and eject our fired cartridge. So long as we're imagining, place a powerful spring against the butt and fire the rifle again. This time the rifle will recoil rearward, but will also return to firing position because of the spring.

Now you understand what a recoil-operated rifle goes through when it cycles. It's just that simple. Add a device to trip the trigger when the rifle is forward and you have a machine gun.

Naturally you can't fix a gun in a vise to have it self-loading, so designers employ the principle to allow the barrel to recoil *within the gun* and set the action parts in motion. So now we can define a recoil-operated gun: *the barrel moves.* And this applies whether it's pistol, rifle, or shotgun and regardless of the amount of barrel movement.

In *short* recoil, the barrel moves a scant fraction of an inch (there are exceptions where the barrel moves more than that, but generally it's around ⅛ inch in the .45 Automatic Colt, and ⅜ inch in the .30-caliber Browning machine gun, and in most systems the barrel moves a similar short distance). In *long* recoil, the barrel moves more—about 3 inches in the Browning Auto-5 shotgun, more than a foot in the 37mm Browning aircraft cannon. Those are the principal differences between long and short recoil. Auto pistols are strictly a short-recoil proposition.

SHORT-RECOIL AUTOS

We will examine two distinct types, typified by the Colt Government Model .45 auto, Model

Browning's original .45-caliber military model was invented in 1905 and adopted in 1911 as the official "government model." When submitted for ordnance trials, the pistol was the first small arm ever tested to complete all its exhaustive tests with a perfect record.

1911, patented by John Browning in 1905, and the German Luger, known as the P-08 (Pistole '08) and also as the Parabellum, certainly one of the most famous of all handguns.

We have already established that the breech end of a gun barrel must be securely locked during firing because of the high gas pressures necessary to drive a bullet. But there is a point at which we can allow the gun to become unlocked, after the pressure has subsided sufficiently to make it safe.

In the short-recoil system, barrel and breech block are tightly and securely locked together. They recoil together for a short distance and then unlock; the barrel stays where it is while the breech block continues rearward. As the breech block comes back forward, it re-engages the barrel and both parts return to firing position, locked again. That sounds simple enough. Let's follow the big .45 Colt through the seven steps:

1. **Firing** is the same, familiar step.
2. **Unlocking** is unique. First, understand that the barrel is tightly locked into the slide (that's the part you pull back to chamber a cartridge, and it also serves as the breech block). The lock consists of two square ridges which engage matching recesses in the slide; these locking surfaces are near the breech end on top of the barrel. The front of the barrel is permitted to slide back and forth in a bushing at the front end of the slide.

Upon firing, the slide and barrel move back

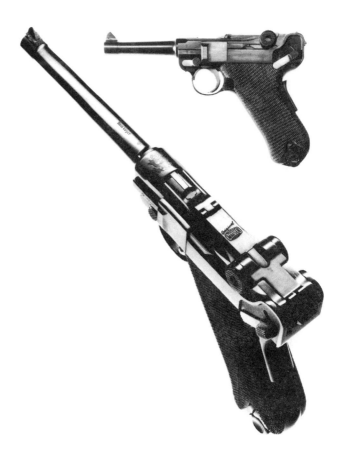

The German Luger pistol, properly called the Parabellum, was adopted by Germany in 1908, has been used by many other nations' armies, and is one of the world's most famous pistols. It is operated by short recoil, as described in the text. When fired, barrel and breech bolt move to the rear until the knurled round knobs engage the sloped surface to their rear. This surface forces the knobs up, which opens the breech. The gun illustrated was one of the last to be manufactured. Until recently the Luger was made by the original Mauser works and imported by Interarms. Luger/Parabellum production was suspended in 1977.

tightly locked together. After about ⅛ inch of travel, the bullet has left the barrel and unlocking is safe, so the breech end of the barrel is pulled down, out of its locking engagement with the slide, by a small link. The barrel now stays where it is while the slide goes all the way to the rear.

3. Extraction is accomplished as the barrel starts to slow down during unlocking. There is primary extraction in this action which breaks the fired cartridge's seal; as the slide continues to the rear it pulls the empty out of the barrel. Another small event happens during the slide's rearward travel: It pushes a small part called the disconnector down, which disengages the trigger from the sear so the gun cannot be fired when the slide comes back forward (not until you relax the trigger and pull it again).

4. Ejection occurs at the rear end of the slide's travel, when the lower edge of the cartridge strikes the fixed ejector and the empty, spinning about the extractor hook, is flipped clear

of the gun. During this rearward movement, the recoil spring has become compressed to drive the slide forward again.

5. Cocking is accomplished by the slide's rear surface, which pushes the hammer back down into cocked position.

The little part shown here is the disconnector on a .45 Auto pistol. The gun will fire only when this part is raised, as it is here. There is a corresponding recess in the slide which allows the disconnector to rise when the gun is ready to fire. Once the slide moves back it pushes this part down and the gun cannot be fired. Every semiautomatic gun of any type has some method of disconnecting the trigger; otherwise it would be a machine gun and fully automatic.

6. Feeding is performed as the slide sweeps forward again and picks up a fresh cartridge from the magazine and pushes it into the chamber.

7. Locking. As the slide chambers the cartridge, it slams against the breech end of the barrel and drives it forward into firing position. As the barrel and slide go forward together, the link forces the barrels' breech end up and the locking lugs into their recesses. The pistol is now ready to be fired again, after the trigger is relaxed to permit the disconnector to re-engage.

Earlier Browning pistols employed two links, one up front, one at the rear, in which barrel and slide were parallel throughout the operating cycle. A single link proved more dependable and simpler—two characteristics of Browning's designs; the simpler and the fewer parts, the more dependable and long-lasting the firearm. This Browning design has been copied throughout the world.

The .45 Auto pistol has a reputation of being hard to shoot accurately. This isn't hard to understand, because the reputation is chiefly among those who try a .45 for the first time. Those who have become good handgun shots know the .45 Auto is a pussycat when compared to the .44 Magnum revolver as far as recoil is concerned. These good shooters also know that the original design leaves something to be desired in the accuracy potential of the gun itself. That's chiefly because the barrel moves and because some barrels are a sloppy fit in the barrel bushing in which the muzzle rides back and forth. For any firearm to deliver consistent shots, the barrel must be in the same precise place from shot to shot, every time. So there came into being a small group of craftsmen called pistol gunsmiths who specialized in "accurizing" the .45 Auto for target shooting. Their work consists of making some new parts to much closer tolerances and of employing small springs here and there to press against the barrel and ensure that it would always be in the same place (see Chapter Twenty-one).

Smith & Wesson addressed this problem a few short years ago in their Model 52 Master auto pistol chambered for the .38 Special cartridge. Their solution called for a round ridge running about the muzzle of the barrel in such a way that you could lower the barrel's breech end in unlocking without altering the fit between muzzle and bushing. This called for extraordinarily careful engineering and manufacture. I understand that S&W still targets each Model 52 and that it must conform to very rigid accuracy standards before it leaves the plant. Colt also has its own "accurized" version of its .45 Auto pistol.

Refinements of this sort are fine on a target pistol; they can get you extra points. But they have no place in a service gun that must function under sometimes rigorous conditions.

THE GERMAN LUGER

The German Luger pistol is properly called the Parabellum, and the 9mm cartridge for which most of these pistols are made is also called the Parabellum. The original design for this gun was by the American Hugo Borchardt; then it was adapted and improved by Georg Luger. The name "Luger" was popularized in America by A. F. Stoeger, the importer who had the gun made in Germany for U.S. sale—models bearing the American eagle.

As near as I can fathom, Stoeger still "owns" the Luger trademark. There was a Parabellum pistol on the market, imported by Interarms in both 9mm and 7.65mm calibers, but manufacture was suspended in 1977. This is the original gun in nearly all respects.

Meantime, Stoeger now imports a "Luger" .22 caliber which is a blowback pistol made to resemble the original Luger, or Parabellum. "Parabellum" may be the correct name, but we'll call it the Luger in this book to comply with popular usage.

For some reason the Luger has always fascinated Americans. It's hard to know just why, though it is a fine pistol and points very naturally. Some of the older original Lugers are now commanding fancy prices from collectors. The Luger, like the .45 Colt, is chambered for a very fine cartridge too—the 9mm Luger or 9mm Parabellum. (Some Lugers are chambered for the 7.65mm Luger cartridge, often called the .30 Luger in America.) First adopted in 1908, the Luger pistol and the 9mm cartridge were German standards for years; the cartridge was also standard for submachine guns. In fact, the 9mm

The top photo shows the Luger toggle-joint pistol in fully locked position with the joint lying flat. When fired, the barrel and toggle are in line, flat down. (The dangling piece shown at the right is the part that connects with the recoil spring, inside the butt. The parts shown include barrel, receiver, and toggle, which have been dismounted from the frame.) The middle photo shows how the toggle joint opens up as recoil begins. The knurled knobs contact a sloping surface on the frame (not shown) which makes them rise. This effectively breaks the "in-line" attitude of the toggle, the same as raising your knees weakens your ability to withstand pressure. The bottom photo shows the toggle joint open in full recoil. In this position, extraction and ejection have occurred, the firing pin has been recocked, and energy has been stored in the recoil spring to drive the parts forward.

Parabellum cartridge is still used by many of the world's armies.

One of those mysterious wild tales about guns and their ammunition concerns 9mm ammunition. It has been widely rumored that certain batches of 9mm service ammunition were loaded to substantially higher than standard pressures during World War II by Germany for use in 9mm submachine guns. There has never been any documentation of that rumor. Military 9mm cartridges have been loaded since about 1904 and by many of the world's nations, so there are bound to be irregularities, changes, differences, and so forth. But there is no truth to the rumor that higher-pressure cartridges were loaded for submachine guns.

The Luger pistol locks in a very unique fashion: It has a toggle joint which provides the lockup. To visualize how this works, imagine yourself flat on your back on the floor. Your shoulders cannot move. Your legs are flat against the floor and your feet are against a heavy, movable object like a safe. Now imagine that someone is pushing that safe toward you with a powerful force. You can hold that safe where it is until someome comes along, places a stick under your knees, and begins to raise them. Suddenly your mechanical advantage is lost and the safe begins to move toward you. The higher your knees are raised, the less resistance you can offer.

With that example in mind, visualize the Luger toggle joint laid out flat along the floor (the pistol's frame). Upon firing, barrel and toggle system move to the rear as a unit. After a very short movement, the knobs on either side of the toggle engage a sloped surface which raises the center of the toggle (your knees). Now the barrel stops where it is and the toggle, carrying the breech bolt, moves all the way to the rear.

That's the basic difference between the two action systems. Instead of pulling back the slide as you do in the Browning system (Colt .45) you simply pull up and back on the Luger's toggle-joint knobs in order to chamber a cartridge and cock the pistol.

OTHER SHORT-RECOIL AUTOS AND VARIATIONS

The Colt and the Luger are the primary types of recoil-operated pistols, most other designs being simply a modification or an adaptation of the Colt. For example, Smith & Wesson's Model 39 utilizes the same basic idea, but its locking and unlocking are provided by cams rather than a link. Otherwise the situation is very similar.

One unique pistol about which much has been written despite the small number of guns actually produced is a special short-recoil-operated gun known as the Auto-Mag. Its lockup is by a rotating bolt which turns the six locking lugs into six matching surfaces in the barrel extension. In this regard the action is close to that used in the Remington pump- and gas-operated high-power rifles. The Auto-Mag is made entirely of stainless steel and only for a few specially designed cartridges made by shortening .30/06 cases; there are Auto-Mags in .357, .41, and .44 caliber. This is a gun only for the very skilled pistoleer and handloader. Its makers claim about 20 percent more velocity than the standard .44 Magnum, and the gun was built strictly for hunting.

A number of firms have recently sprung up that are engaged in the business of making "smaller than Colt" versions of the .45 Auto. Indeed, some of them make these guns by actually shortening existing service pistols, while others work from scratch. The intent is to make a smaller pocket pistol out of the .45, which is a good way to go if you want a smaller version of this power-packed gun and have the necessary cash to pay for it. Most of these variations are shortened from top to bottom as well as fore and aft, so the result is a truly scaled-down pocket .45.

Colt Firearms offers an interesting conversion kit that allows you to convert either a .45 Colt or .38 Super Colt Auto to shoot .22 Long Rifle cartridges—not only to fire them, but to give a reasonable semblance of the recoil generated by the larger cartridges. This is accomplished by what is known as a floating chamber. A new barrel in .22 caliber is supplied (along with a separate slide and other parts), and this is fastened securely in place of the original barrel. It's a fixed barrel; no locking, no barrel movement. As the sketches show, the .22 floating chamber rests directly against the breech block (an integral part of the slide, as you will recall). When the cartridge is fired and the bullet has moved a very short distance, the gas is allowed to bear against the front of the floating chamber. In fact, it gives this movable chamber a good, swift whack—enough to ram the slide all the way back just as the big .45 cartridge does. The floating chamber only moves a fraction of an inch.

This is not recoil operation; its main advantage is that you can develop .45 caliber feel and recoil with the small .22 Long Rifle in this big gun. It permits inexpensive target shooting.

The floating chamber we've just described was an invention of the late David W. Williams, known as "Carbine" Williams because he also invented the short-stroke piston employed by the U.S. Carbine of World War II. Prior to that, he had successfully modified the .30-caliber Browning machine gun to use .22-caliber cartridges for practice shooting. This was accomplished by basically the same method as the Colt conversion. In effect, Williams made a small piston engine in which the .22 was the motivating force, enough to drive the massive .30 Browning breech bolt—quite a bit of force.

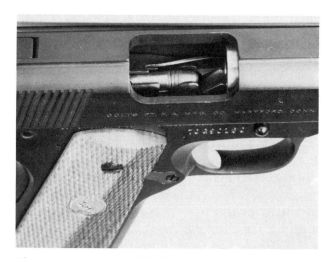

The Colt .45 Auto with .22 conversion unit in place. That's a .22 Long Rifle cartridge in the magazine in position to be fed into the chamber. The magazine lips are most important in any auto pistol, for they determine the angle at which the cartridge is presented. If the lips are too high or too low, a jam will result; a damaged magazine is the most frequent cause of jams in any auto pistol in proper working order with good ammunition.

The most publicized part of Williams' background is that he was serving a term in a North Carolina jail for murder when he whittled out his carbine idea (with the help of a patriotic and sympathetic warden).

An interesting variation in the recoil system is seen in the "double-action" autoloading pistol. Differing only in the trigger action, it represents something of a departure in traditional semiauto-pistol design.

The traditional auto pistol of the Browning type had to be cocked either by pulling the slide back and releasing it, or by manually pulling the hammer back if the gun had an exposed hammer. That meant you could carry the gun in one of two ways: either loaded, cocked, and on safe; or loaded with the hammer in half-cock position. You also could carry the gun with a loaded magazine but without a cartridge in the chamber, which meant that you had to pull the slide back to load and cock the pistol.

But the double-action autoloading pistol changes that. The first of these guns to achieve popularity were the Walther PP and PPK models, along with the Walther P-38 chambered for the 9mm Parabellum cartridge, which became a standard for the German army in 1938. Today's shooter is probably more familiar with the fine Smith & Wesson Model 39 double-action, also chambered for the 9mm cartridge.

In action, these guns are essentially the same as using a double-action revolver for the first shot. That is, you can carry the pistol loaded with a cartridge in the chamber and the hammer down. The hammer can't possibly fire the gun because the firing pin is of the inertia type and isn't long enough to transmit a blow to the primer even if the gun is dropped directly on the hammer. To fire, you simply pull the trigger, which cocks the hammer just as in the double-action revolver. After the first shot the gun works exactly like any other autoloader and the trigger pull is short.

There are many who prefer this sort of handgun for defense purposes. It is just as fast as the revolver for the first shot and faster for repeat shots. It also offers a safer way to carry a loaded pistol than any gun without the double-action feature.

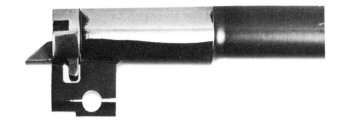

The Colt "conversion unit" consists of a number of parts that render a .45 Auto pistol into a .22. It packs essentially the same recoil as the .45 load, so it's an ideal practice package. The first photo shows the floating chamber, viewed from the top, with a .22 Long Rifle cartridge inserted. You can just see the bullet's nose sticking out at the right; the feed ramp is at the left. The second photo shows the floating chamber at the right, viewed from its front end. At the left is the special barrel which is necessary to the conversion.
The third and fourth photos show the floating chamber in place in the barrel, viewed from the side. The third photo has the chamber all the way forward in unfired position. The fourth photo shows the floating chamber in recoil. Once the bullet clears the floating chamber, gas is then permitted to push the chamber back with enough force to work the slide and accomplish all the steps of operation for semiautomatic fire with as much recoil as the .45 cartridge produces.

I have heard objections to several models of double-action auto, but I have never experienced any trouble myself. The chief objection made is that the guns can be unsafe when dropping the hammer. There is a method on most models to lower the hammer by placing the gun on safe. That is, the safety causes the hammer to fall, and it also rolls a block in the way of the hammer to prevent it from striking the firing pin. Those who criticize these pistols claim the gun will occasionally fire when this is done. I mention this only because it is on the record, but, I have no firsthand knowledge of this occurring.

Another interesting variation on autoloading handguns is a little-known British revolver called the Webley-Fosberry automatic revolver, a true self-loader but in an unusual way. The cylinder on this model had ratchet grooves similar to those on the popular "Yankee" type screwdrivers. Upon firing, the barrel and cylinder recoiled backward together while the frame stayed in place. The cylinder's grooves fitted a pin in the frame which, on recoiling, made the cylinder rotate. The recoil action also pushed the hammer into cocked position. So the Webley-Fosberry was truly an autoloader operated by recoil action. But it was pretty unusual and is seldom seen; it should be considered something of an oddity.

BLOWBACK OPERATION

We said earlier in this book that a firearm must be securely locked at the moment of firing in order to safely contain the gas pressures generated. That statement remains true. However, it's not always necessary to make that lock like a safe door, or a turning bolt like the Mauser rifle's bolt system.

Guns operated by blowback operation do not have a mechanical locking arrangement. Locking is accomplished by inertia (defined as the tendency of a body at rest to remain at rest, and body in motion to remain in motion). Generally speaking, blowback operation is restricted to cartridges developing relatively low chamber pressure. Most handgun cartridges fall into this category, along with the .22. Most of the world's submachine guns are blowback-operated, and

most of them are chambered either for the 9mm Parabellum or the U.S. .45 automatic Colt Pistol (ACP) cartridge. All .22 autoloading rifles and pistols are blowback guns.

John Browning invented blowback operation in about 1895, and it has since been used by gunmakers all over the world.

To visualize why blowback works, you can imagine that you're seated at a long table on which has been placed a long row of books. Move just one book far enough to place both your hands, with palms out, between it and the long row. Now, applying equal force to both hands, spread your hands apart rapidly. You don't have to do it to know the single book will fly the length of the table while the rest of them will tend to remain where they are but will eventually move. Just apply this example to the gun.

Instead of a single book you have a bullet weighing only 40 grains (in .22 caliber). Instead of a long row of books you have a heavy breech block weighing many times as much as the bullet. When you fire the gun, the gas pressure works equally in all directions. The bullet moves first because it's so light. But the gas is also pushing against the breech bolt through the cartridge case, and just as the bullet leaves the muzzle, the inertia of the heavy bolt has been overcome and there is enough remaining pressure to shove it all the way back. Engineers call this remaining gas the "residual pressure"—it's not enough to be harmful but it is enough to work the action. Blowback calls for reasonably delicate timing to be sure the bullet is clear and chamber pressures have subsided enough before the breech bolt opens up.

Otherwise, blowback action is no different from recoil action. Aside from the steps of locking and unlocking, blowback and recoil operations are virtually the same.

In 1907 and 1910, Winchester introduced two blowback rifles chambered for fairly large cartridges, the .351 and .401, both of which are now long gone. These two rifles were used for law-enforcement purposes and were preferred by some hunters. The rifles were, however, quite muzzle-heavy, somewhat ungainly, and poorly balanced. As a result they never really achieved much popularity and were eventually dropped.

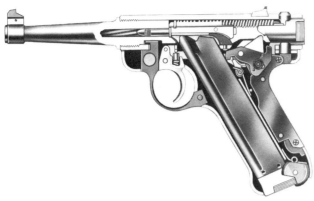

A cutaway view of the Ruger Standard Model .22 auto pistol operated by blowback. Blowback is suitable for most low-pressure cartridges, and the breech is locked by inertia as explained in the text. The Ruger pistol is shown here with 4¾-inch barrel.

The reason they were unbalanced was that they were blowback. As I said earlier, the cartridges were fairly powerful, so a heavy breech block was necessary to keep it closed until the bullet got away. Since there wasn't room for a heavy breech block, Winchester's engineers solved that by an extension rod from the breech bolt up into the forearm, where it was fastened to a large weight. That's what unbalanced this rifle, but without that added weight the bolt would have opened too soon, with disastrous results.

Another interesting blowback gun was the

A very early, and somewhat neglected, Colt pocket .25 Auto pistol is shown at top, and a .22 Long Rifle Smith & Wesson Escort at the bottom. The Colt was a Browning design and was in the line for many years. Smith & Wesson introduced the tiny Escort in about 1971 and dropped it a couple of years later. I've been told the company felt it in the best interests of all concerned that they abandon manufacture of such a concealable pocket gun. Nevertheless, this was a fine gun and I take some credit for its appearance in the first place. Both were blowback-operated.

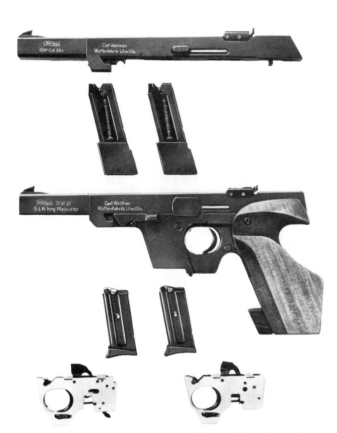

The Walther (Germany) GSP Match Pistol is a blow-back-operated autoloader. In the center of the photo it is shown assembled for .32-caliber S&W wadcutter ammo. At the top is the replaceable .22-caliber barrel; at the bottom are spare magazines and triggers. The gun is imported by Interarms.

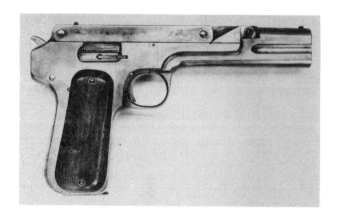

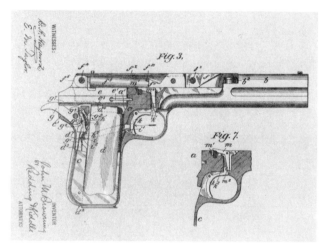
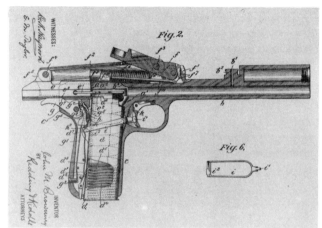

John Browning's first autoloading pistol design was this gas-operated model. It was never produced, because he developed the recoil-operated gun before this gas gun could be put in production. Both photos and the accompanying patent drawings show how the gun works; a small amount of gas is bled from the barrel (the barrel is the lower tube) and blows back the little cap, which jacks the action open. Energy stored in a spring returns the parts to firing position. This gun worked perfectly, and Colt would have manufactured it had the recoil gun not come along. The principle used is very similar to that of the Colt/Browning machine gun of 1895, known as the "potato digger," which had its moving flap under the gun. If the gun was mounted too low it had the effect of digging into the ground, hence the name. (Patent photos courtesy of the National Rifle Association; photos of the gun courtesy of Robert N. Sears).

Swiss Oerlikon 20mm automatic cannon. How could such a whopping high-pressure cartridge work in blowback? It was accomplished by firing from an open bolt which we've already described —and a massive bolt it was, propelled by an enormous spring. When the gun was triggered, the massive bolt flew forward under tremendous speed to strip a cartridge from the magazine and into the chamber. The inventors made this cannon fire just as the bolt was about to close—*it was still moving forward,* and that extra inertia of the moving bolt had to be overcome and turned around. (This system is properly called delayed blowback.)

Blowbacks are balanced by carefully weighting the moving parts and by careful attention to spring tension, all in relation to the cartridge to be used. This will explain why a .22 autoloading pistol or rifle chambered for the .22 Long Rifle High Speed won't work with standard-velocity .22 Long Rifle cartridges. The action needs that slight extra push to operate consistently.

Smith & Wesson, for example, makes a fine .22 target auto pistol called the Model 41. You can buy an interchangeable barrel for this pistol chambered for the .22 Short. The Short is preferred by many Olympic and International pistol shooters because it has less recoil than the .22

Long Rifle and disturbs their aim less, making it easier to get back on target. But the .22 Short cartridge will not work a standard .22 Long Rifle blowback action.

GAS OPERATION

So far as I know, the only gas pistol ever developed was John Browning's very first pistol. As a matter of fact, this was the first gas-operated gun ever recognized as a practical design. Browning had supposedly observed the leaves and grass being blown by the exhaust gas when a firearm was fired on the range, and had decided to try to harness this power to work the action.

His first experiment was with a .44/40 Winchester lever-action rifle, to which he attached a series of rods connected to a small cup fitted over the gun's muzzle with a small hole for the bullet to pass through. In firing, the bullet passed through the hole; the gas behind it blew the cup away and motivated the rods in a swinging arc that also worked the lever of the rifle. Next, Browning applied the principle to a pistol design in 1895.

In a .38-caliber pistol, Browning drilled a small hole near the muzzle and on top. In firing, after the bullet passed the hole, some gas was vented upward, where it pushed a lever connected to the breech block. This lever rotated upward and back in an arc, which served to move the breech block back, causing extraction, ejection, and cocking. On the return or forward stroke, it fed a new cartridge into the chamber and the gun was ready to fire again. Locking was accomplished by the straight-line arrangement of operating lever, connecting rod, and breech block much like the German Luger already discussed.

This was Browning's first autoloading pistol and he took it to Colt in Hartford, where it was test-fired by company officials. It proved very successful in operation; manufacturing rights were acquired by Colt and became the cornerstone upon which a Browning/Colt relationship was begun. From that day until now, no automatic-pistol design ever manufactured by Colt has been other than a basic Browning design.

Browning's gas pistol was never produced, because his autoloading and automatic inventions came so fast on its heels. However, also in 1895, Browning adapted the gas theory to a machine gun. Called the Colt Model 1895, this operational system was similar to that of the pistol just described except that the gas port and operating lever were on the bottom and were, of course, much larger. The Model 1895 was made for both the .30/40 Krag cartridge and the 6mm Lee cartridge. First ordered by the U.S. Navy, the Colt Model 1895 was the first machine gun ever ordered by U.S. forces and saw service in the Boxer Rebellion and Spanish-American War. It was a highly successful design and was eventually succeeded by the 1917 Browning recoil-operated machine gun.

To the best of my knowledge there have been no successful gas pistols ever marketed.

CHAPTER FOUR

BREECH-ACTION LOCKING SYSTEMS

It should be clear by this time that the breech end of the gun barrel must be securely locked in one way or another at the time of firing so that the propellant gas is confined and made to perform its assigned task: to move the bullet or shot charge out of the barrel. It should also be clear that we cannot open this lock until the gas pressure has subsided to a safe level, and that different pressures require different types of locks. By this I mean that a locking arrangement perfectly adequate for a .22 rimfire cartridge is not nearly strong enough to retain the enormous pressures needed to drive a .44 Magnum bullet at high velocity.

The locking system must be strong enough to hold the cartridge or family of cartridges for which the firearm is or will be adapted. Rifle cartridges are generally much more powerful than the hottest handgun, so we are talking about relative figures in terms of firearms in general. Most of the hotter rifle Magnums operate at pressures around 50,000 to 55,000 copper units of pressure, while pistols and revolvers generally operate at substantially lower pressures. For example to quote some figures from DuPont: The .38 Special operates from 10,000 to 15,000 cup, the .45 ACP at about 18,000, and the .41 and .44 Magnums at a husky 40,000 cup. The weaker numbers, of course, operate at far lower pressures. It is also worth noting here that a gun such as the Thompson/Center Contender is available with a barrel for the .30/30 rifle cartridge—which, while not an especially powerful rifle cartridge, is pretty potent in a pistol.

There are two major reasons why you can use far hotter loads and cartridges in rifles than in handguns: there is more beef in the guns, so they are capable of stronger locking; and the shoulder can handle more recoil, supported additionally by the two-handed grip, than the one hand with a handgun. Despite the fact that some brave souls have made themselves handguns to shoot the .45/70 and other whoppers, there is a reasonable limit beyond which most people don't want to go.

Locking systems, which must contain those pressures we've just mentioned, are many and varied. Some are particularly suited to a certain type of action. Inevitably there are some that are better than others, and some just won't handle high pressure. Generally speaking, the lockups found on guns today are suitable for the cartridge they're meant to fire—but often they would not be suitable for any higher pressures.

THE TURNING-BOLT SYSTEM

The turning-bolt system is pure Mauser, developed by the same Peter Paul Mauser that gave the world the famous military rifle which has become the basis for every turning-bolt locking system used in all gundom. At this writing there are two turning-bolt handguns to my knowledge: Remington's Fire Ball, which is often considered more of a rifle than a handgun; and the Auto-Mag, a custom development that handles very powerful cartridges specially made for it.

The turning-bolt system works just like the common door lock which is raised 90° to unlock and then pulled back. The only major difference between the door lock and the gun bolt is that the door lock's pressure comes from the side while the gun lock has a thrust that is in line with the bolt.

Remington's Fire Ball has the same bolt action that was used on their now obsolete Models 600 and 660 and is used on the promotional Remington Mohawk Model 600. These are all rifles— and according to Remington spokesmen, the company does not really know if Fire Ball pistols are bought just for the action, which is then made into a custom rifle, or if they are bought for use as is. (As noted previously, federal law permits making a rifle from this or any other pistol/revolver action, but not reworking any rifle or shotgun action into a pistol!) Remington's Fire Ball is a single-shot, high-velocity pistol that uses a cartridge similar to the popular .222 rifle cartridge.

The Auto-Mag is an autoloading pistol with a turning-bolt lock chambered for some very heavy cartridges. Before the development of this gun the most powerful handgun was the .44 Magnum, and the latter is still the winner among common handguns. It is unlikely that the Auto-Mag will ever become much more than a custom proposition for a small market. Just the same, it's important to note it, since it may be the world's most powerful autoloading handgun.

REVOLVER LOCKING SYSTEMS

When you get into the locking system employed in a revolver you have to forget everything conventional. The term "lock" has an entirely different meaning.

Let's first talk about the single-action, because that departs from double-action locking to a degree. If you accept that the revolver is locked when the cylinder is in place, you will have accepted *part* of the locking of a revolver. In the single-action that means the gun is always locked; you simply rotate the cylinder to load and unload one cartridge at a time through the loading gate.

In a double-action, on the other hand, you swing the whole cylinder out of the gun to load and unload, and when it's swung back into the gun, the gun is loaded and locked. Double-action cylinders are locked in place by a small button at the rear of the frame, below the firing-pin hole, which snaps into a recess in the cylinder. Some models, notably Smith & Wesson, also have a snap lock at the front of the ejector rod which helps hold the cylinder in place. At one time some years ago there was a Smith & Wesson model with an extra lock at the front of the crane (which carries the cylinder in and out). This was called a Triple Lock model and is highly valued today by collectors.

But that's only part of the locking in any revolver. It is obvious that the simple expedient of having the cylinder firmly in the frame provides sufficient locking to hold things together. When

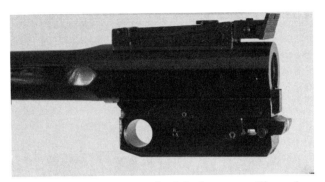

The Thompson/Center pistol locks not unlike a double shotgun. The movable locking bolt is seen at the right, under the chamber; it slips into a corresponding notch in the gun's frame to lock. T/C barrels are interchangeable, making this a very versatile gun.

Everything about a revolver "lock" is different from any other gun. The cylinder is locked into the gun by a pin in a single-action, and by the cylinder latch in a double-action swing-out cylinder. But the cylinder must also be locked in place during firing to align the charge hole with the barrel; the small notches visible in this Ruger cylinder engage a small bolt at the bottom of the frame, which ensures proper alignment during firing.

the cylinder is rotated and a charge hole is aligned with the barrel, there must be provision to hold it in place so the bullet will enter the barrel *exactly* straight and in line. So revolvers are equipped with a small part called the cylinder bolt, which is located in the bottom of the frame, usually just above the trigger. It is the function of this little part to snap up into a notch in the cylinder when the next charge hole is aligned. This serves to lock the cylinder in place and in alignment with the barrel.

So the revolver is locked by virtue of its design—and by that tiny cylinder bolt which locks the cylinder in place so it can't rotate until the gun is cycled.

SINGLE-SHOT LOCKING SYSTEMS

There are several single-shot pistols around, and all of them lock a little differently. The most important of these is the Thompson/Center Contender, usually referred to simply as the T/C. This is a swing-down-barrel affair much like a double shotgun. The barrel swings on a hinge pin, and the lock is a rather massive lug under

the barrel that engages a "bite" or slot. It is activated by an under lever which moves the lock back and forth to lock and unlock. Very simple, and very effective.

Navy Arms in Ridgefield, N. J., is manufacturing an old system known as the Remington Rider or rolling-block action. This was a popular rifle, designed by Joseph Rider and manufactured by Remington for many years beginning in about 1865. The rolling-block was a very simple action consisting of a big hammer behind a sturdy breech block. In operation, the hammer was pulled back conventionally, and the breech

The old Remington rolling-block is again being manufactured, now by Navy Arms. This .357 Magnum is shown cocked with breech plug forward. When the hammer moves forward to fire, its broad surface (seen on either side of the thumbpiece) slips under the breech block, holding the latter secure in the locked position. The hammer must be fully cocked to unlock the gun.

block was also pulled down much as the hammer was. This opened the breech and ejected the fired cartridge, whereupon a fresh cartridge was chambered and the block flipped shut all in one motion. When the hammer came down it helped hold the block closed with a unique interlocking and bracing motion, the hammer moving under the breech block.

As a result of the excellence of this action it was ordered in vast quantities by many foreign governments for military use. The Remington rolling-block is long gone, but the action is far from forgotten, since it is now employed by Navy Arms in a variety of pistol chamberings from .22 to .357 Magnum, at least as of this writing. The action will stand more pressure if demand warrants.

Various single-shot pistols are used by Olympic shooters, and generally manufactured by the Swiss firm Hammerli. Several models of this pistol employ the time-tried Martini falling-block action, which is hinged at the rear of the block; the front end drops to load and unload. Needless to point out, these are rare, elegant, and very expensive shooting machines designed for the single purpose of putting .22 bullets into the 10-ring during International competition.

AUTOLOADER LOCKING SYSTEMS

Aside from the Auto-Mag already mentioned, auto pistols lock in one of three ways: inertia, barrel lug, or toggle joint.

INERTIA LOCKS
The inertia lock is found in most low-powered guns, the range generally running from .22 to .380 and including most everything in between. Not all .380 pistols are inertia locked, though most are; the Star sold by Garcia is locked by a mechanically locked breech.

Inertia locking is also called blowback and was described in the previous chapter. It works because the breech block is much heavier than the bullet, so the bullet moves first. By the time the bullet has reached the muzzle, the block's inertia has been overcome and there is enough residual pressure remaining to move the block to the rear and complete the cycle.

To give an example of how blowback operation can be used only in low-pressure cartridges, it has been computed that it would require a 27-pound breech block to operate in a .30/06 rifle if blowback were employed.

There have been various sytems of delayed or retarded blowback to employ higher-pressure cartridges, but these are not common on any handguns to my knowledge. Their principal applications have been in submachine and machine guns. It is interesting to note that the two most popular submachine-gun cartridges are the 9mm Parabellum and the .45 ACP—both of which are used in many blowback-operated submachine guns. But these guns are much heavier than handguns, and there is insufficient weight in a handgun to employ blowback operation in any handgun for either cartridge.

BARREL-LUG LOCKS
Barrel lugs are employed in most short-recoil-operated auto pistols secured with a mechanically locked breech. The best-known of these systems is that used by John Browning on his .45 Colt pistol, which has two lugs fitting recesses in

The .45 Colt Auto uses a unique locking arrangement perfected by John Browning around 1900 and since copied by many others. The top of the barrel is shown below the underside of the slide. Note the two locking lugs on the barrel to the right of the chamber, which is marked with model and caliber identification. Directly above the lugs you see the recesses in the slide which, when engaged firmly, lock barrel and slide together.

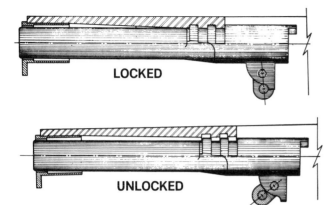

The top of the Luger frame. The two checkered knobs on either side of the action are lifted to open the breech.

Details of the Browning system of locking as used in the .45 Auto are shown by these two sketches. In the upper sketch the gun is locked; you can see the two barrel lugs engaging the slide at the top. In the lower sketch, the barrel and slide have recoiled together about ⅛ inch, and since the "link" (shaded) is pinned to the receiver by the lower pin, it tends to pull the rear end of the barrel down and the lugs out of engagement. The gun is fully unlocked and the slide will now go fully to the rear while the barrel remains where it is. In the counter-recoil stroke, the slide strikes the breech end of the barrel and moves it forward. Then the opposite action takes place via the same link, which now reloads the gun as in the upper sketch.

the slide. A barrel link is used to pull the lugs out of engagement in recoil to unlock and to push them back into engagement on the return stroke to lock the gun.

Other systems, more often using one lug than

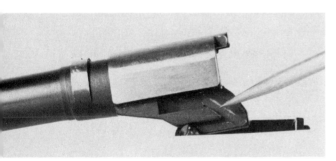

Smith & Wesson's auto pistol is recoil-operated and locks by the single lug you see on top of the barrel. The pointer indicates the surface which forces the barrel down to disengage it from the slide and unlock. At that point the slide moves rearward without the barrel. Locking is accomplished when the barrel moves up the angled surface onto the pin, partially shown below the barrel.

two, cam the rear of the barrel up and down to lock and unlock in the same basic system used on the big .45. Such locking is positive and simple, and it has been employed since about 1900. Many millions of guns have been made all over the world using this or similar systems.

A variation on this system is seen in the Walther P-38, a short-recoil-operated gun which is locked by a vertically sliding locking block under the barrel; the block is cammed up and down to lock and unlock. Aside from this locking system, and the fact that the barrel recoils straight back and forth without dropping down at its breech end, the gun operates very much like those already described.

TOGGLE LOCKS

The toggle-joint lock of the Luger or Parabellum pistol was explained in the previous chapter. It remains the most vivid and visible example of this type of lockup, although there have been other applications, chiefly in machine guns, and in one experimental rifle that came close to adoption in the United States between World Wars I and II. That particular rifle was a delayed-blowback toggle-type action, sort of a marriage of the two systems. A toggle lock can be either in a perfectly straight line or slightly over center; as long as the joint is buckled at the right time the lockup will be secure.

DELAYED-BLOWBACK LOCKING SYSTEM

A unique delayed-blowback locking system is seen in the Hechler & Koch design concept. This West German firm has developed a series of firearms based on a locking arrangement originally employed in a German assault rifle during

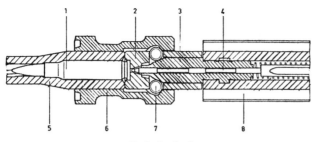

Bolt locked

Hechler & Koch Delayed-Blowback Locking System
1. Cartridge   5. Barrel
2. Bolt head   6. Barrel extension
3. Locking piece   7. Locking roller
4. Firing pin   8. Bolt-head carrier

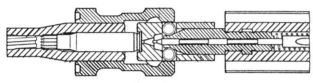

Bolt unlocked

World War II. The system also provided the basis for the Russian AK 47 Assault Rifle and, later, the CETME rifle. Using the same bolt system, Hechler & Koch developed the G-3 automatic rifle adopted by the German armed forces in 1958. A series of autoloading pistols employ the same system; the models are chambered for the 9mm Parabellum and the .45 ACP.

The major parts of this locking system are: the bolt head (2), locking rollers (7), locking piece (3), and bolt-head carrier (8). According to H&K, the system works on the "delayed inertia and symmetrical balance of forces principle." That means that while the gases are forcing the bullet out of the barrel they also are exerting force rearward, through the cartridge case, against the bolt head. In turn, the bolt head pushes against the rollers, which push against the locking piece, which pushes the bolt-head carrier. These forces unlock the bolt by the expedient of letting the rollers move down out of engagement with the barrel extension.

According to the manufacturer, this geometric relationship delays the recoil of the bolt head by a 1:4 ratio. Put another way, this means the bolt head carrier (8) travels four times as far as the bolt head (2) during unlocking as the rollers move out of engagement. It is claimed the weight of the bolt is reduced one-sixteenth of that of the pure inertia bolt which would otherwise be required.

A significant advantage of this system is that it allows a gradual acceleration of the bolt in its extraction movement, which minimizes case tear-off in extraction. This is not very important in pistol ammunition, because extraction is a simple function with these relatively low-powered cartridges, but its application to rifle cartridges is significant.

CHAPTER FIVE

FEEDING SYSTEMS

The feeding of a firearm is defined as the act of moving a fresh cartridge from storage into the firing chamber. This ranges all the way from taking a single cartridge from your pocket and inserting it directly into the barrel of a single-shot firearm to the metallic-disintegrating-link systems employed in the modern machine gun.

Handguns are fed in three basic ways: by hand as in the single-shot as just mentioned, by the magazine system as used in autoloading pistols, and by the revolving-cylinder system as used in revolvers.

Any good feeding system must provide reliability and must feed under any adverse conditions found in the field, including holding the gun right side up, upside down, on either side, or any variations of those positions. Some of the things that dictate the feeding system are the basic gun design, the number of shots desired to be fed, and the shape of the loaded cartridge.

It must also be realized that the problems of feeding are much more acute in military weaponry than in sporting firearms. It's a rare event when the sportsman's life depends on a repeat shot at a target. But it's quite different in both military and law-enforcement situations, where reliability is often a life-or-death matter.

The systems in use today are reliable. They have been in use for many years, and as long as they are designed and manufactured properly — and maintained properly — they will give excellent service.

During World War I, revolvers were manufactured for the .45 Automatic pistol cartridge but, lacking a rim, the cartridges could not be used in a conventional revolver. Smith & Wesson developed these 3-shot "clips," which permitted the use of rimless cartridges in a conventional revolver cylinder.

At the outset we should note that the shape of the loaded cartridge is of great importance in designing the feeding system. For example, one of the easiest cartridges to feed is the .45 ACP (Automatic Colt Pistol), because it has a metal-cased, round-nosed bullet. Feeding the .45 ACP is like steering a fat ferry boat into a wide slip — it's hard to miss, and any deviation will be corrected by the shape of the bullet. And the metal-covered lead bullet resists deformation, which helps it slip into the chamber.

This is the "hand" on the Dan Wesson revolver; it is fastened to the trigger at the bottom. When the trigger is pulled (either single- or double-action) it raises the hand, which rotates the cylinder. The same principle has been employed ever since Sam Colt whittled his first revolver out of wood. The barrel and stock have both been removed in this photo; note that Wesson gives you a square stub on which to mount any grip configuration that suits you.

On the other hand, take the .38 Special wadcutter cartridge with its bullet which is perfectly flat, as flat as a barn door. Both it and the .45 ACP are used in similar handguns! Much more care must be taken to make the .38 Special wadcutter feed reliably, because it must be introduced to the chamber in a perfect attitude or the flat bullet will hang up.

Straight-sided cartridges are easier to feed than rimmed cartridges, because the latter are wider at the rim and, when you have a loaded magazine, the rear part of the cartridges occupies more space than the front. And rimmed cartridges can be loaded in such a way that the rim of a cartridge gets behind the rim of the one below it, so that it will refuse to feed.

So the simplest cartridges of all to feed are those fat, round numbers — the .45 ACP, 9mm Luger or Parabellum, .380, and those of similar shape. That's why these have been so popular for both military use in sidearms and submachine guns and in pocket auto pistols.

REVOLVER FEEDING SYSTEMS

The feeding of revolvers is quite simple and straightforward and really does not require a lot of explanation. Whether you choose to use the word "feed" to mean loading the cylinder is an interesting question. Let's assume the term means loading the cylinder as well as rotating it to align a new cartridge with the barrel. I think this definition is accurate.

Revolver cylinders are generally loaded by hand, by placing each cartridge, one at a time, in the charge holes. There are several quick-load gadgets on the market which will drop six fresh cartridges into the cylinder at a single stroke if you need to do that. (Useful in some target matches as well as in the obvious law-enforcement applications.) During World War I both Colt and Smith & Wesson revolvers were made for military use chambered for the .45 ACP cartridge. This is a rimless cartridge, meaning that it was easy to slip it into the charge hole, but there was nothing to grasp to extract and eject the empty! S&W designed the so-called "half-moon" clips which held three cartridges, and the shooter loaded the cartridges into these clips, then inserted the unit in the revolver. All three were extracted and ejected as a unit.

Now Ruger has developed a method of handling the rimless 9mm cartridge in his double-action revolver by the use of a spring. When you slip the 9mm load into the Ruger, a spring wire slips into the extracting groove, and the empties are removed just as if they were rimmed cases. A photo of this system appears in the next chapter.

Cylinder rotation feeds cartridges into firing position, and the cylinder is rotated by a hand-and-ratchet arrangement. The former is attached to the trigger or hammer and is moved up when the gun is cocked. The ratchet, which the hand engages, is on the rear of the cylinder. Of course there is another part, called the cylinder bolt, which snaps in and out of small notches to lock the cylinder in place once it reaches firing position.

AUTOLOADER FEEDING SYSTEMS

Most autoloaders use one form or another of what is usually called the clip magazine. To be precise, it is a magazine—a "clip" is actually a device to hold cartridges preparatory to loading, as in the early Mauser and Springfield military rifles, which were loaded from a five-shot clip. Pistol magazines really should be called box magazines, but the term "clip magazine" has come into such general use that it's pretty hard to swim upstream against it.

Magazines come in two basic styles: those which align cartridges directly above one another and those which stagger them from side to side. The latter has the advantage of holding more cartridges in a given amount of depth, but it has the disadvantage of requiring a wider magazine. That makes it unhandy for most pistols, because it would require the grip to be too wide. For example, there are 9mm pistols on the market with staggered magazines, but to use the same principle in a .45 would require a gun too fat in the grip to be hand-held comfortably.

The capacity of such magazines is also dependent upon the depth of the gun. A too-long magazine is generally avoided for the simple reasons that it would make the gun too deep through the grip, it would make it hellish to load, and it would require a very long, very strong spring. These actions work very fast, and it's necessary to have ample spring pressure to lift the new cartridge instantly when the slide is

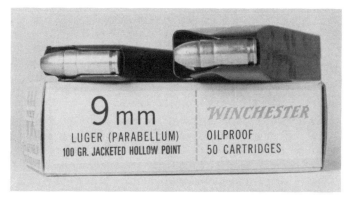

Two Smith & Wesson variations for their Model 39 pistol. At the left, the standard magazine with 8-shot capacity. The pistol is also available as Model 59 with 14-shot magazine, shown at the right. The magazines are not interchangeable.

to the rear and before it starts the forward stroke. Failure to do so means failure to feed.

You can appreciate that spring pressure is just as important for the last shot in the magazine when the spring is at its most relaxed point; it still must have enough strength to shove that last cartridge up fast. Such a strong spring is really hard to compress when you put the last few cartridges in the magazine. For this reason, most .22 pistol magazines (which ordinarily hold ten

A small tool is provided with Luger pistols to assist loading. You slip the tool over the knurled button and depress it, which pulls the follower down. This has another benefit besides making loading easier: It makes it unnecessary to force the last few cartridges by twisting them into the magazine, which would deform the magazine lips.

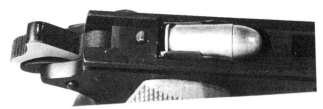

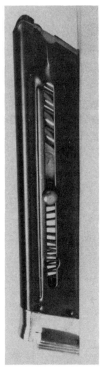

A .45 Auto pistol with slide removed and loaded magazine in place. The magazine lips are very critical, because they determine the angle at which the cartridge is positioned for feeding. If they hold the nose too low or too high, a jam will result.

shots) have a little button alongside that you can grasp. The Luger has a button too but also comes with a combination tool, part of which is meant to slip over the button and help hold down that strong spring.

Another important reason for such aids in loading is that magazine lips are easily bent in trying to force that last cartridge into place. Bent magazine lips mean the cartridge will be positioned at the wrong angle for feeding, and a jam will often result. These lips are also damaged by dropping. I recommend that you always buy two magazines with any auto pistol (many come with an extra at no added cost) for an instant replacement if one becomes damaged, and also for something against which you can compare the one you're using if you experience feeding problems. Feeding problems with any gun using a clip magazine are nearly always the result of bent or battered magazine lips.

These magazines are made of spring steel and are very difficult to repair should they become damaged. The best bet is to buy a new one.

Failure to feed in an auto is generally the result of one of these three things: (1) The cartridge to be fed is held at the wrong angle, which will cause the bullet to strike too high to too low and not enter the chamber. (2) The cartridge is not positioned high enough for the bolt to pick it up, in which event the bolt will come to rest about halfway closed against the side of the cartridge. (3) The action fails to extract cleanly, so that the fired empty interferes with the forward or feeding stroke.

Clip magazines for any rimmed cartridge, such as the .22 rimfire, must be slanted sharply to force each cartridge to lie in such a way that

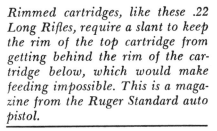

Rimmed cartridges, like these .22 Long Rifles, require a slant to keep the rim of the top cartridge from getting behind the rim of the cartridge below, which would make feeding impossible. This is a magazine from the Ruger Standard auto pistol.

the cartridge above it will have its rim in front of the lower cartridge.

Some years back there was a 32-shot magazine for the Luger which resembled a conventional box magazine with a drum at its bottom. And the old Mauser military pistol had ten- and twenty-shot magazines which were loaded by clip. There have been other variations as well, but by and large these are the most common means of feeding handguns, and they are likely to be the most common forever.

Tubular magazines have no place in a pistol for obvious reasons. Nor do rotary magazines, because they take up too much room. Box magazines, such as are found in most bolt-action rifles, are not as practical as the removable magazines used in pistols, although the principle of operation is the same. And other feeding arrangements characteristic of submachine and machine guns have no place in a handgun either, so that eliminates the belts, drums, gravity hoppers, and the like.

Since feeding is defined as the removal of new cartridges from storage into firing position, it follows that some consideration need be given to the number of cartridges made available. That is pretty simply answered with the revolver, because the diameter of the cylinder dictates the number of charge holes. Conventional revolvers today have anywhere from five to nine charge holes—the former in small, easily concealable .38 Special revolvers and the latter in .22 Long Rifle, for which more holes can be drilled than for a larger caliber.

Auto pistols are limited by the width and depth of the grip. This dimension can be just so fat or the average man can't get his hand around it, and too much depth can be a nuisance, as already explained. The size of the cartridge makes a big difference too, since you can get more 9mm cartridges into the same size grip than you can with the .45s.

The speed of reloading the gun is also a factor, and there's no question that the auto is faster —assuming you have an extra loaded magazine!

CHAPTER SIX

EXTRACTION AND EJECTION

It is important to understand thoroughly the difference between extraction and ejection, which are often confused. Extraction is the withdrawal of the fired cartridge case from the chamber of the barrel. Ejection is the discarding, removal, or tossing out of that case from the gun. Extraction is further broken down into phases; primary extraction is the breaking loose of the case from the chamber walls.

Extraction, expecially ease of extraction, depends not only on the system employed by the specific gun but also on the ammunition: the shape and size of the case, the chamber pressure it generates, the degree of hardness of each lot of brass cases, and cleanliness. Good extraction is also a function of the gun's chamber, which must be clean, smooth, and dimensionally correct.

When a firearm is discharged, the case expands to fill the chamber walls from the same pressure that drives a bullet up the barrel. The higher the power, the tighter the case will be pressed against the chamber walls. If you have a rough or dirty chamber or a dirty cartridge, you can have a stuck case that will be very hard to remove. But all this is relative, since cartridges have varying pressures. The extraction force necessary for a whopping rifle cartridge like the .300 Winchester Magnum is hardly needed to extract a mild cartridge like the .25 Auto pistol.

Fact is, most handgun cartridges do not require primary extraction, so it's not provided. For the record, primary extraction is accomplished by the first movement of the breech bolt,

A unique extractor system was developed by Ruger to handle the 9mm Parabellum rimless cartridge. The little music-wire clips visible in the ratchet slip into the extracting groove and offer sufficient purchase to provide positive extraction. This type of ejection is known as hand ejector, meaning that the heel of the left hand is utilized to push back on the front of the ejector rod, which extracts and ejects all six empties. It can sometimes be hard on the hand.

because such bolts are cammed back by mechanical advantage. A case in point would be the Thompson/Center pistol. This doesn't have a movable breech bolt but rather breaks open like a double shotgun, and the leverage provided by the dropping barrel is substantial. The T/C is chambered for some pretty hot cartridges where primary extraction is a blessing, and it is provided neatly, since the very first downward movement of the barrel slowly begins to move the extractor back with considerable mechanical advantage.

REVOLVER SYSTEMS

Contrast the Thompson/Center single-shot with a revolver like the Model 29 Smith & Wesson .44 Magnum and its extraction. Extraction and ejection is an all-at-once operation in most modern revolvers. Fire all six shots from this .44 Magnum and you swing out the cylinder to reload. Now you have to push back on the ejection rod,

which shoves straight back on all six empties. No mechanical advantage at all—just a straight push. The .44 Magnum is a powerful cartridge, but as long as the gun is in good condition and the charge holes in the cylinder are clean, extraction is not difficult.

If the modern conventional double-action revolver has a disadvantage, it has to be its old (since 1889) hand-ejector system. There is no mechanical advantage whatever, and, especially with a potent load like the .357, .41, and .44 Magnums, ejection can be hard on the heel of your hand. There is a great temptation to push the ejector rod with a block of wood or to ram the ejector rod against a wooden object. This can be done perfectly safely if necessary, but it can also easily result in bending the rod, which can be disastrous. The best way, if you do a lot of shooting with full loads and the heel of your hand gets tender, is to use a glove.

I do not mean to pick on this ejection operation as a serious disadvantage; after all, it's been in use nearly a hundred years. In earlier days both Colt and Smith & Wesson screwed a slightly larger tip on their ejector rods, but modern tips are smaller, and this may be regarded as a form of reverse progress.

A revolver that had a short life span and was one of the tougher ones to extract was the Smith & Wesson .22 Jet. This cartridge case was made by necking down the .357 Magnum to .22 caliber, and the case body was given quite a severe slope. Several problems were posed by this combination. First, it was necessary to have absolutely clean charge holes (they had to be cleaned with lighter fluid), or else the cases would back up on firing and jam against the revolver frame, which prevented cylinder rotation. The total absence of any lubrication in the charge holes obviously made it very likely that fired cases would stick, and that made extraction tough. This .22 Jet produced a hellish roar, enormous flash, and poor sales. It was soon dropped.

Single-action revolvers have the same sort of extraction and ejection in that the cartridges are shoved out by the same kind of straight push. But it's much easier because you poke them out one at a time, and that requires one-sixth the effort. However, it is harder to get at the ejector rod in a single-action because it lies so close to the barrel, so sometimes it too becomes pretty hard to push.

The best revolver extraction and ejection system is that formerly widely used by Smith & Wesson and now used by Harrington & Richardson in a couple of models. As far as I know, these H&R guns are the only ones of current production using the system. Called top-break guns, these revolvers drop their barrels much as does a double shotgun, the barrel being pivoted forward of the cylinder. As the barrel is dropped the extractor is forced back until it reaches a point where all the empties clear the charge holes, whereupon the extractor is permitted to snap back into firing position. Now the holes are empty and ready to reload. The top-break system locks by a small latch at the top of the frame.

Top-break revolvers were made famous by Smith & Wesson in the latter part of the 1800s with several single-action models, the most famous of which were the .44 Russian, made for the Czar, and the .44 American. Extended trials by the army pitted this revolver system against the Colt single-action, and the Colt won despite the reloading efficiency of the Smith & Wesson. The system was, and is, excellent. Today Harrington & Richardson uses it only on .22 caliber revolvers, but the old Smith & Wesson .44s were big guns, quite powerful in their day. Quite possibly the heaviest cartridge used in one of these old revolvers was the .45 S&W used in the Schofield revolver, which was made for the U.S. Cavalry in 1871. It fired a 230-grain bullet with a charge of 28 grains of black powder. The top-break gun succumbed to heavier cartridges that required a solid frame, and a superior extraction and ejection system died with it.

It must be said that extraction in revolvers, both single- and double-action, is something that can and should be improved. The application of some mechanical advantage would be most useful and is not now present on any revolvers except the H&R models mentioned. However, this is not to suggest that the old top break is a superior system; it isn't. The "modern" revolver is far from modern in many respects, and none of the recent improvements in revolvers, good as they are, have addressed themselves to this problem.

The top-break system with its excellent ejection qualities was widely used years ago by Smith & Wesson. It is used today primarily by Harrington & Richardson on many of their fine .22 revolvers. Shown is an H&R Model 999 with the cartridges partially extracted. As the barrel is lowered the cartridges will be ejected. This is a very powerful extraction and ejection system, and I wish more guns employed it today. It's superior to the so-called "hand-ejector" types, but it requires a top-break action.

You might almost call this a "nonejector" model. It's a bottom-of-the-line Harrington & Richardson which can be made at a low cost because the cylinder must be removed from the frame to load or unload. To do so you push the little button visible at the front of the frame, then pull out the rod, which allows removal of the cylinder. Each empty cartridge is then poked out individually by the same rod. Such low-cost revolvers are very useful, since they can be stored in the camper's pack for canoe or fishing or hunting trips and used for emergency.

AUTOLOADER SYSTEMS

Autoloading pistols are a far different proposition from revolvers or single-shots, because the gun provides extraction and ejection automatically. The type of action, whether recoil or blowback, has a bearing on the steps too. For example, a blowback gun has its bolt blown back by the gas generated. Since that pressure comes through the cartridge case, it is obvious that extraction is an automatic function of the design. In fact, most blowback guns will operate without an extractor at all. The role of the extractor in blowback pistols is to act as a pivot for the ejection phase when the rim of the cartridge strikes the ejector. Of course, an extractor is also necessary when you want to remove a cartridge without firing it, but in the course of actual operation, an extractor isn't necessary.

It may be concluded that extraction in any blowback gun is a function of the gun's system of operation—the same gas pressure that blew the bullet out the muzzle is used to blow the fired case out the back and the breech bolt along with it. Ejection in a blowback works the same as in any recoil-operated pistol.

Extraction in a recoil-operated auto pistol,

A Colt .380 pocket auto has a small projection milled into the side of its frame which acts as the ejector. When the cartridge is pulled to the rear by the extractor, its left edge hits the ejector and the cartridge is flipped out of the gun. The pointer shows the ejector; the extractor is visible just over the word "Colt."

however, is entirely different, because the extractor pulls the fired case from the chamber. Although there is often some remaining pressure (called residual pressure) present which aids extraction, the major force is exerted by the mechanical extractor.

In such a gun the breech block or slide is placed in motion by the recoiling barrel, and both parts recoil together for a short distance before the barrel is stopped and the breech block is permitted to travel to the rear alone. During the separation of these parts, extraction occurs, because the barrel has stopped and the extractor, fastened to the breech block, continues to the rear with the fired case.

The separation of these parts is gradual, however—it is not a sharp, instant separation. If it were, the extractor would probably tear through the case rim no matter how little chamber pressure was involved simply because the jolt would be so severe.

For example, in the Colt 1911 .45 Auto, the barrel is unlocked by being pulled down by its link, which is fastened to the frame, resulting in gradual separation. Similarly, the Model 39 Smith & Wesson (and many other autos) are unlocked by a camming of the barrel down out of its engagement with the slide (the breech block) in a gradual manner. And the toggle-joint Luger pistol also has a gradual separation because of the tapered ramps which cam the gun unlocked.

The proper way to visualize this gradual separation is to picture both barrel and breech block as moving rearward tightly locked together. Then the barrel is gradually brought to a halt while the breech block continues to the rear. That is true in most instances, but there are others (the Luger, for example) where the barrel is stopped abruptly but the breech bolt is accelerated, with respect to the barrel's motion, in its rearward movement.

The ejector in nearly all auto pistols is simply a small steel post, sometimes a cut in the frame itself, placed near the back of the opening so that once the breech bolt is far enough to the rear, the post will contact the base of the cartridge and stop its motion. This causes the case to flip around the extractor hook and be flipped out of the gun. Ejection must be fast and positive and

A .25-caliber Colt auto pistol, showing how the firing pin is used to eject the fired cartridge. When fully to the rear the extra-long firing pin is forced farther through its hole to push the cartridge out of the gun. This sort of ejection can be used only with very low-powered cartridges, such as the .25 and .32 auto types.

timed perfectly so that the breech block will be clear on its forward stroke to feed a fresh cartridge from the magazine.

There are a couple of interesting exceptions to this system, seen in very low-powered guns like the .25 Colt Auto and a couple of German designs such as the Ortgies. In these examples, the firing pin acts as the ejector. It is made long enough to have abnormal protrusion. When the slide approaches the rear position the firing pin is stopped, and, with the slide still moving, the firing pin protrudes through its hole far enough to spin the cartridge out of the little gun. This system can be used only on a low-powered gun; if used on a high-pressure cartridge the unsupported firing pin would be blown back out.

The position of the extractor and ejector determines which direction ejection will take place.

Sometimes it is straight up, sometimes directly to the side, and sometimes at about a 45° angle. Aside from the obvious problems with ejection on the target firing line, where a hot empty might drop down the neck of the shooter next to you, the direction of ejection is a matter strictly left to the designer, who will make it fit whatever action design he has in mind. As long as ejection is positive it doesn't matter too much which way the empty flips out.

To cite a few examples of ejection direction: the Luger, a world standard since 1908, flips them straight up; the 1911 Colt .45 at about a 45° angle; the Model 39 Smith & Wesson close to sideways; and the old Colt pocket .380 Auto straight to the side. All these are successful designs—so, as you can see, ejected cases can spin out any old way, just so they clear the gun.

CHAPTER SEVEN

FIRING SYSTEMS

Firing any gun consists of pressing the trigger, which, in turn, releases and/or sets in motion a mechanism or mechanisms that cause the firing pin to strike the primer of the cartridge in the barrel. That's a very simplified definition but a satisfactory one.

Perhaps the simplest system is that seen on many revolvers: The firing pin is part of the hammer. When you pull the trigger the hammer flies forward, and its firing-pin nose enters a hole leading to the primer, which is ignited by the blow. This system was among the first ever used with metallic cartridges, and it's still used on many revolvers as effectively as ever. One small step away from the integral firing pin and hammer is another very common, and very old, method: The firing pin is a separate piece secured in the gun's frame, where it gets whacked by the falling hammer. All modern revolvers work in one of these two ways, and many auto pistols work in the latter way.

Ignition requires a satisfactory blow, and over the many years, engineers have found that one of the most satisfactory firing systems is the combination of a massive hammer with an appropriate firing pin. The system is used not only in handguns but also in the most up-to-date shotgun and rifle designs.

There is very little mystery about the direct-hammer system; it's the same as that used in the cap pistol you had when you were a kid. Place a cap in position where the hammer blow will fall and press the trigger. Bang. The same bang was obtained by putting the same cap on a flat, hard object and whacking it with a carpenter's hammer, as most every kid who ever had a cap pistol learned. We can draw a conclusion here: Ignition requires a satisfactory blow to fire the primer uniformly.

It is important to note that there is a difference in primer sensitivity between rifle ammunition and handgun ammunition. The reason is that the hammer blow in a rifle is stronger—there is space for larger hammers and stronger springs than can be built into a handgun. This fact is of little importance to anyone except a handloader, but it's vital to him because rifle and pistol primers come in the same sizes, and once they stray from their boxes, you can't tell them apart.

Pistol primers are made with softer metal cups to compensate for the lighter firing-pin blow. If you used a rifle primer in a handgun reload, it would sometimes fail to fire and in any case would provide erratic ignition. Using a pistol primer in a hot rifle cartridge (which develops much higher pressures than handgun cartridges) could cause a primer rupture that would spill high pressure gas into the action, with serious results.

Again, this is meaningless unless you reload. But if you do, be sure always to keep primers in their original boxes to avoid any mixup.

THE TRIGGER PULL

This little curved piece of steel that you pull (or press or squeeze) can be simple or complex. The simple trigger is most commonly defined as one which directly engages the hammer. It's seen on most revolvers and on such rifles as the Winchester Model 94 and Marlin Model 336. The upper part of the trigger is formed into a precise shape that is called the sear. It has a finely defined angle that engages a notch in the hammer which is called the sear notch. Pressing the bottom of the trigger to the rear moves the sear forward out of engagement with the hammer, permitting the latter to fly forward under the shove of the big spring usually called the mainspring.

Trigger pulls are good or bad, hard or light, smooth or rough. A good trigger pull should be (1) consistent, (2) crisp, (3) smooth, (4) with as lit-tle movement as possible, (5) heavy enough to be safe, and (6) nonetheless light enough to permit an easy let-off.

The simple trigger can conform to all these requirements, and it will in a properly designed and manufactured revolver (the requirements for auto pistols are a little different; we'll come to them later). One of its controls is the distance from the finger curve to the pin on which it pivots and from that pin to the sear. These dimensions form a simple lever with the mechanical advantages known to all. Additionally, the fit of the sear in the sear notch—which includes the angles formed on both pieces, the depth of the notch, and the hardness and smoothness of these surfaces—will dictate the delicacy of the trigger pull. For the record, these surfaces should be hard and smooth. And of course their angles and the depth of engagement should be carefully controlled.

Some folks are bold enough to stone these surfaces with a hard Arkansas stone to "improve" the pull. This is acceptable when you know what you're doing (which most people don't), but the most important thing to maintain is the angles—and that's much easier said than done. A good way to "improve" the trigger pull on any gun of this type is rough and crude, but it works. Simply place a wide-bladed screwdriver under the tail of the cocked hammer (with an empty gun!) and pry up on the hammer as you pull the trigger. This has the effect of jamming the surfaces together as you pull the trigger and moving the sear out of the sear notch. Several treatments like this will often smooth out a rough pull. You should protect the surfaces under the hammer with a bit of stiff cardboard.

A trigger pull should resemble breaking a glass rod, to use the description that's been common for years. Gradually increasing the finger pressure should result in no perceptible movement of the trigger and should eventually release the firing system, at which point the trigger should stop without further rearward movement. Creep in a trigger cannot be tolerated if you expect any sort of accuracy with any kind of gun. Creep is usually described as being like a creaky, rusty barn gate which lurches and stops, squeaks a little, takes another lurch, and finally fires. Nobody ever shot well with such a trigger, and no modern gun ought to be delivered with creep, although many are.

Different types of guns require different types of firing systems, because of the nature of their design. The simple trigger we've described above is most easily understood, and any other trigger pull is basically the same.

It is comparatively easy to secure a good trigger pull on a revolver. The engagement on any single-action gun is the same as that of any simple trigger such as the Model 94 Winchester rifle. I've already described how this can be accomplished. Double-action revolvers are traditionally fired single-action style in target shooting, so the situation is the same as with a single-action revolver.

When fired double-action, however, the story is quite different. Here the trigger pull is very long and must accomplish all these things: rotate the cylinder, cock the hammer, unlock and re-lock the cylinder. This is accomplished because the long tail of the trigger engages the hammer strut, which only becomes operative in double-action fire, and this motion accomplishes the aforementioned steps. As a result, the pull is long (almost ½ inch) and quite hard. It is difficult to shoot with any precision using the double-action pull. But this pull is not meant for long-range precision shooting; it's meant for fast, close fire, and for this it is superb. You can get the first shot off with a double-action revolver very quickly and, if the range isn't great, with adequate accuracy.

There is more movement present in the trigger pull of an auto gun than of a revolver. That is because the gun must disconnect, which will be described later in this chapter, and such action requires some play in the parts. It is possible to adjust the trigger of a single-action so you can feel very little movement. But that can never be the case with an auto pistol, simply because you have to relax the trigger for the disconnector to re-engage. Auto pistols can have an excellent trigger pull, but they'll always have a little slack or loose movement which must first be taken up before beginning the actual trigger squeeze.

Many early revolvers had a type of trigger that I call a "button" trigger. There are quite common on early Smith & Wesson guns, even the bigger-caliber models. Their operation was essentially the same as a conventional trigger, although their appearance was considerably different and no trigger guard was employed on all the models I've seen.

SIMPLE FIRING PINS

"Simple" isn't really the right word, but by using it I mean pins that are simple to understand; they are those that are directly connected to a hammer. Examples are found on many revolvers, some rifles, and many shotguns, although you can't generally see them in shotguns.

Some of these pins are an integral part of the hammer, and some are a separate part pinned in place. Smith & Wesson, for example, lets its hammers pivot just a few degrees, because the hammer swings in an arc and S&W prefers to make the hole leading to the primer as tight as possible. When you look through this little hole you'll see the primer of a centerfire cartridge, or the rim of a rimfire cartridge. When you pull the trigger and the hammer flies forward, it will hit this primer and ignite the priming charge.

Firing pins used for centerfire and rimfire cartridges must be positioned differently, since one must strike in the middle while the other must strike off center to hit the rim. They must also have different profiles. A rimfire firing pin is flat on the end but may be round, square, or rectan-

A "lifetime" unbreakable firing pin as used by Charter Arms and made from beryllium copper. Many modern revolvers and pistols have firing pins that can be snapped on an empty chamber nearly forever. But it's always wise to make sure the manufacturer has made this claim before doing too much dry-firing.

The Luger pistol's firing system incorporates a spring-driven firing pin. You can see the spring in the rear of the breech bolt. That square, shiny spot is the sear notch, which is caught by the trigger linkage to cock and fire the pistol.

gular in section; they come in all sizes and shapes. Their function, again, is to smack the cartridge's rim hard enough to crush the soft metal and deliver a good sharp whack to the priming compound inside the case. It will be obvious that the larger in area the face of such a pin is, the harder must be the blow.

The centerfire pin, on the other hand, must hit the primer as nearly dead center as possible, and it must deliver a good whack also. It must indent the primer cup with enough force to crush the priming compound, which is located directly under the cup. (This will be discussed in detail in Chapter Fourteen.) The pin, however, must *not* pierce the cup nor allow it to rupture. So the centerfire firing pin must have a spherical nose, very nicely polished and smooth.

The next-simplest firing pin is the combination of firing pin and hammer. It's one of the oldest systems and one of the most reliable. Typical examples are seen in Ruger revolvers. In these guns you can see both the hammer and the rear end of the firing pin, so it's easy to understand. The same system is used in most of the so-called hammerless shoulder guns (which actually have a hammer inside the receiver where you can't see it). These range from the Browning Auto-5, in use since 1900, to the M1 Garand, to the modern gas shotgun. One of the reasons this type of firing system is so widely used is that it's simple and positive.

Finally, the third common system is that used in most bolt-action rifles: the Mauser-type spring-loaded firing pin. It is an excellent system, positive and reliable, and is used in some handguns, a notable example being the Luger pistol.

Those are the basic systems. There are variations, many of which we'll discuss, and, of course, there are a lot of other complicating fac-

tors which we'll also discuss. First, though, the types of firing pins:

The two major types of firing pins are the inertia pin and the supported pin. An example of the inertia pin is found in the .45 Colt Auto. Nearly all others are supported, and an excellent example of the supported pin is that of the Winchester Model 94 rifle. When the hammer goes down it stays down and supports the pin.

A third type of firing pin, formerly used on a couple of sporting .22s but no longer found on anything but machine guns, is the fixed firing pin. This type of pin is machined as a permanent, immovable pin on the bolt face. It's designed to be used only on a gun firing from the open-bolt position, and it works by firing the cartridge as the bolt fully closes. The system is ideal for low-pressure cartridges such as the 9mm and .45 ACP used in machine pistols or submachine guns. But it isn't worth much for any sporting purpose because firing from an open bolt is not conducive to any sort of decent accuracy. (You can't expect the gun to stay still while the bolt is flying forward.)

The inertia firing pin as found on the .45 Colt Auto is a comparatively heavy pin, and it gets a good whack from the big .45 hammer. It needs it because the pin isn't long enough to reach from the hammer to the primer. This means the hammer has to hit the back of the firing pin hard enough to make it go far enough and hard enough on its own momentum to fire the primer. A very limp firing-pin spring holds the pin back in position for the hammer to connect. The advantage to this pin is that it's quite safe to carry the gun with the hammer down on a live cartridge. There's no way the gun can fire until it's cocked.

The .45 is a relatively low-pressure cartridge, which means that the pin need not be supported, because firing-pin support helps hold the pin tightly against the indented primer—against the chamber pressure. The higher the pressure, the more important this is. Inertia firing pins cannot be used in a high-power rifle.

THE BLOW AND INDENTATION

We can establish certain requirements for the firing system (including the primer):

1. The primer must fire consistently with a blow of a certain energy or weight.

2. The primer must not fire when struck with a blow less than the minimum (that is, the primers must not be too sensitive).

3. The primer, or the rim of a rimfire cartridge case, must not rupture or be pierced.

While those limits are required for ignition, there is a far narrower range of specifications within which more nearly perfect ignition will result. And more nearly perfect ignition will produce more nearly perfect accuracy. This explains why target guns are refined to the point where their ignition systems provide the quickest, surest, and most uniform ignition possible.

LOCK TIME
Quickness is known in the trade as lock time—and it's very important to the target shooter, because he has learned to study any number of range conditions to the point where, when he says "Go," he wants that gun to fire instantly. The slightest slowness in lock time can easily make a 9 out of a perfect 10-hold. It's easy to make an action with fast lock time, but quickness is generally associated with light weight, and the combination doesn't always result in consistency. So the problem of lock time in a target gun is considerably more complicated than it sounds at first glance.

Lock time is defined as the elapsed time between the moment the sear releases the firing pin or hammer and the moment the primer is crushed and explodes. It is claimed by several authorities that the quickest locks are those of a finely made double shotgun employing the traditional V-springs. Any action in which the strike is actuated by a rotating hammer is quicker than actions in which the striker is pushed forward by a coiled spring as in a bolt-action rifle. The speed

of hammer rotation depends upon the strength and efficiency of the spring. And the efficiency further depends upon the angle through which the hammer must fall. The locks used in "best" double shotguns have a lock time of approximately .002 second.

MODERN REVOLVER FIRING SYSTEMS

Until the past few years it was considered unsafe to carry a single-action revolver unless the hammer was all the way down on an empty charge hole. The reason was that if the gun was dropped and landed on the hammer spur, the blow was heavy enough to knock the hammer out of the half-cock notch and fire the gun. A number of serious injuries resulted from such accidents.

Some double-action incidents of the same sort were reported over the years, but not as many as with the old single-action guns. Carrying a six-shot gun with only five cartridges was a disadvantage, of course, but it was safe.

All modern revolvers employ a device which prevents this unwanted firing no matter how hard the hammer spur is hit. In fact, there has long been one brand on the market (Iver Johnson, since 1892) with the same fail-safe system now adopted by almost every maker. One method is to utilize what is called a transfer bar—the hammer cannot hit the firing pin until the trigger is pulled to raise the transfer bar between the firing pin and hammer. The hammer then hits the transfer bar, which, in turn, hits the firing pin. If the trigger isn't pulled, the transfer bar is out of position and the hammer cannot reach the firing pin. Other systems utilize the same principle, except they use the bar in reverse fashion and it rises to block the hammer blow unless the trigger is pulled.

The result is a good deal more safety. If your single-action revolver is an older model without either of these modern devices, you are well advised to carry it with the hammer down on an empty charge hole.

I suspect an argument could be made that the transfer-bar system adds a bit of "softness" to the hammer blow because the hammer must hit the bar first. The net effect of this is inevitably a slightly slower lock time (it being necessary to

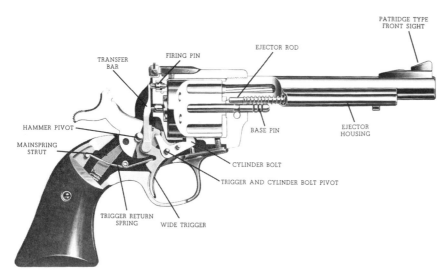

The action of the transfer-bar system is clearly shown in these two photos of a Ruger single-action revolver. In the cutaway (top), the gun is shown with trigger pulled and hammer beginning to fall. Note that when the trigger is pressed, the transfer bar is raised so that its top is behind the firing pin. In the lower photo, with gun at rest position, the transfer bar is in its low position, the top of the bar is below the firing pin, and the hammer cannot possibly reach the firing pin. This revolver can be safely carried with all charge holes loaded.

The action of the transfer bar is also shown in these photos of the Dan Wesson double-action revolver. In the full-cock photo the transfer bar is raised so the hammer will hit the bar and carry it forward to drive the firing pin down. In the photo of the gun at rest, the transfer bar is lowered; the hammer cannot make contact with it, and the hammer itself cannot hit the firing pin. This type of safety device prevents accidental discharge if the gun is dropped.

overcome the inertia of the bar and get it moving to hammer speed), and a softer hammer blow. I assume that the makers have added stronger springs to overcome any tendency toward sponginess, and I have heard no complaints in the accuracy department.

An interesting different way of accomplishing this same function is seen in the new Crusader by High Standard. In this gun the hammer and trigger are geared, and when the trigger is deliberately pulled, the hammer lowers to engage the firing pin. There is no transfer bar of any kind; unless the trigger is pulled the hammer is in the wrong plane to fire the revolver.

FIRING-PIN PROTRUSION

A very important detail in firearms manufacture is the control of firing-pin protrusion. This is usually controlled by the shape of the shoulder behind the striking point. It is most important in high-power centerfire rifle cartridges, which develop enormous chamber pressures. Too much protrusion could easily cause a pierced primer, with the result that gas under pressure would rush back into the bolt body via the firing-pin hole. The normal protrusion in such a rifle is between .055 and .065 inch—roughly $\frac{1}{16}$ inch (.0625). Less protrusion will not give consistent ignition; more will risk a pierced primer.

The same degree of protrusion is not a major requirement of low-pressure cartridges, however, and as discussed in Chapter Six, some smaller autoloading pistols (notably the .25-caliber Browning-designed Colt and several German Ortgies pistols) use a firing pin with abnormally long protrusion which acts as the ejector when the slide is in full recoil.

A rimfire gun also must have a limited protrusion; otherwise snapping the firing pin without a cartridge in the chamber would cause the pin's nose to hit the barrel or cylinder each time. This would soon ruin the pin and would mar the barrel where it must support the rim for consistent ignition.

LUBRICATION

Many of today's lubricants are designed for very cold weather, and if you use one of these you're not going to experience what some hunters have learned the hard way. One day many years ago, when I had a gunsmith shop in New York's Adirondacks, it was bitterly cold. A friend who had been hunting dropped in, quite annoyed because his pet Model 70 Winchester had failed to fire when he had a good buck in his sights an hour or so earlier. Bill sat the rifle down and began complaining, so I picked it up and looked it over. It appeared to be in order, but then I took the firing-pin assembly out of the bolt body and pointed out the trouble. A coating of heavy grease covered the mainspring. It had congealed in the extreme cold and only allowed the firing pin to ooze forward, far too slowly to ignite a cartridge. We cleaned out the grease and dried out the firing-pin recess, and Bill went back to his hunting. The moral is that unless you're using one of the modern light oils specifically made to flow at very low temperatures, you're far better off to keep your firing mechanism clean and dry. If you must lubricate, use powdered graphite.

TYPES OF SPRINGS

There are three types of springs in general use for firing mechanisms: coil, leaf, and V. There is nothing whatever wrong with any of the three types, as long as each is correctly made, hardened, and tempered. The leaf spring is probably the least used of the three today, although you still find it on many older guns. It is quite dependable. However, if not made correctly it has a tendency to break more easily than a coil spring.

The V-spring, which is still used on most of the top grades of double shotguns, also must be made correctly to give good service. When purchased from a reliable maker a V-spring will never fail, but the same cannot be said for a spring from an unreliable maker. As I have said earlier, the V-spring coupled with a correctly designed hammer delivers probably the fastest lock time in gundom.

Today, however, almost every maker uses coil springs. They are cheaper, easier to assemble, easier to make, and totally reliable. Given low-cost manufacture, there is no question they are more dependable than any other type of spring. Some revolvers and most better-grade double shotguns employ a small part called a stirrup between the hammer and the spring. This usually has the effect of slightly accelerating the action. The British call this part a swivel. Since the spring force decreases as it is relaxed, the stirrup, or swivel, tends to maintain the same force throughout the fall of the hammer. This is accomplished by increasing the amount of leverage as the hammer falls.

ELECTRIC IGNITION

Attempts to fire guns electrically date almost as far back as Ben Franklin's kite. In 1881, W. W. Greener wrote in *The Gun and Its Development* of an experiment with electric ignition "forty years ago" in Prague. That would have been about 1840!

The idea was, as it is today, to ignite the powder charge by electrically releasing the firing mechanism. There have been numerous attempts, the most notable to my knowledge having been the High Standard development of about 1960. It was the position of the company that U.S. free-pistol shooters (with the kind of pistols used in International and Olympic matches) ought to use American products. Most American shooters use pistols made by such foreign firms as the Swiss Hammerli. The manufacture of such fine, precise pistols requires an incredible degree of workmanship and time, with the result that there is very little reward for the company that makes these guns. Producing fifteen or twenty pistols for the Olympic team would cost the company far more than they could realize from the sale. The small amount of publicity would scarcely be worth the effort. And this is probably what prompted High Standard to shelve the project. The only thing electric ignition could hope to achieve would be a better trigger release and faster lock time. But, as I have said, these are worthwhile objectives if they can be accomplished.

THE OPEN-BOLT SYSTEM

One remaining firing mechanism should be mentioned briefly even though it's of small interest to sportsmen. That is the open-bolt mechanism employed in machine pistols (all of which fire "pistol cartridges"). As already stated, some

of these have a fixed firing pin, and there is no mystery about that. The gun simply fires as the cartridge is chambered, since the firing pin hits the primer at the same time. Early Thompson submachine guns had a movable hammer and separate firing pin that was a little different. The hammer was shaped liked a triangle, with legs about 5/8 inch long, and was about 3/16 inch thick. It was pinned near the square corner and operated in such a way that as the breech bolt slammed home, the lower end of the hammer struck the gun's frame, causing the hammer to rotate, whereupon the upper end gave the firing pin a whack and fired the cartridge. Other open-bolt guns fire in ways that are somewhat different, but all depend upon the force of the closing bolt to actuate the firing pin fairly similarly.

THE CASELESS EXPERIMENT

A few years ago, Daisy—the air-rifle people—introduced a revolutionary concept which they called V/L, a "shooting system with caseless ammunition." It was revolutionary, it was different, and it was short-lived. But it's of enough interest to describe.

What Daisy did was to take a .22-caliber lead bullet and attach a "short rod of propellant on its base." There was no conventional brass cartridge case and no primer. The ammunition consisted of just a bullet with the propellant stuck to its base. Ignition in the Daisy V/L system was accomplished by heat, from a jet of heated air created by a spring-driven piston behind the firing chamber.

This ingenious system can be compared to the way a diesel engine operates in that the heat generated by compression is sufficient to ignite the propellant. In the case of a diesel it's the fuel mixture; in the Daisy V/L system it was the propellant.

No reasons have ever been given for its failure that I am aware of. I can guess that shooters weren't sufficiently interested in such a departure as one reason. I can also guess that the movement of the big spring and piston were enough to move the gun during their travel motion. To put that another way, lock time in this system had to be very, very slow. I can also imagine that the ammunition-storage problem must have been monumental; you couldn't carry the caseless ammo loose in your pocket. And I should also think propellant deterioration would have been a factor.

Just the same, it was an experiment in a different method of firing, and it worked sufficiently well to get on the market. But obviously it didn't reach sales goals, and the project is now a dead issue.

DISCONNECTORS

It is necessary in any autoloading firearm to have some method of preventing the gun from becoming a machine gun—that is, to ensure that only one shot will be fired with each pull of the trigger. If the sear were permitted to remain in the firing position it would fail to catch the hammer, or firing pin, and one of two things would happen: The gun would fire fully automatically and rip through the entire magazineful of cartridges, or the hammer would slide up into the fired position with insufficient force to fire the gun. The exact design of each gun would govern which of these two events would occur, although sometimes the sensitivity of primers would have a bearing. In either event, the situation is not desirable.

Once an autoloader is fired, the firing system is therefore disconnected—and that permits the sear to engage the hammer or firing pin during the operational cycle and leave the gun reloaded and ready to be fired again by relaxing the trigger, which reconnects the firing system with the trigger. It's not as complicated as it may sound.

In the autoloading pistol—the .45 Colt is a good example—the disconnector connects the trigger with the sear (the sear, in turn, holds the hammer) only when the slide is fully closed, meaning only when the gun is fully locked. This occurs because the top of the disconnector is permitted to rise into a small notch in the bottom surface of the slide. Housed in the frame, the top of the disconnector tends to force itself up about 1/16 inch under spring tension. It's prevented from doing so except when the gun is fully closed. This disconnector has two functions: It will not allow the gun to fire unless the gun is closed and locked, and it disconnects the

trigger from the sear to allow only one shot each time the trigger is pulled.

You may have read or heard that you can prevent an assailant from firing his autoloading pistol if you're quick enough to push back the barrel. While this procedure is certainly not the safest if you're about to be mugged, raped, or shot, it does happen to work. That is, if you push back the barrel of a recoil-operated gun a bit, it will disengage the sear and hammer by disconnecting the disconnector.

That same system, with a few minor changes depending on the gun, appears on every autoloading pistol ever made by Colt (primarily because every autoloading pistol ever made by Colt, right up to today, is a Browning patent) and on other makes as well.

Other autos perform the disconnection in different ways, but the principle is the same: to ensure that only a single shot will be fired with each pull of the trigger.

Attempts to modify a semiautomatic gun to a full auto have been tried many times and should be avoided for three elemental reasons: They rarely work properly for one reason or another depending on the gun; even if successful there would be no way to control the gun because it would empty in one swift roar; and it's illegal. Don't try to do it.

SAFETIES

Safeties are part and parcel of firing systems, because a safety works directly on some element of the firing system.

Revolvers have no manual safety in the usual sense but depend upon either a half-cock notch, the transfer bar system already mentioned which prevents discharge without pulling the trigger, or the rebound position of the hammer. The rebound system allows the hammer to retract slightly after firing and after the trigger is relaxed. (This retraction is necessary anyway; otherwise cylinder rotation would be prevented by a firing pin dug deep into the primer or a fired cartridge.)

This is not to imply that revolvers are not safe—far from it, because the exposed-hammer system has been used on millions and millions of guns. Consider the old Paterson Colt that dates to 1836, plus all the single- and double-action revolvers made over the years. And that doesn't include the Winchester Model 94 (some 4,-000,000 to date) and the Marlin Model 336 (about 3,500,000 to date), all of which are exposed–hammer guns—one of the safest firing systems ever designed.

Autoloaders are another story; they require a manual safety. As a matter of fact, many of them have a combination of safeties of these types: a grip safety, a magazine safety, and the usual thumb safety. Let's examine each of these.

Grip safeties were a John Browning idea that was first applied to the Colt "pocket auto" Model 1903 and patented in 1901. The grip safety is widely used today on most auto pistols and is even included on the German Luger recently imported by Interarms (but discontinued in 1977). A grip safety is simply a movable piece at the rear of the gun's grip; you must hold the pistol in firing position, which depresses the grip safety, in order to fire the gun.

A magazine safety, as its name implies, means that you can't fire the gun unless the magazine is in place. This type of safety is particularly useful for the novice, because you can remove the magazine from any auto and not realize there may still be a cartridge in the chamber. With a magazine safety you can't fire the gun; without it you could.

The thumb safety is a deliberate safety, meaning that you put it on to carry the loaded gun safely and push it off when you are ready to fire. There are some exceptions, and some added functions, with certain of these safeties. On the Smith & Wesson Model 39 double-action auto, for example, the safety can be placed on with the hammer cocked, whereupon the hammer will fall. But the safety rocks a block in front of the hammer, so the hammer cannot reach the firing pin. The result is that you can load a magazine in this gun, cycle the slide, which will chamber a cartridge, and leave the gun cocked with hammer back. Then push the safety on and you drop the hammer. It can't fire even though there's a cartridge in the chamber. While on safe the gun can't be fired, but this gun can be safely carried off safe because it's a double-action and can only be fired deliberately.

The double-action auto pistol has become popular fairly recently. The first important one of these was the German Walther police model (which preceded the famous Walther P-38 of World War II). Its chief advantages are that you can carry a loaded auto pistol with no danger of its firing until desired, and the first shot can be gotten off as quickly as with a double-action revolver. (Otherwise an auto must be carried with the chamber empty, which means you must cycle the slide to chamber a round, or loaded with the manual safety on. Getting into action either way is slower than firing a double-action revolver.) From the first shot on, a double-action auto is fired conventionally. So it will be seen that this firing system possesses the speed advantage of a revolver's first shot and its safety, plus the rapid firepower of the autoloading system.

Over the years there have been various "safeties" on many revolvers. Generally speaking, all of these are now gone, and it's doubtful that they will ever return. Some of the ideas were reasonably good; their demise was occasioned because there is no real need for such a safety on any revolver. It's quite possible that you'll run into an old revolver with some sort of patent safety, but there were too many and they are too unimportant to elaborate upon here.

CHAPTER EIGHT

THE GUN BARREL

The earliest guns were not shoulder-fired; they more nearly resembled small artillery. Early barrels were wood. A bit too much gunpowder and the barrels burst, so they were often wrapped with wire. The wire wrapping added strength, and in fact wire-wrapped artillery barrels were used until comparatively recently. Soon the wooden barrels gave way to metal, and then to improved metals as the science of metallurgy developed.

The methods by which barrels have been made over the years have been closely related to machine-tool development. As I have already stated, the American industrial revolution, when America began to turn from an agricultural society to an industrial one, was formed around two industries: firearms and textile machinery. Of the two, the firearms industry is the older, since it can be traced to the earliest settlers, while the textile industry was not started until 1790.

It would be useless in this book to review some of the older methods of making gun barrels, but it will be of interest to review quickly the methods used during the early and middle 1800s. Barrels were not bored out of solid steel as they are today; rather they were made by wrapping metal around a steel bar, welding the joints, and then withdrawing the bar.

Such barrels are variously called Damascus, twist, stub, or laminated (and sometimes a combination of those names). There are distinct variations in each one of them, but we agreed not to probe this subject too deeply. Early barrels were iron; later ones were usually a combination of iron and steel. Some of the twist barrels (we'll use that term generically) were excellent, being a good combination of steel, with its properties of strength and elasticity, and soft iron. Others were pretty nearly pure iron, which wouldn't stand as much pressure.

Moreover, such barrels' quality also depended on the skills of the various workmen who forged and welded them. It was important to keep scale out of the welds (and very hard to do), and it was equally important to keep the metal at the right temperature (in a charcoal fire) and hammer it correctly to achieve perfect welds. The hammering had another important effect. It strengthened the metal by molecular rearrangement; we know this as forging, and a forged product usually has greater strength than a similar product manufactured by other techniques.

After a twist barrel was rough-formed on the steel bar, called a mandrel, it was rough-ground on the outside and rough-bored on the inside. These operations removed most of the roughness; a visual inspection would now disclose serious imperfections, and if there were any the barrel was scrapped. Assuming no visual defects, the barrel was now proofed by loading it with a prescribed overload and firing it remotely in the confines of a "proof house." Some barrels burst wide open from poor welds or other defects; those that did not were finished and then proofed again.

In England and most other European countries where gun proofing is a government function, this initial proving is called provisional proof. The final proof is called definitive proof.

As steels improved, the gun industry began to bore barrels from solid steel bars. Initially called weldless barrels, they had many advantages over twist barrels. As is usual among gun people, however, there were countless arguments over the relative merits of the two types—and there's no denying the beauty of a fine twist barrel such as a "three-iron stub Damascus." I suspect the development of smokeless powder had as much to do with the demise of twist barrels as anything else. Smokeless, which became popular during the 1890s, developed considerably higher pres-

sures than black powder, so it required stronger barrels. It also burned hotter, so it demanded tougher steel. That's why if you have a fine old gun made during the days of black powder you should not shoot smokeless loads in it unless the barrel is specifically stamped "for smokeless powder." (And that's why, should you own an old twist-barreled shotgun, you should *never* shoot a smokeless load in it.)

Steel is made tough by the addition of certain alloys, and made harder by the addition of other alloys. The most common gun-barrel steel today is known as SAE (for Society of Automotive Engineers) 4140. It's an alloy consisting of chromium and molybdenum, popularly called chrome-moly. This steel is abrasion-resistant, high in tensile strength, and readily machinable. It satisfies the requirements for nearly all gun barrels in use today.

Some of the very hot rifle cartridges, such as the .264 Winchester, 7mm Remington, some Weatherby Magnums, and the .220 Swift, are very hard on barrels. They create such heat that a barrel will be eroded very rapidly. The solution here has been stainless steel. Stainless has all the desirable attributes of SAE 4140, except that it is much more difficult to machine. It adds great abrasion resistance and thus longer barrel life for these hot calibers.

Most .22 rimfire rifles do not develop very hot pressures and do not require a steel as tough as SAE 4140. So most .22 barrels are a softer, milder steel—actually an alloy of carbon and manganese, which is much easier to machine and just as suitable for the purpose. There are many high-power rifles that are used solely for hunting, which means they won't be fired very often, and their barrels also are made of this softer carbon-manganese steel.

The use of stainless steel has been expanding at a great rate in the handgun world (see Chapter Twenty-three for further details on this development). Stainless isn't necessary for hot handgun cartridges, so it is not used for the same reasons that it is for high-power rifle cartridges. It may be stated that stainless steel is used for handgun barrels simply because many new handgun models are *entirely* made of stainless steel (except for grips and adjustable sights).

THE RIFLED BARREL

Nobody knows who invented rifling—the spiral grooves in a gun barrel that give a rotational spin to the projectile to keep it flying point first. Rifling was used in Europe in the sixteenth century, so it has been around a long time.

In the manufacture of a rifled barrel, the bore is first drilled and then reamed up to what is called bore diameter. Let's use the .30 caliber as our example, in which case the barrel is reamed to an exact diameter of .300 inch. Now we have a perfectly smooth, precise hole through the barrel—that is, it appears absolutely smooth but actually has circular tool marks in its surface, no matter how slight. At this point barrels are sometimes honed, or polished, to make this surface even smoother.

Barrel drilling is generally considered the most critical operation in barrel manufacture. The stationary barrel drill is shaped like a V at its drilling end and has a long groove running the full length of the drill as well as a small hole paralleling the groove. The hole is to force cutting oil to the cutting edge and to carry the chips back out along the V-groove. The barrel itself is rotated at very high speed, and the drill is fed into the barrel blank. Assuming there are no flaws in the steel and the bit is properly sharpened, the bore should be drilled dead straight.

Rifling, as we have said, is the system of grooves running down the barrel that give a bullet its spin. Only with the spin will a bullet have stability. This can be compared with throwing a football. Get a good spin, make the ball fly point on, and you can sneak it between two defenders closer together than a pair of chorus girls. Let it tumble end over end and you lose speed, accuracy, and the ball.

We've been using .30 caliber as our example, so let's point out now that a .30-caliber bullet measures .308 inch. That's 8/1000 inch larger than the bore diameter of .300 inch. Therefore the rifling grooves are cut to a depth of .004 inch— making a *groove diameter* of .308 inch, the same as the bullet. The reason for all this is that the bullet must be driven into the rifling, and the rifling must bite into the bullet to make it accept the spin. We call the space between the grooves

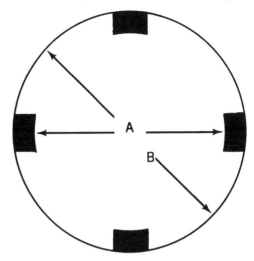

A rifled barrel is first bored to bore diameter, A, and after rifling it also has a groove diameter, B. Bullets are made to groove diameter so they can be forced into the rifling and accept its twist. In a typical .30-caliber rifle, the A dimension shown would be .300 inch and the B dimension would be .308 inch, meaning that each land *(shaded) would have a height of .004 inch. A 30-caliber bullet measures .308 inch.*

the land, and the sketch shows a typical rifling system with dimensions for .30 caliber.

Now—let's mention it again—there are tolerances. Bores usually measure very close to .300 inch. Groove depth can run a little deeper than .308 inch, and it often goes to .3085 or even .309 inch. There is an excellent reason for this. The barrel must perform with ammunition of any and all brands—and vice versa. All of this is controlled by an organization known as the Sporting Arms and Ammunition Manufacturers' Institute (SAAMI, always referred to as "Sammy") which establishes the standards so that your Federal ammunition will fit a Colt, Winchester's ammunition a Smith & Wesson, and so on.

Right here, let's make it clear that a "bullet" is a projectile. Let's not get into the news media's problem of not being able to distinguish a cartridge from a bullet. Bullets are made to tolerances. For example, a set of bullet-forming dies will be used to make several million bullets before the die is retired. That means the die is going to wear so that the first bullet made from this die will be smaller than the last. A bullet die for a huge volume run will be made a little undersized, say .306 inch, and after several million bullets have been formed the die will be producing bullets measuring close to .309 inch. Maybe that doesn't sound like much, but a difference of so little as .001 can raise merry hell with the chamber pressure, if it's the bullet that's bigger than the hole.

Generally speaking, today's ammunition is far closer to dimension than was true fifteen or twenty years ago. We'll get into this in more detail later in this book, but it's important to know that much about bullets for any intelligent understanding of barrels.

Nearly all rifling is to the right. Why? Good question. British guns usually twist to the left, and so does the Colt revolver. Almost everybody else twists to the right. According to the best information I have, the British believe that this side of the equator works better with a left-hand twist. I've heard it said that Colt uses a left-hand twist because the torque of the bullet going through the barrel will tend to tighten the barrel in its threads. Who knows? It really doesn't matter. What does matter is the amount of twist, which is always expressed in one complete turn in so many inches.

RIFLING SYSTEMS

The systems used in handguns are nowhere near as varied as those used in rifles. The reason would seem to be that the same sort of accuracy is neither needed nor particularly wanted. While dozens of different land and groove configurations have appeared in rifles over the years, only a few of them have been copied in handguns. Today, to the best of my knowledge, there are only a couple of systems in use.

Nearly all pistols and revolvers use the standard Enfield system, which has square corners; the number of lands and grooves usually depends on the caliber. This also happens to be the system used in more rifles at present than any other.

Most rifling grooves are cut in the bore, although some are broached (another cutting method) and some are swaged or pushed into shape by using a carbide "button" which is the reverse image of the rifling it produces. Broaching would seem to be the best and easiest way to cut the rifling in a handgun barrel, because these barrels are so short. Broaching a rifle barrel is a different matter entirely.

A broach is a long tool with many cutting edges, somewhat resembling a saw blade except that each tooth is slightly higher than the one before it so each removes a tiny chip as it is forced through the barrel. Cut a 24-inch rifle barrel and you have a far bigger chip than if you cut a 4- or 6-inch handgun barrel.

The twist is given a cutting tool, regardless of the method of rifling, by an attachment that makes the tool rotate as it is either pushed or pulled through the bore. Rate of twist—that is, the number of turns—is predetermined. Sometimes the rate is determined by calculation, but more often it takes experimenting to achieve the most desired rate. Twist is expressed as one turn in so many inches: 1-10 means one complete revolution in 10 inches of barrel length. As a rule, handguns have much slower twists than high-power rifles; the reason is simply that a short, fat handgun bullet does not require as much twist to be stable in flight.

To explain this further, a .30/06 rifle uses a twist of 1 in 10. Although bullets in .30 caliber up to 180 grains do not require a twist faster than 1-12, the .30/06 is loaded with long 220-grain bullets which must also be stabilized. There are some who believe the 10-inch twist in a .30/06 "overstabilizes" bullets weighing 150 and 180 grains, but this is not so in my opinion. I have never believed it a sin to overstabilize, and every accuracy test I've ever made proves my point. But the rule is that long, slim bullets need more twist than short, fat ones. One common extreme would seem to be the .264 Winchester Magnum rifle cartridge, which uses bullets up to 140 grains and is indeed a long and slim slug—and the rifle uses a twist rate of one turn in 9 inches. On the other hand, both Smith & Wesson and Ruger use a rate of one turn in 20 inches for their .44 Magnum barrels. (Interestingly, Ruger, Marlin, Remington, and Winchester have all used one turn in 38 inches for their .44 Magnum *rifles,* all of which use the same ammunition as the handguns!)

I have always wondered about that turtle-slow twist used in the .44 Magnum rifles and suspect it's simply a case of follow the leader. Ruger was first with a .44 rifle, Marlin next. At the time

Marlin was developing its rifle I got a barrel blank and had it rifled by Smith & Wesson with their twist rate. But the barrel was lost at Marlin and never used. Had it been, it's likely it would have worked well, and maybe all .44 Magnum rifles would use a 20-inch twist. Marlin simply followed the Ruger lead, and I suspect the others followed them.

It follows quite logically that accuracy in most handguns need not be that demanded of the rifle. Aside from a few varmint hunters and quite a few target shooters who demand something extra in the way of accuracy, the average guy can never shoot as well as his gun.

POLYGONAL RIFLING

One of the more interesting forms of rifling in use today is the "polygonal" pattern that is employed by West Germany's Hechler & Koch. It resembles the old Newton segmental rifling once used by Charles Newton, the American gun designer and manufacturer. This system doesn't use conventional lands and grooves but rather very shallow and gradual rifling. The company claims reduction of gas leakage, higher velocity, longer bore life, and easier cleaning. These claims seem sound in theory, but if polygonal rifling were really that much better than any other system you can bet others would use it. Hechler and Koch claims it's in use by some English gunmakers for double rifles. Maybe so, But, as noted, it's not that much different from a Newton system used about seventy-five years ago and long since abandoned. This is not to say H&K doesn't have a good barrel—they do. But don't accept all the claims at face value.

COLD-FORMED RIFLING

Another interesting method of producing rifled barrels (though it's used for smoothbores too) is known as cold forming, a rather revolutionary method of manufacturing a rifle barrel that I first learned about in the 1950s when I was a working gunsmith. I was introduced to a Dr. Gerhardt Appel from Germany who had perfected a method of manufacturing hypodermic needles by a cold-forming process before the war. The method was highly successful, and when Germany began World War II, Dr. Appel was enlisted by the German government to produce barrels for the MG 42 machine gun. Apparently, many hundreds of thousands of these barrels were made by the Appel process.

I remember going to Detroit to visit the doctor, who had his big machine set up in a small shop in that machine-tool city. I had the opportunity of discussing the process with Appel and watching the machine make a few barrels, and then I obtained some sample barrels and made quite a few tests on them.

The process is quite complicated to explain, so I'll try to keep it very simple. You must first have a drilled and reamed steel bar; let's say just for the sake of an example that it is about 16 inches long and 1⅜ inches in diameter. Its bore is larger than .30 caliber. Located inside the machine—and this is a giant machine, a little larger than a big station wagon—is a mandrel which contains the rifling in mirror image and to exact dimension. The barrel-to-be is placed in the machine and positioned over the mandrel, and the machine is turned on. At this point, very rapidly revolving shafts begin to whir and rotate; cams force "hammers" to push against the steel bar so rapidly and so forcefully that they actually reduce the steel to a plastic form as it passes over the mandrel. The bar is fed through the machine and, as it passes over the mandrel where the hammers strike it, the inside assumes the reverse shape of the mandrel.

The other thing the cold forming does is elongate the barrel to about 24 inches. What comes out of the machine then is a rifled barrel, longer and slimmer than when it went in. And completely rifled inside with a very smooth finish. Moreover, each and every barrel is theoretically identical as to inside dimension.

The Appel process has a number of advantages. The hammering was a cold forging and it possessed all the advantages of that process, particularly greater strength through rearranged molecules. The smoothness of the internal surface and its surface hardness were very significant advantages, and the speed of producing a barrel was a significant production plus.

But the process, as actually applied by Dr. Appel, had flaws too. Appel had to buy his barrel blanks already drilled—that is, he had no control over the drilling operation. In addition, his barrels were not reamed, which means that the drilled hole had a very rough surface. In the process, despite the heavy hammer forging, these drill marks were not always erased. The second big disadvantage was that the blanks were not straightened before forging, and thus came out just as crooked as they went in. There's no question in my mind that if Dr. Appel had had better blanks to work with, he would have produced a superior product indeed.

In fact, the very nature of the process led me to some pretty exciting thoughts (which were never followed, but I toss them out anyway). I suggested, for instance, that a very thin-walled piece of stainless-steel tubing be inserted in a piece of tough aluminum-alloy tubing and the whole thing forged as a unit. If that worked, you could produce a very light barrel with a very tough surface that ought to give long barrel life and withstand very high pressures. One of its advantages would be that you could use a tougher stainless alloy than now can be used for barrel steel, because the tough alloys are very hard to machine. Forging can produce any rifling configuration desired, and it can even produce the chamber, so the only remaining operations necessary would be to thread the shank to screw it into the action and turn down the outside. I still have an Appel barrel on one of my own rifles — it's a .30-caliber barrel and a very nice clean one inside.

Some companies are using cold forming today, one of them being Winchester, which of course, controls internal surfaces and straightness better than Appel could. The people at Winchester have shed a little more light on the cold-forming process.

Winchester uses what I have referred to here as the Appel process of cold-forming barrels. The machinery is made by three different companies, and Winchester claims to be probably the only major sporting-arms manufacturer that is cold-forming a chamber in a rifle barrel. Winchester further claims these advantages for cold-formed barrels: (1) Bore and rifling surface finish is superior; (2) bore and rifling dimensions are more consistent; (3) the barrel is straighter; and (4) there is anywhere from a 20 to 40 percent saving in material.

I would agree with all these points except to comment that a straighter barrel doesn't necessarily follow. Winchester's procedure *may* produce straighter barrels than the company's competitors but, if true, it's not the result of cold forming alone. There's not much question that cold forming is one of the most interesting production techniques to come along in many years. It may not have the romance of an old, crotchety mechanic feeling his way to hand-rifle a barrel, but there's no doubt it produces excellent barrels — and lots of them in a hurry, which is all to the good for consumers.

LEADING

One of the big problems in some hot handguns is leading — defined as the stripping of bullet metal and a corresponding lead buildup in the rifling. One of the worst offenders in this department has always been the .357 Magnum, due primarily to its speed. When lead builds up it means that each succeeding shot must ride up and over the built-up lead. And each new bullet leaves a little of itself on the pile. Gradually this begins to clog the hole to a dangerous level. The first thing to happen is that accuracy goes to hell. Then if the lead isn't removed it can get to the point where a barrel obstruction exists and the barrel can be damaged.

One result has been to "lap" barrels in this caliber. Lapping is a polishing process which is performed by centering a steel rod in the barrel in such a way that you can pour molten lead around one end of the rod, between the rod and the bore. Then, when the lead hardens, you work the rod back and forth. Some very fine powdered emery dust mixed with oil is applied, and the lap is moved back and forth in the bore. The result smooths out the rifling and brings the bore to a high polish. Often, another operation known as bore honing is employed to polish the bore before the rifling grooves are cut. The object of both operations is to make the bore as smooth as possible with whatever tool marks are left in a fore-and-aft direction.

The remainder of the "cure" for leading is to use a copper gas check on the bullet's base, which greatly reduces any tendency for the barrel to build up lead.

SMOOTHBORES

There are a few smoothbored handgun barrels available, although not very many. Some years ago there were a couple of models of short-barreled guns, most of them capable of one-hand operation, that were made to fire shot cartridges. For one reason or another these are mostly now illegal. There also are some conventional guns that have had their barrels reamed smooth to fire shot loads. The reason is that a small, handy shot cartridge packing a good charge is very handy for snakes or potting a grouse on a hunting trip.

Today the only such gun I know of that's legal is the Thompson/Center Contender with appropriate barrels. This gun comes with a .410 shotgun barrel, or you can also buy their Hot Shot arrangement in .357 or .44 Magnum calibers. These barrels come with either an internal or an external removable choke device. The Hot Shot cartridge is intended for use only in the T/C gun in the appropriate caliber.

This is quite an interesting appendage. Rifling in any gun barrel is not meant for shot charges; it tends to spin the pellets so the pattern disperses too quickly to be of much use. The patented choke device used by T/C is intended to overcome this by an unusual method. The Hot Shot charge contains its shot pellets in a plastic casing which simply rides down the bore like a bullet. The choke device shreds the plastic container and serves to choke the pellets so they have a very effective pattern out to 20 yards. The choke is simply unscrewed (either inside or outside versions) to use the gun with conventional ammunition.

CHAMBERS AND HEADSPACE

That part of any gun barrel in which the cartridge is placed for firing is known as the chamber. It's the charge hole in a revolver cylinder, but its function is identical. Chambers must be cut to exacting specifications so that ammunition of any make (as long as the ammo is made to specification) will fit a gun of any make specified for that particular cartridge. The front end of any chamber must also be "throated" so the

bullet will be able to enter the rifling gradually. This is simply a taper at the end of each land. Revolver barrels are "funneled" to a degree at the breech end to allow for slight misalignment of cylinders.

Headspace is that part of the chamber which prevents further forward movement of the cartridge. Put more simply, it's the amount of room, front to back, that's allowed for the cartridge. This dimension is very critical, for if there is too much headspace the cartridge case is likely to rupture. That dimension is different for the different *types* of cartridge cases. For example, a rimmed cartridge—the .22 Long Rifle, .357 Magnum, etc.—is "headspaced" on the front of the rim. That means it's the rim itself that stops the cartridge's forward movement. On a bottle-necked case such as the .30 Luger or Parabellum, the headspace is the distance from the base of the case to a specified spot on the shoulder of the cartridge. On a straight-sided case which is also rimless—the .45 ACP is a good example—the case mouth is used for headspacing.

You can understand easily how faulty headspace can be the result of either chamber or ammunition. Insufficient headspace will result in a simple jam, because the cartridge won't go in far enough to close the action. But too much space can, and usually will, cause more serious problems, running all the way to a burst case which can spill high-pressure gas into the action. A reloader can create this condition easily if he doesn't watch what he's doing. For example, it is quite easy to trim back the case mouth of a .45 ACP case excessively so that the case can go in too far and create a dangerous condition.

PROOFING

It is normal in the United States for a manufacturer of any firearm to "proof" his product by firing an overload and then examining the gun to check results. These overloads, called "blue pills" in the industry, are loaded by the major ammunition companies to predetermined levels and sold only to gun manufacturers. The ordinary procedure is to fire one proof load, then a magazineful of standard ammunition to check for function. Many makers also target their guns to align the sights correctly, and some guns are shipped with a target that had actually been used during these tests.

Once the gun has passed proof, the maker stamps his proof mark on the gun. This mark is usually a trademark of one kind or another, but sometimes it is so well hidden it defies anyone to locate or identify it.

In Europe, on the other hand, proofing is done by the government to standards set by that government. These are generally very much the same no matter where they are proofed, but the point is that our system differs from that employed elsewhere. Of the two systems, I much prefer ours; not only is it more democratic but it results in far lower cost than if each maker had to trundle down to a government proof house with a batch of guns every day. You can rest assured that if any producer put shoddy guns on the market he wouldn't last very long. Nor do we need another government bureau to fatten federal spending.

Quite likely the most restrictive gun proofing is that done in England, although most English proof is in shotguns and very little of it is handguns. While the English recognize the proof marks of major American companies, nearly all others must undergo English proof when imported into England. I understand the guns American citizens lent Britishers in the Home Guard during the dark, early days of World War II had to be proofed before they were issued!

HOW BARRELS ARE FASTENED

Handgun barrels are fastened in a rather wide variety of ways. Revolver barrels, which are usually a one-piece forging with their sights, ejector-rod protecting shroud, and other appendages, are screwed tightly into the frame. Tip-down barrels like a couple of Harrington & Richardson models are a one-piece forging with their hinge.

Autoloading pistol barrels are fastened by links and pins and bushings in the case of recoil-operated models. Blowback auto barrels are sometimes fitted into slots to prevent back-and-forth movement while the slide holds them in the slots. Other blowback barrels are screwed and/or pinned into the frame or receiver.

Smith & Wesson clings to a very old method of pinning its revolver barrels once they are tightly screwed home. This pin is totally unnecessary but it's a hangover from the old days. Nobody else uses a pin, unless he's making an out-and-out copy of a S&W model.

The Dan Wesson revolver barrel is unique and should be mentioned separately. You can buy this gun with any number of different barrels, and they are interchangeable within a few seconds. The barrel itself is very thin, but a shroud of the correct length slips over the barrel tube, presenting a "normal" appearance. To assemble this gun you screw the barrel of your choice into the frame, slip the .006-inch gauge between cylinder and barrel, and screw the barrel home. Then slip on the shroud and screw on the muzzle nut, tightening the nut with the special wrench provided. Slip out the gauge and you're ready to go.

One of the problems with any recoil-operated auto gun in terms of its accuracy is that the barrel must be free to move. And it doesn't always come back to the same, exact position in the firing cycle. We'll have more to say about this in Chapter Twenty-one, but it should be noted here. A gun meant for military operation, like the .45 Colt, which is probably the world's best sidearm for the purpose, must be free enough to work in all kinds of climate, wet or dry; in all temperatures, hot and cold; and with all kinds of abuse. That means you can't enjoy the luxury of "target-type" gun fitting, because the gun would jam in service use. Yet the same gun has been used for target shooting for years, which has resulted in some novel refinements to make the barrel come back to the same position for each shot. One of the most important parts of these "accurizing" jobs, as they are called, is the barrel bushing at the muzzle end.

The barrel must be pulled down to unlock during the cycling of the gun, meaning that the front end must tip slightly, which prevents a snug fit. This problem has been solved uniquely in the Smith & Wesson Model 52 .38 Master by forming a sort of ball joint on the barrel. This joint allows the barrel to tip for unlocking but does not change its relation to the bushing—a very neat solution, though a complicated shape to generate in production. There are other methods of retaining auto pistol barrels, but they are primarily variations on what I've explained.

Single-shot handgun barrels are fastened differently, the major exception being the Remington Fire Ball, which is fastened like a rifle barrel: screwed tightly into its receiver. The Thompson/Center has a hinged barrel which hooks onto the frame somewhat like a double shotgun barrel, except that the pin is removed to change barrels. T/C barrels can be interchanged at will.

BARREL LENGTH

The length of a handgun barrel affects many things, most of which are discussed in other chapters. One of the most important effects of length is velocity, and this is discussed in Chapter Eighteen.

Barrel length also affects the portability of a handgun. It can render it an undercover job with 2-inch barrel, or a Buntline Special with a 12-inch or even longer tube. This business about barrel lengths has been the subject of much pointless discussion lately as the government set about to define such terms as "Saturday-night special" and some other equally stupid things in a so-called effort to reduce the number of "concealable" handguns. The government came up with some sort of silly mathematical formula whereby barrel length combined with overall length and overall depth and Lord knows what else equaled a gun you couldn't conceal.

To get around this bit of foolishness, some manufacturers altered their designs. It's a bit like making a racing sloop to fit the 12-meter classification; you change one line here and you've got to change six other specifications to wind up with the right result. Adding ½ inch of barrel or slanting the grip to give a longer overall length is hardly conducive to progress.

Other guns were simply dropped just because the maker felt that it was in the best interest not to manufacture it any longer. One example of this that I know about firsthand is the tiny Smith & Wesson .22 Escort, a fine little .22 auto that you could hide in your palm. Yet it packed a dandy wallop and was a perfect "social gun" for a lady, for an undercover agent, or for any vest-pocket use. S&W marketed it for a few years, then took it off the market just because the company felt it would be good public relations. Or perhaps because it would have been bad public relations to keep on making it. It is a shame that the climate is such that this fine little gun had to be dropped.

Longer and heavier barrels are generally preferred for target shooting, chiefly because they present a longer sighting radius and can be held steadier. Of course, the handgunning varminter will use a scope, so sighting radius means little, but the longer barrel will give him slightly better ballistics and better performance.

There is a tendency of late to add ribs to handgun barrels. Some of these are of the ventilated variety and others are solid. The latter are most useful for adding weight, while the former add to appearance as much as anything. Either type of rib will aid sighting. Even if you have a

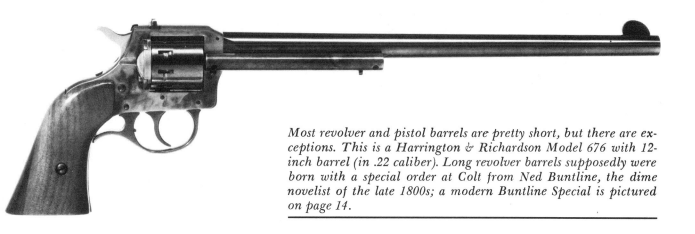

Most revolver and pistol barrels are pretty short, but there are exceptions. This is a Harrington & Richardson Model 676 with 12-inch barrel (in .22 caliber). Long revolver barrels supposedly were born with a special order at Colt from Ned Buntline, the dime novelist of the late 1800s; a modern Buntline Special is pictured on page 14.

gun without a rib, all is not lost, Poly-Choke makes ribs for many handguns as well as shotguns, and they are easily fastened permanently with some of the fine epoxies on the market.

RECOIL COMPENSATORS

These are the gadgets that you fasten to a gun's muzzle to reduce recoil. Or, an alternate method is to cut ports directly into the barrel to achieve the same purpose.

The theory is that by deflecting gas up and slightly to the rear you help hold the barrel down and forward. The theory is fine. And for most of these devices or methods there is documentary evidence to prove that they work. They

The latest method of employing gases to reduce jump and recoil is known as "Mag-na-porting"—a system of electrically cut holes in the barrel near the muzzle. The theory is that the vented gas spurts force the barrel down and forward to accomplish the desired objectives. Such venting also often increases the muzzle blast and can make shooting quite unpleasant.

do work. But they have side effects that are not so pleasant. For example, when gas is diverted to the rear it seems to funnel directly into your ear, or the ear of someone nearby. It can be regarded as a swap: less recoil for more noise.

Despite the proof that these things work, you are dealing with emotions and personal reactions to recoil. These are vastly different things. To say that an 8-pound .30/06 rifle delivers so many foot-pounds of free recoil is really meaningless, because it's the "felt recoil" of the shooter that counts. If his particular 8-pound .30/06 is stocked in a way that he gets his chops whacked every shot, his rifle hurts him badly. The same rifle with another stock would probably suit him perfectly and he'd be happy. Or he could add a recoil reducer, which might have the same effect.

I have been around long enough to have seen a couple of generations of these things come and go. Harry Pope, the late great barrelmaker, used to say: "The only holes that should be drilled in a rifle barrel ought to be as close to the muzzle as possible, and just in front of it." Pope didn't comment on the handgun for the record that I know of, but I suspect he'd have said the same thing. I agree with Pope completely, because I don't mind recoil particularly; I admit some guns hurt me, but I dislike ear-splitting noise a hell of a lot more.

Before we wrap up this discussion about handgun barrels it should be repeated that federal law prohibits rendering a rifle into a handgun. This means you cannot saw off the barrel of a rifle, cut its stock down and make a handgun. Not legally you can't.

This despite the fact that Remington makes two guns on the same action. Its Mohawk 600 in .243, .308, and other calibers is a popular hunting rifle, very lightweight and handy. The very same action is used to make the Fire Ball pistol. But *you* cannot take a Mohawk 600 and make a pistol out of the action.

Navy Arms in Ridgefield, N. J., sells a single-shot handgun which is a copy of the old Remington Rider rolling-block action on which Remington made both rifles and pistols years ago. It's legal for Navy Arms to sell these, but *you* cannot buy an old rolling-block rifle and make a handgun out of it.

CHAPTER NINE

HANDGUN GRIPS

I have rather large hands—not large enough to palm a basketball, but larger than average. And I can get by with most American handgun grips of the better grades, better with some than with others.

There are few hands alike. Some come with short or long fingers, fat or skinny fingers, meaty or leathery palms. It's obvious that the grip that fits any one of these extremes isn't going to fit the rest. And the grips meant to fit the average hand won't fit the extremes either.

Some guns are restricted to certain grip sizes because of the gun frame's size, shape, or configuration. The small pocket autos are typical examples of guns that are so small that even a tiny hand can't get a decent hold.

And some of the hard-recoiling guns present special problems. For example, shooting the .44 Magnum presents different problems with different guns. Using a Ruger single-action, a style which does not have the typical "double-action hump" on the rear edge of the grip, can be damned painful because the gun spins through the hand until it's stopped by the hammer smashing your flesh at the web between thumb and forefinger. That smarts. On the other hand, the big Smith & Wesson .44 has that hump, which prevents the gun from squirming down through your hand. Yet the S&W has its own pain-inflicting style, since its checkering is sharp and the abrasion resulting also smarts. I find it pays to wear a light glove when shooting any .44 Magnum; better to let the buckskin take the rub.

GRIP MATERIALS

Handgun grips, or stocks, are made from a wide variety of woods and plastics. A few generations back, many grips were made from "hard rubber," and I don't know what that term meant. They also were made of Bakelite at one time, which I believe was a trade name for some hard material which could be molded. There was a time when mother-of-pearl handles were the vogue, which led to plastic imitations of the genuine. Happily those appear to be a thing of the past. Another material once used for handgun grips was bone, and the stocks made from bone were called "stag" grips. They were quite attractive, and I still have a very old Colt revolver with a set of "genuine stag" grips. The plastic imitation might have ruined the popularity of stag grips, though they were hard to tell from the real thing—and what's the use of having the real thing if it doesn't look any better than a fake?

Back when I started shooting, a revolver's grips were confined to the shape dictated by the frame. And that always left too much space behind the trigger guard. Frank Pachmayr solved that one with a slick, simple rubber adaptor that fitted this curve and made shooting much more comfortable and better. Today, many guns on the market have wood grips which fill in this space.

Pistol and revolver stocks don't generate the same amount of emotion that rifle and shotgun stocks do. I suppose that's because the grips are

Some pistols have a forearm, like this Thompson/Center with heavy barrel and scope. The forearm on any one-hand gun is generally useless except for resting, in which case it is an important addition. Resting any gun directly on the barrel will throw the shot off because it inhibits barrel vibration. But you can rest on the forearm and achieve top accuracy.

so small that you wouldn't see enough pretty grain to excite you even if it was there. Some grips today are made of American walnut, some of other hardwoods, and many of various plastics. I really don't think it matters much what they are made of, except that I do prefer wood grips to plastic.

A possible exception to what I've just said is the stainless-steel handgun. I'm looking at a brushed-finish stainless-steel Model 66 Smith & Wesson revolver in .357 Magnum. Its stocks are a rather light-colored wood called Goncalo Alves, which, I understand, comes from South America. S&W uses this wood on some of its higher-grade Magnum models. There's no question that this wood nicely complements the finish on this stainless revolver, but I'm not sure it's necessary to go clear to South America for any grip material.

Handgun grips are, after all, very small pieces of wood; you could make grips for several handguns out of the scrap from one rifle or shotgun stock.

GRIP SHAPE

A recent trend in revolvers makes a lot of sense. Typical of this trend is the shank type used by Dan Wesson; it is simply a square shank on the

This old Colt revolver in my collection has a "stag" grip—that is, it's made of bone. Note also that there is a Pachmayr grip adaptor installed, a necessity on most older revolvers.

metal frame. This means the grip itself can be a single piece of wood and can be shaped to any desired configuration; the frame does not pose any limits. It also provides a very simple means of removing the grip without marring either frame or grip.

The kind of grip necessary on a handgun depends upon the use to which the gun will be put. A gun that sits in your bedside-table drawer won't need much in the way of a grip, because you will probably use the gun only in an emergency and at very short range. A gun that is used for formal target shooting requires a totally different sort of grip, because you must wring out every micromillimeter of good shooting contained in the gun. And you can only do that with a good hold.

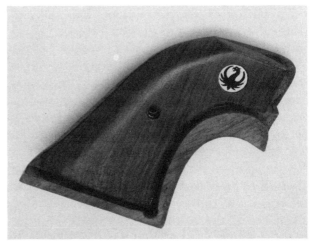

A Ruger single-action factory grip overlaid on a custom grip. This points out the added wood on the latter, which often results in a more functional grip. This is especially true at the forward end (right in the photo) where the middle finger supports most of the gun's weight.

The old (bottom) and the new in revolver factory grips. Both are Smith & Wessons. The top gun is a modern Magnum with grips that are much more comfortable than those on the older gun below.

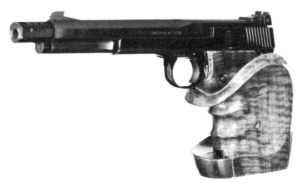

A pair of gussied-up target stocks from Steve Herrett. These are precisely made to fit a specific shooter's hand, which will produce better scores. One is an autoloading .22 and the other a single-shot free pistol.

The various guns in between have varying requirements in between. The special-purpose target gun with hand-fitting target stocks is not particularly portable, so it won't do for such sporting uses as on fishing or camping trips, nor as a sidearm on a big-game hunt. Yet these latter uses require fine shooting, and fine shooting requires good grips. Often it requires better grips than those supplied with the gun.

The shape of a grip is often dictated by the frame, but it also is dictated by tradition. A grip should *look* good. And people are accustomed to looking at the traditional grips used on handguns for more than a century. But a grip that looks good doesn't always shoot good!

As far as I know, the man most responsible for better stocks today is Steve Herrett of the handgun-grip company that bears his name. Herrett points out that a human hand is fatter along the lower edge than at the upper part of the palm. But most conventional revolver stocks are flared at the bottom. This is pure tradition; that's the way a stock is supposed to look. But just replace those grips with a set of Herrett's and feel the difference. Now you can see what Herrett means, because his stocks are swollen at the top where the meat is thin. I don't think the Herrett stocks *look* as good. But they *feel* much better and they make you shoot better scores. And that, in the final analysis, is what it's all about.

A grip must also be shaped so that it fits the hand well enough for fast repeat shots. Some grips are so poorly shaped that a hard-recoiling gun will squirm like a live thing in your hand. In such a case, repeat shots are difficult, and if your life is on the line that can make a big difference. Some hard-recoiling guns are not necessarily the big Magnums—a .38 Special pocket model can kick pretty hard because it's so light. And if you are using such a gun as a pocket model, I suggest you consider better grips. They may make the gun slightly less concealable, but if they also make it a much better shooter in repeat shots, that would be a good swap.

There are a number of firms that make stocks such as Steve Herrett supplies, and I do not necessarily mean to single him out. Some replacement stocks are very poorly made, though, and you should examine the merchandise for proper fit before you buy. I'm talking now about the fit of wood to metal, which can be very bad.

Many handgun grips are checkered, and many are not. Checkering, whether on a rifle, shotgun, or handgun, is a functional addition. It's meant to give you a better grip. Some guns need to be tightly held when they are fired; otherwise they would slip through your hands. Others, giving less recoil, do not need so tight a

Standard .45 Auto grips on the right compared with Herrett custom target grips. The gun on the left will be much more comfortable and will produce far better scores.

Steve Herrett stocks on a Ruger single-action and a Smith & Wesson pocket .38 Special revolver. While these stocks may look strange, that's because you're used to seeing conventional grips. The Herrett stocks will fit anyone better because there is more wood up high, where the hand is less meaty. Standard stocks are the reverse—flared at the bottom where the hand is also fatter.

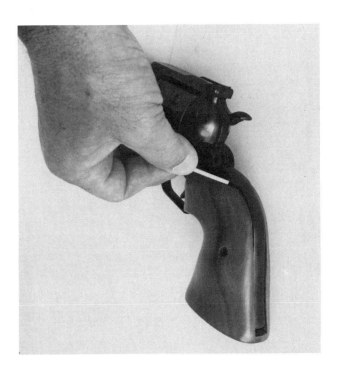

A very poor fit in a pair of replacement grips for this single-action Ruger revolver. Anytime you can stick a match between wood and metal the product is a shoddy one. Note also the gaps around the frame where the fit should be tight.

grip. I would frankly like to see checkering on all stocks because of its function. But I admit a single-action gun doesn't look as good with checkered wood grips as with plain grips. This is not entirely tradition, because Colt made many Model P guns with checkered hard-rubber grips that are as much a tradition as plain wood.

On the other hand, Smith & Wesson checkers its Magnums with such sharp-pointed diamonds that they hurt like hell when you shoot. This particularly applies to the .41 and .44 Magnums with full loads—the checkering on these guns goes through your palm like a rasp.

CHAPTER TEN

SIGHTS

Sights are provided on any gun for the simple, single purpose of helping aim or point the arm toward the target so the bullet will arrive where you want it to. Generally speaking, pistols and revolvers are the most difficult types of guns to sight with any degree of precision.

There are several reasons why this is so. The most obvious reason is that a pistol or revolver is generally held at arm's length, which makes holding wobbly and uncertain when compared with a shoulder arm because there is far less support. The most important reason is that it is impossible for the eye, wonderful organ that it is, to focus on front and rear sights and the target at the same time. This is simply a physical impossibility, and we'll have more to say about this in a few moments. A third reason is that many handguns come equipped with lousy sights.

Sights are not needed on all types of handguns. In fact, those stubby models designed for undercover use would usually be as efficient with no sights at all. (Yet a 2-inch-barreled gun will shoot with surprising accuracy under ideal conditions). The reason is that these guns are normally used at such short range that *pointing* is sufficient aiming. And, as usually supplied, these guns are equipped with such poor sighting equipment that they may be said to have no sights at all.

The ordinary "service" revolver or pistol has essentially the same sights as the short gun I've just described. If a revolver, the rear sight is a notch machined down the top strap, and the front sight is essentially the same thing: a post machined on the muzzle end of the barrel. Service auto pistols generally have nonadjustable sights slipped into dovetail slots at the rear with a front sight fitted (often by pinning) at the muzzle. These pistol sights are adjusted by knocking the rear sight back and forth for windage, but there is no elevation adjustment. Some models have provision for windage adjustment with a little more finesse, but they are still rudimentary.

I suppose it is felt that this is all the sighting equipment needed for "service" work with a pistol or revolver. The most popular police revolver in the world is the Smith & Wesson Model 10 .38 Military & Police, chambered for .38 Special. The sights are described as "Front: Fixed $\frac{1}{8}$-inch serrated ramp. Rear: square notch." These are rudimentary sights. They haven't changed appreciably in a hundred years. They cannot be adjusted—you can file them and obtain some elevation changes, but there is no way in the world to make windage adjustment.

This is obviously enough to satisfy the market, but I think cops would take more interest in shooting, and develop accurate shooting as a result, if they were equipped with better sights. Lest you think I'm picking on Smith & Wesson, let me add that Colt, Ruger, and most others offer the same sort of "sights" on their service revolvers. This could be a case of following the leader; it could also be a case of price competition, because the addition of decent sights would boost the cost. But it's also important to note that the market doesn't know any better and is satisfied with last century's sighting equipment.

Target shooters demand finer sights, and these are generally available in good quality on certain target models produced by the gunmakers. And there are many custom sight makers doing a hotcake business for those who want something a bit better or perhaps something tailored to their shooting form that they don't feel is met by factory production. In general it may be said that the factory product in these models is excellent and needs little improvement. But many custom sights are made for such guns as the Service Model .45 Colt Auto and the Model 39 Smith & Wesson, which has only windage adjustment, and both guns can be

made to shoot much more accurately with better adjustable sights.

Early sights on percussion revolvers consisted of a post at the muzzle and a notch filed in the hammer, which became the rear sight when the revolver was cocked. These are still seen on cap-and-ball percussion revolvers, and the current replicas being sold have copied the old "sight" system. Those sights, believe it or not, were actually inferior, and cruder, than sights found on older flintlock pistols! Many of the latter had front and rear sights in dovetail slots, which at least were stationary and which could be adjusted. In the latter sense they were just as up to date as the rear sight still furnished by Colt on their Service Model .45. Needless to add, any sight notch on a revolver's hammer is not a very precise rear sight.

The sad fact about pistol and revolver sights is that the average person is such a lousy shot with these guns that he doesn't know enough to want better sights. They probably wouldn't help him, because his basic ability is inadequate. Such a person, if he really wants to become proficient with the handgun, should buy a book on shooting and seek competent instruction so he'll know where he's going. Shooting a pistol is not difficult, and a little concentration, larded with a little help, will pay quick dividends.

Some guns come equipped with a rear sight adjustable for windage and front sight for elevation. The Harrington & Richardson Model 999 is one such revolver. This is a fine little gun in terms of dollar value and its sights are very good.

For the record, the best shooting is normally done with wide, square sights. The front sight should be about $\frac{1}{8}$ inch wide and flat on top. The notch in the rear sight should be wide enough to accommodate the front sight with sufficient clearance on both sides and, of course, should also be square. Some front sights are red, some rear sights have a white outline for definition. If you like a red front sight but yours is black, it's an easy thing to paint it with a little red nail polish.

Slide-mounted sights such as those found on most autos suffer from recoil and from movement. The recoil of a handgun is a tremendous movement—much greater than on a rifle because the handgun is so small and so light by comparison. Consequently, handgun recoil can knock a poorly made or inadequately fastened sight out of alignment. The movement of a slide also can contribute to inaccuracy. For example, many .22 auto pistols mount their rear sights on the slide, while front sights are on the barrel at the muzzle. The result, when you have one sight on a movable slide and the other on a fixed barrel, can result in loss of alignment through wear and movement. Not all .22s suffer from this, however, since the Ruger, Browning, and others provide for rear-sight mounting on fixed parts. Each gun does this in a different way, but the result is the same. Another gun that handles the problem well is the Smith & Wesson Model 41, in which the slide moves under a top extension and both sights are on fixed, immovable parts.

While this is desirable, it must be noted that the loss of accuracy from a slide-mounted sight is negligible for any practical purpose. It is an important feature for a highly refined target pistol, but isn't that big a deal for an ordinary "fun gun" for sport and plinking.

CUSTOM SIGHTS

One of the popular makers of custom sights is the Miniature Machine Company of Deming, N. M. Most of the MMC business is supplying ad-

This is a new, patented adjustable rear sight from Austin Behlert, the New Jersey custom pistol gunsmith. A number of small firms manufacture excellent adjustable sights for pistol and revolver use. By comparison, sights furnished by the manufacturers are generally pretty poor.

Miniature Machine Company makes a fine line of adjustable sights; this sample is shown on the .45 Colt Auto. The standard .45 sight is a nonadjustable notched block in a slot. The MMC replacement, and others by different makers, fit the same slot.

justable rear sights for service automatic pistols. The installation of most of these sights, however, requires a bit of gunsmithing, and you are advised to have the sights fitted by a good gunsmith or have your local dealer ship your gun to the sight manufacturer for installation. There are a number of crack pistol gunsmiths—Austin Behlert, Pachmayr, and others—who can handle such a job. And there are a number of small firms specializing in sight work, such as Micro, Bo-Mar, and Austin Behlert. Bo-Mar is well known for its fine ribs and extended ribs. The competitive shooter as well as the sportsman who expects good accuracy should inform himself about these products.

You can also have decent sights mounted on almost any revolver, although the job will require extensive gunsmithing on a service revolver. But the results will be well worth the effort and cost. The average service revolver is capable of far finer accuracy than its sights.

The sportsman as well as the target shooter benefits from better sights. If your planned pistol use is for potting an occasional grouse, beheading a poisonous snake, popping a snapping turtle, or any of the hundred and one other sporting uses for a pistol, then you'll need better sights than most revolvers and pistols come with from the factory. Shots of this type demand just as fine shooting as a paper target, and nothing less should be tolerated in sighting equipment.

Frankly, I think the manufacturers of service revolvers and pistols should machine their frames so custom sights could be installed with a minimum amount of fuss. It's past time to take this step, which need not raise the cost of production significantly. If this were done the buyer could install the sight of his choice much as he does with a rifle. Hardly anyone who knows anything about shooting uses the sights rifles bear when you buy them. They are replaced by either a scope or a peep sight, and you can buy any one of dozens of makes because they are all made to fit the make and model of rifle you bought. There's no reason this can't be done with pistols and revolvers too.

SCOPES

Scoping a pistol or revolver started out as a fad, I'm sure—I think the first time it was done on a large scale was by Dave Bushnell. In those early days very few handguns were scope-equipped, but the business today is increasing by leaps and bounds.

The first thing that had to be resolved in a scope for any handgun was the matter of eye relief. Up till then all scopes were made for rifle use, and you positioned the scope so that it was about 2½ to 3½ inches from your eye. This figure is known as eye relief. It was obvious that you couldn't hold a revolver so close that your

eye was only around 3 inches from the scope. It would be an awkward position, and it's likely the recoil would slam the gun into your head.

But I suspect the real motivation to develop a scope with longer eye relief was that vast numbers of Winchester Model 94 rifles were in use. The old 94 is a top-ejecting rifle, and you can't mount a scope centered on this rifle. (Offset mounts have long been available, but they are not satisfactory because your head can't snug the stock.) The solution was to develop a long-eye-relief scope so it could be mounted forward of the receiver; then the top ejection wouldn't be in the way. This was done, and such scopes have found some happiness on 94 rifles. As a by-product the way was cleared for scoping a handgun, and that's now an immensely popular marriage.

The only disadvantage to a pistol or revolver with scope aboard is that it is bulky, awkward, and cumbersome. You can't keep the gun in its original box. You can't carry it in most holsters, and a mighty big pocket would be otherwise required. This objection has been overcome to a degree by the S.D. Myres Saddle Company, which makes a shoulder holster for large-frame guns with scopes attached. Still, carrying a big .44 Magnum revolver with a scope is quite a load, but this shoulder holster is the best bet yet.

Bushnell has done a lot for the handgun scope shooter. Here is a Bushnell Phantom scope on a Smith & Wesson .41 Magnum with which I have shot groups as small as 3 inches at 100 yards over sandbags. The only criticism I have of a scoped handgun is that it is bulky and awkward.

There are some typical scope terms which I'll explain before we proceed with our discussion:

Field of view: The width of the area you can see at 100 yards. Normally the higher power a scope has, the smaller the field of view.

Eye relief: The distance from your eye where you can see the complete field of view. Generally this is around $2\frac{1}{2}$ to $3\frac{1}{2}$ inches, and this distance is necessary to protect your head from a hard-recoiling rifle. Scopes for pistols and revolvers have an eye relief of from 10 to 24 inches.

Variable power: A variable-power scope can be changed in power by turning an adjustment. A scope designated 3-9X, for example, has a range of power (magnification) from 3X to 9X or anywhere between.

Fixed power: A fixed-power scope has one power which cannot be changed.

Lenses: Glass or plastic lenses provide the magnification. Plastic lenses are molded, have some surface irregularity, are easily scratched, and absorb moisture. Glass lenses are ground to precise specifications, are heavier than plastic, and do not absorb moisture. Glass lenses are usually coated, which increases light transmission (making better visibility at dawn and dusk). Coated lenses transmit 90 percent of available light, uncoated lenses only about 55 percent.

Reticle: The sighting or aiming point in a scope. Most of today's scopes have "centered" reticles, which means that they always remain in the center of the field of view when corrections are made. Older scopes moved the reticle across the field of view and sometimes wound up way off center. The most common is the cross-hair reticle, but there are many other variations, from tapered posts to dots.

Parallax: The most difficult word for anyone to understand in scope language. Briefly, and somewhat oversimply, it means focus. More precisely, it occurs when the reticle is not positioned at the actual optical center of the scope. Some scopes, notably precise target scopes, can be adjusted for parallax at different ranges by moving the reticle back and forth until it's optically centered. You can tell when parallax is present (it should not be) by placing the scope on a firm rest and, without touching it, moving your head back and forth, up and down. The reticle should not move across the target. If it does, parallax is present. You can eliminate parallax at only one distance, except with adjustable target scopes. Most hunting scopes are parallax-free at 100 yards, and this provides minimum parallax at other distances. To check your scope, make the test at a precise 100 yards.

Adjustments: Most scopes are internally adjustable for windage and elevation, but there are a couple of brands on the market that are nonadjustable, in which case they require a mount with adjustments built in. The literature accompanying each scope will tell you the value of each increment of adjustment. A scope is just as easy to adjust as any other sight; in fact, it's easier than most iron sights. A quality scope will give very precise adjustments, but some lower-cost and low-quality scopes cannot be depended upon for precise adjustments.

A variable scope has adjustment for power, usually with a ring, which should turn with considerable resistance to prevent accidental turning.

Fogging: In the early days it wasn't wise to bring a scoped gun into a warm room or cabin from the outside cold. The inside would fog up as the moisture in the air contacted the cold tube and condensed. Next morning the reverse happened; the warm moist air now in the tube would fog in the cold outside. Many shots were missed because of fogged scopes until hunters learned to leave their guns out in the cold all night. Now fogging is a thing of the past in any quality scope (as long as its owner doesn't remove the seal) because they have been filled with moisture-free nitrogen in manufacture and permanently sealed. The seal is the secret, and a scope is a smart thing to leave alone when it comes to repairs.

Resolution: Strictly speaking, resolution is the ability of a lens to separate objects, such as two stars that are very close together. More loosely, it is a measure of crispness; good resolution means crisp detail throughout the field of view, without distortion or curvature anywhere in the viewing area.

Eyepiece: The piece at the rear, or eye, end of

the scope that you can screw back and forth. It contains the ocular lens.

Objective: The front end of a scope containing the objective lens.

Turret: The sealed housing containing the windage and elevation adjustment systems.

Ejector system: A system of lenses located in the approximate middle of the scope which reinvert the image. It is important to realize that you do not really look *through* a scope, you look *into* it. And you see an image—as opposed to looking directly at the object. You know that when you look into the ground glass of many cameras the image is upside down. It's the same in a scope. The erector lenses invert the upside-down image so you see it right side up. Scopes which maintain the reticle in the center of the field accomplish this feat by moving the entire erector system (containing the reticle) when you make adjustments. The old way moved only the reticle.

These are the most important terms, with fairly concise explanations. There are other terms which you need not get into unless you plan to be an optical engineer. And there are other things, like mounts, which we'll discuss later.

You should also be aware that scope manufacturers realize the public doesn't really know much about scopes, so the public can be fooled. Sometimes a manufacturer's literature will tell you what he wants you to know. He will tell you the truth, but will sometimes stop short of telling you the whole truth. Whatever can be told that will make his product look better than his competitor's is probably what you'll read in product literature. Of course, this happens with just about any product made and sold in America.

There are some excellent scopes being made here in the United States, and there are excellent scopes being made in Japan and parts of Europe. Many of these are in widely varying price categories, and you'll have to study the specifications carefully. Imported scopes are usually less expensive than domestic ones, although that gap is closing.

The average person doesn't really know why scopes are so excellent as aiming devices. They usually think only in terms of magnification. But the most wonderful single thing about a scope is that it places everything in the same plane.

Earlier, I said that the eye couldn't focus on front and rear sights and the target at the same time. Scopes eliminate that completely. A scope simply plasters the aiming point on the target—in the same plane as the target. You don't have to line up two sights with the target; you simply find the target in the scope, place the reticle where you want the bullet to hit, and shoot. What could be simpler? That advantage applies to rifles as well as handguns, of course, but, if anything, it's even more important with a pistol or revolver.

Don't get the idea you can stand up on two feet, poke your left hand into your pocket, hold the gun at arm's length, and do much in the way of good shooting. To take advantage of a scoped gun you should use either a two-hand hold or a rest. You're not trying out for the Olympics, you're trying to knock the head off a grouse or a snake or something equally difficult, and you need all the help you can get.

Scopes used on handguns are in the lower magnification powers, and that's as it should be. There isn't much use for a lot of power. Thompson/Center, which has made a serious study of the single-shot pistol's sporting uses, imports a scope known as the Lobo; its magnification is 1½X. Leupold has a 2X, Bushnell a 1.3X and a 2.5X, and so it goes. All these are low-power scopes, but that's enough magnification.

I've had one of the first Bushnell pistol scopes on a Smith & Wesson .41 Magnum ever since the gun came out. It's about 1.3X, and I've done some great shooting with the combination. For example, I have fired groups at 100 yards as small as 3 inches with the outfit. That is by using all six charge holes and with factory ammunition. A lot of people will agree that's pretty good *rifle* accuracy.

On another occasion I was on a fishing trip in the north country and had this gun along. We camped on the shore of a lake and there was a small stump some 500 yards from shore. I took one sighting shot to see how far the bullet would drop at that distance, then held over, and the next shot hit the stump! That's pretty fair country accuracy for a revolver, and a scope

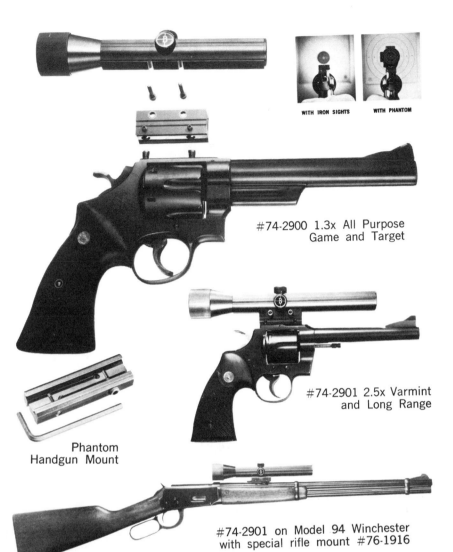

#74-2900 1.3x All Purpose Game and Target

WITH IRON SIGHTS   WITH PHANTOM

Phantom Handgun Mount

#74-2901 2.5x Varmint and Long Range

#74-2901 on Model 94 Winchester with special rifle mount #76-1916

This series of photos shows most of the pistol/revolver scope spectrum. Note that mounts fit on the gun (in many cases) without any machining, that there are two scopes offered, and that the same scopes can be mounted on top-ejecting rifles like the Model 94 Winchester because the scopes have longer eye relief than rifle scopes. Note also how the target appears fuzzy with open sights, clear with a scope.

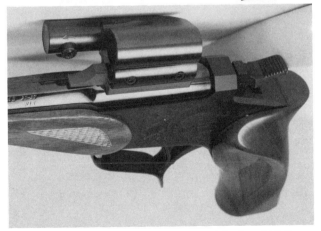

The Thompson/Center Contender with the T/C Insta-Sight mounted. It is a most interesting small sight that works very well on this pistol. One of its advantages is that it takes up relatively little space. This T/C barrel is chambered for the .25/35, an old favorite of mine.

shows what you can do when you can reduce the aiming error.

Thompson/Center is now out with a gadget called the Insta-Sight, which is best defined as a method of placing an aiming point on the target. It is not a scope; it has no magnification. It is, however, an optical instrument. This clever unit consists of two tubes. The light (target) comes into the front end of one tube, and you look into the rear end of the second tube. In between, the image is prismed up and back and a reticle is superimposed. The sight has adjustments.

In use, you simply look into the tube, see the target, and place the reticle or aiming point where you want the bullet. This device has the advantages of a scope in that it puts everything

This dramatic photo gives some idea of the recoil from a pistol or revolver, in this case the Colt .45 Auto. The scope is a Leupold in Leupold mounts. According to Leupold, the scope was subjected to a "G force" of 2,000 when fired. Lesser G forces of 750 and 800 were noted when the slide reached the rear or full-open position and when it reached the forward position again. In case you've forgotten, a G is the measure of the pull of gravity at sea level; 2,000 Gs is roughly the same as a car hitting a stone wall at 135 mph. Note that while the gun is in full recoil, the hand has not yet begun to absorb the recoil. Photo courtesy of Leupold.

in the same plane. There are no sights to align; as with a scope, you simply place the aiming point on the target. It also is far smaller and less bulky than a scope and should prove popular. Its lack of magnification is not particularly detrimental; as already explained, there is very small use for magnification in any scope used on a pistol or revolver.

RECOIL PROBLEMS
WITH HANDGUN SCOPES

Mounting a scope on a pistol or revolver poses unique problems that are simply not present in a rifle, no matter how much recoil that rifle may have. Maynard Buehler, the well-known scope-mount builder, has done a lot of experimenting to prove his mounts by installing them on the hardest-kicking rifles he has ever found. These include .600 Nitro Express double rifles, 4-bore rifles, even antitank rifles and automatic aircraft cannon. Buehler states the recoil of a .44 Magnum or a .30 Herrett is worse!

In tests made by Leupold, a measuring device called an accelerometer was constructed. It was found that the .45 Auto pistol subjected a scope to three sharp jolts varying between 750 and 2,000 Gs. (One G is the measure of the pull of gravity at sea level.) A whack amounting to 2,000 Gs is, according to Leupold, akin to that of the

The Leupold 2X scope mounted on a Colt .45 with special Leupold mounts. See text for accelerometer results with this pistol as measured by Leupold. The company points out that this mount requires precise gunsmithing because the slots must be milled in the slide.

deceleration of a car traveling 135 miles an hour when it hits a solid brick wall. And that's just a .45 Auto, which is far from the magnitude of cartridges like the .30 Herrett and .44 Magnum.

Maynard Buehler, the scope-mount manufacturer, has developed a recoil sleeve for hard-recoiling pistols and revolvers. It's shown here behind the front scope ring (photographed in the white, before bluing, for illustrative purposes) on this Auto-Mag, which is a hard-recoiling custom pistol. Buehler has put scope mounts on all manner of guns up to and including aircraft cannon; he states the recoil shock is greatest on heavy-calibered pistols and revolvers.

Buehler has developed a recoil sleeve which he recommends on .30 Herretts and .44 Magnums (with Leupold 2X scope) to lessen the strain on the mount. There's no question that some study is indicated before you mount any scope on one of these hellbender guns. If a .45 ACP generates 2,000 Gs, a .44 Magnum and some of the other wildcats must generate fearful G force. And the result can be a breakdown, or breakup, of a scope's whole optical system. You need a scope that can take the recoil and not lose adjustment, and you need a mount that can stand the gaff. As you can see, it's a large order.

Thus scoping any pistol or any revolver calls for good mounts, properly fitted. Some screw holes are very shallow, and you will have to watch carefully to make sure that the screws don't bottom in the holes before they are tight. If so, the screws must be ground off ever so little until the screws wind home properly, using as much of the threads as possible. Then both screws and holes should be cleaned with lighter fluid and Loctite should be applied to all the screws. It's a good idea to place Loctite under the bases too, especially on the big guns.

SCOPED HANDGUNS FOR HUNTING AND SPORT

I have not recommended, and do not recommend, using any one-hand gun for big-game hunting. There are some who do use these guns for big game, and as long as they are excellent shots and can place a bullet precisely I have no quarrel. But I still think it's in the nature of a stunt. Needless to say, such a hunter will be backed up with a capable friend toting a big rifle.

Many handgun shooters like to shoot varmints at long distances, and this is a great sport. The use of a handgun as an emergency arm is also logical. It isn't a bad idea to have a big revolver on the hip when you're in dangerous-game country. Whether you're hunting or working, it just makes good sense.

Packing a handgun on a canoe trip where weight is a factor makes a lot of sense and a scoped handgun will do a lot more for you than an unscoped one. I think my own choice for such a gun and for such a trip would be a scoped Thompson/Center in either .25/35 or .22 Hornet. An extra barrel for the .22 Long Rifle would be handy too. That combination could save a life by enabling one to shoot some meat in the event provisions ran out.

CHAPTER ELEVEN

BLACKPOWDER GUNS AND OTHER MISCELLANY

There has always been a strong interest in the older guns used in America, especially among collectors. Over a period of years, those with an interest in these old guns began to shoot them. Eventually, the National Muzzle Loading Rifle Association was formed and interest in shooting the old guns began to grow.

But it soon became obvious that it didn't make good sense to shoot the genuine antiques—they should be preserved to protect their value. As a result, small gunsmiths began to manufacture replicas as faithfully as possible but with modern components—which means better steel and better parts.

While there were quite a large number of people in this business, with varying degrees of expertise, it remained for a sharp Southerner named Turner Kirkland, who owns Dixie Gun Works and puts out a catalog as thick as your thumb, to make these guns on a production basis.

In 1955 Kirkland started selling Kentucky rifles—new ones, that is—which were made in Belgium. What Kirkland began has become a rout today, with an interest in black-powder guns that defies imagination. Today, Kirkland has a host of competitors, though he still sells thousands of these rifles every year.

Nor is the black-powder business restricted to Kentucky rifles. Far from it. Today's market includes Kentucky or Kentucky-type flintlocks, percussion copies, plains rifles like the Hawken made by Thompson/Center in New Hampshire,

An original, and very valuable, sample of a muzzleloading Colt percussion revolver. The owners of these guns do not — should not — fire them. Their value is such that it's much wiser to shoot replicas and save the originals.

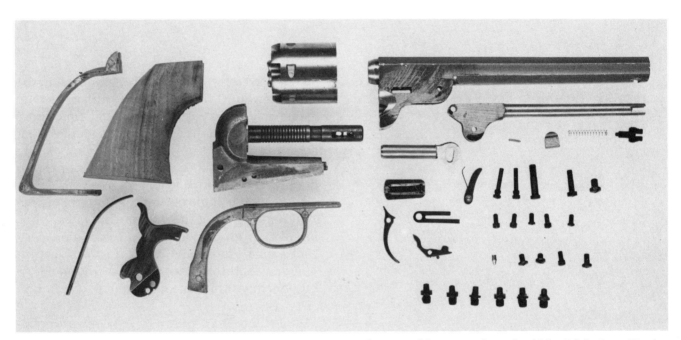

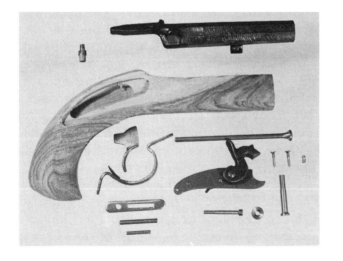

These two kits are made and sold by Dixie Gun Works. The long-barreled revolver is a replica of the Colt 1851 Navy, and the short single-shot is an "overcoat pistol" kit. These kits are becoming quite popular. If you're handy with tools, you can easily complete the gun. Kits are also offered for rifles, both percussion and flintlock, and are available from other makers as well.

and handguns galore. Colt, Lyman (the gunsight people), and many more are offering blackpowder revolvers that are copies of the old Army dragoon models, smaller Navy models . . . and who knows what else will come along.

The vast interest in muzzleloader shooting has led Colt and many others, including Lyman, to manufacture replicas of the old guns. This is a Colt 1851 Navy replica of current manufacture, a percussion muzzleloader. Note that the notch at the tip of the hammer is employed as the rear sight.

Henry Deringer of Philadelphia made some of the smallest, neatest, and best small pistols during the early and middle 1800s. They were known as back-action locks, because the hammer spring was in the rear part of the lock plate, which allowed a shorter barrel. Deringer's pistols were so popular that they were copied and the name "derringer" (with double r) was adopted as generic for the type of gun. This is a modern replica of the "Philadelphia derringer," by CVA (Connecticut Valley Arms), and is available as a finished product or in kit form.

It remained for a new outfit called Connecticut Valley Arms to come up with the idea of selling a do-it-yourself kit. CVA furnishes all the ingredients and all you have to do is a little fitting here and there plus finishing the stock. (It's really not that simple—if you buy a kit you'll have quite a bit of work to do, and you'll have to be good to match the quality of the finished product you can buy for a little more money.)

These "replicas" of older guns are available both in flint and percussion systems. A flintlock requires a lot more babying, since it's all too easy to get the powder in the pan damp, in which case the gun won't fire.

Let's run through how these guns work very briefly. Any muzzleloading gun is loaded from the muzzle, naturally. First, the gun must be clean inside. If it is a percussion-cap gun, you should fire a cap or two before you load the gun (from each charge hole if it's a revolver) to make sure these holes are clean. Then the proper amount of powder is poured into the barrel, or

The reintroduced Colt 3rd Model Dragoon Revolver. Made like the original, it is in .44 caliber with an engraved scene around the cylinder. However, the gun has been dropped again in 1977.

Ruger Old Army model percussion revolver. Note that Ruger has not just copied the old models but rather has put his design talents toward improving the old designs, which is evidenced by the modern rear sight. The same model is available in stainless steel at slight added cost.

into each charge hole of the revolver, and the ball is seated with the seater built into the gun.

With the percussion system, you simply place a percussion cap over the nipple. When the hammer comes down it fires the cap (just like a toy cap pistol) and a bit of flame squirts through the hole into the barrel, where the main charge of black powder rests.

A flintlock is another story. The flint is clamped to the top of the hammer, and when you pull the trigger to release the hammer, it allows the flint to strike a vertically standing piece of steel called the frizzen. This contact sends a shower of sparks into a depression right under the frizzen called the pan, which contains some fine priming powder. The sparks set this priming powder afire, and it produces the flame which travels through the touch hole into the barrel to the main charge. As you can appreciate, you've got to keep your powder dry or else the gun won't fire. Which means that if you hunt with a flintlock you will experience problems in the damp brush or in a rain or fog—or if you may have to stoop to get under some brush, inadvertently raise the frizzen, and the powder in the pan will slip away! If nothing else, you'll learn that our ancestors didn't have it as easy as we do.

In any event, there is currently a great rebirth in black-powder shooting and hunting. It may well be the fastest-growing part of the gun sport today. Just how much of this interest can be at-

tributed to the nation's bicentennial is hard to estimate; I doubt if it's very much. It just happens to be fun, and that stupid 1968 so-called gun-control law doesn't include these older guns. Another interesting aspect is that many states now have what they refer to as a "primitive weapons" season, meaning that black-powder hunters can take to the woods (often at the same time as the bow-and-arrow crowd) during their own season.

The word "replica" is often confusing. Copies of older guns are called replicas, and so are some fake products that don't shoot and are not meant to shoot. Just what the appeal of these particular "replicas" is I don't know. But they exist, often for a few dollars. At a distance, they look like a gun; but up close they are a pure fake.

One of the things contributing to the boom in black-powder interest today is the introduction of Pyrodex powder, which is discussed in Chapter Fifteen. This is a new substitute for black powder, with all the attributes of black powder but few of the disadvantages. Another is that a number of bullet makers, like Hornady, now supply ready-formed round balls and lead bullets, so the chore of casting your own lead slugs is removed if you prefer it that way.

These old, or newly manufactured old, single-action revolvers operate much like the modern ones. The instructions that accompany the gun will advise you how to operate it, and these should be followed closely.

One of the firms specializing in replicas is Classic Arms International of Lynbrook, N. Y., which has a line of finished guns and kits. I obtained a sample of their Ethan Allen Pepperbox, a four-barreled affair which they label "America's first double-action pistol." That designation is a little stretched, since you have to rotate the barrel unit by hand, but pulling the trigger does raise the hammer and let it fall. This model shoots a .345-inch-diameter round ball with a charge of 12 grains of FFFG black powder. I fired the sample with Pyrodex, and it gave satisfactory results—which means it worked and the balls came out along with a huge billowing smoke cloud. Since there are no sights on this gun, accuracy is suitable for across the card table. That's about what the gun was made for in the first place. The gun is nicely made and nicely finished.

Classic Arms International, a Long Island, N.Y., firm, manufactures a line of interesting replicas in finished and kit form that are fun to shoot. The triple-barreled gun is a "duckfoot" model which sprays three lead balls down an alley in classic clearing fashion. The double-barreled "snake eyes" model was meant to be used by riverboat gamblers. The four-barreled gun is known as the Ethan Allen Pepperbox and is claimed to be the first double-action revolver. It isn't really that, but its barrels are rotated by hand and all that's needed to fire is a pull on the trigger, which cocks and releases the hammer.

I have also fired sample Colt and Lyman replicas with satisfactory results, using Pyrodex and Hornady balls. It's easy to see how someone can get hung up on these oldies, as long as he doesn't mind the smells and all the mess that go along with them.

PART TWO

AMMUNITION AND BALLISTICS

INTRODUCTION

Part Two of this book is concerned primarily with ammunition: what it contains and how it performs, both inside the gun and once it's airborne, and what happens when it arrives at the target. This is sometimes referred to as the science of ballistics—internal ballistics for the events within the gun and external ballistics for the rest of it.

As a science, ballistics is deep, mysterious, and dependent on higher mathematics. We'll avoid that sort of thing, because it's of interest to hardly anyone, least of all you—or me for that matter. What really counts is the practical business of what happens, and we'll explore these events in some detail in language that will be meaningful to you and help you to understand why your particular gun does what it does, or perhaps why it doesn't do what it ought to do.

There are some other subjects covered in Part Two, including handgun decoration, law-enforcement uses of handguns, and miscellaneous opinions on various aspects of handguns.

Before we get started, a few definitions are in order so we know what we're talking about when these terms come up.

Cartridge: A cartridge is a complete unit consisting of the brass case, primer, propellant powder, and bullet or shot charge. (Yes, as explained elsewhere, there are shot loads used in handguns.)

Primer: This is the very tiny component which is exploded by the firing pin's blow and which, in turn, ignites the powder. Primers are very sensitive, very powerful—and very small.

Powder: The propellant. When ignited, it burns to generate gas, which propels the bullet or shot charge.

Caliber: A term used to measure the bore of a firearm but having no relation to its power or performance. In fact, the measurements are often meaningless. For example, .38-caliber guns are actually .357 inch in caliber, all of which will be explained in due course.

Magnum: The word simply means big. But this word has been employed so loosely in the gun world that it has little meaning and is not necessarily descriptive. Magnum means different things among the three broad classes of firearms, too. In a shotgun, the word simply means a larger charge of shot with a corresponding increase in powder. It does not mean higher velocity, because there is a limit to the speed at which a round pellet may be efficiently driven. In a rifle the word *usually* means a more powerful cartridge, as in .300 Winchester Magnum or .300 Weatherby Magnum. In the revolver the word also usually means more power, as in .357, .41, or .44 Magnum. But, as we shall see, the word in handgunnery also carries the myth of punishment to the shooter.

By way of interest, Smith & Wesson copyrighted the word "Magnum" for handgun use, although from what I know about copyright law, I doubt the company has properly protected the copyright; I suspect if it ever came to a legal test, Magnum would be as generic as aspirin, linoleum, thermos, and other trade names have become. All these and more were once copyrighted trade names, but copyright was lost through failure to protect it properly.

There are many myths concerning the performance of handgun ammunition, many of them foisted upon the public by newspaper and general magazine writers and editors who have no idea what they're talking about. In fact, these people seem to delight in deliberately misleading the general public. For example, many bleeding-heart groups think the expanding bullet shouldn't be used by police. The media appear to encourage this opinion with false ballistic information.

One case in point is the so-called dumdum bullet. It's an alliterative term which appeals to newspapermen, but they don't know what it really means. Dum-Dum was an arsenal in India, and in the late 1800s, a British army captain there nipped the noses off military rifle bullets, which made them expanding bullets. For a brief period, such bullets were made and used by the British against the Dervishes, but the practice soon stopped, because these jacketed bullets then had lead exposed at both ends and often the lead was blown out of the bullet, leaving the jacket in the bore. The next shot, with a barrel obstruction, exploded the rifle. The result was a very short life for the dumdum—except in newspaper parlance, where it still lives.

Another word used casually by these writers is cordite—a British gunpowder which is supposed to cause a mysterious, easily definable odor. The British have employed cordite as a satisfactory propellant for many years. It is a smokeless powder and a good one. Its odor isn't any more definable than the word "dumdum," but it will continue to be used by fiction writers, both in newspapers and in pulp books.

CHAPTER TWELVE

AMMUNITION

Ammunition consists of centerfire and rimfire types. Today, with the increasing popularity of muzzleloading, we also have to contend with those old types. In fact, the muzzleloader may be a good place to start, because it's the simplest form of ammunition.

Long ago, "ammunition" consisted of powder and shot—and some form of igniting the powder, although the method of ignition was not truly part of the ammunition at that time. Back then, the powder was black powder and the shot was round balls.

To use a muzzleloader you poured the required amount of powder down the bore, or into the charge holes of a revolver, and seated a ball on top of the powder. In the very early days ignition was accomplished by sticking a smoldering wick through a little hole in the breech that touched and ignited the powder. The next refinements had to do with ignition. First came the wheellock, which was wound up like a watch mainspring and spun rapidly against a flint to throw a shower of sparks which ignited the powder. This was followed by a reversal of the parts; the flint was clamped into a large hammer which fell against an upright steel part called the frizzen, which caused the sparking. This was the flintlock, and it was popular for many years. Today there is renewed interest in the flintlock as well as in the percussion system which replaced it.

Perhaps one of the greatest inventions—and one of the shortest-lived—in all gun history was the percussion cap. Invented in about 1840, it soon replaced the flintlock because it was faster, more efficient, and more dependable. But it lasted only until the development of "fixed ammunition," meaning the self-contained cartridge as we know it today. The first successful modern cartridge was first used in about 1854, so you can see how quickly the percussion cap was abandoned. But its considerable impact is still seen in the fact that the cap was simply moved, from the nipple at the breech of the barrel to its present place inside the cartridge.

With percussion-cap ignition the flint system was eliminated entirely. The pan and frizzen were replaced with a little part known as the nipple, which stuck up and rearward and had a small hole that extended into the barrel, where the main charge of powder lay. Instead of a shower of sparks provided by the flint against steel, the percussion cap employed fulminate of mercury, a violent explosive detonated by a percussion blow. This cap, of soft metal, was placed over the nipple. When the big hammer, with a concave face to help contain the explosion, came down it fired the cap and its flame rushed through the nipple's hole into the powder.

The first of the modern cartridges was the result of a development by a Frenchman, Louis Flobert. Exhibited at the Paris Exposition in 1851, it consisted of a pinch of percussion-cap explosive material encased in a small copper cup with a bullet perched on top. Flobert exhibited the little cartridge along with a small rifle he had developed for target shooting. The development caused little stir, but it was observed by two Americans named Horace Smith and Daniel Wesson. They returned with the idea and added a very small charge of black powder to the combination. Thus was born, in 1854, the .22 Short cartridge. (It wasn't called the Short then, for there was no other .22.) Today's .22 Short is hardly changed from the 1854 version in outward appearance. This was the first successful modern cartridge and was entirely self-contained.

The history of ammunition development is hard to separate from that of rifles, shotguns, and handguns. Smith & Wesson's .22 Short (S&W made ammunition in those days) was first

used in revolvers. At about the same time, as has been recounted in Chapter One, a man named Rollin White patented a relatively simple idea: drilling the charge holes clear through the revolver cylinder. Such a practice was necessary for the successful use of self-contained ammunition. Smith & Wesson bought the patent, vigorously defended it, and quickly established a stranglehold on the market. It was a classic case of a new company vaulting into a dominant market position because it had a better idea. The remainder of American pistol makers had to wait until the patent expired in 1869 before they could get on this bandwagon.

Meantime, ammunition was developing rapidly in other ways. The rimfire cartridge was excellent for low-pressure cartridges, but its basic weakness was that its rim had to be crushed by the firing-pin blow for ignition. This meant the cartridge-case material had to be soft enough to crush, and thus too soft to hold high pressures.

The result was the centerfire cartridge, and development went on at a fast pace. The same principle of centerfire ignition applies to rifles, handguns, and shotguns although there are differences. The blow of a handgun firing pin is weaker than that of most rifle or shotgun firing pins because the guns are smaller, and therefore the primers are made softer in handgun ammunition. Handgun ammo also does not develop as high pressure as high-power rifle ammunition, so a softer primer is acceptable. The shotgun primer must be hotter than that used in rifles, chiefly because the flame must travel a longer path and many shotgun powders are harder to ignite.

Thus despite the apparent similarities between rifle and handgun ammunition there are important differences. The handgun is designed to be small and portable and to be used at short distances. It is not expected to place a small, high-velocity bullet into a varmint at 400 or 500 yards (although there are some special-purpose handguns meant to do just that). Nor is it expected to place a heavy bullet in a precise spot in an elephant's head to penetrate the massive bone and reach the brain.

The short-barreled one-hand gun must achieve its velocity in a barrel from one-fourth to one-twelfth as long as the average rifle barrel, so it follows that its ammunition requirements are quite different.

And, since the handgun is much lighter and is fired by one hand, it does not have the size, weight, or support that is offered by the shoulder-fired rifle. The heavy rifle can handle a whopping cartridge like the .458 Winchester Magnum, a cartridge which, if ever built in a handgun, would most likely tear the hand right off the shooter.

So we now see that there are physical limitations on the power a handgun can achieve. Except for a few very special purpose guns, handguns are much less potent than rifles.

A handgun cartridge must use a faster-burning powder to generate its maximum velocity in a barrel not much longer than 6 inches, and it must achieve respectable velocity in a 2-inch barrel. By contrast, if you cut a rifle barrel to only 2 inches long, the powder wouldn't burn and the bullet would be shoved out by the primer's thrust, spilling unburned powder on the ground. (Note too that federal law dictates that a rifle barrel must be a minimum of 16 inches long.)

Nor can a handgun generate too much chamber pressure, simply because there is no way to provide enough metal to withstand high pressures. You have only to look at a revolver cylinder bored full of holes, leaving a minimum amount of steel to contain the pressure, to realize these limits. Any increase in pressure means a corresponding beefing up of the steel—in six directions—and that means a much larger revolver frame and a heavier gun that soon takes it out of the handgun class.

That's another reason most handgun cartridges are straight and not bottlenecked like most high-power rifle cartridges. A straight cartridge allows the pressure to get out much quicker. The result is that you can use faster-burning powders in a handgun, and, in fact, handgun powder accidentally loaded in a rifle will blow the rifle apart like a bomb.

Still, there are cartridges used interchangeably in rifles and handguns. Chief among these is the .22 Long Rifle, the most useful cartridge ever developed, which produces excellent results in both types of firearm. Another is the .22 WMR (Winchester Magnum Rimfire), which also produces good results in both.

The biggest standard handgun cartridge is the .44 Magnum, and two very popular rifles are made for this revolver cartridge. The rifles are used in wooded country by many deer hunters with excellent results. But aside from these particular cartridges, there are very few rifles made for handgun cartridges. This was not true years ago when the .44/40 Winchester was a popular number in the old Winchester rifles and Colt revolvers and a man could use the same ammo in either gun.

MAGNUMS

Today there are four standard handgun cartridges known as Magnums: the .22 WMR, .357, .41, and .44. The first is a rimfire developed by Winchester, and the remainder were all developed by Smith & Wesson (with an assist from the ammunition makers, notably Remington). There were two recent attempts to produce the .22 Jet (officially the .22 centerfire Magnum) and the .256 Winchester Magnum. Neither was successful and neither should have been.

I don't think the .22 WMR deserves the Magnum title, but the term has become so vague that it's not worth arguing about. The remaining three, the .357, .41, and .44 Magnums, are legitimate powerhouses and are properly called by the name Magnum. Yet, the .41 was primarily developed for police work (and supplied with two factory loads, one mild and one hot), and here the term has been disastrous. For the .41, excellent though it is, has suffered from the use of the word.

This is a strange circumstance indeed. The word "Magnum" suggests extra power, and thoughtless civil liberty activists fly into a rage because police are considering buying Magnum guns that will help save their lives. These people, apparently, would rather have a cop die than a crook shot seriously. In addition, many cops were afraid of the Magnum despite the fact that it's really no more difficult to master than the .38 Special. We'll have more to say about this later, but it is important to note here that the very use of the word "Magnum" has various effects on various people.

It was back in about 1935 that the .357 Magnum rocked the gun world. While several people have claimed parenthood, the best information seems to be that Major Daniel Wesson himself is the person most responsible for its development, for he was seeking a gun with more sock than the old .38 Special. And he succeeded. When first announced, one of the biggest claims for the .357 was that it could, by God, drive through the block of an auto engine. That was some claim then, and auto blocks were dutifully blown to hell by early experimenters. I don't know what the story would be today. The way modern cars are built, you could likely do the same thing with a standard .22 Long Rifle. But cars in the '30s were massive, with equally massive cast-iron blocks, and, you may recall, some were used by the likes of John Dillinger, Pretty Boy Floyd, Baby Face Nelson, Machine Gun Kelly, and other offensive characters. Officers often had to slug it out in a firefight, and it was deemed useful that a bullet could down a car much as a big rifle can down a stampeding elephant.

All too many times the gangster would get away with his car shot full of holes. Most of the problem was marksmanship, for a .38 Special in the tires would have konked even Dillinger's favorite Ford V-8. So the point about the .357 being a car killer really was pretty moot, but I can remember it being made.

SHOT CARTRIDGES

Sportsmen have long tried to use various shot cartridges in handguns, with mixed results. There have been guns manufactured as single-shot .410 pistols, although there have been complications because of federal laws. There is today a barrel for the Thompson/Center Contender in .410 bore which is legal.

Omark Industries has perfected shot cartridges for revolver (and rifle) use with these three offerings: .357 Magnum, .22 Winchester Magnum Rimfire, and .44 Magnum. The .357 and .44 cartridges are loaded with No. 9 shot, the .22 with No. 12. A load is available in .22 Long Rifle. These cartridges perform very well at short range, and enclosing the shot in a plastic capsule has resulted in good patterns. Formerly, any shot load fired through a rifled barrel spread the pellets so rapidly that they were largely ineffective. These loads are useful for such targets as dangerous snakes and very little else.

These extra-long cartridges are produced by Thompson/Center for the Contender single-shot exclusively. Available in .357 and .44 Magnum, and known as Hot Shots, these power packages deliver as much payload as a .410 shotgun. In use, the shot container is driven through the bore and is shredded by a special device at the muzzle. The gun may also be used with conventional ammunition.

Shot cartridges have been on the market for many years in .22 Long Rifle caliber. Containing only a pinch of No. 12 shot, they have been notably useless in either handgun or rifle, largely because the rifling spins the shot into a wild, wide pattern at very short range.

Some shooters have bored out revolver barrels to remove the rifling and produce a semblance of choke at the muzzle. Some of these guns, especially in larger calibers such as .44 Special and .45 Colt, have been very useful and have produced good patterns.

Today there are several cartridges loaded with shot that do a fine job of shooting even in a rifled bore because the shot is contained in a plastic container which rides right through the bore without being affected by the rifling. CCI produces some excellent shot cartridges, and Thompson/Center has its Hot Shot ammo along the same lines for its guns exclusively.

EXPERIMENTAL AMMUNITION

Over the years there have been other attempts at "different" methods of producing ammunition, but so far none have made it commercially. One of these developments was called "caseless" ammunition and was produced (in a rifle) by Daisy, the air-gun company. This ammo consisted of a lead bullet with a bit of what appeared to be cotton plastered to its base. There was no primer,

and the ignition was accomplished by a diesel effect when a heavy spring compressed air to high heat to ignite the propellant. This development is now dead.

Another was something called the Gyrojet Rocket. It was a true rocket. That is, the projectile was loaded with a solid burning fuel in its base, and it kept accelerating until burnout. Among the major disadvantages of this gadget was that rockets start slowly; thus lock time was very long and any movement of the gun resulted in inaccuracy. I don't think the gun world was ready for a rocket pistol, and the idea died fast.

Experiments continue to develop caseless ammunition, mostly because of military interest, where reduction of both cost and weight would be a great advantage. Will these ever see their way onto dealer's shelves and be used by the average sportsman? Not in my time, and most likely not in yours either.

Another weirdo was the Dardick gun, which used what was essentially a .38 Special except that the cartridge consisted of a plastic case which was roughly triangular with rounded sides and corners. The advantage to the Dardick was that its magazine could hold more ammo because there was less empty space. Dardick spent a couple of years tooling up, produced a few guns and some ammunition, and then the whole thing died. Dardick called his cartridges "trounds"—everybody else called them silly.

CHAPTER THIRTEEN

CALIBERS

RIMFIRE AND CENTERFIRE: THE DIFFERENCES

A rimfire cartridge—the .22 Long Rifle, Long, and Short are the most common rimfires today—is one in which the priming mixture is placed all around the inside of the rim so that a blow by the firing pin on any part of the rim will ignite the cartridge. Ignition in any cartridge is accomplished by a hammer blow on the priming mixture, a sensitive, very high-energy mixture whose only function is to ignite the powder. When the powder burns it generates gas which drives the bullet out of the gun. Exploding the primer might be likened to placing a tiny pinch of priming mix on an anvil, then hitting it with a hammer. In a firearm you substitute the firing pin for the hammer, and in the case of a rimfire cartridge, the back of the rim is supported either by the barrel or by the edge of the cylinder in a revolver.

A centerfire cartridge differs in that the primer is in a self-contained capsule containing its own anvil. Primer flame rushes through a flash hole into the main body of the cartridge to ignite the powder. In both rimfire and centerfire cartridges, ignition is similar; it's just the physical form that's different. Only centerfire cartridges may be reloaded.

Since rimfire cartridges must be comparatively soft to permit the gun's firing pin to crush the rim and set off the primer, it follows that rimfire cartridges cannot be loaded to as high

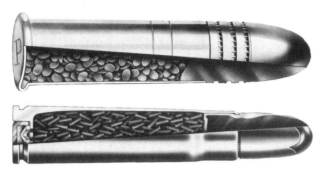

The differences between centerfire (below) and rimfire (above) ignition systems are shown by these cutaway sketches. Note that the rimfire priming compound is spread around the inside of the rim and that the rim metal is quite thin at this point. The centerfire primer consists of cup, priming compound, and anvil. Also shown is the flashhole leading from the primer pocket into the main body of the cartridge case. It can easily be seen that a centerfire cartridge is much stronger than a rimfire.

pressures as centerfire cartridges. If they were, the case would rupture and spill propellant gas into the works of the gun. This gas is under extremely high pressure and could ruin the gun. A centerfire cartridge has a separate primer, and the case doesn't get crushed during ignition, so it can be made much tougher and much thicker. The result is that you can utilize higher chamber pressures and obtain higher velocities using centerfire ammunition. That's why all high-velocity rifle and pistol cartridges are centerfire. Today's most powerful rimfire is the .22 Winchester Magnum Rimfire (WMR).

The advantages of rimfire cartridges are (1) that they're low-powered, and thus suitable for target shooting as well as small-game and pest shooting, and (2) they are considerably less expensive than centerfire ammunition, because the latter is more expensive to manufacture. The main advantage of a centerfire is that its stronger construction permits high velocity, more power and greater performance. The centerfire cartridge may also be reloaded, which cuts the cost of target shooting enormously.

HANDGUN AMMUNITION

.22 Short, rimfire. Developed in 1854, the .22 Short was the world's first complete metallic cartridge. Virtually the only obvious change in the Short from 1854 to today is the current use of smokeless powder and a nonfouling primer compound. Shorts are very popular and useful, especially in a cellar target range because the noise level is very low. At one time the .22 Short was extremely well made for target shooting, and many excellent rifles were made for its exclusive use. There is a trend back in that direction, primarily in target handguns. Guns which are chambered exclusively for Shorts will not accommodate Longs or Long Rifles. Shorts may also be used in revolvers chambered for the Long Rifle, but they are not powerful enough to work the action of .22 Long Rifle autoloading pistols.

Shorts are manufactured in both standard and high-velocity ammunition, and hollowpoint bullets are loaded in some brands. The Short is most useful for target shooting where little noise is desired. It is not as suitable as the Long Rifle for small-game shooting.

.22 Long, rimfire. This is a miserable cartridge that uses the Short bullet and the Long Rifle case and powder charge. There is nothing to recommend the Long, and the only reason I can see for its continued existence is that too many people simply ask for ".22 Longs" when they really mean Long Rifles, and most clerks don't know the difference. I'm even willing to bet that if Longs were dropped entirely nobody would even be aware of it. I do not advise using the Long in any firearm.

.22 Long Rifle, rimfire. This is certainly the most useful cartridge ever developed, and the world's most popular. Millions of these cartridges are produced every year all over the world. Long Rifles are available in standard and high-velocity loadings and in hollowpoint styles. The hollowpoint is a very destructive bullet on small game and pests at short range. Special match ammunition, loaded in various American and imported brands, is remarkably good target ammunition. A .22 Long Rifle cartridge case is the same in diameter and case head dimensions as the Short, but it's longer and the bullet is heavier. Shorts may be fired in a Long Rifle chamber, but Long Rifles will not enter a Short chamber. It is perfectly acceptable to fire Shorts in a handgun or rifle made to fire both (Longs too, for that matter), but it isn't advisable to fire Shorts in a good target arm especially made for the Long Rifle. No harm will come from firing a few shots, but prolonged use should be avoided.

Standard and target .22 Long Rifle ammunition is loaded to a velocity just below the speed of sound (approximately 1100 fps at sea level), because the bullet is not shaped for supersonic flight. High-speed ammunition is loaded over the speed of sound, however, and as a rule develops poorer accuracy. The differences are minor—enough to be noticed by the expert target shooter but not by anyone else.

All .22 rimfire cartridges are suitable for both rifle and handgun use, though Shorts and standard-velocity Long Rifles usually will not cycle an autoloader made for high-velocity Long Rifle cartridges.

Stinger .22, rimfire. An interesting new development (1976–77) is the Stinger .22 produced by Omark Industries. It features a slightly longer .22 Long Rifle cartridge case, a slightly lighter bullet, and considerably more velocity.

It reminds me of the .22 Hornet when it first came along in the early '30s. I was twelve years old when it was announced officially but I didn't learn about it right away. It was my "understanding" that the more powerful Hornet could goose up any .22 rifle—the common knowledge was that you could fire Hornets in an ordinary .22 rifle. That was far from true, but we all accepted it as gospel, and with money as scarce as it was in the early Depression, there was no chance of a young teenager getting hold of one and I remained ignorant about the Hornet for years.

But the Stinger is a different proposition. It does fit ordinary .22s, and that's what it's meant to be fired in. It gives 25 percent more velocity than a .22 Long Rifle *high-speed* in a rifle. And that's a significant improvement, especially when coupled with a flatter trajectory over 100 yards (3½ inches less drop).

In a pistol or revolver it's quite safe to use Stingers, and the new ammo gives proportionately better speeds too. According to Omark, a 4-inch barrel will produce about 1150–1200 fps, and a 6-inch barrel about 1300–1350 fps.

There are a couple of cautions to be observed, however. The Stinger case is about 1/10 longer than standard, which means that if your gun has been fired considerably without cleaning you may have some fouling built up in the area immediately in front of the chamber. The solution is a good cleaning with a solvent like Hoppe's No. 9; no other cautions need be observed. Failure to remove this fouling could result in the Stinger cartridges jamming in the fouling and producing difficult chambering and extraction.

Omark also reports that the Stinger does not function reliably in some pistols. They specifically mention the Sterling pocket automatic and the Llama M15; the latter does not have a chamber, bore, and groove that conforms with U.S. specifications. It is safe to assume that such problems may soon be corrected, and you should consult the manufacturer or importer for precise details.

The Stinger performs very well in modern guns in good condition, and I have fired enough of them in both rifles and handguns to be much impressed. I have not shot enough live game or varmints to offer much of an opinion, but other sources tell me to use head shots on any edible game. The Stinger is very destructive.

.22 Winchester Magnum Rimfire. This has been one of the most confusing cartridges ever developed. It really needn't be, but I've found more people have asked questions about the uses of this cartridge than any other I can think of.

A good deal of the mixup occurred when Winchester developed the cartridge and placed it on the market before there was ever a gun to fire it! For reasons best known to Winchester, they made the Magnum Rimfire with a slightly larger-diameter bullet than all other .22 rimfires. Other rimfires are .222 inch; the Magnum is .224 inch, a difference of 2/1000 inch. That doesn't sound like much, but it's too much to safely shoot a Magnum through a standard .22 barrel even if the gun were chambered for it. The larger bullet would meet with too much resistance and pressures would be too high for safety. Conclusion number one is that the Magnum requires a barrel with slightly larger bore and groove dimensions (.224 inch happens to be the size used for .22 centerfire rifle cartridges like the .22/250, .222, etc.).

The Magnum cartridge is different in size also; it's fatter and longer than a .22 Long Rifle. This is a common safety procedure when a new cartridge is developed—make it big enough so

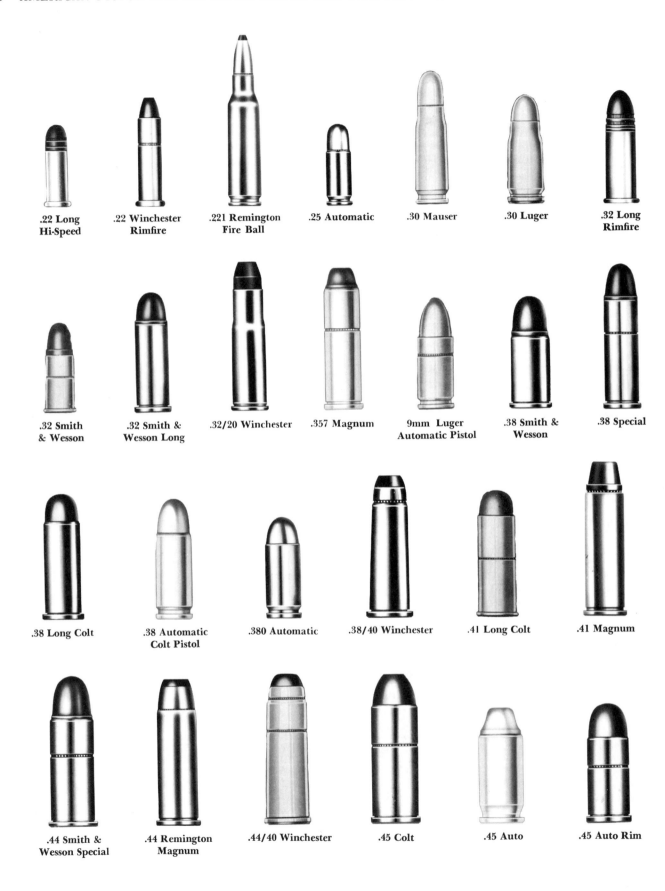

.22 Long
Hi-Speed

.22 Winchester
Rimfire

.221 Remington
Fire Ball

.25 Automatic

.30 Mauser

.30 Luger

.32 Long
Rimfire

.32 Smith
& Wesson

.32 Smith &
Wesson Long

.32/20 Winchester

.357 Magnum

9mm Luger
Automatic Pistol

.38 Smith &
Wesson

.38 Special

.38 Long Colt

.38 Automatic
Colt Pistol

.380 Automatic

.38/40 Winchester

.41 Long Colt

.41 Magnum

.44 Smith &
Wesson Special

.44 Remington
Magnum

.44/40 Winchester

.45 Colt

.45 Auto

.45 Auto Rim

A typical revolver for the .22 WMR with extra cylinder for .22 Long Rifle. A revolver is the only kind of firearm that can handle this combination, because the chambers are of different size, which rules out any firearm with the chamber cut directly in the barrel. With a revolver, you can simply switch cylinders and fire either cartridge. This is the Harrington & Richardson Model 676 with 4½-inch barrel.

nobody can get it in the wrong gun and cause trouble.

The first guns ever made for the .22 WMR were revolvers, made especially for the cartridge with barrels bored and rifled to the larger dimension. These handguns could not be used for .22 Long Rifle ammunition because the chambers were too large; a Long Rifle would fit sloppily and, if it did fire, there would be a danger that the case would have to expand farther than its elastic limit and a rupture would result. Thus conclusion number two is that guns made *exclusively* for the .22 Magnum will not fire any other cartridge.

But we're not through yet! We have stated that it isn't safe to drive an oversize bullet through a barrel. But it *is* safe to drive a slightly undersize soft-lead bullet through a larger barrel. Revolver makers, led by Ruger, decided to supply a .22 Magnum Rimfire handgun with an extra cylinder for the .22 Long Rifle, making the gun do double duty. Under the gas pressure, the Long Rifle bullet easily swells to fit the larger barrel and it works perfectly.

This interchangeability, however, can only work with a revolver because it alone can offer extra chambers with an extra cylinder. Rifles chambered for Magnum may only be fired with

Magnum cartridges. There are no auto pistols for this cartridge, but if there were, they would be restricted to WMR ammunition, the same as a rifle. You can buy a Magnum revolver with Long Rifle cylinder, but you cannot buy a Long Rifle revolver with a Magnum cylinder.

In spite of all the confusion, the WMR is a fine cartridge in either rifle or revolver. Its rifle velocity is 2000 fps; 6½-inch revolver barrels give it 1550 fps. It is a cartridge for the sportsman, and its best use is small-game and pest shooting.

.22 Winchester Rim Fire (WRF). The same cartridge was issued by Remington and known as the .22 Remington Special; they are identical and may be interchanged. The WRF is an old cartridge dating from black-powder days. It was longer than a Long Rifle and used a larger bullet (.228 inch). At one time several popular revolvers were made in this caliber, although its main use was in the Winchester Model 1890 rifle (and a Remington autoloader). The WRF is obsolete today, although ammunition was still listed in 1977.

.22 BB Cap and CB Cap. There used to be a couple of smaller .22 caliber cartridges but both are now obsolete. One was the .22 BB Cap, with BB standing for "bullet breech." It was a very short cartridge case with 20-grain bullet. Made originally for Flobert rifles (a French make), the BB Caps were quite accurate in revolvers and suitable for indoor target practice because of their low noise level. The .22 CB Cap—CB stands for "conical ball"—used the same short case as the BB Cap but a 29-grain .22 Short bullet. It has a little more power and noise than the BB Cap.

.22 Jet. This cartridge is even more confusing than the .22 WMR, perhaps because one of its names is the .22 Center Fire Magnum. The cartridge was developed jointly by Remington and Smith & Wesson. It is simply the .357 Magnum necked down to .22 caliber. Unlike the Rimfire Magnum, its bullet diameter is .222 inch, same as the Long Rifle. The Smith & Wesson revolver made for the .22 Jet came with a hammer convertible from rimfire to centerfire and two tiny firing pins, one for rimfire and one for centerfire. Six adaptors were supplied, and you slipped these adaptors into the revolver's charge holes loaded with Long Rifles, flipped the hammer converter, and were in business. The same revolver is used for either cartridge; it's only necessary to use the adaptors and set the hammer right. A spare cylinder for .22 Long Rifle was available as an extra if ordered with the gun.

The Jet was a very high-powered handgun even though it has a small bore. Although it is not to be recommended, black bear have been bagged with it. However, the convertible Jet is a good handgun for the man who wants two guns in one, since it shoots splendidly as a target or plinking gun in .22 Long Rifle, and converts readily to high-power Jet for small game and big varmints.

The Jet cartridge, however, has a severe taper, and unless the charge holes are clean and dry, cartridges will back up in firing and wedge tightly against the rear face of the revolver frame and put the gun out of commission because the cylinder can't be turned. The maker recommends cleaning the charge holes thoroughly with lighter fluid before firing Jet ammunition to prevent this. My own Jet worked perfectly when I followed these instructions.

The Jet is now a dead issue; very few revolvers were made and the whole thing is best forgotten. At one time Marlin considered making a rifle for the cartridge but gave up the idea. Today the best use for a Smith & Wesson Jet revolver is to keep it as a collector's item; their value will continue to increase.

.221 Fire Ball. The Remington Fire Ball is a handgun, although it might as well be classified as a one-handed rifle, since Remington developed a bolt action for the gun which has subsequently been used for several rifles. Nevertheless, it is a handgun, and is manufactured as such. It's also very potent. The cartridge is the .222 Remington shortened up a bit, and it's among the hottest handguns going in terms of velocity. It is useful for small game as well as for big varmints.

Remington apparently thinks many of these guns are purchased simply for their actions, and that the buyers then build a custom rifle using the Fire Ball action as a base. There is considerable reason to think this may be the case; the action is the same as that used on the Mohawk 600 rifle. (A Remington promotional brand name, this model is available in .243, .308, and similar cartridges.)

.22 Hornet. The .22 Hornet was first popular just before 1930. It was the first of the varmint cartridges as we know them today, and one of the interesting things about this cartridge is that it was the first cartridge made available commercially before there was a commercial rifle made for it. The reason was that it had captured the imagination of riflemen and the demand was heavy. Before the legitimate Hornet cartridge, shooters used cases for the old .22 Winchester Center Fire (a black-powder number).

Many custom-built Hornet handguns have been made over the years, because the cartridge is a natural for handgun use, being very powerful for such a gun. Now the Thompson/Center single-shot is made for .22 Hornet and is quite popular. T/C claims it is the most accurate centerfire cartridge in their gun.

.25 Automatic. The smallest centerfire cartridge is made for tiny pocket autoloading pistols. In Europe, where it originated, it's known as the 6.35mm. It's commonly supposed that the .25 Auto is a fairly powerful cartridge, and most people think it more potent than the .22 Long Rifle, probably because it has a larger bore. However, the .25 Auto is very decidedly less powerful than a .22, and its only real claim to fame is that it fits a very tiny handgun fully capable of being palmed out of sight.

.256 Winchester Magnum. Like the .22 Magnum Rimfire, this is another cartridge that Winchester created before a gun was developed or even planned. And, like the .22 Jet, this number is made by necking the .357 Magnum cartridge to .25 caliber. The .256 is red-hot, a fierce handgun for the varmint hunter.

A .256 single-shot pistol was made by Ruger for a short period. Marlin also made a lever-action rifle in this caliber for a while. Both are now obsolete. The .256 lingers on in the Thompson/Center pistol along with the .22 Jet. Both were rather surprising developments in that there was no need for them and they were and are generally useless.

.30 Mauser (7.63mm, also known as the 7.72mm Russian). This is a high-velocity cartridge made primarily for the old Mauser autoloading pistol. It was once seen in this country in some quantity, especially after World War I, but is rapidly becoming a collector's item. It shoots an 85-grain bullet at a muzzle velocity of 1323 fps with a chamber pressure of 29,000 units. A hot gun indeed, and, incidentally, a favorite of Winston Churchill's during the Boer War.

.30 Luger (7.65mm Luger). Some years ago, Luger pistols enjoyed a good sale in this country, and the .30 Luger was a red-hot handgun. It is seldom seen today, although American ammunition is still loaded. The .30 Luger is not as hot a cartridge as the .30 Mauser but the pistol was much more popular. The most popular Luger was, and is, the 9mm.

Luger pistols have been imported to the United States by Interarms and were manufactured by Mauser in West Germany. However, production of this great pistol ceased in 1976 and, it is claimed, will not be resumed. The Stoeger company, which owns the name "Luger" in the United States, now imports a "Luger .22" which is a totally different gun and should not be confused with the old Pistole '08. Interarms branded their Lugers "Parabellum."

.30 U.S. Carbine. Available in Ruger and Thompson/Center guns; the latter claims a velocity of 1800 fps with 110-grain ammunition. If ever there was a poorer cartridge for almost any purpose it would be hard to imagine. The .30

Carbine was developed during World War II for a small carbine with which service troops were generally armed. It is said that the little gun was highly thought of . . . by anyone who never had to use it in combat.

Since the war there have been many attempts to make a deer rifle out of it, but that was doomed to defeat because the cartridge lacks the necessary power. It has no more value in a handgun than in a rifle, though it does have more bark and bite in a one-hand gun than a shoulder arm. But the .30 U.S. Carbine has to rank very high on any list of useless cartridges.

.32 Automatic. One step above the .25 Auto, the .32 Auto is known in Europe as the 7.65mm. (But it should not be confused with the .30 Luger. The Luger is a powerful and potent cartridge; the .32 Auto is not.) This .32 is frequently called the .32 ACP (Automatic Colt Pistol). It was once quite popular here and abroad as a pocket-pistol cartridge but is not much in evidence today.

.32 Smith & Wesson. A small cartridge once popular for pocket revolvers, now nearly obsolete—as it should be.

.32 Smith & Wesson Long. Also known as the .32 Colt New Police or Colt Police Positive. Another old, small cartridge only a cut above the .32 S&W and not much more useful.

.32/20 Winchester. This was once a quite popular rifle cartridge that doubled as a potent handgun cartridge. The double-digit name is a holdover from black-powder days like the .30/30, .45/70, etc. The first number indicates the caliber, the second the powder charge in grains of black powder—the standard method of naming rifle cartridges in days gone by. No revolvers are made for the .32/20 any longer, but if you should pick up a used gun in this caliber it will do a good job for you on small game and varmints. One caution: .32/20 ammunition is available in high-speed and standard; use *only* the standard velocity in a revolver.

The .32/20 deserves a better fate in handguns. It is a fine revolver cartridge, and the gun makers would do well to throw out some of the weak, useless oldies they are still making and pick up the .32/20 again. It is a fine cartridge for the sportsman.

.32 Rimfires. At one time there were a number

of guns made for the quite weak .32 Long and .32 Short rimfire. Ammunition is not made any more, and should you locate a batch of old ammo, you'll likely find it won't fire very often. The priming mix tends to fall out of the rim in this old ammo. Which is just as well.

.38 Smith & Wesson. The same cartridge is also known as the .38 Colt New Police. It is known best as a pocket-revolver cartridge with somewhat more power than the various .32s, somewhat less power than the .38 Special. It used to be quite popular for pocket use. These cartridges may not be chambered or fired in .38 Special or .357 Magnum revolvers.

.38 Special. Next to the .22, the .38 Special is easily the most versatile and popular handgun cartridge going. It's practically the law-enforcement standard in America and many other nations. This cartridge is said to be extremely well balanced, by which we mean that it's large enough to have considerable knockdown power and penetration, yet is not so large that it can't be made for a compact revolver for pocket or holster use. It's been around so long and been popular for so many years that an enormous number of loads are made for it, and members of the handloading fraternity can, and frequently do, extend even these loads.

Some .38 Special revolvers are available that are made on a heavier frame, and these will safely handle a .38 Special high-speed load, which comes quite close to the .357 Magnum in performance. Only heavy-frame revolvers so designated should be used for these loads, however. These heavier loads are now designated +P and are so stamped on the cartridge head. Older ammunition is not so identified, however, and, once cartridges stray from their boxes, there's no way to identify them. If there's any doubt in your mind about what guns can and what guns cannot use this +P ammunition, write to the manufacturer, giving the model and serial number of your gun. Accept nobody else's word.

Designed in about 1902, the .38 Special is still a great revolver cartridge and is bound to last a great many more years. The number ".38" came about this way. A very popular cap-and-ball (muzzleloading) revolver was the .36 caliber, the "pocket" gun of the mid-1800s. When successful metallic cartridges were invented, the .36-caliber handgun was highly popular and it became standard practice to convert these guns to metallic cartridge use. The conversion consisted of machining off the nipples at the rear of the cylinder, boring the charge holes through, and installing a filler to keep the cylinder close to the barrel. Conversions were made for both rimfire and centerfire ammunition, and since the .36-caliber barrels were not changed, the guns retained their original caliber. But a new name was necessary to avoid confusion, so the number .38 was adopted for no particular reason that is clear today. The fact remains that .38s are really .35s (although they can as well be legitimately called .36, since the measurements run between .35 and .36 inch). There isn't too much legitimacy in cartridge nomenclature, however.

.38 Long Colt. This cartridge was the official sidearm of our armed forces for many years and was made in double-action revolvers. The cartridge was abandoned when it proved incapable of stopping the Moros during the Philippine Insurrection, and the .45 Auto was adopted. The .38 Long Colt is also the ancestor of the .38 Special. In addition, there is a .38 Short Colt cartridge; both are still loaded. Despite their antiquity and general uselessness today when better cartridges abound, there are still a great number of the old Smith & Wesson and Colt revolvers chambered for .38 Long Colt because it was the service cartridge for some years. You can shoot either of these cartridges in .38 Special and .357 Magnum revolvers.

.357 Magnum. Here's where more confusion enters the scene. In spite of the names and numbers, .38 Special and .357 Magnum have the same bore dimensions and thus the same bullet diameter. However, the .357 is a longer cartridge and more powerful. The actual bullet diameter of both is .357 inch.

The .357 Magnum is a revolver cartridge and a mighty good one. It was introduced in 1935 and remained the world's most potent handgun load for twenty years until the .44 Magnum came along. While the .357 is a plenty potent cartridge, the revolver may also be fired with .38 Special ammunition, so one can shoot what amounts to a "reduced load" and still retain full load capacity. For this reason, many experts recommend the purchase of a .357 Magnum over a .38 Special, for the reverse is impossible; you can't fire Magnum cartridges in a .38 Special revolver. Standard .357 loading is a 158-grain bullet at a muzzle velocity of 1410 fps—and that's real slick performance.

.380 Automatic (ACP). Also known as the 9mm Browning Short, this cartridge has been widely used since about 1908 in various pocket auto-loading pistols by both civilians and the military. It is a good deal more powerful than the .32 Auto cartridge, an interesting point since these two cartridges are the most popular among the "pocket-automatic" pistols.

There is increased interest in .380 pocket pistols today. At one time the only model seen was the Colt, which was manufactured from the early 1900s until recently. A few Brownings were imported, but the guns were never really popular. Colt .380s were issued to officers of general rank during World War II. Now there is a new crop of .380s, many of them made in America by companies which didn't exist a few years ago. While the .380 is not a very powerful cartridge it is suitable for the purpose and much more reliable than any of the smaller bores in similar guns.

.38 Automatic Colt Pistol (ACP). This is a potent cartridge that resembles the 9mm Luger but is more powerful. It was originally designed in 1904 for government competitions, but the .45 was chosen instead. Ammunition for this cartridge is loaded in two velocity levels, a standard load for older handguns and a hot number called the Super .38 for modern pistols clearly designated for it. As the name implies, the .38 ACP is adaptable only to autoloading pistols.

9mm Luger. Commonly known as the Parabellum in Europe. Hardly anyone needs an introduction to this cartridge; it has been used and is still used by more of the world's nations as a service sidearm than any other. A great variety of autoloading pistols have been made for the 9mm cartridge. The original gun design was by the American Hugo Borchardt; the design was further improved by Georg Luger and adopted by the German government in 1908 (and called Pistole '08).

A certain amount of confusion exists with regard to the 9mm Luger or Parabellum ammunition. Some claim that a hotter version of the cartridge was loaded for submachine-gun use and that this ammunition should not be used in pistols. However, tests by this country's fore-most independent ballistics laboratory, the H. P. White Company, indicate no appreciable difference and reach the conclusion that any 9mm Luger or Parabellum ammunition is safe with any well-made pistol in good condition. (This does not include "proof-test" cartridges, which are overloaded for use by gun manufacturers and are never released for sale.)

The 9mm, as well as .45 auto, cartridge is also widely employed in submachine guns all over the world. While designed as an autoloading pistol cartridge, Ruger has adapted one of his revolvers to fire the rimless 9mm Luger cartridge. Some years ago the 9mm was loaded with an odd-shaped bullet which had a flat-nosed cone instead of the usual rounded shape. This was known as a "truncated-cone" bullet. There is considerable interest today in 9mm double-action pistols for law-enforcement use.

.38/40. Also known as .38 Winchester, like the .32/20 this is a holdover from black-powder days and retains the black-powder designation: .38 indicates the bore and 40 indicates the powder charge in grains. The .38/40 was one of those cartridges suitable for use both in rifles and revolvers. Also like the .32/20, this cartridge was loaded in both high-velocity and standard type. Only the standard may be safely used in revolvers. Though named ".38," this is really a .40-caliber cartridge using a bullet .400 inch in diameter.

.41 Short Colt and .41 Long Colt. At one time the .41 Colt was a rather popular revolver, but it is long gone today. Cartridges are interchangeable, but the old .41 Colts are not interchangeable with the .41 Magnum. The Colt numbers used a .406-inch lead bullet; the .41 Magnum is a true .410 inch.

.41 Magnum. This interesting cartridge is designed for two purposes and is available in two loads. A standard-velocity load with lead bullet is designed for law-enforcement use, and a Magnum load is made for the hunter who wants to hunt big bears with a handgun. The .41 is second only to the big .44 Magnum in terms of sheer power when using the Magnum load. It's not much harder to handle than a .38 Special when using the police load but has much greater stopping power because of its bigger bullet. It is for revolver use only.

For reasons which are not clear, the .41 Magnum has become controversial. A demand for it was created by certain law-enforcement officers and several gun writers. Its developers, Smith & Wesson, saw no real need for it but they yielded to the demand. Once the gun was marketed, however, it was immediately met with lukewarm enthusiasm and much scorn. Certain gun writers (who should have known better) severely criticized it. Those who had demanded the gun virtually lost interest once it had been developed.

The .41 is, in fact, one of the great handgun cartridges. It deserves a better fate and a good deal more recognition than it's getting. I was in at the beginning of the .41 Magnum story because the advertising agency with which I was connected handled the initial advertisements for the .41 Magnum and I worked closely with the company's president, William Gunn.

The .41 is a fine handgun indeed. A number of police forces have adopted it and, so far as I know now, are generally more pleased with it than with the .38 Special. I hope Smith & Wesson continues to push it, and perhaps through a better marketing effort its popularity will increase. One happy note: Winchester has begun to make ammunition for it (the cartridge was developed by Remington while S&W developed the gun, and for a long while ammunition was available only in Remington brand).

.44/40. Also known as the .44 Winchester, this was a great old rifle cartridge in its day—which was long ago. This is probably the best-known rifle/revolver combination cartridge of all time. Those who tamed the West did much of it with lever-action Winchester rifles and Colt revolvers both chambered for the same .44/40 cartridge. There was an obvious advantage in being able to use the same ammunition for both long gun and revolver.

Smokeless powder is credited with the demise of this idea, for the first powders were such that they burned well in rifles but were too slow in the short handgun barrels, and so the results were not favorable. The old Colt Model P Peacemaker was first chambered in .44/40 in 1878.

.44 Smith & Wesson Special. Back in 1871, S&W pioneered the first of a long line of great .44 cartridges. First was the .44 S&W American. It was followed shortly by the .44 S&W Russian, made for and standardized by the Russian army.

Next in line was the .44 S&W Special, consisting of the Russian bullet but with a longer cartridge case to handle the then-new smokeless powder. Many handgun experts favored the .44 Special for big-game hunting, claiming it had far better stopping power than even the .357 Magnum.

The .44 Special came close to obsolescence except for its use as a lower-powered load in the .44 Magnum, but it has been saved from that fate by Charter Arms, which is making a fine undercover .44. Make no mistake, the .44 Special is a very powerful handgun.

Many claim that rather than build the new .41 Magnum, Smith & Wesson would have served the shooting world better by producing a "military and police" version of the .44 Magnum, for use with .44 Special and .44 Magnum ammo. The claim has much merit.

.44 Magnum. The last of the S&W .44 developments, the big Magnum was developed jointly by S&W and Remington. This is the biggest, heaviest, and most powerful revolver manufactured to date. The .44 and .41 Magnums are the only revolvers made which can safely handle big, dangerous North American game. In Magnum loads, both cartridges are furnished with a soft-point bullet, which should be used for game shooting. I would suggest the use of either .44 Special ammunition or an equivalent handload for regular shooting practice in the big .44. Full-power .44 loads can become uncomfortable.

The .44 Magnum makes a lie out of what I just said about the .44/40: It makes a very effective carbine for deer hunting! Ruger and Marlin make an autoloader and lever rifle respectively and both are very popular.

.45 Auto. This has been the official sidearm of the U.S. armed forces since 1911. The big .45 has two big claims to popularity: It's a great man-stopper and thus a great war pistol, and it's a favorite for target shooting, principally because much pistol marksmanship is service-oriented. During World War I, many thousands of double-action revolvers were manufactured for this cartridge. A rimless case, the .45 Auto does not lend itself to revolver-cylinder use because there's no rim to prevent it from sliding in too deeply and no way to extract and eject. "Half-moon" clips, each holding three cartridges by the extracting grooves, were developed and used

Ruger New Model Blackhawk

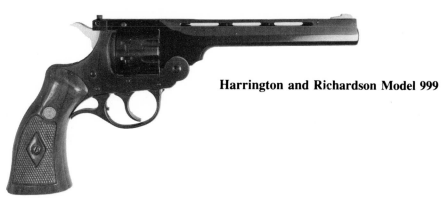

Harrington and Richardson Model 999

Colt Python

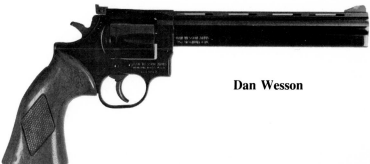

Dan Wesson

CENTER FIRE PISTOL & REVOLVER CARTRIDGES

25 Auto. 256 Win. 30 Luger 32 Auto. 32 S&W 32 S&W Long 32 Short Colt 32 Long Colt 32-20 Win. 357 Mag. 9mm Luger 38 S&W 38 Special 38 Special S.M.

CALIBER	BULLET WT. GRS.	BULLET TYPE	SYMBOL WINCHESTER	SYMBOL WESTERN	PRIMER
25 Automatic (6.35mm)	50	FMC	W25AP	25AP	1½-108
256 Winchester Magnum Super-X	60	OPE (HP)	—	2561P	6½-116
30 Luger (7.65mm)	93	FMC	W30LP	30LP	1½-108
32 Automatic	71	FMC	W32AP	32AP	1½-108
32 Smith & Wesson (inside lubricated)	85	Lead	W32SWP	32SWP	1½-108
32 Smith & Wesson Long (inside lubricated)	98	Lead	W32SWLP	32SWLP	1½-108
32 Short Colt (greased)	80	Lead	—	32SCP	1½-108
32 Long Colt (inside lubricated)	82	Lead	—	32LCP	1½-108
32 Colt New Police (inside lubricated)	98	Lead	W32CNP	—	1½-108
32-20 Winchester (inside lubricated)	100	Lead	W32201	32201	6½-116
32-20 Winchester	100	SP	W32202	32202	6½-116
357 Magnum Jacketed Hollow Point Super-X	110	JHP	—	3573P	1½-108
357 Magnum Jacketed Hollow Point Super-X	125	JHP	—	3576P	1½-108
357 Magnum Super-X (inside lubricated)	158	Lead	—	3571P	1½-108
357 Magnum Jacketed Hollow Point Super-X	158	JHP	—	3574P	1½-108
357 Magnum Jacketed Soft Point Super-X	158	JSP	—	3575P	1½-108
357 Magnum Metal Piercing Super-X (inside lubricated, lead bearing)	158	Met. Pierc.	—	3572P	1½-108
9mm Luger (Parabellum)	95	JSP	W9MMJSP	—	1½-108
9mm Luger (Parabellum)	100	PP	W9MMPP	—	1½-108
9mm Luger (Parabellum)	100	JHP	W9MMJHP	—	1½-108
9mm Luger (Parabellum)	115	FMC	W9LP	—	1½-108
38 Smith & Wesson (inside lubricated)	145	Lead	W38SWP	38SWP	1½-108
38 Special (inside lubricated)	158	Lead	W38S1P	38S1P	1½-108
38 Special Metal Point (inside lubricated, lead bearing)	158	Met. Pt.	W38S2P	38S2P	1½-108
38 Special Super Police (inside lubricated)	200	Lead	W38S3P	38S3P	1½-108
38 Special Super-X Jacketed Hollow Point +P	110	JHP	—	38S6PH	1½-108
38 Special Super-X Jacketed Hollow Point +P	125	JHP	W38S7PH	—	1½-108
38 Special Super-X +P	130	FMC	—	38S8P	1½-108
38 Special Super-X (inside lubricated) +P	150	Lead	—	38S4P	1½-108
38 Special Metal Piercing Super-X (inside lubricated, lead bearing) +P	150	Met. Pierc.	—	38S5P	1½-108
38 Special Super-X (inside lubricated) +P	158	Lead-HP	W38SPD	—	1½-108
38 Special Super-X Semi-Wad Cutter (inside lubricated) +P	158	Lead-SWC	W38WCP	—	1½-108
38 Special Super-Match and Match Mid-Range Clean Cutting (inside lubricated)	148	Lead-WC	W38SMRP	38SMRP	1½-108
38 Special Super Match (inside lubricated)	158	Lead	—	38SMP	1½-108
38 Short Colt (greased)	130	Lead	—	38SCP	1½-108
38 Long Colt (inside lubricated)	150	Lead	—	38LCP	1½-108
38 Automatic Super-X +P (For use only in 38 Colt Super and Colt Commander Automatic Pistols)	125	JHP	W38A3P	38A3P	1½-108
38 Automatic Super-X +P (For use only in 38 Colt Super and Colt Commander Automatic Pistols)	130	FMC	W38A1P	38A1P	1½-108
38 Automatic (For all 38 Colt Automatic Pistols)	130	FMC	W38A2P	38A2P	1½-108
380 Automatic	95	FMC	W380AP	380AP	1½-108
38-40 Winchester	180	SP	W3840	3840	7-111
41 Remington Magnum Super-X (inside lubricant)	210	Lead	W41MP	—	7-111F
41 Remington Magnum Super-X Jacketed Soft Point	210	JSP	W41MJSP	—	7-111F
44 Smith & Wesson Special (inside lubricated)	246	Lead	W44SP	—	7-111
44 Remington Magnum Super-X (Gas Check) (inside lubricated)	240	Lead	—	44MP	7-111F
44-40 Winchester	200	SP	W4440	4440	7-111
45 Colt (inside lubricated)	255	Lead	W45CP	45CP	7-111
45 Automatic	230	FMC	W45A1P	45A1P	7-111
45 Automatic Super-Match Clean Cutting	185	FMC-WC	—	45AWCP	7-111

Met. Pierc.—Metal Piercing   FMC—Full Metal Case   SP—Soft Point   JHP—Jacketed Hollow Point   JSP— Jacketed Soft Point   Met. Pt.—Metal Point   OPE—Open Point Expan
HP—Hollow Point   PP—Power Point   WC—Wad Cutter   SWC—Semi Wad Cutter
Test barrels are used to determine ballistics figures. Individual firearms may differ from these test barrel statistics.

38 Short Colt | 38 Long Colt | 38 Auto. | 380 Auto. | 38-40 Win. | 41 Rem. Mag. | 44 S&W | 44 Rem. Mag. | 44-40 Win. | 45 Colt | 45 Auto. | 45 Auto. S.M.

VELOCITY-FPS			ENERGY FT./LBS.			MID RANGE TRAJECTORY INCHES		BARREL LENGTH INCHES
MUZZLE	50 YDS.	100 YDS.	MUZZLE	50 YDS.	100 YDS.	50 YDS.	100 YDS.	
810	755	700	73	63	54	1.8	7.7	2
2350	2030	1760	735	550	415	0.3	1.1	8½
1220	1110	1040	305	255	225	0.9	3.5	4½
905	855	810	130	115	97	1.4	5.8	4
680	645	610	90	81	73	2.5	10.5	3
705	670	635	115	98	88	2.3	10.5	4
745	665	590	100	79	62	2.2	9.9	4
755	715	675	100	93	83	2.0	8.7	4
680	635	595	100	88	77	2.5	11.0	4
1030	970	920	270	210	190	1.2	4.4	6
1030	970	920	270	210	190	1.2	4.4	6
1295	1094	975	410	292	232	0.8	3.5	4 V
1450	1240	1090	583	427	330	0.6	2.8	4 V
1235	1104	1015	535	428	361	0.8	3.5	4 V
1235	1104	1015	535	428	361	0.8	3.5	4 V
1235	1104	1015	535	428	361	0.8	3.5	4 V
1235	1104	1015	535	428	361	0.8	3.5	4 V
1355	1140	1008	387	274	214	0.7	3.3	4 V
1320	1114	991	387	275	218	0.7	3.4	4 V
1320	1114	991	387	275	218	0.7	3.4	4 V
1155	1047	971	341	280	241	0.9	3.9	4 V
685	650	620	150	135	125	2.4	10.0	4
755	723	693	200	183	168	2.0	8.3	4 V
755	723	693	200	183	168	2.0	8.3	4 V
635	614	594	179	168	157	2.8	11.5	4 V
1020	945	887	254	218	192	1.1	4.8	4 V
945	898	858	248	224	204	1.3	5.4	4 V
950	910	880	260	240	225	1.3	5.2	4 V
910	870	835	276	252	232	1.4	5.7	4 V
910	870	835	276	252	232	1.4	5.7	4 V
915	878	844	294	270	250	1.4	5.6	4 V
915	878	844	294	270	250	1.4	5.6	4 V
710	634	566	166	132	105	2.4	10.8	4 V
755	723	693	200	183	168	2.0	8.3	4 V
730	685	645	150	130	115	2.2	9.4	6
730	700	670	175	165	150	2.1	8.8	6
1245	1105	1010	430	340	285	0.8	3.6	5
1245	1120	1035	450	365	310	0.8	3.4	5
1040	980	925	310	275	245	1.0	4.7	4½
955	865	785	190	160	130	1.4	5.9	3¾
975	920	870	380	340	300	1.5	5.4	5
965	898	842	434	376	331	1.3	5.4	4 V
1300	1162	1062	778	630	526	0.7	3.2	4 V
755	725	695	310	285	265	2.0	8.3	6½
1350	1186	1069	971	749	608	0.7	3.1	4 V
975	920	865	420	375	330	0.5	5.7	7½
860	820	780	410	375	340	1.6	6.6	5½
810	776	745	335	308	284	1.7	7.2	5
770	707	650	244	205	174	2.0	8.7	5

+P Ammunition with (+P) on the case head stamp is loaded to higher pressure. Use only in firearms designated for this cartridge and so recommended by the gun manufacturer.

V—Data is based on velocity obtained from 4" vented barrels for revolver cartridges (38 Special, 357 Magnum, 41 Rem Mag and 44 Rem Mag) and unvented (solid) test barrels of the length specified for 9mm and 45 auto pistols.

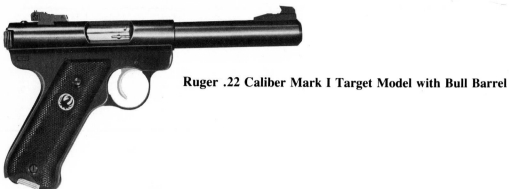

Ruger .22 Caliber Mark I Target Model with Bull Barrel

Smith & Wesson Model 39

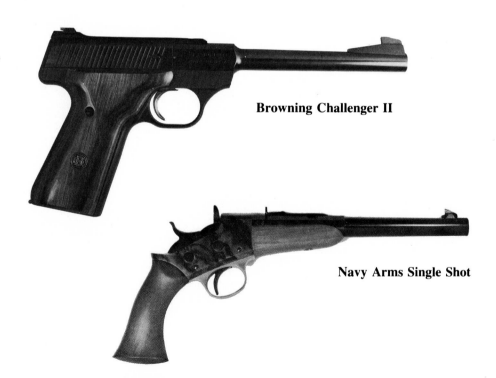

Browning Challenger II

Navy Arms Single Shot

in conjunction with the revolvers. The .45 is loaded today in a variety of loads.

.45 Auto Rim. This cartridge is simply a different version of the .45 Auto, made with a rim for use in revolvers. Other specifications remain about the same.

.45 Colt. A little bigger in bore diameter than the .44 Magnum, the big .45 Colt is far less powerful. It's quite possibly the best-known and most famous revolver cartridge, thanks largely to popularization of Westerns both in paperbacks and on TV.

Though factory ammunition in .45 Colt is downloaded because there are so many old revolvers in use, it can be handloaded to very nearly .44 Magnum performance. Such loads must be used only in revolvers of new manufacture, however. This combination does make a fine, powerful revolver capable of handling any game the .41 or .44 Magnum can handle.

INTERCHANGEABILITY OF HANDGUN CARTRIDGES

Interchangeability among cartridges is often confusing to many shooters. The best rule to follow if you don't know is never to fire any cartridge that is identified differently from the load stamped on the gun barrel. This will keep you out of trouble. There are, however, times when it's useful to know just exactly what you can shoot in a gun.

.22 Short, Long, and Long Rifle. These three popular rimfires are made to the same diameter and differ only in length, bullet weight, and powder charge. They may be used interchangeably in any revolver chambered for the longest, the .22 Long Rifle. However, they are not interchangeable in .22 auto pistols for the simple reason that Longs and Shorts do not develop enough pressure to operate the actions. A very few target .22 auto pistols are manufactured for the .22 Short cartridge, and these will not accept any other cartridge.

It is entirely possible to fire Shorts in a .22 Long Rifle auto if you single-load; this sometimes is a useful procedure in a basement range where you want to keep the noise level low. But the continued practice is not wise because the Short cartridge isn't long enough for the bullet

to rest against the rifling, which means the bullet must take a running jump straight ahead before it hits the rifling and begins to spin. The best bet is to use nothing but Long Rifles.

The .22 Long, as already explained, is a bastard cartridge made by marrying the .22 Long Rifle case with the Short's bullet.

In the rimfire .22s you have a choice of high-speed and regular ammo, and any modern .22 handgun is perfectly adaptable to either. However, the regular, sometimes called standard, develops a little less pressure, and a rare gun is sometimes found that will fail to drive the slide back far enough on occasion to pick up a new cartridge. This is very rare, however, and is only mentioned because it can happen. Should you find such an auto pistol, simply switch to high-speed ammo and the trouble will stop.

Early .22 auto pistols—that is, those made during and before the early 1930s—were made for standard ammunition, because there were no high-speeds in those days. The springs in these guns are not strong enough for use with high-speed cartridges and the recoil will eventually be harmful to the gun. You aren't very likely to run across one of these old-timers, though it can happen. If you do, have a gunsmith check it out to determine if the gun has been converted for use with high-speed ammo.

The .22 WRF and .22 Remington Special are the same. They are also obsolete, and it would be foolish to buy any second-hand gun chambered for either.

.22 Winchester Rimfire Magnum (WRM). This cartridge is a rimfire .22 but it differs from the Short, Long, and Long Rifle considerably. It is not interchangeable with any other cartridge.

However—and there has been a lot of confusion with regard to the use of this cartridge—*revolvers* chambered for the .22 WRM can be used with Short, Long, and Long Rifle cartridges—but *only* when an extra cylinder is obtained.

The WRM is a longer and fatter cartridge than the standard .22 rimfires. It also uses a slightly larger copper-jacketed bullet. (See the explanation under the cartridge description for its proper use.)

The chart of interchangeable cartridges on the following page is reprinted by courtesy of Remington Arms Company, Inc.

INTERCHANGEABILITY CHART
Cartridges in groups shown below will interchange.

RIMFIRE
.22 W.R.F.
.22 Remington Special
.22 Win. M/1890
    in a .22 Win. Magnum Rimfire but not conversely

CENTERFIRE
.25 Automatic
.25 Automatic Colt Pistol (ACP)
.25 (6.35) Auto. Pistol
6.35mm Browning

.32 Colt Automatic
.32 Auto. Colt Pistol (ACP)
.32 (7.65mm) Auto. Pistol
7.65mm Automatic Pistol
7.65mm Browning (not interchangeable w/7.65mm Luger)

.32 Short Colt in
.32 Long Colt but not conversely
SEE NOTE C

.32 S&W in
.32 S&W Long but not conversely

.32 S&W Long
.32 Colt New Police
.32 Colt Police Positive

.32/20 Colt LMR
.32/20 WCF
.32/20 Win. and Marlin
SEE NOTES A and G

.38 S&W
.38 Colt New Police
.380 Webley

.38 Colt Special
.38 S&W Special
.38 Targetmaster
.38 S&W Spec. Mid-Range
.38 Special (+P)
.38/44 Special (+P)
.38 Special
.38 Special Flat Point
SEE NOTES B & D

.38 Short Colt in
.38 Long Colt but not conversely.
    Both can be used in .38 Spec.

.38 Marlin*
.38 Win.
SEE NOTE A

.38 Remington*
.38/40 Win.
.38 WCF*
SEE NOTE A

.38 Automatic in
.38 Super (+P) but not conversely

.380 Automatic
9mm Browning Short (Corto Kurz)

9mm Luger
9mm Parabellum
SEE NOTE E

.44 S&W Spec. in .44 Magnum but not conversely
SEE NOTE F

.44 Marlin
.44 Win.
.44 Remington
.44/40 Win.
.44 WCF

NOTE A: * High-speed cartridges must not be used in revolvers. They should be used only in rifles made especially for them.
NOTE B: Ammunition with (+P) on the case headstamp is loaded to higher pressures. Use only in firearms designated for this cartridge and so recommended by the gun manufacturer.
NOTE C: Not for use in revolvers chambered for .32 S&W or .32 S&W Long.

NOTE D: All .38 Special cartridges can be used in .357 Magnum revolvers but not conversely.
NOTE E: 9mm submachine-gun cartridges should not be used in handguns.
NOTE F: .44 Russian and .44 S&W Special can be used in .44 Remington Magnum revolvers but not conversely.
NOTE G: Not to be used in Win. M66 and M73.

EUROPEAN DESIGNATIONS
Europe uses the metric system, so ammunition loaded there is often identical with American, except that it carries a different name. The following chart will be found helpful. You may use European ammunition, identified correctly according to the chart, in your handgun that's made for the American equivalent, or vice versa.

AMERICAN	EUROPEAN
.25 Automatic (ACP)	6.35mm Browning
.30 Luger	7.65mm (Parabellum)
.30 Mauser	7.63 Militaire
.32 Automatic (ACP)	7.65mm Browning
.380 Automatic (ACP)	9mm Browning Short (Corto Kurz)
9mm Luger	9mm Luger (Parabellum)

NAMES AND NUMBERS

The identification methods used for cartridges are often confusing—and often meaningless. There are not as many names (as opposed to numbers) used for handgun cartridges as there are for rifles, and that may be a blessing.

I suspect the first modern cartridge to acquire a name that achieved lasting popularity was the .22 Hornet back around 1930. From then on the names came thick and fast in a blur of confusion, but today's trend is more digit-oriented.

The various shorts and longs need no elaboration; they have pretty straightforward names that are self-descriptive. Winchester for many years followed the practice of calling a cartridge either WCF for Winchester Center Fire or WRF for Winchester Rim Fire. That practice was dropped a long time ago, but it's still seen on old ammunition boxes, old catalogs, and old gun barrels.

Black-powder loads used the double-number system that we've mentioned—.32/20, .44/40, etc.—but the period also saw another set of numbers often used which indicated the weight of the bullet, also in grains. Thus a .45/70/500 was a .45-caliber cartridge using 70 grains of powder pushing a 500-grain bullet.

Names, numbers, or combinations of them are not necessarily meaningful at all. The .22 rimfires, for example, are all made with bullets measuring about .224 inch (however, while that's what is listed for a .22 Long Rifle bullet, I've found most rimfire bores formerly were .222 inch). But the .22 WMR is .224 inch, and the .22 WRF is .228 inch. .22 Short and Long are the same as the .22 Long Rifle.

In the world of .22 centerfires, the .22 Jet is .222 inch while the .221 Fire Ball is .224 inch—the same as most .22 centerfire rifle cartridges.

For many years Remington has had the habit of sticking its name on cartridges that make one wonder. For example, they legitimized two excellent wildcat rifle cartridges a few years ago, the .22/250 and .25/06. The .22/250 has been around since the early 1930s when Grove Wotkyns necked the .250/3000 Savage down to .22 caliber. And the .25/06 is even older. But when Remington gave them respectability and parenthood they also gave them their name, so now we

have the ".22/250 Remington" and the ".25/06 Remington." Other developments which were entirely Remington's, like the .222 Remington, 8mm Remington Magnum, and so on are a different story.

With both the .44 and .41 Magnum developments, Remington shared the work with Smith & Wesson. One company developed the gun, the other the ammo, and the research was of course shared with considerable "joint development." However, when the cartridges came out they were called ".44 Remington Magnum," etc. They are so head-stamped, and that's what appears on the boxes too. Winchester and Federal have followed suit, so the practice is universal. This is not to say Remington can't call these any damned thing they want to, but I do think the practice is being stretched a bit.

Cartridge identification is a lot more bastardized in rifle lingo than it is in the world of handguns, but there are some real doozies the handgunner has to live with too.

WILDCATS

A wildcat cartridge is one that is not available in factory-loaded ammunition. It does not have the respectability of parenthood; it is a bastard. Wildcat cartridges, however, are very useful. A vast number of cartridges either were wildcats and have been adopted or were developed by large factories by the standard methods used by wildcatters for years.

There has not been nearly as much wildcat activity in the handgun world as in the rifle world. The past few years, however, have seen an increased activity in handgun wildcats and a reduced number of rifle wildcats. The reason for this is pretty easy to understand: Just about all that need be done with rifle cartridges has been done, while the handgun world has been pure virgin territory.

In addition to a number of rifle cartridges being used in handguns (most notably in the Thompson/Center, which has embraced the .22 Hornet, .218 Bee, .222 Remington, .25/35, .30 U.S. Carbine, and .30/30—rifle cartridges every one), there are many wildcats.

Again, these are most notably in the T/C single-shot gun. Among them at present are: .22

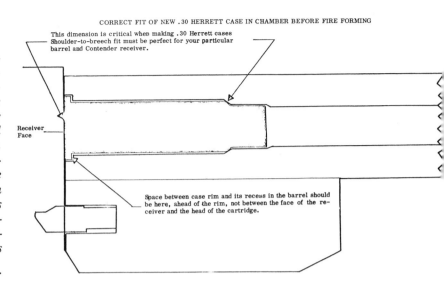

CORRECT FIT OF NEW .30 HERRETT CASE IN CHAMBER BEFORE FIRE FORMING

This dimension is critical when making .30 Herrett cases Shoulder-to-breech fit must be perfect for your particular barrel and Contender receiver.

Receiver Face

Space between case rim and its recess in the barrel should be here, ahead of the rim, not between the face of the receiver and the head of the cartridge.

A switch on the normal rule of headspace is seen in this diagram for forming brass for the .30 Herrett, a wildcat cartridge. In this example, the .30/30 empty case is advanced into the sizing die slowly, until the gun will just barely close on the case but with the latter offering considerable resistance. Put another way, this headspace is measured like a rimless case, not a rimmed case, even though the case is a rimmed one. According to the manufacturer, this cartridge is more accurate and safer when proper instructions are followed.

K Hornet, something called the .357/44 Bain & Davis, plus the .30 and .357 Herrett. The .22 K Hornet is an old and well-known wildcat, one of the very first. It came about in the 1930s when the late Lyle Kilbourn, a well-known gunsmith, made a reamer that opened up the standard Hornet chamber. Firing a standard Hornet cartridge in the K chamber allowed the brass case to swell and accept the larger shape. Then the case could be reloaded with more powder and give higher velocities. The K Hornet was very popular, and it improved Hornet performance quite a bit. Lyle Kilbourn finally quit gunsmithing and went to work for Lyman in their reloading department. He passed away during the 1960s, but he left behind him a deep imprint on the wildcatting world.

Steve Herrett, of the Herrett handgun stock company, is also a wildcatter, and he has popularized two of his own wildcats which are both available only in the T/C pistol. Herrett's wildcats are based on .30/30 rifle cartridges. One is shortened and necked to .30 caliber and the other to .357. By using a fatter case body with less taper than the original .30/30, you get very hot performance from these two numbers. Herrett himself has killed a number of game animals with the guns. T/C calls these the hottest handgun cartridges going and quotes a muzzle velocity of 2108 fps with a 158-grain .357 bullet. Compared to 1425 fps for the factory-loaded .357 Magnum, Herrett's indeed gives excellent performance.

The Bain & Davis creation is a .44 Magnum case necked down to .357 caliber. Another set of wildcats is for a gun known as the Auto Mag, a custom-made recoil-operated pistol developed solely for hunting. The cases are in two sizes, .357 and .44, and the brass is made from .308 or .30/06 rifle cartridge cases which are shortened and necked appropriately. Offhand, the Auto-Mag looks and sounds like a real hellbender, but it's not really that much hotter than either a .357 or .44 Magnum revolver. In fact, the standard cartridges in the 10-inch-barreled Thompson/Center give just about the same performance as does the Auto Mag. In order to tame the Auto Mag a bit it is probably desirable to have the barrel Mag-na-ported or otherwise vented to keep the muzzle down on the rest.

There are a few other handgun wildcats, and there will doubtless be more as time goes by. The limiting factors are weight, because there's just so much you can hold at arm's length and still have some control, and power, because the hand can stand just so much recoil. The introduction of such an adaptable gun as the Thompson/Center, coupled with its brute strength, has made pistol wildcatting much more viable than it ever was before. Creation of a gun as complicated as the Auto Mag doesn't help much because it can't be sold in volume at a realistic cost. About the only advantage the Auto Mag has over the T/C is that it's a repeater. On the other hand, the T/C has more variables and is made in production.

Wildcatting a revolver is a tough proposition,

because there's a vast amount of engineering in these guns and it doesn't pay to upset the balances unless you know what you're doing. As a result there is very little of it done. Wildcatting an autoloader is no easier because of the delicate timing balance necessary plus feeding problems when you begin to introduce new elements for which the gun was not designed. These are the main reasons why there was really very little handgun wildcatting before the T/C, and why, since its introduction, wildcat cartridges have begun to proliferate.

COMMENTS ON SOME OF THE HANDGUN CARTRIDGES

Handgun cartridges in existence before World War II and still standard. .25 ACP (Automatic Colt Pistol), .30 Luger, .32 S&W Long, 9mm Luger or Parabellum, Colt Super .38, .38 Special, .380 ACP, .357 Magnum, .44 Special, .45 ACP, .45 Auto Rim, and .45 Colt.

Among these I'd think the .30 Luger is due for quick departure. Fact is, the Luger pistol itself has been dropped from production in both calibers. To the best of my knowledge the Luger (now called the Parabellum and recently manufactured by Mauser, imported by Interarms) was the only gun currently chambered for the .30 Luger cartridge.

The .32 S&W Long should have gone long ago, but S&W still lists a couple of models for this old one. If there is any excuse for a .32-caliber revolver today it ought to be the .32/20, which had a lot more snap than these other oldies. The .45 Auto Rim is a cartridge intended to be used in revolvers chambered for the .45 Auto cartridge. The story goes back to World War I. When that war came along our sidearm was the 1911 Model Auto pistol, designed by John Browning and made by Colt, chambered for the .45 ACP, a rimless cartridge. You can't use a rimless cartridge in a revolver because there's no rim to use for extraction. It was necessary to get a lot of guns in a hurry, and Smith & Wesson designed the old "half moon" clips, each of which held three .45 cartridges and thus made revolver function possible with the .45 cartridge. Both Colt and S&W made revolvers for use with these clips during World War I.

The .45 Auto Rim is simply the standard .45 Auto cartridge except that it's made with a rim, for use in these revolvers. There are a lot of the World War I guns still in use, and S&W still makes a revolver for the .45 ACP.

The .45 Colt has the distinction of being the oldest remaining centerfire cartridge going, certainly in America and most likely in the world. Work was started on the Colt Single Action Army revolver in 1871 and the cartridge was apparently designed at that time. Actual production started in 1872, so it's just one year older than the .45/70. At least, that's what my sources tell me, for what little it may be worth.

Of more importance is the fact that the .45 Colt is still one hell of a fine revolver cartridge. The factory load is pretty light, because there are so many old guns around, but if you have a modern revolver chambered for the .45 Colt, made out of good steel, you can handload this old-timer so it's a real hummer.

A few years ago the .380 ACP was among the obsolete, but, as noted elsewhere, it's back and flourishing again as a very popular and very useful pocket pistol cartridge.

Obsolete handgun cartridges for which U.S. guns were made when World War II started. .32 ACP, .32 New Police, .32 Short S&W, .32/20, .38 S&W, .38 New Police, .38/40, .44/40 and .455 Webley.

There's also a bit of competitiveness going here with some of these names; the .32 S&W and the .32 New Police (which was a Colt name) were interchangeable, as were the .38s of the same names. S&W tacked its name on one; Colt called its the New Police. The ancient .44/40 was chambered very early, in 1878, in the Colt single-action army revolver because it was such a popular rifle cartridge and gave a man the option of using both guns with the same ammunition. That was a very popular combination for many years. The .44/40 was a pretty mild number, though, and more potent rifles soon pushed it over the hump and into oblivion. The .455 Webley was made here for reasons nobody knows, or if anyone does he won't admit it. This is an English revolver cartridge, a nice big fat one not much unlike the .45 Auto except a little less powerful (slightly heavier bullet but with less velocity).

All things considered, there isn't much missed in this list.

Handgun cartridges developed since World War II. .22 WMR, .22 Jet, .221 Remington, .256 Magnum, .41 Magnum and .44 Magnum.

Already, two of these are gone, as is only just. They were a pair of losers, and let's look at them a moment. First, the .22 Jet. Firing the Jet cartridge in the S&W revolver was a rather uncanny, and unsettling, experience. It made a roar you wouldn't believe and belched a huge flame. It also delivered remarkable speeds, and it was very, very difficult to extract all six fired cartridges. You had to make certain the charge holes were cleaned, preferably with lighter fluid, before shooting, or they'd set back in the holes and prevent the cylinder from rotating.

All together, the Jet was ill conceived and it didn't last very long on the market.

At just about the same time, for reasons known only to the company, Winchester developed a little cartridge they called the .256 Winchester Magnum. Like the Jet, it was the .357 cartridge necked down to .25 caliber. I understand that both S&W and Colt fooled around with it and tried to make a handgun to hold it but that it couldn't be done safely. Then Marlin worked with both cases in their Model 56 and produced a few rifles in .256 (none in Jet). Also Ruger made a single-shot pistol for the .256 known as the Hawkeye for a brief period.

Why companies with such know-how and apparent market intelligence got off on such nutty tacks is hard to understand. These things were doomed from the start, as should have been known. I suspect the .221 Fire Ball is kept around for vague reasons too. It can't be a best seller and there isn't a great deal of reason for its existence.

The big .44 Magnum is here to stay, of course,

and that's as it should be, for this is one of the finest revolvers going. As most people are aware, it also shoots the .44 Special, an older and milder load, so even if you're not a reloader, you can enjoy the big gun with mild loads as well as having the full powerhouses in reserve. And between the excellent S&W and Ruger models available the handgunner has ample choice.

The .41 Magnum is a little harder to understand. It was developed primarily for the purpose of law enforcement, with two totally different loads. One of these is a mild load with sharp-shouldered lead bullet which is meant for "street work"; its energy is supposed to be expended within the "target" and not rip through to harm innocent bystanders as some of the smaller bores tend to do. It's also meant to be a real stopper in the true sense of the word, meaning that it should offer the police officer a bigger gun than the crook is liable to have and thus a better chance of overpowering him. (There have been too many cases of cops being killed by crooks with equal or more powerful guns.)

The .22 WMR has proved to be one of the finest and most popular cartridges for revolver use. It is particularly adapted to the revolver, as a matter of fact, because in this type of gun, and only in this type of gun, it's interchangeable with the .22 Long Rifle.

By buying a .22 WMR revolver with extra cylinder for the .22 LR you have a fine combination indeed. The Long Rifle for cheap practice and for most regular use, then the added power of the WMR when wanted. There are those who wonder why the WMR was ever built, and for rifle use it's not an easy question to answer. But the cartridge really comes into its own in the revolver and must be listed as one of the more important handgun cartridge developments to come along.

CHAPTER FOURTEEN

CASES
AND
PRIMERS

Cartridge cases are divided into two broad categories: metallic and shotgun. Those categories are quite obvious. Metallics deal with both rimfire and centerfire numbers, and while the rimfire cartridge, as we have already explained, is considerably softer than the centerfire, both are commonly made of brass.

Rimfire brass is soft, centerfire cartridge brass is hard. In fact, "cartridge brass," as it is known in the brass industry, is the hardest and toughest in existence. Cartridge brass is the very best brass alloy in the industry.

Any metal can be softened by annealing—that's what the word means. For example, steel is hardened by heating and then quenching in water, oil, or air, depending on the properties of the particular alloy. Steel can be annealed by heating it to a specified temperature and then allowing it to cool slowly (often by placing it in a furnace and then turning off the furnace to let it cool overnight).

Brass works the opposite: You heat and quench to soften brass. Brass cartridge cases are made by a method known as drawing, in which you start by punching out a slug which resembles a coin of the proper thickness and diameter to finish up to the proper size. This "coin" or slug is then formed through a succession of punch and die operations which gradually form it into the elongated shape familiar to us as a cartridge. Each time the brass goes through an operation it is "work-hardened"—which is the same as when you bend a piece of metal back and forth until it breaks. You are work-hardening that metal by the bending operation until it becomes crystalline and snaps apart.

To avoid that, cartridge cases are annealed frequently during the forming operations so that the brass remains strong, tough, and elastic. It must be strong, because the cartridge case is the weakest part of the gun/ammo combination—and in some instances it must hold enormous chamber pressures. Naturally, the case is held in place by the gun barrel and breech bolt securely locked, as we have discussed. But any rupture of the brass case will result in the spilling of gas under very high pressure. Since that spilled gas can't go forward because there's a bullet sealing the bore, it must go backward—or sideways.

A case must also be tough and elastic because it should not only hold those pressures but it ought to spring back a bit after the pressure has subsided, which will help ease extraction. Most of today's cartridge cases fit these requirements very well. It wasn't always so, however, and in the early days of metallic cartridges there were numerous failures, often with distinctly unpleasant results.

During World War II when brass was in critical supply, many experiments were made with steel cases both in the Allied armies and on the German side. While these worked and many millions of pistol and submachine-gun cartridges (9mm and .45 ACP) were made of steel, the practice was stopped as soon as enough brass became available. So far as I can recall, these experiments with rifle ammunition were never really practical.

It is critical that the base (rear) of the centerfire cartridge be as hard as possible. This is accomplished by the work-hardening principle already mentioned. Following the final drawing operation which determines the final shape, the case has its primer pocket and flash hole punched into place. This serves to further harden the brass. Then the cartridge identification, manufacturer and caliber, is stamped, which further hardens the head. These operations make the head quite hard, and, as a matter of interest, the hardness can be controlled by the amount of name and number stamping as well as its depth. The more and the deeper, the harder will be the brass at this critical point.

Extracting grooves are machined after final shaping, and if additional annealing is required to soften the case mouth, the cases are often placed standing in water to keep the bases cold and hard.

Since cases come in both straight and bottleneck versions, it follows that some require more drawing than others. However, few handgun cases are of bottleneck design.

A few years ago there was an abortive attempt to neck the .357 Magnum case to .22 and .25 caliber for revolver use. These were bottlenecked cases, and there are a couple of others, but nearly all handgun cartridges are either straight-sided or very slightly tapered.

When smokeless powder came into general use during the 1890s, the higher pressures generated demanded better cartridge cases than black powder required. By the same token, smokeless also demanded stronger guns. The usual way to accomplish such development is by the introduction of new cartridges to accompany new guns. An example is the .357 Magnum introduced by Smith & Wesson in 1935. Using the same-diameter cartridge case as the .38 Special, the new Magnum case was made longer so that it was impossible to load the more powerful cartridges in any .38 Special revolver. (You can fire .38 Specials in .357 Magnum guns, however.)

With an old cartridge like the .45 Colt, which has been in existence since 1873, the situation is quite different. Factory-loaded ammunition must be loaded to a pressure level that is safe in old revolvers made around 1873, because some of these old-timers still exist. Never mind that a .45 Colt revolver made today will stand heavy loads—you can't buy ammunition that will do the modern gun justice, although you can handload it. Despite the excellence of the .45 Colt with hot handloads in a modern handgun, this load will never approach its potential in over-the-counter ammo. The reloader is as well off with either the .44 Magnum or the .45 Colt, but the nonreloader is going to be better off with the .44 Magnum.

Other old cartridges—the .38/40 and .44/40 are two examples—were once popular because of the immense popularity of lever-action rifles in the American West. Using a sixgun chambered for the same cartridge as your rifle meant only one size of ammunition had to be carried.

This is true again today with the .44 Magnum, available in both single- and double-action revolvers and lever-action and autoloading rifles.

HEADSPACE

Headspace was discussed in Chapter Nine in connection with the gun barrel. It is important to repeat here that, first, there must be a compatible relationship between the cartridge case and the chamber cut in the gun barrel, and second, that a condition of too much space, known as excessive headspace, can result in a ruptured case with unpleasant results.

A condition of excessive headspace can be created by either cartridge or gun-barrel chamber. Either way, the result is the same.

To repeat what I said in Chapter Nine, we define "headspace" as the distance from the bolt face (in locked position) to that point that stops further forward movement of the cartridge case. This differs with rimmed, rimless, belted, and straight-sided cartridges like the .45 ACP pistol cartridge.

"IMPROVED" CASES

For many years custom gunsmiths and experimental riflemen have sought to improve the performance of existing cartridges by changing the shape and usually increasing powder capacity. But there has been very little of this sort of experimenting in the handgun field.

An example is found in the Weatherby line of rifle cartridges. Roy Weatherby started as a wildcatter—his first popular cartridge was the .300 Weatherby Magnum, which he made in those days by "fire-forming" a .300 H&H Magnum cartridge in his bigger chamber. This permitted the brass case to expand and fill the big chamber and allowed the shooter to reload using more powder and developing higher velocity. Weatherby is not a wildcatter today because he has his own branded ammunition; thus he made the leap from bastardy to respectability.

There are a few pistoleers around who engage in that old rifleman's game. Most of them use such guns as the single-shot Thompson/Center Contender because it's an easy gun to adapt and because the maker obliges by furnishing almost any kind of a cartridge a wild-eyed experimenter

dreams up. Another hellbender is the autoloading Auto-Mag, which has a solid lockup and develops enormous power.

Of course the handgun itself is limited by many factors. The .458 Winchester Magnum rifle, which is the most popular cartridge going for Africa's big game, is no fun to shoot, let alone the even bigger .460 Weatherby Magnum. But you can handle these big rifles if you don't mind a little kick. There's no way the average pistol shooter can handle anything bigger than the .44 Magnum, though. Anything heavier would be extremely punishing to the shooter's hand. (I confess that I wear a glove to fire the .44 Magnum.) Still, some braver than I like heavier hand cannons. I've even heard of a special gun being made in .45/70 for one-hand use!

Yet another restriction with any semiautomatic pistol is the amount of power required to work the action. Too little and the gun will fail to operate; too much and the gun will be slammed too hard and its parts will be damaged.

Some years ago a character named Dardick developed a strange gun which employed a strange cartridge. I've always felt the whole scheme was just something to float a stock issue, but that's just my opinion. In any event, the whole thing was ridiculous and came to naught. Dardick's cartridge was a queer plastic unit shaped like a triangle with rounded sides. It has a .38-caliber bullet, and powder and primer at the other end in more or less conventional fashion. These "trounds," as Dardick called them, were fed up out of a magazine which was quite fat and held a large supply. Because of the triangular shape the magazine had a large capacity. But the gun was ugly as sin and the concept unsound, and the whole thing died.

Dardick's dream occurred in the 1950s while I was toiling for *The American Rifleman* magazine, and a lady reporter for one of the national newsweeklies called me one day and asked about the Dardick. She had planned to write it up, but I advised her not to, and she took the suggestion.

SHOT CARTRIDGES

The handgunner has considerable legitimate use for shot loads, although the rifled bore of a handgun generally makes the pattern useless for any killing beyond a few feet.

Probably the most common shot cartridge is the .22 Long Rifle shot cartridge containing a few dust-size shot with the case crimped together at the mouth. These cartridges are pretty useless. Now the CCI Division of Omark has solved an old problem by encasing the shot charge in a plastic container. Available in a number of standard cases (.22 Long Rifle, .22 WMR, .357, and .44 Magnum), these loads produce excellent results and will serve the handgun-packing camper, fisherman, and hunter well by killing dangerous snakes, grouse for the pot, or whatever legitimate use is desired. The cartridge cases used by CCI are standard.

PRIMERS

The primer is a very tiny pinch of a very violent chemical that explodes when hit or crushed. Its flame then saturates and ignites the main powder charge. The amount of priming compound necessary isn't any larger than the small amount you could get on the very end of a toothpick. If you placed this on a flat surface and hit it with a hammer it would explode.

Essentially the same thing happens in your cartridge. In the rimfire the priming mixture is spread around the inside of the rim. The firing pin crushes any part of the rim between it and the breech end of the barrel (rear of a revolver cylinder), and this explodes the mixture.

A centerfire cartridge contains its own primer as a self-contained unit. It has a small cup of soft

A Winchester primer shown unfired and complete at left. Next, the anvil removed from the primer; then the bottom of the fired primer; and then the top of a fired primer. The anvil is a very hard piece of brass and, just as its name implies, serves as a seat for the priming compound. The firing pin crushes the compound on the anvil and causes ignition.

metal; the priming mix is directly under the cup and is held in place by a thin paper washer. Then a separate anvil is inserted which is raised in the center and composed of hard metal; the anvil has two or three legs depending on the manufacturer. When the firing pin comes down it crushes the priming mix between the pin and anvil, causing the mix to explode, whereupon the flames rush through the anvil's legs and through the flash hole into the main body of the cartridge to saturate the powder with flame for ignition.

The only difference in a Berdan primer is that its anvil is built into the cartridge case; otherwise they work the same. As I said, primers are very violent and only a very small amount is required. In manufacture, the mix is handled wet (for safety) and in very small batches, for the same purpose. It is handled by workers from behind protective barriers, and storage facilities have roofs and walls that are easily blown away, with heavy earthen walls between them to confine any accidents to as small an area as possible.

Primers come in two basic sizes for metallic cartridges, which are known as "large rifle" and "small rifle." "Large pistol" and "small pistol" are the same size and you can't tell them apart by looking at them. (There are a few exceptions in size, but these are the most common.) As stated earlier in this book, handgun primers have softer cups because the firing-pin blows are weaker. This is no problem for the average shooter, but the reloader must be careful not to mix his primers, since a handgun primer, even though it's the same size, will present the possibility of a rupture when used in a rifle because of its weaker cup. On the other hand, a tough rifle primer will not provide uniform inition in a handgun because the metal is too hard for the hammer blow.

Manufacturers carefully list the uses for the primer sizes they make. Reloading manuals also tell you what primers to use with loads they recommend. You should be careful to keep primers in their original boxes and to follow the recommendations given. Should any primers stray from their original boxes, it's better to discard them than to guess. Primers may be effectively "killed" by placing them in oil.

Which brings up the fact that primer pockets

are usually sealed in manufacture against penetration by oil, or any petroleum product. A bit of varnish provides a satisfactory seal, although the military also insists on "staking" primers in place, which consists of upsetting a bit of the case head around the top of the primer to reduce the size of the pocket and so lock the primer in place. Staking isn't really necessary, and I think its only benefit is to further work-harden the case head. I have never had the slightest problem with handloaded ammunition that was not sealed, and I've often used loads that were assembled years earlier.

Sometimes a primer will produce what is known as a hangfire, which means that something has happened to deteriorate the primer, resulting in a noticeable delay between the firing-pin blow and ignition. I suspect the major cause of this rare event is improper storage. The result is almost like firing a flintlock, where there is also a delay. After the last war I recall acquiring some old .270 cartridges which produced a uniform hangfire for some reason. This box of ammo could always be depended upon to produce the described hangfire. In this case the hangfire was rather quick, but they have been known to have a delay of up to a couple of seconds—long enough to move the muzzle dangerously. While you are most unlikely to experience a hangfire, should it ever happen, the safe procedure to follow is the old army rule: Don't move anything until you count to ten. Keep the gun pointed downrange at all times. It is not safe to assume a hangfire won't go off until you've gotten to the ten count, when you know the case is a dud.

PERCUSSION-CAP GUNS

With the vast increase in black-powder pistol and rifle shooting, it is useful to know that the elements of a percussion-cap system are basically the same as those for a cartridge gun. There is no cartridge case, since the powder is poured directly into the barrel, or into the charge holes of a revolver. Then a bullet or ball is seated on top of the powder by ramming it home.

Percussion firearms have a small hole in the breech end of their barrels, or at the rear of each charge hole in a revolver's cylinder, and these holes are the seats for an upward-extending part called the nipple. Nipples also contain a hole which aligns with the hole in the barrel or charge hole. To fire the gun, you place a percussion cap over the nipple. When the hammer comes down it whacks the cap; the nipple acts as an anvil and the flame travels through the hole into the barrel, where it ignites the powder charge. Percussion hammers are deeply concave to help keep the bits of soft percussion-cap material from flying about. One must be careful not to snap the hammer on a nipple without a cap in place or the nipple will be damaged.

A flintlock fires quite differently, since the ignition comes from the flint, clamped in the hammer, which strikes a vertical plate called the frizzen. The hammer blow creates a shower of sparks and shoves the frizzen up and forward, exposing the "pan," which contains fine priming powder and into which the sparks fall. The result ignites this fine powder and flame passes through the flash hole into the barrel to ignite the main charge.

CHAPTER FIFTEEN

PROPELLANTS

We have discussed the fact that the priming compound *explodes,* and that the result of that small explosion is to ignite the powder—our propellant. Powder *burns.* It does not explode. There are varying requirements for today's gunpowder, and it requires a different kind of powder to drive a charge of shot, to drive a large-diameter pistol bullet at moderate speed, to drive a small, high-velocity rifle bullet at tremendous speed, or to drive a heavy artillery shell many miles. The same *basic* kind of propellant can be used for each, but many modifications must be made to provide a suitable powder for each of these, and many more, specific uses.

The gun barrel has often been compared to the internal-combustion engine. The piston is replaced by a bullet or shot charge. (And a new "piston" is required for each shot.) The gun barrel, however, more closely resembles a diesel engine than the gas internal-combustion engine, because the gasoline-operated engine is driven by an explosion. A diesel engine, on the other hand, develops a relatively slow thrust *throughout the piston stroke.*

So too does the gun work, for we cannot generate the necessary chamber pressure with an explosion. Rather we must make this pressure build gradually in order to gradually accelerate the flight of the bullet down the barrel. Otherwise the result would be disaster. The pressures developed in the barrel would be beyond the ability of the barrel to contain them. Similarly, different situations occur in the many different types of shotgun or rifle or pistol, and the propellant chosen for each individual cartridge and bullet weight must be compatible with those components, with the guns in the field chambered for that particular cartridge, and with the uses to which such guns and ammunition will be employed.

BLACK POWDER

The first discovery of a fuel that would burn without atmospheric oxygen was the mixture of charcoal, sulfur, and saltpeter which was known as gunpowder for several hundred years. During that long period its composition changed little, although its appearance and methods of manufacture changed. Later it was formed into rough grains and graded by sifting; still later it was compacted by forming it into cakes under considerable pressure before being broken up for use. These efforts helped control combustion speed so that the pressures generated by combustion were distributed more evenly as the projectile traveled the length of the bore.

Black powder also has been widely used as an explosive in mining and quarrying and for blowing up enemy fortifications. Black powder is available in fine through coarse granulations (FFFFG, known as 4FG, to FG); you use the coarser granulations with larger-bore rifles and heavier projectiles. The finer powders are for shotguns, pistols, and the "pans" of flintlocks.

Now there is a new substitute for black powder on the market. Called Pyrodex, it is exclusively distributed by Bruce Hodgdon, the nation's principal powder vendor for reloaders.

Pyrodex is intended to be loaded bulk for bulk with black powder, meaning that if you load a certain-sized scoop of black powder you should use the same scoop for Pyrodex. This charge of pyrodex will weigh from 15 to 20 percent *less* than black powder. For example, 8 grains of Pyrodex has the same bulk as 10 grains of black powder by weight, but the bulk is the same. On the bulk-for-bulk basis, Pyrodex gives pressure and velocity that are identical with those of black powder for all practical purposes. If you are loading black powder by weight and want to load Pyrodex the same way, reduce your charge by 20 percent and you will get the same results.

Black powder was made by DuPont from the company's beginning in 1802 until a few years ago, when manufacture was finally stopped for economic reasons. The abandonment of black powder by DuPont preceded by about a year the tremendous rebirth of black-powder shooting in America. And this left shooters pretty high and dry, though the gap was filled, largely by Hodgdon, by importing black powder from Scotland.

Meantime, they were working on Pyrodex, which is not an explosive and hence can be shipped by most common carriers. (For example, black powder must be shipped by freight, but Pyrodex can be sent by UPS.) And that's a big advantage; it means Pyrodex can be shipped by the same means as smokeless powder.

Pyrodex is loaded the same as black powder. It burns slightly cleaner and leaves slightly less of that awful fouling in the bore. But it produces the same dense cloud of smelly smoke that warms the heart of any black-powder shooter. Two basic varieties of Pyrodex are available as this is written: one for rifles and pistols and the other for shotgun use. I understand there will soon be a variety for cannon hobbyists.

SMOKELESS POWDER

It is generally claimed that the invention of a Frenchman named Pelouze in 1838 sealed the doom of black powder as a propellant. Pelouze discovered that an explosive could be made by "nitrating cotton"—which means treating cotton with nitric acid. That's an oversimplification, of course, but the result is an explosive known as guncotton. Or, to put it another way, the result was a nitrocellulose—cotton being of the wood-fiber family and "nitro-" referring to nitric acid.

The active agent in any explosive of this type or in smokeless powder is the nitrogen atom in combination with two oxygen atoms (NO_2). Originally, the combination contained potassium, which fouled gun barrels. Then the chemists found they could remove the potassium by means of sulfuric acid and add it to a simple hydrocarbon like glycerin. The result is nitroglycerin which is uncertain and awkward to handle as a liquid, so it was mixed with sawdust or some other porous substance and molded into sticks, and became dynamite.

That stringy stuff that looks like spaghetti is cordite, an English propellant that is smokeless. It is what we call a double-base powder, meaning that it contains both nitrocellulose and nitroglycerin. Some American powders are double-base, but we do not use cordite. At the right is shown a typical American powder, one of the DuPont IMR powders.

Left to right: Black powder, DuPont IMR 4227, IMR 4350, and Winchester-Western Ball Powder #785.

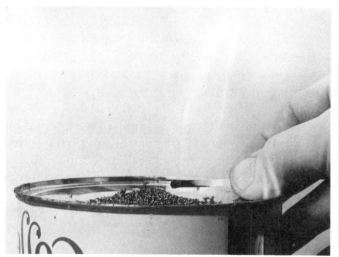

Smokeless powder, when lighted in the open as on this coffee can, burns comparatively slowly. It is not an explosive, but a flammable solid. Note that it is perfectly safe to light with a match held in the hand as at left. At right, the powder is burning. This is not to suggest the flame isn't a brisk one, but it's not an explosion. Under the confinement of a cartridge case, smokeless powder burns very much faster of course. Black powder, on the other hand, should never be lighted in this manner. It will go up with some violence and, indeed, can be used as a substitute for dynamite as an explosive.

Instead of glycerin we use cellulose in the form of wood pulp or cotton, treat it with nitric and sulfuric acids, and get nitrocellulose, the chief ingredient of smokeless powder. But this material is too light and loose to pack into a cartridge, so it is dissolved with ether and alcohol or acetone to make a plastic mass that can be molded into rods resembling spaghetti. This process was discovered by a French government chemist named Vieille in 1885.

That, basically, is how smokeless powder is made—the nitrocellulose variety which we also call a "single-base" powder. There also is a "double-base" powder which came about in 1878, when the Swedish chemist Alfred Nobel thought of dissolving guncotton in nitroglycerin. Nobel made a huge fortune out of his discovery, and, apparently appalled at the thought of what he had left behind, he left his fortune to fund the Nobel Prizes.

In any event, Nobel's invention is known as cordite, and it is, for our purposes here, a smokeless powder containing both nitrocellulose and nitroglycerin—which is why we also call it a double-base powder. Some double-base powders are harder on a barrel than single-base powders, but this is more often true with the English cordite than with the American double-base powders. For the record, the line of DuPont powders known as IMR (for Improved Military Rifle) are single-base powders. A few of the powders in the Hercules line are double-base. Otherwise most of the powders available to the American reloader are of the single-base variety (that is, nitrocellulose).

There is still another type of powder known as Ball Powder, an invention of the Western Cartridge Company (now part of Winchester-Western) in the early 1930s. Ball Powder is made essentially the same as any other nitrocellulose powder (which it is) except that it is made into an emulsion, which forms small droplets on the surface that can be removed in that form. The process greatly reduces time and cost in manufacture, and we'll have more to say about Ball Powder in a few moments. The important thing to remember is that it's simply another form of nitrocellulose containing a small addition of nitroglycerin and is a double-base powder.

We have mentioned *types* of smokeless powder, but it is important to know that these three types can be manufactured in an endless variety of *rates of burning*. By this I mean that you need a much faster burning powder for a shotgun or pistol cartridge than for a big rifle Magnum, which requires a comparatively slow-burning powder. Any of these types can be manufactured to deliver a desired burning rate.

Long ago it was discovered that just like pieces of wood, small-size grains burn faster than larger grains. Take a piece of 2×4 pine 6 inches long and split it into a couple of dozen pieces and it will burn a good deal faster than if left whole. The same exact thing happens with gunpowder, because you are increasing the exposed surface of a given amount of powder. The greater that surface, the faster it will burn.

A Col. Rodman of the U.S. Army discovered that you could perforate powder grains, which would increase the rate of burning even further. Now you had an exposed area inside the grain of powder and burning was from both within and without.

Burning rate, then, is controlled by the size of powder grains or, more precisely, by the amount of surface area exposed. It is important to keep this in mind, because the same basic *type* of powder is used in 16-inch naval guns as is used in small arms. But the individual powder grains for the big artillery are several times the size of a whole box of .22 Hornet cartridges.

Burning rates are further controlled by coating the powder grains with graphite. So, with nitrocellulose (single-base) and with nitrocellulose-nitroglycerin (double-base) powders we control the rates of burning by the size of their grains, by the amount of surface area, and by a retardant coating of graphite.

One further point about Ball Powder: it too can be controlled, and this control is exercised by rolling the spherical grains, while in plastic form, into flats like little pancakes. These can be rolled thick or thin, or they can be left in tiny spheres. Ball Powder also is coated to retard burning.

As you can see, smokeless powder can be made in endless varieties. Powders made for large cannon are perforated many times. In the trade, the perforating machine for rifle powder is known as the "macaroni press." The powder, in plastic form, is forced through a die, from which it emerges as a long, continuous strip with a tiny hole in the middle. It is then cut into small lengths and dried.

It is interesting to realize that a gun is a very inefficient engine when it comes to conversion of the energy of combustion into work—that is, the moving of a projectile. It has been computed that the energy of the moving projectile accounts for only about 32 percent of the propellant's energy. The heat of the gun, including friction loss, takes up 22 percent, the rotation of the projectile 0.14 percent, recoil 0.12 percent. The balance, about 45 percent is lost. These figures were computed for artillery and were published in *Steel* magazine in 1942. They will vary slightly for small arms, but not appreciably; they furnish a rough idea of the general waste of power in firearms.

The total power inherent in gunpowder is also of interest. For example, cellulose-nitrate powder gives out about 3600 BTU per pound as compared with over 15,000 BTU for a pound of semibituminous coal.

Powders must be mated to their loads with extreme care. It is very easy to use the wrong powder with disastrous results (by which I mean, to use an extreme example, that if you loaded an artillery piece with fast-burning pistol powder you would blow the gun and its crew clear to hell and beyond, because it would develop pressure far too fast for the projectile to move before maximum pressure was achieved). Powder is made in huge lots or batches, and while extreme control is exercised, the lot may or may not turn out exactly as desired.

For example, let's say DuPont wishes to make a new lot of powder for handloaders—say SR 7625, a popular handgun and shotgun powder (these powders are called "canister lots"). Their supply of SR 7625 is low and must be replenished. So they manufacture a lot of powder with the hope that it will turn out to be SR 7625. It may or may not. DuPont won't know until the powder is manufactured and tested, retested, and tested some more, because every lot must be exactly like every other lot. Should it fail to duplicate SR 7625 exactly, it is given another number and will be sold to one of the ammunition-loading companies, which, in turn, will experiment with this powder to mate it to one of its own batches of ammunition. It will be loaded to achieve specified pressures, velocity, and accuracy in a particular load.

This is one point the reloader must understand completely. Sometimes he will pull the bullet from a factory-loaded cartridge and examine the powder. It *looks* like 2400, so he thinks it is 2400. It is not, and the wrong conclusion can lead to trouble. Reloaders should—indeed they must—stick to the canister lots of powders available to them and follow the guidelines given by the manufacturers.

There have been times when a powder manufacturer manufactured a canister lot of powder and then *could not duplicate it* to restock dealers' shelves! That's one of the reasons a powder is occasionally taken off the market—there was not necessarily anything wrong with the powder, but it simply could not be duplicated with the precision necessary for a canister lot. The canister powder lot you buy tomorrow will exactly duplicate the lot you bought in 1948.

One of the problems with gunpowders is that they occupy a limited space in the cartridge case, held back by the bullet. When the powder is ignited it begins to generate gas, and the gas begins to move the bullet, which leaves more space for the gas to occupy. Then the gas, filling this void, tends to lose pressure, simply because the same amount of gas now occupies more space. The solution lies in the perforation of powder grains.

As a powder grain burns from the outside, it gets smaller and smaller, which reduces the burning area and so reduces the amount of gas given off. But if it burns from within, the surface keeps expanding and more gas is given off. Thus the thrust against the bullet is maintained and, with the proper blend of powder, is actually increased so that it is maintained all the way to the muzzle.

The correct powder for a given load can be achieved by the size of the grain, including the size of the perforation. In some cannon powders, each grain sometimes has as many as seven perforations. When we use the term "progressive powder," we mean a powder that will rapidly build its pressure (called the pressure curve, which I'll discuss more fully later) to start the bullet moving but will then maintain that thrust all the way to the muzzle, at which point the pressure will have dropped substantially. A pressure curve builds very steeply, then gradually tapers down as the bullet reaches the muzzle, but the push keeps pushing all the way down the barrel. Another advantage to progressive powders is that they develop maximum velocities without attaining extraordinarily high pressures. Such high pressures can be very hard on a gun mechanism, and they are also generally accompanied by very high temperatures.

Powders used in both pistols and shotguns, while progressive to a degree, are much quicker than those used in rifles. One example of this is that these powders are usually (but not always) small, very flat and thin grains. That means they burn much faster.

Burning rate is also a function of the heat within the cartridge case—which builds when a bullet is harder and slower to move. For example, it takes much longer to move the 180-grain bullet in a .300 Winchester Magnum than it does to move a pistol bullet, regardless of the weight and caliber of that pistol bullet. One of the prime reasons is that most pistol cartridges are straight cases, not bottlenecked, which offers much more room for the gas to push against. When gas starts to build in the rifle cartridge, it turns back against itself, and this hastens the rate of burning. The slower the bullet moves, the more this gas feeds on itself, so to speak, and the more rapidly gas is created.

With a pistol or shotgun, where the bullet or shot charge starts to move quicker than in a rifle, the gas must also be built quicker in order to provide the thrust necessary. Moreover, the pistol powder must achieve its top velocity in a barrel that is much shorter than a rifle barrel. The average rifle barrel is from 20 to 24 inches long, while the average handgun barrel varies from 4 to 6 inches—a vast difference.

To take a cartridge like the popular .22 Long Rifle as an example, since it is widely used in both handguns and rifles, it becomes obvious that a higher velocity will be achieved in the rifle. (Actually, a .22 Long Rifle attains its maximum velocity in 16 inches of barrel length. A rifle barrel longer than that actually loses a very small amount of velocity due to added friction. On the other hand, the same cartridge fired from a 2-inch-barreled pistol delivers substantially lower velocity.)

An understanding of the different requirements for propellants for the various types of small arms is interesting, and it is essential if you are a handloader. Mixing powders could be hazardous because, as we've seen, pistol and shotgun powders are much faster and would wreck a rifle if a "rifle charge" of pistol powder were inadvertently loaded in a rifle. Some handgun powders are so powerful that a double load is possible even in a small handgun cartridge, and this, too, could wreck the handgun. A blown-up handgun is no fun. Though the gun is hand-held a long way from your body and face in normal shooting, you can easily damage your hand seriously. You must be very careful to use the right components and then see that unused quantities are quickly replaced in their original containers to avoid any possibility of a mixup.

BLANK POWDER

A blank cartridge has the sole function of making a loud noise. It is used in starter's pistols at track meets, in salute cannons by yachtsmen, and in formal military formations as a salute over a grave or as an honorary salute for dignitaries.

This powder must burn with most extreme rapidity and must produce a suitable noise. It also must do this with no resistance from bullet or shot charge—nothing but a paper wad over the case muzzle to hold the powder in place. Blank powder must never be used in any loaded ammunition. It is the fastest-burning of all powders; a tiny pinch of it, if loaded behind any bullet, would cause the gun to blow up like a bomb. (In fact, hand grenades are loaded with a small amount of "blank powder," to give you some idea of its power.) Should you run across blank cartridges, as military surplus or whatever, use them as blanks if you wish, but do not, under any circumstances, try to salvage the powder. (Also, do not reload blank military cartridges with full loads. Blanks are often loaded with cartridge cases that are not up to standard, and they are not suitable for full-load use.)

At one time, there was a powder widely used in .22 Long Rifle match ammunition called Lesmok Powder. It was a mixture of guncotton and black powder, it gave off more smoke than smokeless but less than black powder and gave superb accuracy. Happily, it has now gone off the market; one of its other faults was that its manufacture was extremely hazardous.

CORDITE

This British powder, which we have mentioned before, is a double-base powder with a rather high nitroglycerin content. It has been widely claimed that cordite is very hard on gun barrels — that it erodes them very quickly in comparison with most American powders. The point may well be moot, since the British have clung to cordite for years and have been using it for both military and sporting purposes in many parts of the world. Cordite is a satisfactory propellant.

One of the most unusual things about cordite is the physical form in which it is loaded: long sections that resemble long, thin spaghetti. The "grains," unlike those in American powders, are usually as long as the length from the base of the cartridge case to the base of the bullet. This is pretty startling when one first breaks down a British cartridge loaded with cordite.

The method of loading cordite in manufacture is also of interest, since it differs widely from our practices. The powder is inserted before the cartridge case is necked. That is, after all final case operations are completed, including primer seating, the strands of cordite are inserted, a glazed cardboard disc is inserted over the powder, and *then the case is necked.* Otherwise it would be impossible to get those long strands of spaghettilike cordite in place after necking. After necking, the bullet is seated and then the round is finished.

BULLET DESIGN, CONSTRUC- TION, AND BEHAVIOR

It should be obvious, once you think about it, that the single most important object in all gundom is the bullet. Everything else is a mere vehicle to get that bullet precisely where you want it. And, once it arrives, it must do what you expect it to. That can be simply stated, and you can easily accept it as fact because it's so logical. But bullets are called upon to do many things—some of them very different. So there are many kinds of bullets, some of which are multipurpose (or at least will serve several roles) and others which are of no earthly use save for their single special role. Bullet design, construction, and behavior are most interesting subjects, are vastly more complicated than you may imagine, and are one of the most important things you will learn from this study.

Before we get into the whys and wherefores of bullet design, how they are made and how they act or react when hitting the target, let's first define the word "bullet."

I think nothing infuriates a gun buff so much as to have people refer to ammunition as "bullets." A bullet is a projectile. Period. It is a single projectile fired from either a rifle or pistol or revolver. It is nothing else. It is not a shotgun slug, even though that slug somewhat resembles a bullet.

There are hundreds of different kinds of bullets. We'll talk about the most important ones, and we'll discuss enough of the reasons behind the various designs so that you will be able to analyze other bullet styles as you come across them. Some pretty weird things are often attributed to bullets that are ballistically impossible, usually by the newspaper or broadcasting commentators who don't know what they're talking about. But sometimes you see things in serious gun publications which are just as wildly foolish.

In today's scheme of firearms there are three common styles of bullet: jacketed, pure lead, and disintegrating. The jacketed bullet is the most common. It is composed of a lead core surrounded by a jacket of either soft copper-nickel alloy or mild steel. A pure lead bullet (which isn't really pure lead because there is usually a little antimony added to the lead) is most often found in .22 rimfire ammunition and revolver loads. Lead bullets are often equipped with a copper base, called a gas check, that helps protect the soft lead from the hot propellant gas. The disintegrating bullet is found in certain .22 Short cartridges and is composed of lead mixed with other elements which cause it to disintegrate instantly on impact. These cartridges are usually used in gallery shooting and are of little interest to the serious gunner. Their purpose is to permit close-range target shooting (often of the exhibition type) with the employment of a suitable steel backstop. The bullet breaks up into dust on impact, and there is no danger whatever from a ricochet.

A bullet's weight, shape, and length control its air resistance, and affect its length of flight. Its construction (including balance) controls its accuracy and the ability to transmit its energy to the target (that is, its "killing power"). And, as we shall see, there are special-purpose bullets designed to do one specific task and nothing more.

Bullets may also be categorized by shape: spherical, conical, wadcutter and sharp shoulder. Among handgun bullets the most common types are: lead, lead with gas check, jacketed soft point, wadcutter, metal-piercing, hollowpoint (both lead and jacketed), and sharp-shoulder (often called the Keith design after Elmer Keith, the gun writer).

In the world of rifles there are proprietary types of bullet construction which do not exist in handgun bullets. Among these are the Winchester-Western Silvertip, the Remington Core-Lokt, and others.

Basically you should understand that the bullets used in autoloading pistols are generally of the full-metal-jacketed type, because this type aids feeding out of the magazine, while soft lead bullets could easily jam against the breech end of the barrel and fail to feed. A revolver, on the other hand, can digest any cartridge with any form of bullet that's compatible with the load, because it's fed by hand into the charge hole.

Some of these bullets are single-purpose affairs, and one of these is the metal-piercing bullet loaded for the sole purpose of law-enforcement use to rip through auto bodies. The same bullet is loaded in .38 Special and .357 Magnum (they are the same size in spite of the differing caliber designations). I shouldn't be surprised if a load of quail shot would penetrate today's car bodies just as well.

Another special bullet is the wadcutter, which has an absolutely flat nose. It's shaped just like a small tin can. Viewed from the side, a wadcutter loaded cartridge doesn't look loaded because the nose of the bullet is even with the case mouth. The purpose of the wadcutter is to cut clean holes in a target and make scoring easier. Targets shot with these bullets appear to be punched by a paper punch. While they are suitable for the ranges over which matches are usually fired, these bullets have no long-range attributes at all.

It has not gone unnoticed that a wadcutter makes an ideal bullet for close-range defensive shooting. Hitting like a small barn door, such a bullet can do serious damage to an assailant.

The sharp-shoulder of Keith-design bullet is meant to combine the wadcutter effect with longer-range characteristics. And it accomplishes this very well. In fact, this may be the single most popular revolver bullet shape in use. Its sharp shoulder cuts clean holes in a target and helps produce substantial shocking power, while its nose (which appears to be a nose stuck on a wadcutter) produces reasonable flight characteristics, and the bullet can be used for long-range handgun shooting.

LEAD BULLETS

Lead bullets, used almost entirely for .22 and pistol ammunition, are made either by casting

Above Left: Cylindrical 100-pound lead billets moving along a conveyor to an extrusion press that will squeeze them into lead wire from which bullet cores will be made. Above Right: After leaving the extrusion press the lead wire is coiled in barrels. Left: The wire is then fed into a battery of machines that cut it into preformed sections of the exact weight required for the bullets being manufactured. Bullet cores are then placed into drawn jackets before final forming.

molten metal in a specific mold, many of which have as many as six cavities and will cast that number of bullets at a time, or by cold-forming them from lead wire. The latter process is used by the larger plants, the former by most reloaders. Either way produces good bullets as long as proper procedures are used. At one time, all bullets were made of lead—or a lead alloy, because it has been customary for many years to add another metal to lead to increase the

hardness slightly. In the early days this metal was often mercury (quicksilver); today it's tin, antimony, or both.

Once cast or formed, the bullet is usually *sized* by running it through a sizing die, which also inserts a lubricant into the grooves. Lead bullets therefore are often cast slightly oversize and sized down to exact bore size. The lubricant is forced into the lubricating grooves, which are called cannelures. It is important that lead bullets be lubricated, or else lead will strip off the bullet and adhere to the barrel. This is especially important with higher-velocity ammunition, and one of the chief offenders in this category is the .357 Magnum bullet.

Bullet diameter is also most important. When a cartridge is ignited, the first thing that happens is that the brass case opens up to fill the chamber. This action releases the hold the case neck had on the bullet. At this point, since the bullet hasn't yet moved, a little gas spurts past the bullet and into the barrel. The better the fit of bullet to bore, the less gas will escape. (Such escaping gas does two things: It wastes power and it causes "gas cutting" of the bullet, because the heat of the gas is higher than the melting point of the bullet.)

In olden days, when the propellant was black powder, it was necessary to make bullets quite a bit smaller than barrel diameter. This was because the powder rapidly fouled the bore and soon bullets had to ride over this fouling, causing considerable loss of accuracy. This was especially true with breechloading rifles (in muzzle-loaders the fouling was pushed back down the barrel behind the bullet during loading).

Older riflemen learned that they could often fire up to about ten shots with good accuracy, then the fouling would have accumulated to the point where accuracy suffered badly. This isn't true today with smokeless powder, of course, and a rifle like a .22 can be fired almost forever with no barrel cleaning whatsoever.

Today's higher velocities, especially with some of the hotter revolver loads, call for rather hard bullets. It's probably safe to say that all bullets used these days, whether factory or home-cast, are hardened, usually with antimony. The harder bullet helps prevent skidding—that forward movement of the bullet before it begins to accept the rifling twist. As will become apparent when you think about it for a moment, a bullet will tend to want to move straight ahead down the gun barrel. But it must accept the rifling twist and begin to turn. The softer the metal, the more the tendency to keep moving ahead. The shooter calls this skidding, and the result is undesirable.

Another device used to help prevent skidding, to prevent the hot gases from melting the bases of lead bullets, and at the same time to help prevent leading the barrel is to apply a gas check. This is a small copper-alloy cup that's fitted over the bullet's base (bullets must be specially cast for a gas check) and effectively seals the bullet's base. The cup extends up the side of the bullet about 1/16 inch.

Gas checks are widely used in such cartridges as the .357, .41, and .44 Magnum revolver loads as well as in some .38 Specials. They also are used on many high-powered rifle lead bullets because they permit faster speeds in addition to the other advantages already listed.

Gas checks are really a necessity to prevent leading, especially in the hotter numbers. As already stated, one of the worst offenders in the leading department is the .357 Magnum. Unless precautions are taken, lead from bullets builds up in the rifling to a point where accuracy almost disappears. Indeed, many .357 barrels are honed and lapped in manufacture to make them as smooth as humanly possible, and the use of gas checks is also a great aid.

.22 BULLETS

Bullets loaded for .22 firearms are generally of two basic types: hollowpoint and solid-lead. Target .22 ammo is loaded with much more carefully made bullets. An interesting point about the .22-caliber bullet is that it's designed for subsonic flight, which means that high-velocity loads will not shoot as accurately as standard velocity loads.

Most .22 ammo is greased in conventional fashion, and you should keep it clean, usually by keeping it in the original container until ready to load. Putting a greased .22 cartridge in your pocket, or dropping it on the ground, means it will pick up dirt, which, if fired, will scratch the barrel.

For this purpose some .22s are loaded with bullets clad with an alloy which doesn't require the lubricant in the ordinary sense. These cartridges can usually be carried loosely in your pocket and won't pick up dirt.

SPHERICAL BULLETS

Early lead bullets were spherical, or as nearly spherical as they could be made. Now, the flight of a round ball is an interesting thing, because it involves some laws of physics that we don't ordinarily think about.

A round ball is a miserable shape for the retention of velocity, because the faster it is driven the sooner it slows down! That's because air resistance varies as the square of the velocity. Double the velocity and you increase the air resistance by four times. Treble the velocity and air resistance increases nine times. And so on. As a result of this law of physics there are practical limits beyond which it simply makes no sense to increase the speed of a round ball.

It was discovered long ago that an elongated bullet—sometimes called a slug—produced better ballistic qualities than the sphere, and that shape has been in common use ever since. Just about the only place you'll find spheres today is in shotgun pellets and muzzleloading replicas.

METAL-CASED BULLETS

When smokeless powder came along, lead bullets were found unsatisfactory with the higher temperatures and higher velocities obtainable with the new powders. The approximate date of this development was about 1885. There was, in fact, a UMC (Union Metallic Cartridge Co.—the firm which later bought Remington Arms) bullet marketed in 1884 with a jacketed bullet for the .45/90 Winchester rifle.

Smokeless and lead bullets didn't mix, because the bases of the bullets melted and the bullets skidded in the rifling. Experiments with harder, solid materials were unsatisfactory because they were too light; it was evident that lead was necessary because it had the required density and weight to sustain velocity. The result was to use lead as a bullet core and provide a jacket to surround that core which would solve the problems.

One of the first metals used for jacket material was the so-called German silver—also called cupro-nickel and composed of 60 percent copper and 40 percent nickel. But this was expensive and was soon replaced by gilding metal, which is still used—a composition of copper with 5–10 percent zinc added. In Europe, on the other hand, a mild steel was used for bullet-jacket material, and it is still used by most European ammo companies. Of course, a steel-jacketed bullet tends to rust, so it is lightly plated with a copper compound. The term "steel jacket" is accurately applied to some European ammunition. It is accurately applied to only a very few U.S. loads, such as the .458 Winchester Magnum "solid" (full metal case and labeled FMC), because this jacket toughness is required to get through the nearly 3 feet of bone structure in an elephant's head. The simple test for a steel jacket is to use a magnet. Mild-steel jackets are no harder on rifle barrels than gilding-metal jackets.

Bullet jackets are manufactured the same way that cartridge cases are made—by punching out small discs from metal strips of the correct size and thickness. Then, through successive punch-press operations, these coinlike slugs are drawn and formed into bullet jackets.

A bullet may be formed one of two major ways: with open base, in which event the lead core is seated from the rear, or the other way around. Most hunting bullets have solid bases with the lead core seated from the front. In this case the jacket material is thinner at the nose end to facilitate its unrolling and allow the bullet to expand on impact. Full-metal-case bullets (those with a solid jacket at the nose end) are generally used for target shooting and for auto pistols.

Expanding, softpoint, or hollowpoint bullets are constructed along very similar lines, since they are all closed at the base and the lead cores are inserted from the front. After core insertion, the front end of the jacket is closed in a die to the desired degree. Both bullets are of the expanding type, so that word, in itself, is not really very descriptive. The important feature of these types is that their jackets are closed at the rear, open at the front.

This special bullet from Hornady (available to reloaders) is a hollowpoint with no lead exposed at the nose. It's a .45 caliber, intended for reloading in the .45 Auto. The purpose of the style is to provide better feeding into the chamber. The jacket is slightly thinner at the nose and has serrated markings for strategic weakening of the jacket to ensure low-velocity expansion.

The rush toward higher and higher muzzle velocities posed other problems that hadn't been considered before. One of the first problems noted was that the cupro-nickel jacket material used by the military through World War I, actually until about 1922, caused barrels to foul badly. Sometimes this happened at speeds about 2700 fps; in other rifles and other calibers it occurred at lower velocities. In either event, the cupro-nickel jackets caused thick metal fouling in the bore in the form of smears and lumps, usually on top of the lands, often to a depth of up to .004 inch. The fouling interfered with accuracy, raised pressures, and was hellish to remove. The same thing did not occur with gilding metal, which was also cheaper, and it soon replaced cupro-nickel.

Meanwhile, John Browning was working on his autoloading pistols, and work was proceeding along the same lines in Europe. It became quickly evident that jacketed bullets, of the type shooters used to call "full-metal-patch," meaning with a jacket that completely enclosed the nose, were necessary for best feeding in auto pistols.

THE ROUNDNOSE SOLID-JACKET BULLET

Roundnose bullets with solid jackets—called "full patch" by the military—were a military development because they conformed to the Geneva Convention. This was before the development of pointed bullets. As a military bullet, the roundnose, such as was employed by our .30/40 Krag and .30/03 Springfield, both of which weighed 220 grains, was not a great success. Its weight was also against it, for muzzle velocities were relatively low, and the shape prevented good long-range ballistics.

This type of bullet tends to drill a straight hole when it reaches the target. It does not deflect easily, as does a pointed bullet, nor does it expand readily. Its military use was a success except for the range limitations just noted. In military terms, it was a better wounder than a killer—and the military rationale is that it's better to wound an enemy soldier than to kill him. (If he's killed, that's the end of it. But if wounded, he requires care, and that occupies other soldiers. So a wounded man, as opposed to a dead one, is more effective in terms of reducing the enemy's strength.)

One of the early lessons the U.S. government learned relating to a bullet's stopping power was in the Philippine rebellion in the late 1800s. The army was then armed with an old-timer known as the .38 Long Colt cartridge. This was a slower performer than the .38 Special. In the Philippines it was soon found that the Moro savages kept on coming even after absorbing a number of .38 bullets. With their knives and machetes swinging, they dispatched many U.S. soldiers despite being mortally wounded themselves. Clearly, the word went back to Washington, a better stopper was needed in a sidearm.

The result was development of the .45 ACP (Automatic Colt Pistol), which had then, as it has now, a jacketed, fat, round-nosed slug that has gained a reputation around the world since the early 1900s as a great man-stopper. Whether it killed or not was not important. What was expected of the fat .45 was that it would slam its target so hard and with such force that the target would be put out of commission.

The only other use for roundnose full-metal-clad bullets is in game bullets required for deep, straight penetration. The major example is elephant hunting, because the roundnose slug tends to follow a straight path, whereas a pointed bullet will be deflected. Bullets such as the .458 Winchester Magnum "solid" have a steel jacket that is quite thick, and they do an excellent job of penetrating.

MISCELLANEOUS BULLETS

Handguns today are used for such a wide variety of shooting sports that it's almost impossible to define all of them. For example, the .221 Remington Fire Ball greatly resembles the .222 Remington varmint rifle cartridge. And the Fire Ball rips its hellbending 50-grain bullet out of the Fire Ball pistol at a ferocious 2650 fps.

In the world of wildcat pistol cartridges (a wildcat is a nonstandard cartridge made by hobby shooters from other cases), the .30 and .357 Herrett used in Thompson/Center Contender pistols breathe more fire than St. George's dragon. Both are made on the .30/30 rifle case!

At the other end of the ladder you have such puny, peaceful cartridges as the .25 ACP, which nudges a 50-grain bullet along at a modest 810 fps. You can almost outwalk the little .25, or at least you can almost catch it in a baseball mitt.

Such handguns are also used for a wide variety of purposes—from home defense and pocket concealment for the little ones to big-game hunting with the hotter numbers. Steve Herrett, the pistol-stock maker who designed his versions on the .30/30 cases, has killed several heads of big game with these cartridges. So it follows that the bullet requirements run the full gamut from punching clean holes in paper targets to cleanly killing small and big game to stopping a human assailant bent on doing you harm.

Consequently the requirements of handgun bullets cover a very wide range, from the requirements of a game rifle to the military and law-enforcement needs of shooting people. However, so few people hunt big game with a pistol, or varmints either, that I do not consider it within the scope of this book to go into rifle-bullet design and construction. There are a couple of examples, however, which should certainly be covered.

The .44 Magnum is important for its use in a revolver by many big-game guides who need whopping sidearm power when backing up their clients. This is especially true where the game is dangerous. And the .44 Magnum is also used in rifles by deer hunters. This is a softpoint bullet, jacketed rather thinly because its velocities are not particularly fast (compared to a high-power rifle). Bullet expansion is controlled by the toughness of bullet-jacket material and its thickness—the tougher and thicker, the more resistance to expansion. And when velocity increases, resistance to expansion must also increase, or else the bullet will unravel. This is borne out by the .444 Marlin rifle cartridge loaded by Remington. Unfortunately, Remington chose to load the .44 Magnum revolver bullet in this big rifle case, and the result is that the higher velocity breaks the bullet up on impact. The .444 Marlin must be handloaded (Hornady makes a good bullet) for maximum performance.

To some degree, without the rifle ramifications, both the .41 and .357 Magnums with jacketed-bullet ammunition are in the same category as the .44.

At one time pistol power was measured by the number of pine boards 7/8 inch thick, and placed an inch apart, that were penetrated. The test's only real usefulness was in determining how many pine boards were penetrated, and this particular statistic has been abandoned.

While we will discuss it more fully in Chapter Twenty-four, the late General Julian Hatcher developed a measuring system, called RSP for "relative stopping power," which is still widely used and remains one of the most reliable ways to measure bullet performance. It does not, however, provide a factor for bullet style, which is its major weakness. You can use the Hatcher formula and insert your own factor if you choose, but its value may or may not be right. Various tables have been proposed a number of times for a rifle's reliability on certain game. One of these was promoted by the late John Taylor, who wrote a number of interesting books on shooting African game. His *African Rifles and Cartridges,* published by Samworth, is excellent; even though Taylor himself was a rogue, he was a good, entertaining, and quite logical writer.

Another chart was advanced many years ago by Elmer Keith, and others have proposed similar charts, including one by Fulton North. Save the Hatcher formula, none of these other gentlemen ever told how he arrived at any of the figures, so one can only assume it was done by some gut feeling. They probably started off with the rating numbers and then filled in the gaps with some sort of mumbo-jumbo.

With very few exceptions, a handgun's bullet is called upon to perform a vastly different role than that of a rifle. And the chief reason is that the handgun is a close-range gun, not meant to shoot at any great distances. Yet some of today's one-hand guns are capable of great shooting and, when properly scoped, will deliver astounding accuracy and performance once you take the time to learn how to use the gun. And when the right loads are employed, you can expect the bullet to do the job expected of it.

Chapter Seventeen

THE BULLET'S FLIGHT

There are two common misconceptions that I should like to clear up at the start of this chapter. The first is that one must always blame himself when he misses—because the gun is never at fault. This remains a "fact" to the uninitiated, because he always thinks the blame lies with the shooter. After all, what can be wrong with the gun? This is silly just on the face of it, because, as you know by now if you've read this far into this book, there are errors galore in manufacture. And there are plenty of things that can happen to the flight of a bullet both inside and outside the barrel that some folks will never understand.

The second misconception is that a study of ballistics is dull and complicated. It can be both and, indeed, often is, but we'll keep things simple and easy to understand to help you appreciate what goes on—and why. So dig right in. We'll start off with that thing that resembles a piston engine. We don't use gasoline as a fuel, nor a spark from a plug for ignition. And our "piston" gets shot out of the bore every time. But what we have is very much like the piston engine in your family car.

This is a book about pistols and revolvers. However, pistols and revolvers use rifled bores and are affected by the same laws of ballistics that affect a rifle bullet. Some of the examples I will use apply to rifles, or were determined and/ or proved for rifle use. But the principles still apply to any bullet driven out of any rifled bore

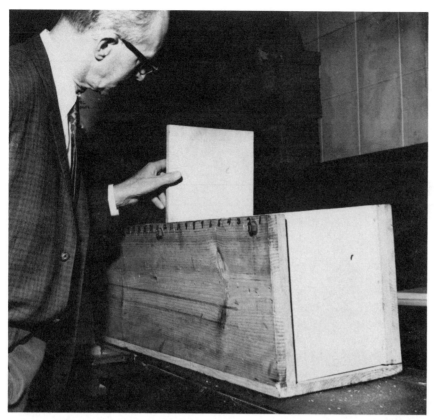

For many years a standard test was "penetration of ⅞-inch pine boards." The first photo shows how these were set up, placed an inch apart in a special box. The other photo shows three bullets that have been test-fired in the box: on the left a 158-grain lead bullet .357 Magnum, which penetrated 11 boards; in the center a .44 Magnum 240-grain softpoint, which slammed through 12 boards; and finally a .41 Magnum with 210-softpoint bullet that slipped through 13 boards. This test has now been pretty well abandoned because it merely tests penetration through pine boards and has little relevance to how a bullet will perform in any other target.

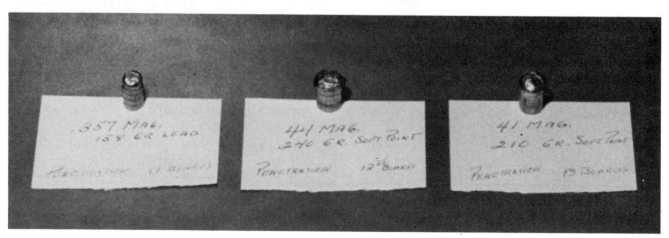

—be it of a conventional rifle, a pistol, a revolver, or an artillery piece.

ALIGNMENT OF BULLET AND BORE

We first must digress to those days, not really so long ago, when it's safe to assume the manufacturing rule was simply to assure easy and uncomplicated insertion of the cartridge into the chamber of the barrel. I believe it is also safe to say that this rule would still be followed were it not for the serious dedication to better accuracy that a few lone men took as a goal; they set out to find out why a rifle wouldn't put every shot through the same hole every time it was fired.

One of these early experimenters was the late Dr. Franklin W. Mann who experimented from about 1894 until about World War I and whose scholarly work *The Bullet's Flight from Powder*

Another old test rarely used any more is shooting into yellow laundry soap. In the first photo a cake of old Octagon soap has been blasted by the .41 Magnum lead bullet load. The other photo offers adequate proof that the .22 Long Rifle hollowpoint blows a better hole than the .25 Automatic. Both fired bullets are shown; the .25-caliber appears at the left. Laundry soap has a consistency similar to that of flesh, and such tests have some degree of reliability.

to Target, published in 1909, is a classic. Much of the basic research and findings of Dr. Mann are as true today as they were three-quarters of a century ago. The next group of experimenters to make real progress were the modern benchrest shooters, who got started in 1947. These men spent their own money seeking answers to accuracy problems that most others didn't care about.

During years as recent as the 1930s and '40s, if you had a rifle—even one of those highly touted bolt-action rifles that were supposed to be very accurate—that would shoot groups at 100 yards of around 4 inches and you wrote to the factory and complained, they'd reply: "That meets our standards of accuracy." That would be your answer, and they would do nothing about it. Actually, they really didn't know how to correct it.

The benchrest shooters found out what made rifles shoot better and they set about making them shoot better. Much of the credit for publicizing what benchresters were doing is due to the late Warren Page's writing in *Field & Stream* over the years. Warren simply never let go of the objective. Other writers covered the subject on occasion, but Warren Page kept at it until things got done. It was this same group that gave birth to today's far finer accuracy, which is largely the result of better bullets. That same movement provided the climate and knowledge that led Sierra, Hornady, and Speer into better bullet manufacture, a move which was followed by Winchester, Remington, and Federal. I may be wrong, but the first bullet I ever saw to come out of one of the big factories that was on a par with those custom bullets was the 80-grain .243 Winchester bullet loaded by Winchester in their first ammo for that rifle.

Today, everybody has learned how to make accurate bullets. They learned it, every one of them, from these experimental riflemen who discovered what happened inside a rifle barrel because they had a compelling desire to know.

Dr. Mann, for example, was a physician when he patented and manufactured a machine for grinding the "green bones" in a slaughterhouse. There was, as it turned out, quite a market for such a machine, and the doctor made a fortune, did not have to practice medicine, and spent the rest of his life seeking the secret of rifle accuracy.

His first experiments dealt with the seating of a bullet in the rifled bore. Being unsatisfied with the misalignment of bore to bullet in conventional cartridges, he made a reamer to permit seating a perfectly tapered bullet (which had been made with the same reamer) directly into the bore ahead of the cartridge. This was a separately seated bullet. The charged cartridge case was then inserted behind the bullet. The doctor used cartridge cases that had been fired in the same rifle previously, so they fitted the chamber perfectly.

That particular experiment was deemed useless because it opened up more problems than it solved. The search for better accuracy took the lid off Pandora's box.

Just the same, note in your mind that a bullet must be seated accurately and uniformly so that it will enter the rifling with the axis of the bullet perfectly coinciding with the axis of the bore.

While you ponder the common sense of that one for a moment, think about the *millions* of bullets being made *every day*. Not just by Winchester, Remington, and Federal. Not just by Sierra, Hornady, Speer, Norma, and so on and on. The shooter has a right to expect that every one of those bullets will be seated just so in his own barrel. A barrel might have been made by Colt, Dan Wesson, Browning, Winchester, Remington, Marlin, Smith & Wesson, Harrington & Richardson, Savage, Champlin, Biesen, and who knows how many more custom gunsmiths, let alone all the imports. As we have said earlier, all these good folks work to tolerances. Some are very close. Some are closer than that. Some, alas, are also a bit loose. But one thing is sure: None of them is perfect. You still want your cartridge case to lie in your chamber so that your bullet is in perfect position for its ride down the barrel when you press the trigger.

The alignment depends upon the accuracy with which the chamber was cut and its alignment with the axis of the bore. It depends on the cartridge case—its fit in the chamber and the bullet's seat in the cartridge-case neck. And it depends upon the throat (or leade, as Col. Townsend Whelen used to call it), that short taper at the breech end of the rifling lands just ahead of the chamber. You see, a bullet is *groove diameter* (.308 inch in a .30-caliber rifle), while the tops of the lands are *bore diameter* (.300 inch). The throat gives the lands a sloping surface which (1) permits you to seat the cartridge in the barrel, and (2) allows the bullet to slowly cut its way into the rifling.

We also have the peculiar case of the revolver, in which the bullet takes a running jump out of the charge hole and into the barrel. To shoot with accuracy, it must enter the bore centrally and retain its alignment without bumping and sliding its way like a ferryboat entering a slip during a high wind and tide.

BULLET SIZE AND BORE SIZE

The bullet must be of a size that can be forced into the rifling and accept the rotation. The ideal size is generally considered to be exactly groove diameter, or very slightly smaller. About .0005 inch smaller is ideal. In actual practice bullets run smaller than that ideal, and many groove diameters run larger, too. If you want a finely tuned target gun you'll do well to get one bored and rifled to exact size and have your bullets as stated above for best results.

Today's bullet dies are made of carbide, which can produce several million bullets before noticeable wear. In older days, before carbide bullet dies, it was the custom to make a bullet-forming die in .30 caliber to a diameter of .306 inch (this for .308-inch barrels). After running a few hundred thousand bullets the die would be worn to .308 or .3085 inch—at which point it was scrapped. There can be vast differences in the performance of a bullet measuring .306 inch and one measuring .3085 inch.

For reasons that are unfathomable, some of these rules do not apply to every barrel. Take a perfectly made rifle barrel—let's say it is a .22-caliber and measures a perfect .2240 inch, which we can measure very precisely today with an air gauge. This barrel might deliver its best accuracy with bullets measuring exactly .2240 inch, or might do better with bullets .0001 inch smaller, or .0002 inch smaller, or . . . You simply won't know until you try.

There is another system of rifling that involves a somewhat different ratio of bullet to bore: the multigroove system, among the best known of which is Marlin's Micro-Groove. Marlin developed this and put it into production in about 1953, at which time they used varying numbers of lands and grooves depending upon the caliber. In .30 caliber they used about sixteen lands and grooves—that's four times the norm—but I understand they have now reduced the number somewhat. In any event, the theory behind the Marlin system is a little different from that behind conventional rifling.

Marlin figures that a greater number of shallow grooves get a firmer but gentler grip on the bullet. We'll get to the theoretical advantage of that in a moment. First, though, remember your groove diameter must still be .308 inch minimum for a .30-caliber bullet—which means the Marlin system consists of shallower lands, or else it would displace too much metal and that would boost pressures too high. Instead of having a .300-inch bore diameter, Marlin's Micro-Groove system has a bore diameter of about .304 inch. While this is different, it is quite acceptable, and, in fact, the Marlin brand has achieved quite a reputation for accuracy.

A gentler, firmer grip on the bullet tends to distort the bullet less. Imagine, if you will, that the bullet jacket is thicker on one side than the other (which can be the case, because there are tolerances here too). The gentle grip will tend to dig into the jacket more uniformly; the conventional grip will force the bullet toward the jacket side of least resistance.

Now, here's where we begin to get into something. A nonuniform bullet jacket means there's more lead on one side than the other. The lead is heavier than the jacket. Thus the center of gravity doesn't coincide with the center of form.

As this unbalanced bullet is forced through the barrel, its center of gravity is made to rotate around its center of form. There is nothing else the bullet can do, since it is confined by the bore. Upon leaving the muzzle, however, the bullet tends to want to rotate around its center of gravity. This is something we'll spend more time on in the second part of this chapter. For now, accept the fact that it introduces an error because it unbalances the bullet.

With the conventional system, the more pronounced this unbalancing, the more off center the bullet will lie, while with the gentler grip of the multigroove system the less off center the

bullet will tend to lie in the bore. That is the theory behind all the multigroove systems, and while I've never made enough tests to offer convincing proof that it works, I have made some tests, none of them particularly scientific but enough to make me believe that there is something to it.

BEARING AREA

That part of a bullet which is made to full diameter is called the bearing area. It isn't the same with all bullets. Since the bullet is tapered or rounded at the nose, it follows that at some point the bullet is reduced from the full diameter. Indeed, some rifle bullets have been manufactured deliberately with two sections of different dimensions. These are commonly called two-diameter bullets, and usually the rear part of these bullets is made to full groove diameter, while the rest of the bullet is then reduced to bore diameter. The theory is that the section that is groove diameter will fill the grooves, accept the rifling twist, and seal the bore against the propellant gas. The forward section is intended to ride the tops of the lands and therefore provide more stability (and concentricity) without increasing the force necessary to drive the bullet into the lands. It will be obvious that the longer the bearing area, the more force is required to drive the bullet through the barrel.

A parallel can be seen in artillery (an artillery piece is basically a damned big rifle, and many of the same things occur), where the shell (in artillery, the projectile is called a shell) itself is usually made of steel and is made to bore diameter. That is, the basic shell can slide down the barrel, riding on top of the lands. But an artillery shell is made with a big copper band around its middle called a rotating band. It's the function of this band to accept the rifling, giving the shell its spin, and seal the bore.

SEALING THE BORE

Sealing the bore (which is known by a 50-cent word: "obturation") is essential if the gas is to thrust against the bullet. Otherwise gas pressure would be wasted, and, in fact, the gas squeezing past the bullet under intense pressure and white-hot heat will "gas-cut" both barrel and bullet, causing poor accuracy and barrel wear.

We have previously mentioned that most bullets are a bit smaller than groove diameter, and you may well ask if gas isn't lost with each shot you fire. No significant amount is lost. That's because the bullet is hit so hard and fast by the intense blow of the propellant that it swells to fit the barrel. This is called upsetting—the same word that's used in forging when a red-hot piece of steel is whacked by the big drop-forge hammer and "upset" to a larger diameter.

This is why, to offer a common explanation, you can shoot both .22 WMR and .22 Long Rifle cartridges in the same revolver barrel. A .22 WMR has a jacketed bullet measuring .224 inch; the .22 Long Rifle's lead bullet is .222 inch. By using *different cylinders* you can fire either cartridge through the same barrel because the soft-lead .22 Long Rifle bullet will upset to fill the .224 grooves. In fact, many barrels for .22 rifles are made to .224 inch.

Other factors that affect upsetting are thickness and hardness of bullet jacket, whether it's an open-point bullet with base closed or a full-metal-cased bullet with lead exposed at the base. Rest assured that any bullet will upset, some more readily than others. This can be proved by the simple expedient of taking a picture with a high-speed camera at the muzzle; a tiny puff of gas can be seen escaping from the muzzle before the bullet leaves.

The high-speed motion-picture camera has done wonders for gun designers because it can capture things the eye can never see. However, we still have to theorize about what happens inside the barrel—there's no way to *see* what goes on in there.

The late Dr. Mann spent some forty years experimenting off and on to determine how quickly a bullet is upset in the bore. These tests were all made with lead bullets, and the results are interesting. The experiments were made by using different barrel lengths and catching the bullets in oiled sawdust, which recovered them in unmutilated condition. He found that even when using a barrel as short as ¼ inch (which actually left most of the bullet out in the air before firing), the base of the bullet was found to be approximately doubled in size when recovered.

As is normal when experimenting with something new, Dr. Mann soon learned that he was generating more questions than he was answering. He finally concluded, however, that the base of a lead bullet was actually upset *before* the bullet was in motion.

Later, in 1906, Dr. Mann performed the same basic experiment to determine when a jacketed bullet upset, using a .25-caliber Marlin barrel. An unfired bullet had a diameter of .258 inch and, after firing from a barrel only 1.32 inch long, had expanded to a diameter of .430— nearly double. It may be concluded from these tests that jacketed or lead, the bullet is upset to fill the grooves before the bullet is set in motion.

The first action of the powder gas is to expand the brass cartridge case and release the bullet. It is at this point that a bit of gas squirts past the bullet. It is also true that no bullet completely fills the remote corners of the groove bottoms, so there's always a little leakage here.

THE BALANCED BULLET

While it becomes more apparent after the bullet is airborne and hence is of more interest in the second part of this chapter, the balanced bullet is also of importance internally because here is where it gets its thrust.

A bullet can be compared with a gyroscope or a spinning top, because, due to its rotation, that's precisely what it is. Everyone has experimented

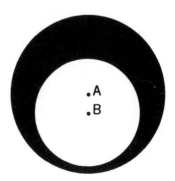

In this diagram of an unbalanced bullet, the shaded area represents the jacket. A is the center of form and B the center of gravity. When these centers do not exactly coincide, the bullet is forced to rotate around its center of form while in the barrel; once airborne, it will tend to revolve around its center of gravity. The result is an inaccurate (and unpredictable) flight.

Typical pistol/revolver bullets: left to right, a lead bullet with copper gas check seated on its base as is typically found in some .357 Magnum loads and others; a metal-penetrating bullet for law-enforcement use; typical metal-pointed bullet for use in autoloading pistols to provide sure feeding; a wadcutter, so called because it cuts clean holes in target paper; and a plain lead bullet. These are the common configurations found in most ammunition. (Photo courtesy Remington Arms)

Common revolver bullets are the wadcutter, left, and the sharp-shoulder type generally referred to as Keith-style. The wadcutter is intended for target shooting, but the flat-nosed shape also provides an excellent "stopper" at short range, though the bullet is not useful at distant targets. The Keith style, named after writer Elmer Keith, is a sort of wadcutter with a nose, and its performance combines some of the excellent characteristics of the wadcutter with greater distance capabilities. It is a very popular, good-performing revolver bullet. Note that both these lead bullets have grooves for lubricant which are known as cannelures, and that the wadcutter has a crimping groove near the top into which the case mouth is squeezed when the bullet is seated.

with toy tops as a youngster. A cheap top will spin for a few seconds, or perhaps a minute or two. What you may not know is that very precisely made tops have been made and spun in laboratories—in which case they are able to spin for hours. The ideal would be a top that would spin for days and, when it finally stopped rotating, would simply stand on its point. That's almost as impossible as perpetual motion, but it would be the ultimate.

Just as a top must be perfectly balanced to spin a long time, so must a bullet be perfectly balanced to fly true. I believe the first person to discover this was Dr. Mann, who performed endless experiments with tops and who then deliberately unbalanced bullets and was able to predict their erratic flight.

When you consider modern bullets, some of which are composed of several parts, everything must be in perfect balance. Consider the Winchester-Western Silvertip, the Remington Core-Lokt, the Nosler Partition, and so on—there are many bullets with more components than a simple jacket and lead core. And it was the modern benchrest shooter who finally learned that consistent jackets and cores (he was the first to suspect trouble with the lead cores) were the secret to better accuracy.

Not only does the unbalanced bullet not fly true, but it sets up its erratic flight characteristics while still in the bore. For accurate rifle shooting, the bullet must be balanced, and it must properly fit the bore it's shot out of.

TWIST

The rate of twist in a barrel must be fast enough to stabilize the bullet that will be used. Twist, which gives the bullet its rotation, is the same thing that makes a forward pass with a football fly true. Insufficient twist and the pass is a blooper; insufficient twist to a bullet and the bullet begins to tip and yaw and finally turn end over end, and the result is not only erratic flight, but also short flight and no accuracy whatever.

We discussed twist to some degree in Chapter Eight as well as various forms of rifling. It is of vital importance that a bullet be given the correct twist for accurate flight characteristics. While precise twist rates are often worked out by scientific means, the old rules of thumb are as good. And if you're in doubt the only way to get a reliable answer is by experimenting.

Generally speaking, the longer a bullet, the faster must be the rate of twist. You can take two bullets of identical weight, one a roundnose and one a spitzer (which will be a bit longer), and one will be stabilized while the longer one will not. There is a school of thought that a bullet should be just stabilized and that it's a sin of sorts to "overstabilize." This is a theory I've never bought. I don't think you can overstabilize any bullet.

IGNITION

Normal ignition takes place in about .0002 second. Smokeless powder is more difficult to ignite than black and requires a stronger primer. The larger the powder charge, the stronger must be the primer to achieve fast ignition. This is why, as we discussed in Chapter Fifteen, there are many variations in modern primers. A powder charge must be ignited not just near the primer; the whole powder charge must be saturated with flame. This should explain why a hotter primer is necessary to ignite the big charge behind a .300 Winchester Magnum as compared with the small charge behind a .38 Special.

The gas builds up what we call chamber pressure, which we can measure with appropriate gauges. It's of interest to note what a "pressure curve" looks like. It shows that the maximum pressure is achieved very rapidly. The graph illustrated here shows clearly why the breech end of a barrel must be the heaviest, and it also shows why cutting a few inches off the muzzle doesn't reduce velocity too much.

Pressure is measured by a complicated means. A hole is drilled into the barrel at the chamber and a small steel plug is inserted. A small disc of known characteristics is placed on top of this plug. Upon firing, the disc is crushed, and the amount of crushing can be measured and computed into a factor. This used to be called "pounds per square inch." The British used "tons" rather than pounds, and they meant the British long ton. However, the figure was not really pounds, or tons, or anything else save a measurement. It could be a comparative measurement—that is, you could compare the figures for a .30/06 vs. a .222, for example. But to say the .30/06 developed 50,000 pounds per square inch of chamber pressure was not necessarily correct.

Now the pressure designation has been changed to a mysterious designation of "cup"—meaning copper units of pressure. Mysterious or not, it's a good deal more descriptive, and more accurate, than the old psi. So far as I know, the British still use tons of pressure, but that's not really of any importance since the figures are relative. You know, for instance, that a tough, strong, modern action can safely be operated at a level of so many psi or cup or whatever you choose to call it. You also know that some of the older actions are not as strong and shouldn't be loaded with ammo developing more than a specified pressure.

While copper discs are used for high-power rifles, lead discs are used for lower-pressure cartridges such as shotgun shells and some handgun cartridges. These are designated "lup" —lead units of pressure. Both cup and lup designations are interchangeable with the old psi term; it's simply a change in nomenclature. A revolver which used to be said to develop 30,000 psi of breech pressure now develops 30,000 lup.

The effect of heat on pressure must not be overlooked. It has been noted by many American riflemen that the English seemingly underload their ammunition, and it is often won-

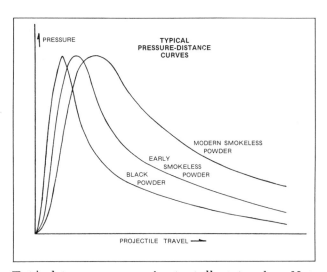

Typical pressure curves for propellant powders. Note that pressure builds rapidly at the breech end and then tails off toward the muzzle. This is why barrels must be larger at the breech end than at the muzzle. Note too that modern smokeless powders build their pressure more slowly (progressively) than earlier powders and that they sustain the delivery of propellant gas at a higher level all the way to the muzzle.

dered why. Similarly, our military ammunition is loaded a bit lighter than a good many people think it can be.

The reason is that heat has a serious effect on pressure, and military ammunition must be capable of operating satisfactorily in any part of the world. British gunmakers customarily serve clients who traditionally hunt in the tropics, where the heat boosts pressures. Many American experimental riflemen have noted that if they're shooting in the hot summer sun in the desert and leave their ammo exposed to the sun, it will generate fearful pressures. The reloader should always bear this in mind, for a handload near maximum that might be perfectly suitable in Quebec in the fall could be hot enough to cause trouble in the desert of Arizona in August.

BARREL TIME AND TOTAL TIME

We have mentioned barrel time, and earlier we mentioned lock time and ignition time. Now we can combine these various times and note that they accumulate and become more significant. They won't mean much to the average shooter, but they are of supreme importance to the target marksman. Let's take a look, and remember that there are big variations in guns, cartridges, barrel lengths, powders used, etc. The time intervals from the moment the trigger releases the sear until the time when the bullet leaves the muzzle look like this:

lock time	.002	to	.0057 second
ignition time	.0002		.0002
barrel time	.0007		.001
total time	.0029		.0069

Pretty fast either way, isn't it? Yet the slowest total time is more than twice as slow as the quickest. Enough to "pull" a 9 from a perfect 10-hold on the target!

CARTRIDGE SHAPE

In the early days of smokeless powder it was the natural thing to try the new powder in existing straight-sided black-powder cartridges. But things didn't work so well, because a lot had to be learned about smokeless (and its ignition), and the shooters of those days did not have the vari-

ety of powders available that we have today. The result was that it was hard to make the powder burn fast enough and hard to develop uniform pressure.

This led to more and more experiments with the bottlenecked case, which tends to hold more powder in a given bore diameter and to turn back part of the developing gases and help churn the remainder into faster burning. There were also many experiments with shoulder angles, though steep shoulder angles were hard to form and caused resistance among manufacturers. But they also feared the added boiler room and its larger capacity.

Aside from a very few exceptions, cartridges used in pistols and revolvers are straight-sided and not bottlenecked. The reason is quite simple: There is not the capacity to handle such high pressures in most handguns as are generated in rifles. The most visible exception to this rule is the Thompson/Center single-shot, which must be regarded as among the strongest handgun actions ever developed. It handles, among others, the .30/30, .25/35, and .22 Hornet standard rifle cartridges, plus such fearsome wildcats as the .30 Herrett. All of these are bottlenecked cases. Another standard bottlenecked case is the .30 Luger, but it's far from a popular one, nor is it very potent.

VELOCITY VS. TWIST

A fast twist is more necessary for longer, heavier bullets than for those of short length and lighter weight. Another factor in this relationship is velocity. For example, a .250/3000 Savage with a twist of 1 turn in 14 inches will not stabilize a 117-grain bullet. But the same barrel, if chambered to the .25/06, would stabilize the 117-grain bullet, because the bullet would be driven faster. The higher the velocity, the higher the rate of spin, and so a faster cartridge can sometimes use a slower twist.

There isn't much you can do about the twist you have. You can determine what that twist is by measuring it yourself, using a close-fitting cleaning rod and measuring the distance it takes for the rod to turn once. This is difficult with a short barrel. Or you can write and ask the manufacturer, giving the model and serial number (sometimes twists are changed without notice). Manufacturers sometimes make mistakes in twist too, and when this comes to light they simply change it without telling the public. When that happens nobody knows about it except a few reloaders who find out the hard way when a long bullet won't stabilize.

LOADING DENSITY

Loading density refers to the amount of powder in a given case. If the case is full of powder, with the bullet seated to touch the powder, the density may be stated as 100 percent. Depending upon the size of the case, its wall thickness (which will be found to vary from one brand to another and among lots of the same brand), the weight of the bullet, and the powder used, the density may vary considerably. Consider, for example, a reloaded cartridge with a reduced load. The loading density might be 50 percent or less.

If the gun is carried muzzle up and then slowly brought into firing position, the powder will lie near the primer. On the other hand, if the gun is carried muzzle down, the reverse would occur and the result in terms of ignition and performance would vary.

Cartridges work more efficiently when the loading density is at or near 100 percent, because the ignition is more uniform. Still, no matter what is done to control uniformity in everything, results will vary.

By this I mean that you can take the same barrel and carefully select your components by weighing them and making every test you can determine so as to make everything absolutely alike. Then fire them and you will get variations in velocity that often amount to as much as 100 fps from shot to shot. Sometimes more. There is no explanation for such happenings that I know of. They occur more with certain cartridges than with others. Nobody knows why.

Nor, as a matter of fact, does the rifle/cartridge combination that shows the most consistent velocity necessarily shoot with the most accuracy. These are among the many things about ballistics that cannot be explained.

Similarly, it will be found that a given barrel will usually show a preference for one kind of powder than another, other things being equal.

Other barrels will digest just about any reasonable load regardless of the powder.

RECOIL, JUMP, AND VIBRATION

When a gun is fired, the propellant gas expands in all directions. It shoves the case walls against the chamber walls. It shoves backward against the case, which, in turn, pushes against the bolt face, and this rearward thrust extends throughout the entire gun until it shoves against your hand. It also pushes against the bullet. And it shoves with the same force in all these directions at once. Naturally the bullet gets out of the barrel quickly, because it's so light by comparison with the bulk of the gun — but it's this same force that creates recoil.

When a handgun is fired, the pressure or resistance on the grip is exerted below the line of recoil, which is a continuation of the axis of the bore. That makes the gun not only move to the rear but pivot on the spot providing that resistance, so the gun tends to move not only backward but upward as well. This tendency is known as jump. Its degree of severity depends on how far below the line of recoil that point lies as well as on the configuration of the grip itself and the caliber.

There is some movement of the gun, any gun, before the projectile leaves the bore. This will vary to some very slight degree among the various cartridges, bullet weights, powder charges, barrel lengths, and so on, but *every* gun moves somewhat before the bullet leaves the muzzle.

If you've ever observed a benchrest shooter in action you will note that he takes extraordinary pains to place his heavy rifle precisely the same each time he shoots. And he holds the rifle exactly the same each time — the same cheek pressure against the stock, the same part of the forearm resting, the same touch of the shooting hand against the stock and trigger guard. Everything the same. That's because the rifle, regardless of the caliber, is going to be in motion as the bullet exits. And if there's something different about the shooter's hold, his touch, or anything, the result will show at the target.

That's true with a very heavy rifle, and it's even more true with a pistol or revolver because the handgun is so much lighter. Other things

The author's hand absorbing the recoil of a .44 Magnum revolver. Note that the web of the hand, behind the hammer, is under considerable force. We took a large number of photos to get this photo and found that the bullet was several feet downrange before the actual recoil showed up in a photo, though the gun does start its movement while the bullet is still in the barrel. The muzzle streaks are grains of powder that were ignited late. Photo was taken at Remington Arms ballistic lab and is used here courtesy of Smith & Wesson.

being equal, the recoil of a handgun is much more violent than that of a shoulder arm.

At one time there used to be arguments about whether or not a gun moved before the bullet was on its way. All such chatter ceased long ago when the high-speed camera went to work and proved the point.

Only a very small part of recoil is actually felt by the shooter before the bullet leaves, and it's really only that part that we are concerned with here in our discussion of interior ballistics. I reproduce here a photo of a .44 Magnum Smith & Wesson revolver in the act of being fired. This photo was taken at the Remington Arms ballistics laboratory in Bridgeport, Conn., and the hand holding the gun is mine. We were trying to show vividly the effect of this big gun's recoil as it crushed the hand. Using a standard 4×5 camera triggered by the report of the gun, we experimented with Polaroid film until we got the desired effect. It took quite a while, and, as a matter of fact, the bullet was about 3 feet downrange when this photo was snapped.

My point is that the recoil, or the part of the recoil, that affects the flight of a bullet isn't felt at all. What you feel happens after the event is all over. Nevertheless, we must acknowledge that the psychological effect of the recoil you know is coming your way has an effect on the accuracy of your shot. Very few men will react to firing a .22 Long Rifle the same way as a .44 Magnum.

The third factor in gun movement before the bullet leaves is vibration. There are two phases to vibration. The first is relatively minor and is caused by the movement of the firing mechanism itself. When the sear releases the firing pin or hammer, parts are set in motion, and no matter how fast they move or how light they are, they set up movement. For instance, when a heavy hammer flies up and hits a firing pin it sets up a vibration.

But this minor vibration is quickly obliterated by the vibration caused by firing. This takes the form of many events, which depend on the type of action, how the gun is constructed, how it is held by the shooter, and so on. The vibration possibilities are virtually infinite. But the most important vibration is the one set up by the barrel itself. As you know, barrels come in varying lengths, dimensions, configurations, and bore diameters. They are chambered for a wide variety of cartridges, developing varying forces. And handgun barrels are fastened to their actions in varying ways.

As the gun tends to rotate around the center of its resistance, the butt, there is also a tendency for the barrel to flip down in a counterreaction. This downflip—which we usually simply call vibration—is partly the result of the upward jump of the gun as a unit, and mostly the result of the vibration of firing, which we're coming to in a moment. Suffice it to say, for an explanation of this brief negative flip, that it resembles what happens when you suddenly move your hand up and back with a fly rod in your hand. The rod tip tends to stay where it is, or to flip down in reaction. The gun barrel does the same thing to a far lesser degree; the degree depends on the configuration of the barrel itself.

Firing a gun is akin to whacking a piece of pipe held in a vise with a big hammer. It shakes and vibrates. The way it shakes and vibrates depends on how it's held, how hard you hit it, the size of the hammer, the wall thickness of the pipe, and many other factors that you can think of as well as I. That's just what happens to a barrel, which should help explain why it must be firmly secured in its receiver, why the breeching must be tight, and why everything must remain the same for shot after shot.

They used to talk about "nodes" of vibration and how it was best if a bullet emerged at a certain point in the node. Some theorized how this could be determined by placing strings loosely over a barrel and whacking the tube with a hammer to see where the strings gathered. Then, with some formula they wouldn't divulge, they'd say this barrel should be 27¹⁵/₁₆ inches long.

It didn't mean a thing. They didn't know what the hell they were talking about, and this node stuff finally went out the window. It had some validity, though, in that, depending on the load used, bullets emerged from the muzzle at different points in the vibration of the barrel. That explains why sometimes you can sight in with one weight of bullet, or one brand of ammunition, then switch to another weight or brand and find your point of impact is off. It may be up, down, or to one side or the other. This simply means the barrel is in a different phase of its movement (or the gun in a different phase of recoil) when this bullet emerges.

Jump and vibration can very seriously affect the shot, as we have seen. The amount they affect that shot depends, in addition to those things already mentioned, on the way the shooter handles his gun. And if you really want

to have a shot go wild, just rest the barrel against a tree or fencepost. It's perfectly OK to rest your *hand* on anything that's handy, or to rest your forearm on your hat atop a rock, stump, or what-have-you. But don't let that barrel touch anything, or you'll upset the vibration and your shot will miss by a country mile.

The rule, then, is to eliminate all the possible factors you can think of that will affect jump and vibration. You must get to the point where you do this automatically without thinking of it. And that means constant practice.

Barrel jump and vibration are far more serious with longer barrels. They are no factor at all with any of the short-barreled pistols or revolvers. But when you get to some of the 10-inch-long tubes on some guns—Thompson/Center, Auto-Mag, and others—then these factors begin to manifest themselves.

BULLET DEFORMATION IN THE BORE

In their work to determine ballistic coefficients for downrange ballistics, the Omark/Speer bullet technicians in Lewiston, Idaho, reasoned that actual firing tests were needed to prove, or disprove, their results. The reason was that too many factors occur *after* firing.

To put that another way, it is unrealistic to simply inspect a bullet visually and calculate your ballistics from that shape. That may or may not be the shape in which the bullet leaves the muzzle. Speer found that there was considerable deformation that took place in the bullet at the moment of firing, while the bullet was still in the bore. Most of this can be attributed to inertia "slump" or "setback." They found, for example, that the base of the bullet began to move before the nose did, tending to make the bullet shorter and more cylindrical. They also found that the exposed lead nose of spitzer bullets flowed backward, part of it into the expanded jacket and part of it merely shorn off.

The leading factors influencing these results are the alloy of the lead core (i.e., its toughness), jacket strength and thickness, pressure of the lands being forced into the bullet (this may be one of the places where the shallow multigroove system like Marlin's Micro-Groove is a big advantage), rifling shape and finish, and the "brisance" of the powder (which means the shattering effect of the propellant powder) or how sudden and sharp is the blow of the gases against the base of the bullet.

These results are most interesting, and I'm sure they opened up avenues for study that had not been considered. It must be admitted that now we have the Speer data, the same thing could have been deduced from Dr. Mann's studies. But it wasn't until the advent of high-speed photography, which plainly shows a spitzer bullet entirely sans point and with a blunter shape than it had before firing emerging from the muzzle of a high-powered rifle that we had proof.

I noted long ago that bullets with battered noses seemed to shoot as well as perfectly formed bullets from the same batch. But it never occurred to me to wonder why. The reason would now seem to be that any high-velocity rifle bullet with a lead-exposed tip is going to make its flight without that tip anyway. On the other hand, it is the base of the bullet that must be perfect for top accuracy. If a bullet's base is a little squeehawed or angled in any way, that bullet is not going to perform along with the rest of the box. This applies to rifles and pistols alike.

MUZZLE BLAST

We all recognize muzzle blast as the nasty, sharp, piercing noise that bellows from a gun's muzzle. And we also know that the more powerful the cartridge and the shorter the barrel, the worse the blast effect. It is for this reason that everyone who shoots should always wear ear protection, except while hunting. The blast is a useless by-product of firing and has no desirable effects whatever. It does not help propel the projectile and it represents wasted power. A bit of this power is utilized in gas-operated guns, but except in a couple of the very earliest gas guns, the gas is bled from a point behind the muzzle, so it has nothing to do with muzzle blast.

Muzzle blast has been utilized by some devices to help reduce recoil and jump. There have always been mixed opinions concerning the actual work performed by these devices. This too I have already commented on earlier in this book and won't repeat it here. You will find muzzle-blast diverters on some artillery barrels, especially tank weapons. These may or may not help reduce recoil, but they do provide a useful service in diverting the gases sideways. Otherwise some of the gas would escape directly down and, given a dusty terrain, would raise such a cloud of dust that the tank crew could not see through it.

Contrary to some beliefs, bleeding a bit of gas to make a gas gun work does not rob the bullet (or shot charge) of enough propelling force to amount to anything at all. It may be stated categorically that a gas gun develops just as much velocity as does any other gun.

EFFICIENCY

The firearm is not a very efficient "engine," but we can draw some conclusions with regard to its efficiency that are proportionate to bore diameter. For instance, a .22-caliber is about 22 percent efficient while a .45-caliber is about 45 percent efficient. In fact, as a rule of thumb the efficiency percentage roughly equals the bore size. I've used .22 and .45 caliber as the approximate limits on either end, .22 caliber being approximately as small as is practical and .45 caliber just about as large as you want to go without having undue recoil.

These figures are empirical and were derived from an examination of many centerfire cartridges. They are by no means meant to be anything more than approximate. Efficiency rises as caliber gets larger because the projectile's base area increases with the square of the caliber.

There are vast, and ballistically complicated, differences between pistols and revolvers. Primarily these result from the differences between the chamber in the pistol's barrel, which resembles that in rifles, and the revolver's cylinder, which contains the chambers or charge holes. A pistol barrel is measured like a rifle barrel, from the face of the closed breechblock to the muzzle. A revolver's barrel length is construed to be from the front of the cylinder (or the rear of the barrel) to the muzzle. Since the cylinder has length, which varies roughly from 1³⁄₁₆ to 1³⁄₄ inches, it really ought to be added to the barrel length to make a valid comparison.

If you wish to put this another way, comparing a 5-inch-barreled pistol and a 5-inch-barreled revolver is like comparing apples and bananas. Add the cylinder length of about 1½ inches and the revolver has a "real barrel length" of 6½ inches. It also has that gap, which steals a little of the push. And it has that ferry-slip funnel at the breech end of the barrel to steer a wayward bullet into the hole.

As we have discussed elsewhere, there are many parts that have some bearing on charge-hole alignment in a revolver, and this is something that must be considered because it has an effect on interior ballistics. The revolver is a very strange breed of firearm, with laws unto itself—and with major differences in concept and construction that make it sometimes very difficult to compare with its close cousin the pistol.

EXTERNAL BALLISTICS

Thus far we have been dealing with internal ballistics. External ballistics deals with the bullet's flight after it leaves the muzzle. The path of this flight is called the trajectory, and it's a parabolic curve—which means that it is a curve but that the curve decreases faster at the latter part of its flight than it ascends at the beginning. You could compare this curve to the throw to home plate by an outfielder—the ball starts out at high speed and moves relatively straight, but the farther it goes the slower it goes and it falls faster and faster. The same thing happens to a golf ball.

No bullet goes in a straight line. That's an impossibility, because there's a thing called gravity that makes its influence felt on the bullet the moment it is out of the bore and thus unsupported. If we want the bullet to go farther we must raise the muzzle, which is accomplished by raising the rear sight, which in effect depresses the butt (or raises the muzzle).

The other major factor that influences the flight of a bullet is air resistance. If you fired a bullet in a vacuum, the maximum velocity achieved would continue until the bullet hit the ground, pulled down to earth by gravity. On the moon, for example, where the force of gravity is also far less than on earth, a bullet would travel an enormous distance. I suppose that distance could be computed, but I don't know what purpose the calculation would serve. I believe one of the moon-walking astronauts whacked a golf ball as a stunt.

There was a time, before the U.S. space program began, when many of these things were hard to understand because the average person knew nothing of speeds in excess of the speed of sound, zero gravity, and the lack of atmosphere. The space talk during the years since this program began has made it easier to understand the flight of a bullet and its problems.

Let's first point out that a bullet is not self-propelled like a rocket or an airplane. The initial thrust that it gets inside the barrel is all the propulsion it will receive. It travels in the earth's atmosphere, which means it must contend with both air resistance and gravity—and these forces are something to consider. From the space program you get an idea of air resistance because you know that a space vehicle can burn up from air resistance even at extremely high altitudes, where the air is very thin, let alone at sea level. And you know that any supersonic aircraft makes a sound wave, or sonic boom. So does any bullet that flies faster than the speed of sound (which means virtually all bullets except a number of slow-moving pistol bullets). Consequently you can't silence any gun except one that shoots a slug moving below the speed of sound—another fact that's constantly ignored by newspaper and other fiction writers. You can silence the muzzle blast and the report of the gun's firing won't be heard. But you cannot silence the flight of the projectile, because it will make the sonic boom—the sharp crack you hear when a bullet goes overhead. Anyone who has ever been in the target pits has heard this crack with every shot fired. (You cannot silence *any* revolver, because of the gas and noise loss from the gap between cylinder and barrel.)

AIR RESISTANCE

You know that air resistance is a very powerful force, for nearly all of us have experienced strong winds. On a still, quiet day you can walk slowly along and give no thought to air resistance at all. But on a windy day it's a totally different matter; given a strong enough breeze you have to lean into the wind, and walking against it becomes very difficult as the wind velocity increases. Those of you who have experienced winds of hurricane force are aware that it can blow houses down and barns away and has even been known to drive a straw into the side of a wooden building. Consider then what happens when you fire a bullet on a still day!

A .22 Long Rifle bullet leaves the muzzle of a rifle at about 1100 fps (which is also roughly the velocity of a shotgun pellet). That velocity can be translated into a wind of 752 miles an hour. Keep in mind that winds of "hurricane force" are those in excess of 75 mph.

A .30-caliber bullet leaves the muzzle at 2700 fps; it strikes a wind force of 1841 miles per hour! That's enough to slow the bullet down to a speed of 1460 fps at 100 yards and only 1068 fps at 1,000 yards. The .357 Magnum with 158-grain semijacketed hollowpoint bullet leaves the muzzle of an 8⅜-inch "conventional" barrel, according to Remington figures, at a speed of 1550 fps. But that speed has been slowed to 1190 fps at 100 yards, due to air resistance.

Bullets travel through the air with varying degrees of efficiency depending on their shape, weight, and diameter. It takes no imagination to know that a wadcutter bullet, which is as flat on the front end as a barn door, is going to meet severe air resistance. On the other hand, a pointed, boat-tailed spitzer bullet will have considerably better ballistics because it will slip through the air better. You can also use the analogy of aircraft-frame design—noting that planes designed for supersonic flight are very streamlined. At this writing the only commercial supersonic airplane on this side of the iron curtain is the needle-nosed Anglo-French Concorde, a very streamlined aircraft indeed.

Another point of comparison is found in the racing sailboat, which has a very sharp bow to slice through the water and a tapered stern to allow the water to return to its previous position easily and without "taildragging." Water and air are two very different things and they present different problems, but the resistance to penetration is fairly similar. If you push a trim, slim sailboat and stop the power, it will glide a long distance in the water. Do the same with a flat-ended barge and it won't go far. Bullets behave the same way.

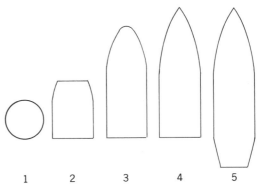

From left to right are shown projectiles with poor-to-excellent flight characteristics. The round ball is the worst possible shape because its air resistance increases in proportion to the square of its velocity. Figure 2 is a typical pistol bullet shape, suitable for short-range shooting. Figure 3 is a blunt-nosed, elongated projectile approximately similar to those used in rifles of the .30/30 class. Figure 4 is the most common shape employed, the flat-based spitzer bullet and Figure 5 is the same basic shape as No. 4, but with a boat tail to reduce tail drag.

The sketch shows five general forms of bullet. From left to right they range from terrible to excellent in their ability to retain velocity. A round ball is next to useless. Bullet number 2, a short, blunt form, is better than a round ball but not suitable for very long range shooting at all. A longer roundnose bullet as represented by bullet number 3 is better—its point is not so blunt and its length is longer. The longer length provides better ballistics, and we use the term "sectional density" to indicate this. Bullets with high sectional density—that is, a long weight-to-length ratio—perform better at longer ranges than bullets with low sectional density. The bullets in this illustration go from low to high sectional density, reading from left to right.

Bullet number 4, with its sharp point, will penetrate the air better than any of the shapes to its left. It represents the most common type of high-powered rifle bullet in use in the world today. But the boat-tailed bullet, number 5, is the best shape of all in terms of velocity retention and long-range performance.

Bullet cores are made of lead, the best metal for the purpose to provide a relatively cheap core material which will produce high sectional density. Any lighter metal would fail to meet that goal. You can readily appreciate this if you throw a golf ball and Ping-Pong ball with as much force as you can. Both balls are roughly similar in size and you know without trying it which will fly the farthest. Similarly, you can look at two bullets of different shape and tell at a glance which bullet will sustain its velocity best.

By taking a bullet's weight, diameter, shape, and material into consideration we can establish an index which ballisticians call a "ballistic coefficient." They define it as the index of a bullet's ability to overcome resistance in flight relative to the performance of a standard projectile used to compute ballistic tables.

Before we leave this subject, we should comment a little further on the round ball—not because it's available in factory ammunition, for it isn't, but because there is so much black-powder shooting today that many round balls are again in use. I said earlier that a round ball was the worst possible shape for a projectile. It merits that rating because you can drive a round ball just so fast; no further increase in velocity is an advantage, because the air resistance increases proportionate to the square of the velocity. In other words, double the velocity and the air resistance is increased four times. Treble the velocity and resistance is boosted to nine times. And so on. Thus there are practical limits to the velocity of any round ball. Though you can increase the actual muzzle velocity, air resistance slows it so fast that its practical increase is lost. This is one reason that most shotgun loads develop an optimum velocity in the vicinity of 1100 to 1200 fps regardless of gauge; any higher speed would be wasted.

GRAVITY

Gravity pulls everything toward the earth as soon as it is unsupported. In the case of a projectile, the gun barrel supports it, but the moment a bullet leaves the muzzle it begins to drop, and it continues to drop at an accelerating rate. It should be noted that the bullet drops from the line which is a continuation of the axis of the bore. (In the case of a long-range shot, when the barrel is elevated slightly, the bullet will rise. But it will fall from the continuation of that line—

and that's what we're talking about.) That line, by the way, is called the angle of departure or line of departure.

If you were to hold a pistol or rifle perfectly level and fire it, and at the same precise moment were to drop a bullet of the same size and weight from the same height, both bullets would strike the ground (assuming a level surface such as water) at the same instant. The reason is that the pull of gravity is the same; even though one bullet has forward momentum, that will not affect the pull of gravity at all, other things being the same.

When any body falls from the pull of gravity, its velocity accelerates at a constant rate until air resistance finally prevents it from falling any faster. These are things you probably learned in a physics class, and they apply to all falling objects. In the first second of a bullet's flight it will drop 16.1 feet below the line of departure. To cite one simple example with a 150-grain bullet from the .30/06 at a muzzle velocity of 2700 fps, its time of flight for the first 100 yards is .116 second, and in that length of time the bullet will drop 2.4 inches. This means that if we aimed the rifle so the bore axis were exactly in line with the target at 100 yards and we fired the rifle, the bullet would hit 2.4 inches below that line.

OTHER FACTORS THAT AFFECT TRAJECTORY

Gravity and air resistance are the two major factors affecting the flight of a bullet, but they are by no means the only things, as we're about to find out. But before we go any further, let's digress and discuss a few basics about the flight of a projectile.

Our interest lies primarily along two lines: the actual line of sight (which can be defined as the straight line from sight to target), and the flight path of the bullet. The bullet does not travel in a straight line, as we have already determined; its path is the other line we are interested in, and our concern is to make the bullet pass through the line of sight at the target. This is called sighting in, or zeroing in, and is accomplished by moving the barrel's muzzle up or down (by moving the sight the opposite way) until the path of the bullet exactly coincides with the line of sight at the range for which we wish to sight in.

Ballistics tables must of necessity be accepted as a guide. They are quite accurate, since the ballisticians have gone to great lengths to compute (and I mean the word "compute" literally, because they have fed into computers all the necessary data) the trajectory of an ideal bullet of the particular shape under discussion. These calculations take into effect the velocity, gravity, rate of rotation, barometric pressure, temperature, humidity, altitude, and size and shape of the bullet. Firing tests determined the drag characteristics, which are defined as the rate at which a bullet decelerates. The drag function usually employed is either that determined by Col. Ingalls, or a set of figures that is compatible with a mathematical model built by Mayevski and used in Krupp test firings in 1881 for a projectile with the same approximate shape as a modern bullet. Tests have indicated that Mayevski's findings (as used by Hornady in his reloading handbook) are compatible with Ingalls' as used by the late Gen. Hatcher in his ballistics work. Indeed, most ballisticians have apparently used Ingalls' tables. The reason one or the other of these standards is used is that otherwise empirical findings would have to be learned for each and every bullet shape, and the job would hardly be worth the tremendous time expended. By plugging in one of the standards the computer can tell us, in a matter of moments, all we need to know. Indeed, the figures will be more precise than the real result! Let's take a look at some of the other things that can affect the bullet's flight—which can make all calculations more or less useless.

DRIFT

Another word sometimes used is "crawl," and I like that word better, for it means the very slight sideways or crablike movement of a bullet caused by its rotational speed. To explain this I think it is simplest to build a picture in your mind of spinning a cylindrical object, say a baseball bat, and then carefully dropping it in still water. As soon as the splash subsides and as long as the bat is still rotating, it will begin to crawl sideways in the direction in which it is turning.

While the effect is much, much less, a rifle bullet does the same thing in flight. Assuming a right-hand twist of rifling, thus a right-hand rotation, the bullet will crawl slightly to the right. This isn't a big deal; a 150-grain .30/06 drifts just 13 inches to the right at a range of 1,000 yards.

YAW, TIP, AND AIR SPIRAL

While there is no such thing as a perfect bullet, today's bullets are remarkably close to that ideal —a good deal closer than they were before World War II, for example.

A little while ago we talked about the unbalanced bullet and said that every bullet is unbalanced to some degree, simply because we can't make things absolutely perfect. For our example here we will exaggerate the errors for the sake of clarity. Bullet imbalance occurs when a gilding-metal jacket is thicker on one side than the other, meaning that there will be more lead on the thin side. That means, in turn, that the bullet's center of gravity will not coincide with its center of form. As this bullet goes down the barrel it is made to rotate around its center of form, simply because the barrel holds it there. Meantime, the center of gravity is also rotating around the center of form.

But once the bullet leaves the barrel, it tends to rotate around the center of gravity. A greatly exaggerated example is seen if you tie a stone to a string, rapidly revolve it around, and then let go. The stone will fly off in a tangent to the circle in which it was held by the string. The bullet does the same thing, except that it is not nearly so noticeable. Eventually, the bullet will be rotating around its center of gravity rather than its center of form, but its flight will be unpredictable. It will not print on the same place at the target as will a more nearly perfect bullet.

Dr. Mann proved this long, long ago, deliberately unbalancing bullets by drilling holes in their bases and then placing them in the chamber so they would emerge from the muzzle with the light side up. By such placement, he could predict the flight. But you can't do that because you don't know in what ways the bullet is unbalanced.

166 AMERICAN PISTOL AND REVOLVER DESIGN AND PERFORMANCE

The error just described is called the "center-of-gravity spiral," because the bullet flies in the tangent described, which is a spiral whose diameter is very small and whose pitch is the same as the pitch of rifling.

Dr. Mann called this the X error, and he spent a long time solving and explaining it. He then found another error (which he dubbed the Y error) and discovered that it was due to a tipping bullet. A tipping bullet may be said to wobble as it passes through the air and does not fly truly point-on. Such a bullet is also an imperfect one, though it may not necessarily be unbalanced. Like the unbalanced bullet, though, it will have an error which is due to air resistance to the tipping, or yawing, of the bullet.

The extent of this error is dependent upon the shape of the bullet, the amount of tipping, the speed, and the number of gyrations per second. Interestingly, sometimes these two errors can cancel each other and the shot will print dead center.

A tipping bullet can occur from a number of sources. There can be damage to the muzzle of the rifle, a bullet's base may have been deformed, it may not have been seated concentrically in the cartridge case, or it may have become a bit bent in the case by rough handling.

However, and fortunately, we have at last learned how to make bullets that are close to perfection. Even though there are still more worlds to conquer in ballistics, bullets are no longer the problem they once were.

ALTITUDE AND TEMPERATURE
Any rise in temperature will increase velocity, since it increases pressure, as we discussed a few pages back. If you're shooting in the desert in hot weather it will pay you to sight in again under those conditions. Similarly, the higher the elevation the less air resistance.

The main lesson to be learned from this is that you must make the proper allowances, check your sighting, and be aware of the changes that can take place. Some of the extremes really can make a vast difference. For example, if you were to work up a load in the hot desert of the Southwest during summertime and then used the

same load in the Arctic during winter, the difference would be very noticeable.

UP-AND-DOWN SHOOTING
It's an old rule of thumb that one tends to shoot too high when shooting at sharp angles either up or down. And it's a fact. The reason is very simple, when you think about it, and it only applies to extremes—and only at distances of 200 yards or more; at shorter ranges the effect is minimal.

For example, if you are shooting at an angle of 45° (either up or down; it makes no difference), you're forming an equilateral right triangle. In this triangle the actual distance from you to the target may be 150 yards—but the level distance is only 100 yards. And it's over the level distance that the force of gravity applies. If you hold for a 150-yard shot, your bullet will be high (not so high as to cause a miss at that short distance, but you can easily see that a 300-yard shot would simply be a miss).

To carry this example to an extreme, you might be shooting almost vertically downward. In this case your range would be virtually zero and if you held for the exact distance you'd shoot far over the target.

WIND DEFLECTION
The wind has a decided effect on the flight of any bullet. You might assume that a fat, heavy slug like the .45/70 rifle bullet weighing 405 grains would be pretty hard for the wind to move. That heavy weight really ought to fly a straight path. Yet a relatively mild breeze of only 15 mph will move that bullet exactly 2 inches off course at 300 yards. And a milder puff of only 10 mph will blow the .22 Long Rifle bullet 3.29 inches at 100 yards. So the wind is a big factor.

Despite what might seem logical, a sharp-pointed bullet at good velocity will be less affected by the wind than a short, fat one. The reason is simply that the latter bullet has more time for the wind to push against it. The fatter bullet also provides more air resistance, and one theory claims the wind not only affects the bullet but also the wall of massed air surrounding the bullet that's been built up by air resistance.

It must be acknowledged that the foregoing ballistics factors are all of much more importance to the rifleman than to any pistol or revolver shooter. Yet the same rules apply, and you should know them. Any handgunner who scopes his gun and expects to make hits at long range must understand them.

VELOCITY AND ENERGY

The speed of bullets is measured by very accurate instruments called chronographs. In use, the bullet breaks two screens set at a predetermined distance from one another. Passing through the first screen starts an electrical circuit; passing the second one stops it. The time is recorded in milliseconds, and these are translated into feet per second. The usual rule is to fire a minimum of ten shots and average the results, because there will always be a variation between shots.

Energy is a unit of work, and it is expressed in foot-pounds. One foot-pound is the energy required to lift 1 pound a distance of 1 foot. You can compute energy by squaring the velocity, multiplying that by the bullet's weight in grains, and dividing the result by 450,250. It's a lot easier to read it out of a catalog, since the ammo makers have done all the work for you. However —and this is very important—remember well the preceding chapter in which we disussed the ability of certain bullets to *transmit* their energy to the target.

SECTIONAL DENSITY AND BALLISTIC COEFFICIENT

These are terms employed by the ballistician, and aside from a brief definition, we aren't going to spend much time with them here. Sectional density is the relationship of a bullet's weight to its diameter. Bullets with higher sectional density, which means very long in relation to their diameter, hold their velocity better than short, blunt bullets with low sectional density.

The ballistic coefficient is a figure used to determine ballistics by computer. Expressed mathematically, it is the ratio of a bullet's weight to the product of the square of its diameter and its form factor.

A typical example of bullets with different velocity retention is to compare the 110-grain .30/06 bullet with the 180-grain .30/06 bullet. The 110-grain slug leaves the muzzle at the flashy speed of 3420 fps, but at 300 yards it has slowed down to 1970 fps. On the other hand, the 180-grain slug leaves the muzzle at a less sensational speed of 2700 fps, but at 300 yards it's still moving smartly at 2190 fps—220 fps faster than the 110-grain slug. Assuming both were fired at the same identical moment, at somewhere between 300 and 500 yards the 180-grain bullet would overtake and pass the 110-grain bullet.

There are countless other examples, but the moral is that you should study ballistics beyond the first column in the lists. Pick a load that is delivering energy, with a bullet that's capable of transmitting that energy.

CHAPTER EIGHTEEN

BARREL LENGTH AND VELOCITY

For some strange reason it is exceedingly hard to determine precise velocities of handgun cartridges. For example, the Winchester catalog states that "test barrels are used to determine ballistic figures. Individual firearms may differ from these test barrel statistics." I'll say they may differ. In the first place, while Winchester tells us what barrel length they use, you can bet the speed out of your gun with different barrel length will be a lot different from the speed of the same cartridge out of this test barrel.

Remington, in its 1977 catalog, has begun to indicate that there are discrepancies, because it lists velocities with both a "solid" and a "vented" barrel—4 inches long in .38 Special, .357, .41, and .44 Magnum barrels. This is to allow for the gap between a revolver cylinder and barrel. At the very least this is a big step forward and should be much appreciated by the American gunner. Even so, there is a lot more to be learned and made available. One can only hope the big companies will begin to determine figures and share them with us.

Barrel length is one factor affecting velocity. Another factor is that velocity is lost in a revolver because of the gap between barrel and cylinder. There is some loss of velocity simply because some of the power has been sapped. But how much? And how does it vary with the differences in the gap? It will be apparent that each revolver made has its own gap clearance.

Some of this information exists but is hard to find. Most of the major manufacturers have not been able to shed much light on the subject. Still, by ferreting out what does exist, one can come up with some interesting answers to the big question: What's my actual velocity out of a handgun with 2-inch (or 4-inch or 6-inch) barrel? You'll still have to do some figuring in most cases, but this will help guide you.

The information appearing in this chapter has been gleaned from such sources as Remington Arms Company, Browning, the late General Julian Hatcher in *The American Rifleman*, the H. P. White Co. and, most important, *Gun Digest*. These sources are hereby acknowledged.

It will be evident that the prospective handgun buyer will be interested in knowing the velocity loss in a .22 pistol if he chooses a 4-inch instead of a 6-inch barrel, or if he chooses a 4-inch revolver instead of a 6-inch pistol. (You must also keep in mind that pistol and revolver barrels are measured differently. A pistol barrel, like every other gun except a revolver, includes the chamber. But a revolver barrel is measured from in front of the cylinder, so, to be consistent, it would be logical to add the length of the cylinder, although it's never done.)

REVOLVER GAS LOSS

The velocity loss in any revolver depends on the gas pressure, the gap, and the bore diameter. Only the Dan Wesson revolver can control this gap which it does because of its unique barrel-fastening system.

Another thing you will notice about revolvers if you measure these gaps is that they vary from one side to the other. For example, measure the gap with a standard feeler gauge and you'll get a gap of, say .005 inch. Then rotate the cylinder halfway and recheck. You may get less or you may get more, but you'll rarely get the same. That's because it is extremely difficult to hold such close tolerances in manufacture.

Just for the exercise I measured a number of revolvers. Their gaps are shown below—maximum gap, that is. In some cases they were tighter halfway around.

As you can see, there is a wide range of gaps here, and these are all high-quality guns just picked out of the case at random. There also is some fore-and-aft play in any revolver's cylinder, which can vary from almost zero to as much

MAXIMUM GAP (INCHES)

Ruger Security Six, .357	.004
Colt Single Action Army, .45 Colt	.005
S&W Model 29, .44 Magnum	.006
Colt Python, .357	.007
Colt Single Action Army, .357	.004
S&W Model 66, .357	.007
Ruger Blackhawk, early model, .44	.004
Ruger Bearcat .22	.0015
Colt Official Police .22*	.0015
S&W Model 58 .41 Magnum	.005
S&W Model 57 .41 Magnum	.007

* This is a very old model, made during the early 1930s or possibly earlier. Note that it, and the Ruger Bearcat (now discontinued), had the tightest gap of the whole group. I have not included the Dan Wesson because that gun can be adjusted. The sample Wesson gun I have can be set at .002 inch even though the gauge that comes with the gun is .006 inch.

as .008 inch or more. This play results in an interesting situation because it can be an advantage (to velocity) when play exists because the firing-pin blow drives the cylinder forward closer to the barrel. The part called the hand, which pushes up and forward to rotate the cylinder, also exerts some force on the cylinder.

Some experimenters have found that a fore-and-aft play of .008 inch or more tended to produce another exciting phenomenon: The cylinder would back up violently in firing—enough to drive the hammer back to full-cock position! And if the trigger remains depressed the gun will fire again. (That can occur only with guns where the hand is pinned to the hammer, not with those with hand pinned to the trigger.) So, for example, if you're firing a single-action gun and the cylinder is free to move back and forth .008 inch or more, it's possible to have a fully automatic gun.

It will be obvious that some gap must exist between cylinder and barrel in order for the cylinder to rotate. Moreover, clearance is necessary to allow for residue, gunk, and other foreign matter to build up without preventing cylinder rotation. In normal manufacture this gap seems to run around .005 inch, although the extremes run from about .0015 inch to .007 inch. Manufacturers obviously would like to leave as much gap as possible for ease in production but still hold the minimum as best they possibly can for optimum performance.

What do you lose by this gap? And what do you gain when the gap is nice and snug rather

VELOCITY AND ENERGY GUIDE FOR VARIOUS BULLETS

CALIBER	BULLET	MUZZLE VELOCITY FEET PER SECOND	ENERGY (MUZZLE) FOOT POUNDS	BARREL LENGTH
.357 Mag. Vent. BBL.	125 Semi-Jacketed H.P.	1450	583	4″
	158 Semi-Jacketed H.P.	1235	535	4″
	158 Soft Point	1235	535	4″
	158 Metal Point	1235	535	4″
	158 Lead	1235	535	4″
.357 Mag. Conventional	125 Semi-Jacketed H.P.	1675	780	8⅜″
	158 Semi-Jacketed H.P.	1550	845	8⅜″
	158 Soft Point	1550	845	8⅜″
	158 Metal Point	1410	695	8⅜″
	158 Lead	1410	695	8⅜″
.38 Special Vent. BBL.	95 Semi-Jacketed H.P. (+P)	1175	291	4″
	125 Semi-Jacketed H.P. (+P)	945	248	4″
	148 Targetmaster, Lead W.C.	710	166	4″
	158 Targetmaster, Lead	755	200	4″
	158 Lead	755	200	4″
	158 Semi-Wadcutter	755	200	4″
	158 Metal Point	755	200	4″
	158 Lead (+P)	915	294	4″
	200 Lead	635	179	4″
.38 Special Conventional	95 Semi-Jacketed H.P. (+P)	985	205	2″
	125 Semi-Jacketed H.P. (+P)	1210	405	6″
	148 Targetmaster, Lead W.C.	770	195	6″
	158 Targetmaster, Lead	855	255	6″
	158 Lead	855	255	6″
	158 Semi-Wadcutter	855	255	6″
	158 Metal Point	855	255	6″
	158 Lead (+P)	1090	415	6″
	200 Lead	730	235	6″
.41 Mag. Vent. BBL.	210 Soft Point	1300	773	4″
	210 Lead	965	434	4″
.41 Mag. Conventional	210 Soft Point	1500	1050	8⅜″
	210 Lead	1050	515	8⅜″
.44 Rem. Mag. Vent. BBL.	240 Lead	1350	971	4″
	240 Soft Point	1180	741	4″
	240 Semi-Jacketed H.P.	1180	741	4″
.44 Rem. Mag. Conventional	240 Lead	1470	1150	6½″
	240 Soft Point	1470	1150	6½″
	240 Semi-Jacketed H.P.	1470	1150	6½″
	240 Lead (Med. Vel.)	1000	533	6½″

NOTE: The .41 Magnum with soft point bullet loses less velocity than the .44 when going from solid to vented barrel. For example, the .41 loses only 200 fps when dropping from an 8⅜ inch conventional barrel to 4 inch vented. The .44 loses 290 fps when going from 6½ inch conventional to 4 inch vented. This would seem to indicate more consistency for the .41, but no reasons are given for the phenomenon. Given these circumstances it would be logical to expect the .41 to have a greater velocity loss than the .44.

than sloppy? There is some information available, and probably the most reliable and up-to-date is that supplied by Remington in its 1977 catalog. The controls established in these tests are as follows. The cartridge case was laid horizontally to assure the powder was evenly distributed. The cylinder gap was controlled at exactly .008 inch and the barrel length was a constant 4 inches long.

Despite the fact that Remington has given us

this vented-barrel information in its catalog, it's not of much value because none of the conventional barrels listed are of the same 4-inch length! It's a comparison of apples and oranges and is included for its interest rather than its value.

In independent tests it has been noted that the greatest velocity loss occurs during the first .001 inch and then steadily drops from that point to a maximum. The following figures are based on a special test gun with carefully controlled cases: Caliber .38 Special with handloaded 127-grain bullet.

GAP (inches)	MUZZLE VELOCITY (fps)
.000	985
.001	965
.002	955
.004	935
.006	920
.008	905
.010	890
.012	865
.015	835
.020	795

This is not really so much of a loss as you might imagine. A gap of .015 inch is 1/64 inch, quite a lot. If you accept the fact that a gap of about .006 inch is as close to standard as you can get, you note that less than 10 percent velocity loss is realized from .006 to .015 inch. You will get a bigger loss with higher-velocity cartridges, as might be expected.

It also must be brought out that the above figures indicate clearly that these variations are *within the normal velocity fluctuations of ammunition.* In other words, a given load will produce velocities that vary more than a reasonable variation in cylinder gap. You have to take at least ten shots and average them to provide meaningful data.

Since there are many other factors that influence velocity, such as the ammunition itself, the dimension and condition of the bore, the alignment of cylinder and barrel, and so on, there is evidence to suggest that you might as well forget about the velocity loss due to the gap between cylinder and barrel. In any well-made revolver

this gap will be small enough not to cause any meaningful loss of speed.

One more interesting experiment may be found interesting: an independent research lab some years ago made a test with the .22 Long Rifle cartridge—with a 1/4-inch hole (precisely .250 inch) drilled exactly 1 inch forward of the breech end of the barrel, just ahead of the bullet. You would think such a hole (which is larger than the .22-caliber bore) would drain all the propellant gas. The results:

BARREL LENGTH	AVERAGE VELOCITY
20-inch solid barrel	1027 fps
10-inch solid barrel	1065 fps
4-inch solid barrel	931 fps
2½-inch solid barrel	900 fps
20-inch as above with hole	612 fps

The test, as far as I know, was never repeated and is noted for its interest. The point is that a bullet gets its start damned quick. Note too from the above that the maximum-length barrel listed shows less velocity than the 10-inch, further evidence that a .22 Long Rifle cartridge develops its maximum velocity at about 14 to 16 inches of barrel length.

WHAT PRICE DO YOU PAY FOR SHORT BARRELS?

Aside from such oddities as the Buntline models, the longest conventional revolver barrel is Smith & Wesson's 8⅜-inch, which is furnished in Magnum calibers. Thompson/Center offers a 10-inch model, but most conventional pistol and revolver barrels run from 2 inches to 6 or 7½ inches maximum. Upon what criteria should you base a buying decision? What will you sacrifice in terms of velocity and performance if you go the shorter barrel route?

The most important real advantage to any longer barrel is the increased sighting radius, which permits closer holding, but that is not the subject of this chapter. The actual choice you will make should depend primarily on the uses to which you will put the gun. By this I mean that if you want a light, compact revolver to be carried unobtrusively, then go ahead and choose the 2-inch barrel. Such a gun will be used only at ranges so short that a reasonable loss in velocity can be accepted.

If, on the other hand, your intended use is hunting or target shooting, then a totally different set of criteria come into play. For a gun that's to be carried on the hip on a fishing or camping trip or as a sidearm on a hunting trip, the barrel can be either 4-inch or 6-inch, your choice. As you will see, there will be a velocity difference but not so much as you might believe.

It has been hard to come by reliable figures for the varying barrel lengths, but there is now sufficient data on hand to make a reasonably good guess, bearing in mind that individual guns will vary and that ammunition varies no matter how carefully it's loaded.

The following figures are from Winchester-Western for the .22 WMR with 40-grain jacketed bullet. These are old figures, and I do not know if they were taken in a revolver barrel with its cylinder-to-barrel gap, though I doubt it. The last figure *is* for a revolver barrel, and note that there is no significant loss that can be attributed to the gap.

CALIBER .22 WINCHESTER
MAGNUM RIMFIRE
Barrel Length vs. Velocity

BARREL LENGTH (inches)	VELOCITY (ft./sec.)
24	2000
22	2000
20	1990
18	1970
16	1940
14	1900
12	1850
10	1780
8	1690
6	1560
4	1350
6½-inch revolver barrel (7.9-inch breech face to muzzle)	1550

Remington has furnished an interesting comparison of velocity and barrel length for the .357 Magnum and .38 Special cartridges:

EFFECT OF BARREL CUTDOWN ON
MUZZLE VELOCITIES

BARREL LENGTH (inches)	.357 MAG. 158 gr.	.38 SPECIAL 148 gr. WC	158 gr.
8⅜	1410		
6½	1370		
6	1340	770	855
5	1280	765	850
4	1220	755	840
3½	1180	745	825
3	1140	735	810
2	1050	700	775

Other tests have been made from time to time, and some of them have been written up in *The American Rifleman* over the years. In most of these cases, standard revolvers were purchased and the tests were conducted by sawing the barrels shorter, an inch at a time. These tests were generally conducted by a reliable independent research lab with proper equipment.

Written up by the late Gen. Hatcher, the tests were made with Colt and Smith & Wesson revolvers chambered for the .357 Magnum cartridge. Tested were both the .357 and .38 Special cartridges. The results were so closely parallel to those from Remington listed above that they do not need repeating here. The only discrepancy of any significance is that the Remington figures are slightly higher for the .357 in 8⅜-inch and 6½-inch barrels. And the difference is only 80 fps faster in both instances, which would be within normal variations from shot to shot even under laboratory conditions.

It will be noted that, in .357 Magnum, the difference between a 6-inch and the longer 8⅜-inch barrel is pretty negligible. There is no reason under the sun to choose the longer barrel that I think makes any sense. It has long been a mystery to me why Smith & Wesson settled on that odd barrel length of 8⅜ inches; the first model was 8¾ inches. It may as well have been an even 8 inches, and even then I doubt whether anyone could tell the difference in either appearance or performance.

Now look at the .38 Special. Note that when you drop from a 6-inch barrel to a 2-incher you lose less than 100 fps of velocity! Think that will mean anything at the usual ranges at which a 2-inch barrel gun is used? And Hatcher's figures exactly conform with Remington's.

While there is no data available on the subject, it will follow that certain special-purpose guns such as the Thompson/Center in rifle calibers such as the .22 Hornet, .25/35, and so forth, as well as the .221 Remington Fire Ball, will do much better with the longer barrels. This is because, being rifle cartridges, they are loaded with powder designed to achieve its maximum thrust in a longer barrel. A straight-sided pistol cartridge like the .38 or .357 uses a faster powder and gets rid of the bullet quicker at higher initial speed.

Smith & Wesson's Model 29 revolver in .44 Magnum is offered with 4-inch, 6½-inch, and 8⅜-inch barrels. Which barrel length should you buy? Some years ago a test was made and reported in *The American Rifleman* which showed some interesting numbers:

BARREL LENGTH (inches)	VELOCITY (ft./sec.)*
8⅜	1500
6½	1430
4	1350

* I have averaged the reported figures from two brands of ammunition.

As with the .357, you don't lose enough from 8⅜ to 6½ inches to even think about. And if the shorter, handier 4-inch tube is a strong consideration, you need not worry too much about losing performance either. These figures were taken from a revolver, by cutting off the barrel of the same gun, so they are quite reliable.

What about downrange performance? After all, a lot of handguns are being used for hunting today, so how do these slugs stack up when they get out to, say, 100 yards? Remington worked out some calculated downrange ballistics for the .41 Magnum some years back which is still valid. Computed for both 6-inch and 8¾-inch barrels, here's what the figures look like:

.41 MAGNUM DOWNRANGE BALLISTICS (CALCULATED)

RANGE (yards)	VELOCITY (fps)	ENERGY (ft./lbs.)	DROP (inches)
6-inch-barrel revolver			
210-grain softpoint bullet			
0	1350	850	—
50	1220	695	2.8
100	1130	595	10.7
210-grain lead bullet			
0	990	455	—
50	935	410	4.4
100	885	365	18.4
8¾-inch-barrel revolver			
210-grain softpoint			
0	1500	1049	—
50	1350	850	2.0
100	1220	694	9.3
210-grain lead bullet			
0	1050	515	—
50	985	450	4.1
100	930	405	17.0

This gun, in S&W brand, is now made with 8⅜-, 6-, and 4-inch barrels, so the 8¾-inch used in determining these figures will be off by an amount not much thicker than the paper this is written on. If these numbers provide any real justification to go to the longer barrel, it escapes my comprehension. I am not a handgun hunter, though I have one of the first Model 57 Smith & Wesson revolvers in .41 Magnum with 6-inch barrel. This gun has been mounted with a Bushnell scope and I've done some pretty great target shooting with it at long distances.

I have, for instance, fired groups as small as 3 inches at 100 yards (using all six charge holes) from benchrest. I also have done some nifty plinking deep in the bush, popping stumps sticking out of the water at distances around 500 or 600 yards. This doesn't mean the .41 is meant to be used beyond a maximum of 100 yards, because I don't think it should be. But these Magnum guns will blister a bullet out in good shape, and if you can hold your gun and judge your distance you can do a whole lot better than is generally thought.

One of the most comprehensive treatments of this matter of handgun barrel length vs. velocity was provided in the 1969 issue of *Gun Digest*. The figures are calculated, not measured, but they agree closely enough with the measured figures we have available to be a reasonable guide.

Reprinted by permission of the Gun Digest Company:

SPERBECK'S TABLE OF COMPARATIVE BALLISTICS—PISTOL AND REVOLVER CARTRIDGES (Revised 2nd Edition)

This table provides up-to-date ballistics for popular American cartridges adapted to revolvers and automatic pistols, when used in arms with barrels of different lengths. New cartridges have been added.

The velocity figures in this table have been obtained by the application of two ballistic principles.

The first principle can be stated as follows: Any change in barrel length affects the velocity of a rifled arm. In rifles, the velocity varies approximately 25 foot-seconds per inch above and below standard length. As rifle cartridges produce higher velocities than pistol and revolver cartridges, this reduced velocity in shorter-barreled rifles is not important. In pistols and revolvers, a change in barrel length affects the velocity to a much greater extent. While the rate of variation depends upon a number of uncertain factors, it is estimated that the average variation is 2 to 3 times greater than is the case with rifles. In pistols and revolvers with barrels of different lengths, the variation in velocity is an important consideration.

The second ballistic principle is this: As barrel length in pistols and revolvers decreases, the rate of loss in velocity increases.

The standard formula was employed to determine the energy figures, in relation to bullet weight and velocity.

These ballistics are relative values, and not absolute values: thus they are intended mainly for the purpose of showing the approximate differences between the various barrel lengths. No attempt has ever been made to arrive at absolute values in a comprehensive work of this kind.

This table does not include all of the barrel lengths which have been manufactured. The lengths listed herein represent a balanced assortment which the author considers the most important.

NOTE: An asterisk (*) indicates barrel lengths for which average velocities have been determined by loading companies; these barrel lengths and velocities are the basis of this table.

CARTRIDGE	BULLET WEIGHT Grains	BARREL LENGTH Inches	MUZZLE VELOCITY Ft. Secs.	MUZZLE ENERGY Ft. Lbs.
22 Long Rifle Standard Velocity	40	2	700	44
	40	2½	740	48
	40	3¼	800	57
	40	4	850	64
	40	4½	880	69
	40	*6	950	80
	40	*6	970	83
25 Automatic 6.35mm	50	*2	810	73
	50	2½	860	82

CARTRIDGE	BULLET WEIGHT Grains	BARREL LENGTH Inches	MUZZLE VELOCITY Ft. Secs.	MUZZLE ENERGY Ft. Lbs.
30 Luger 7.65mm Parabellum	93	3⅝	1135	266
	93	*4½	1220	307
32 Automatic 7.65mm	71	3¼	915	132
	71	3½	930	136
	71	3¾	945	141
	71	*4	960	145
32 Smith & Wesson S&W Short	85	2½	645	79
	85	*3	680	87
	85	3½	715	97
	85	4	745	105
	85	4½	775	113
	85	5	805	122
	85	6	860	140
	88	2½	645	81
	88	*3	680	90
	88	3½	715	100
	88	4	745	108
	88	4½	775	117
	88	5	805	127
	88	6	860	145
32 S&W Long	98	2	560	64
	98	2½	600	78
	98	3¼	650	92
	98	3½	675	99
	98	*4	705	108
	98	4¼	725	114
	98	4½	740	119
	98	5	775	131
	98	6	830	150
32 Colt New Police Police Positive	98	2	535	62
	98	2½	575	72
	98	3¼	625	85
	98	*4	680	100
	98	4½	715	111
	98	5	750	122
	98	6	805	141
	100	2	535	64
	100	2½	575	73
	100	3¼	625	87
	100	*4	680	103
	100	4½	715	114
	100	5	750	125
	100	6	805	144
32-20 Winchester Standard Velocity	100	4	905	182
	100	5	970	209
	100	*6	1030	235
357 Magnum Lead Bullet	158	3½	1065	398
	158	4	1115	436
	158	5	1190	497
	158	6	1260	557
	158	*8⅜	1410	697
357 Magnum Soft Point Bullet	158	3½	1200	505
	158	4	1250	548
	158	5	1325	616
	158	6	1395	682
	158	*8⅜	1550	843

SPERBECK'S TABLE OF COMPARATIVE BALLISTICS—PISTOL AND REVOLVER CARTRIDGES (Revised 2nd Edition) (Cont'd)

CARTRIDGE	BULLET WEIGHT Grains	BARREL LENGTH Inches	MUZZLE VELOCITY Ft. Secs.	MUZZLE ENERGY Ft. Lbs.
9mm Luger	115	*4	1140	332
	115	4½	1185	359
	124	*4	1120	345
	124	4½	1160	371
38 Short Colt	125	4	625	108
	125	5	680	128
	125	*6	730	148
	130	4	625	113
	130	5	680	134
	130	*6	730	154
38 Long Colt	150	4	625	130
	150	5	680	154
	150	*6	730	178
38 Smith & Wesson	145	2	550	97
	145	2½	585	110
	145	3¼	640	132
	145	*4	685	151
	145	4½	715	165
	145	5	740	176
	145	6	785	198
	146	2	550	98
	146	2½	585	111
	146	3¼	640	133
	146	*4	685	152
	146	4½	715	166
	146	5	740	178
	146	6	785	200
38 Colt New Police Police Positive	150	2	545	99
	150	2½	580	112
	150	3¼	635	134
	150	*4	680	154
	150	4½	710	168
	150	5	735	180
	150	6	785	205
38 Special S&W Special and Colt Special Regular Full Charge	158	2	615	133
	158	3½	715	179
	158	4	750	197
	158	4½	780	213
	158	5	805	227
	158	*6	855	256
	158	6½	880	272
	158	7½	925	300
38 Special Super Police Load	200	2	500	111
	200	3½	595	157
	200	4	625	174
	200	5	680	205
	200	*6	730	237
	200	6½	755	253

CARTRIDGE	BULLET WEIGHT Grains	BARREL LENGTH Inches	MUZZLE VELOCITY Ft. Secs.	MUZZLE ENERGY Ft. Lbs.
38 Special 38/44	150	2	805	216
	150	3½	910	276
	150	4	945	298
	150	5	1005	336
	150	*6	1060	374
	150	6½	1085	392
High Speed Loads	158	2	830	242
	158	3½	940	310
	158	4	975	334
	158	5	1035	376
	158	*6	1090	417
	158	6½	1115	436
380 Automatic 9mm	95	3⅛	915	177
	95	3½	940	186
	95	*3¾	955	192
	95	5	1020	220
38 Super Automatic	130	4¼	1220	430
	130	*5	1280	473
38-40 Winchester Standard Velocity	180	*5	975	380
	180	6	1035	428
	180	7½	1105	488
41 Magnum Lead Bullet	210	4	795	295
	210	6	925	399
	210	*8⅜	1050	514
41 Magnum Soft Point Bullet	210	4	1210	683
	210	6	1355	856
	210	*8⅜	1500	1049
44 Magnum	240	*6½	1470	1150
	240	8⅜	1595	1356
44 S&W Special	246	4	615	207
	246	4½	645	227
	246	5	675	249
	246	5½	705	272
	246	6	730	291
	246	*6½	755	311
	246	7½	800	350
44-40 Winchester Standard Velocity	200	4½	825	302
	200	5½	880	344
	200	*7½	975	422
45 Colt	250	4½	810	364
	250	*5½	860	410
	250	7½	950	501
	255	4½	810	372
	255	*5½	860	418
	255	7½	950	511
45 Automatic Regular Full Charge	230	4¼	810	335
	230	*5	850	369
45 Auto Rim	230	4½	755	291
	230	*5½	810	335
	230	7½	900	414

CHAPTER NINETEEN

HANDLOADING

Years ago, everybody handloaded. That was because all guns were muzzleloaders and that's the way they had to be loaded.

In the early days of "fixed ammunition," many shooters also reloaded; they cast their own bullets by melting lead and pouring it into molds, then reloaded their cartridges by hand. Shotgun shooters reloaded by buying powder, shot, and wads in bulk and reloading.

The business of reloading as we know it today was really started in about 1884 by a retired army man named John H. Barlow. He called his business the Ideal Manufacturing Company. Some years later, in 1910, it was sold to Marlin, and when Marlin went on the auction block following World War I, the Ideal business was sold to Lyman. It's still part of the Lyman operation.

Reloading staggered along during the period roughly between World Wars I and II; factory-loaded ammo got much better, was more available, and wasn't all that costly. Reloading got its biggest boost at the end of World War II, mostly because shooters found they could reload better ammunition than they could buy.

When World War II ended there was a shortage of nearly everything. Sporting ammunition hadn't been made for years and was in critically short supply. So was smokeless powder, except surplus, and so were the remaining components—cases, bullets, primers. To fill this demand a lot of small people, who at that time didn't really have a dime to their name but had ideas and guts, got into the business.

For one, Bruce Hodgdon bought up surplus military rifle powder and, with increasing business and income, began experimenting with different powders. In the bullet business, the benchrest rifle shooters learned the secret of better bullets, and a few small manufacturers caught on quick. First there was the Sierra group, which at that time was called Harris Machine Company and was led by Clint Harris, Frank Snow, Jim Spivey, and Loren Harbour. Harris was soon bought out; the rest made a pile of money and eventually sold out to Leisure Group and are now part of Lyman for marketing purposes.

Meantime, a fellow named Joyce Hornady was a distributor for Speer bullets, made up in Lewiston, Idaho. Joyce also learned how to make bullets and started his own company. Today he owns the Pacific Tool Co. and even makes his own factory-loaded ammo under the Frontier brand. Shortly after that, Vernon and Ray Speer learned how to make good bullets, and the Speer organization moved into high gear. It's now part of Omark Industries, which makes rimfire ammunition and primers and imports ammunition from DWM, the famous West German company.

A fellow named Fred Huntington worked in his father's dry-cleaning business originally, then began manufacturing bullet-making dies, which he called the Rock Chuck Bullet Swage—RCBS. Soon he got into reloading dies, then tools, and finally dropped the bullet swages entirely. RCBS is the world's largest maker of reloading dies today and has recently been bought by Omark Industries.

I could go on and on with such stories. The point I'm making here, though, is that the large companies—Winchester-Western, Remington-Peters, and Federal—were sound asleep. They let these other businesses spring up. They didn't think reloading was here to stay; they thought shooters would return to their senses—and their hardware and sporting-goods stores. The result was that Speer, Hornady, Sierra, and Nosler and the others got firmly established with dealers across America, and by the time the giants woke up, they weren't needed. Nor wanted. Today they're after that market, but it's hard sledding for them.

Centerfire rifle, pistol, and shotgun cartridges are reloadable—by the simple expedient of removing the fired primer, squeezing the cartridge case back to its original size to permit easy chambering, and seating a new primer, powder charge, and bullet. The procedure isn't quite that simple, of course, but neither is it very complicated, and reloading has been one of America's fastest-growing businesses since the last war.

There are many real advantages to reloading. Perhaps the most popular is that it saves considerable money. The reloader is forced to learn quite a bit about his ammunition if he expects to perform the operation, so he becomes a better shooter because he is more knowledgeable. Another advantage is that reloading offers you more flexibility in your shooting. For example, there are numerous styles and weights of bullet as well as many powders with varying burning speeds that allow you to develop special loads for special purposes.

Contrary to some old wives' notions, reloading is a very safe hobby. As we have already explained, smokeless powder is not an explosive and may be handled readily. Primers should be handled with care but need not be considered especially dangerous. As a matter of fact, there's a great deal more danger involved with the can of gasoline stored in your garage for the power mower than there is with storing powder or primers.

If you want to start reloading, or even if you want to consider it, the first step is to buy one of the handloader's manuals sold at your local gun store. These books may be depended upon to offer sound advice on reloading procedures and actual suggested loads. They list powder, bullet weight, and velocity of all loads. Nobody should consider reloading without first studying a manual thoroughly.

WHAT YOU HAVE TO BUY

The major items you'll need are a reloading press, dies, and a powder scale (in addition to a supply of primers, powder, and bullets, of course). The press is a rather heavy, bench-mounted tool with a big handle and is capable of powerful leverage. It has a movable shell holder, which is raised and lowered by the handle, and a threaded hole on top for the dies. To use it, you place a die in the threaded hole and a fired cartridge in the shell holder and raise (or lower, depending on the tool design) the handle. This will force the case into the die. Reversing the handle stroke will pull the shell out of the die.

Most pistol reloading dies are now made in sets of three dies. The first is a resizing die which does nothing but restore the fired case, which has expanded to fit the gun's chamber from breech pressure, to original size. After resizing, it will fit the chamber of any standard gun.

Your second die performs two steps. It knocks out the fired primer with a long, slender decapping rod that fits into the flash hole and simply pushes the primer out. Another section of the decapping rod correctly sizes the inside of the case mouth for the new bullet you will seat, and a flared portion of the rod, which must be very carefully adjusted, will slightly bell the case mouth. This is to permit easy seating of a soft lead bullet which would otherwise be scraped or cut by the sharp brass. As the case is removed from this second die, a new primer is seated by the primer-seating device in the press.

You now remove the primed cartridge from the press and charge it with powder, place the bullet in the mouth of the case, and, using your bullet-seating die, run it back in the tool. This die is adjusted to push the bullet in to the proper depth; then it crimps the case mouth into the bullet.

A good crimp is very important for two reasons. First, and most obvious, the recoil of a handgun will snap the gun backward, tending to pull the bullet forward and out of the case. This is inertia at work, since the bullet tends to stay where it is while the cartridge case is yanked backward severely by the gun. Magnum revolvers are the worst offenders in this department. If the bullets move ahead, they will prevent cylinder rotation.

The second reason for crimp is that the resistance to blowing out the bullet is needed to allow

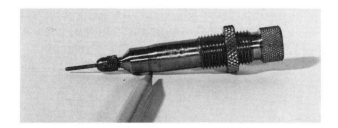

Straight-mouth cases such as this .44 Magnum revolver cartridge are flared at the mouth before bullet seating. The top photo shows the expander, and the lower photo shows the case and a bullet. This bullet is a semijacketed one which can be driven at good speed without leading the barrel.

full pressure to build up within the case. If the bullet moves too soon, peak pressure will never be achieved and poor velocity will result.

You can throw your powder charges from a measure, or you can weigh them individually with a scale. Since a scale is required to set a measure, it follows that the scale is a required item. The measure makes reloading a lot faster, but you can reload without it.

Primers and powder must be purchased. Bullets may be purchased, or you may cast them yourself if you prefer. Lead bullets are easily cast, and lead is obtainable from many sources. After casting, you will have to size and lubricate your bullets in another tool.

Most police departments reload their ammunition. They use high-speed tools that are not required by the average sportsman. If they didn't reload, the cost of ammunition would prove prohibitive for much practice. The hobby of reloading is strongly suggested to anyone who wants to do much shooting and who really wants to learn more about guns and shooting.

The reader interested in reloading is advised to buy a Hornady, Speer, or Lyman reloading handbook at any gun store. These handbooks cost only a few dollars and thoroughly explain the necessary procedures.

CHAPTER TWENTY

WHIMS,
ENGRAVING,
AND
ACCESSORIES

I suppose you could call engraving a whim, but that's a bit deprecating. Engraving is too fine an adornment to be so termed. I suspect the main reason a person likes an engraved gun is that it looks better. Engraving also adds to the value, and a nicely engraved gun should be treated carefully and handled gently.

Engraving is often used to personalize a gun with the owner's name or initials or with whatever he seeks to embellish it, such as certain animals or birds. And a presentation gun is often inscribed with the recipient's name and sometimes the reason for the occasion justifying that presentation.

During the past few years there has been a rash of guns that commemorate certain things, events, persons, or places. Collectively, these are known as commemoratives. In the handgun world the best-known commemoratives are those produced by Colt and commemorating famous battles of earlier wars. Another well-known commemorative was the Smith & Wesson Texas Ranger gun, made in limited numbers and handsomely engraved.

It's called "factory engraving" when you order a gun engraved by the manufacturer. Usually the maker will list several grades of engraving and you can pick and choose what you want according to your likes or your budget. You also can get custom engravers such as Alvin White and John Warren to do the work. The art of engraving consists of cutting the steel with hard steel tools called gravers, which are usually

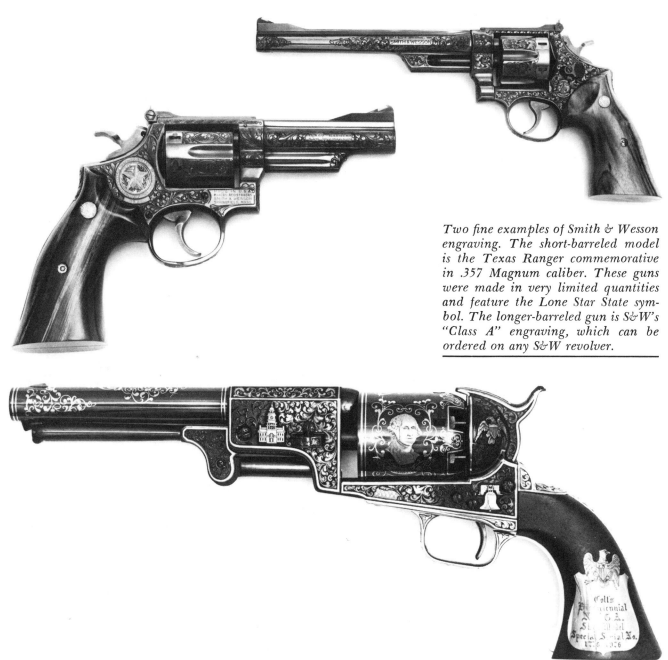

Two fine examples of Smith & Wesson engraving. The short-barreled model is the Texas Ranger commemorative in .357 Magnum caliber. These guns were made in very limited quantities and feature the Lone Star State symbol. The longer-barreled gun is S&W's "Class A" engraving, which can be ordered on any S&W revolver.

Once each year, in conjunction with an industry trade show, Colt auctions off a highly decorated revolver. This one was auctioned at the 1976 Bicentennial show and brought a record sum. The gun is richly engraved and decorated with inlaid work.

urged by small hammers when you're working on steel. The same craftsmen can inlay gold, silver, and ivory and carve the inlays into birds, animals, initials, or whatever you want. But you're going to pay plenty for good engraving.

It's been said that such adornment doesn't make a gun shoot any better. That's a fact. But as the late Captain Edward Crossman used to argue: "You're right, but a necktie doesn't help to keep you warm either." For those who love fine guns there is no question that engraving done tastefully adds a lot to the enjoyment. If engraving is not for you, don't buy it. But don't knock it either.

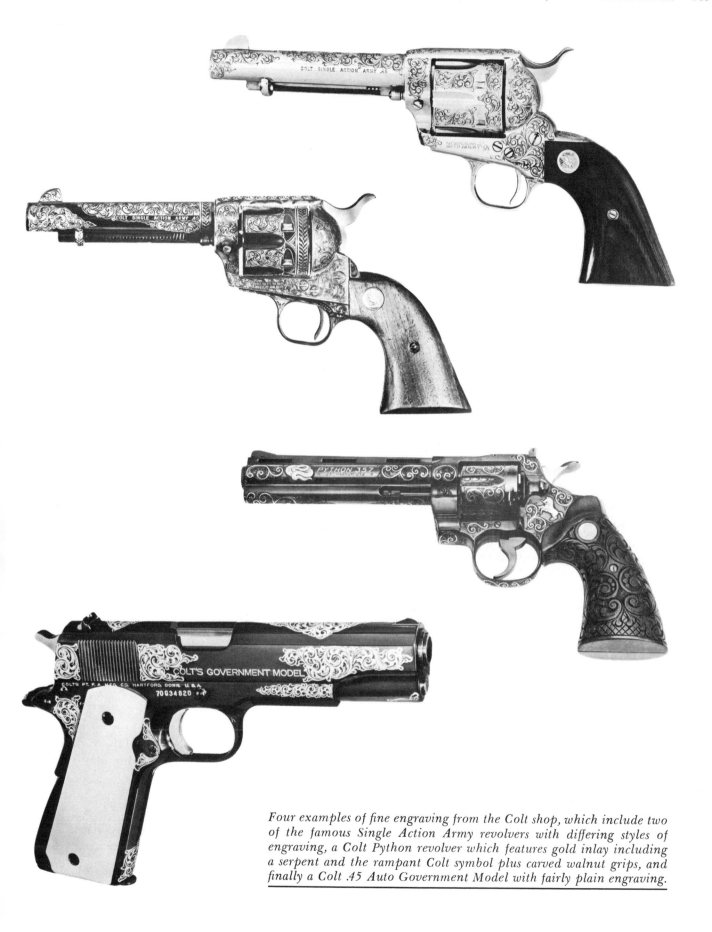

Four examples of fine engraving from the Colt shop, which include two of the famous Single Action Army revolvers with differing styles of engraving, a Colt Python revolver which features gold inlay including a serpent and the rampant Colt symbol plus carved walnut grips, and finally a Colt .45 Auto Government Model with fairly plain engraving.

FINISH

The finish on modern handguns is usually one of two types: the traditional blue or the increasingly popular stainless steel. The latter is a bright finish often toned down to a "brushed" finish by a rapidly spinning wire-brush wheel. There was a time when many revolvers were nickel-plated. Contrary to popular opinion, the nickel wasn't to produce a flashy effect but was intended to resist rusting in a service arm. I've never liked the glare of a nickel-plated gun but admit the finish does provide a measure of protection. Now that stainless guns are here in such numbers it seems a good time to drop the nickel-plated finish; it will hardly be missed.

Gun blue is produced by a process best described as controlled rusting. You can achieve the same thing, if you're very careful, by taking a nicely polished piece of steel and making it rust. Then you wipe off the rust with steel wool, and you'll note the metal has gotten ever so slightly darker. Repeat the process and it gets still darker. Repeat until the desired degree of darkness is obtained and you have a blued piece of steel. That's a somewhat oversimplified description of what has come to be known as rust bluing, the sort found on better-grade guns and on all double-barrel shotguns.

Since World War II a newer process has been used which is often referred to as "sheep dip." It produces a very similar result in far less time. Only the true gun buff can appreciate the older rust bluing; nearly all guns on the market today (except double shotguns) are blued by the sheep-dip method. This is a dip that produces considerably higher temperatures than rust bluing and its chemicals attack soft solder, so double-shotgun barrels are not blued in the "modern" manner.

The quality of bluing, or of any finish for that matter, depends on the quality of the finish on the steel before bluing. Produce a poor polishing job and you'll produce a poor blue job. Good polishing is one of the hardest things to accomplish in gunmaking, regardless of whether it's a long gun or a handgun. The common impression that you can "shoeshine" and buff your way to a good polish in a few moments is pure fantasy. Buffing has a nasty habit of pulling the steel out of holes on one side as well as rounding corners that should be square. Shoeshining leaves waves as you look down a barrel and is best left to the shoeshine boys. Good polishing takes skilled men, skilled hands, the right equipment, and plenty of care. There is no finer finish put on guns than that appearing on guns made by Winchester, Smith & Wesson, Colt, and a very few others.

Bluing can also be produced by heat and oil. This is a satisfactory way to reblue a screw head or some similar part but cannot be used on major parts because it will result in an uneven finish and would draw the temper of any hardened part. You simply polish the part nicely, then heat it in a flame until it starts to color. At that point, wipe it with a piece of oil-soaked rag (like burlap) and you'll get a rich, deep blue. It will not be as permanent a finish as the other methods and is no more than a way to touch up a small part.

Some guns are colored by case-hardening. Case-hardening means hardening a piece of steel by driving carbon into the surface. It also results in mottled colors of blues and browns that are quite attractive. You can take a piece of mild steel—that is, common cold-rolled steel (which does not have the alloys possessed in tool steel, which can be hardened)—and case-harden it so the surface will be very hard while retaining a soft, tough core. A hard surface is desirable on parts that must retain their shape, such as the sear and sear notch. Place the steel in some sort of container so it can be buried in a carbon-rich substance—which can be bone, cyanide, or other materials supplied for the purpose. Then place the whole thing in an oven and bring it up to red heat. The longer it soaks in red heat the deeper the carbon will penetrate. Then the steel is removed and quenched in water.

The result will be a piece of steel with a glass-hard surface, and if you've used the right kind of hardening agent you'll have the very attractive finish found on Smith & Wesson hammers and triggers, Colt Single Action frames, and many old shotgun and rifle receivers. There is quite a trick to doing this operation and it's not to be taken lightly; don't let anybody try it on your pet gun unless he comes highly recommended.

The stainless-steel handgun is here to stay,

and it's a fine and quite natural development. A handgun that won't rust is highly desirable, long-lasting and relatively carefree. Its finish is another matter, however. While the appearance of a stainless-steel finish looks good in the gun case, in the store, in your hand, or wherever, it's also a bright and shiny object that can be seen for miles. Stainless can't be blued in the usual sense, since bluing is a controlled rusting process. But stainless can be blued after a fashion (the Europeans have done it for years), and it should be. This is especially true with a service handgun; a cop can't afford to have a flicker of light catch his gun and attract attention to his position at a critical moment.

Pretty as stainless finishes are—and that brushed stainless is handsome—manufacturers ought to figure out a way to dull them for the safety of the user.

Sometime back in the 1950s there was one of the craziest developments of all time in gun finishes: guns in color. In my 1959 issue of *Gun Digest* I find listed the High Standard Sentinel, a short-barreled nine-shot .22-caliber revolver available in gold, turquoise, or pink Duratone! As I remember, High Standard was not the only offender; there were some long guns with brilliant finishes that looked like a peacock during the rut. These finishes were applied to alloy metal (which in gun language means an aluminum alloy), which was finished by a process called anodizing. Scope tubes and many lightweight gun parts are made of aluminum alloys, properly finished by anodizing to a color matching gun blue. Those damned pink handguns went off the market fast, and they haven't been mourned.

SILENCERS

The silencer has three things going against it: it's illegal, it's big and bulky, and it will not silence the flight of any bullet traveling faster than the speed of sound.

By federal law, these devices were outlawed in 1934. A silencer is simply a device, attached to the muzzle, which absorbs the sound waves of the report at the muzzle. That means it must be rather bulky, because it sticks out in front of the muzzle and contains enough material to soak up the noise.

In earlier and more innocent times it was hard to explain to people what a sonic boom was. Today it's in the news almost daily with talk about the SST and the space programs. The speed of sound is about 1100 fps at sea level, which means that any bullet exceeding that velocity can't be silenced. It creates its own sonic boom, the sharp "crack" you hear and that cannot be quieted even though you can muffle the muzzle's boom.

Moreover, a revolver can't be quieted because of the gap between cylinder and barrel. So the silencer, despite novels to the contrary, is almost totally useless. You are advised that it is best not to fool around with such a device if one should be offered to you for sale or if you are tempted to try to make your own.

CUSTOM WORK

Aside from the practice of "accurizing," which we will discuss in Chapter Twenty-one, there really isn't much in the way of custom work in handguns—not compared to rifles, there isn't.

There is increased activity in making handgun wildcat cartridges, as we've already discussed, and this is particularly true with such handguns as the Thompson/Center, the Remington Fire Ball, the Navy Arms rolling-block, and other such single-shot types. Some handgun actions are built from scratch, as is the case with the Auto-Mag, a custom proposition.

You are again cautioned that federal law prohibits the manufacture of any handgun *based on a rifle or shotgun action*. If you want to make, or have a custom gunsmith make for you, a special handgun, you are obliged to begin with an action that was originally manufactured as a handgun. This despite the fact that Remington's Fire Ball action is identical with their Mohawk Model 600 (and some now-discontinued Remington brand models) and the Navy Arms rolling-block is a re-creation of the old Remington rolling-block rifle that was once very popular. Federal law, on the other hand, doesn't mind if you make a rifle from a pistol action! Such are the contradictions and inconsistencies in the law.

Custom handgun stocks are available (see Chapter Nine). Or you can make your own without much trouble. It's certainly a far simpler job than stocking a rifle or shotgun. One maker, Dan Wesson, supplies a stock blank that's already inletted but unshaped; you can whittle out whatever pleases you. There are enough high-quality custom grips on the market at modest prices that there's no point in making your own unless you have time to whittle or have some specific requirement that you don't think can be met with any ready-made item.

Custom work on revolvers is tricky and can be risky. Barrel removal on a revolver requires the proper equipment. Only the skilled and experienced specialized pistol gunsmith ought to tackle such work. Revolver-cylinder work also calls for very precise work within the limits of the particular revolver's strength.

As a result there is really very little custom revolver work going on that involves rebarreling (except replacement in the same caliber), and there is also very little cylinder work. Frankly, I think the average gun owner is well advised to take such jobs back to the manufacturer's repair or service department rather than have it tackled by a gunsmith unless the latter is skilled in handgun work.

The sort of custom work that is done to revolvers includes such things as removal of hammer spurs and rounding of some corners for fast-draw situations so these obstructions won't catch on clothes. At one time it was fairly common to remove the front of trigger guards so the finger could more easily contact the trigger. If this is still done I haven't heard much about it lately.

Most revolvers seem to come complete with square, sharp corners in many places. Quite a few shooters have complained about this, especially police officers—or former officers become gun writers. They may have a point, but as a former gunsmith myself (though not a pistol-smith) I have always believed a square corner should be a square corner. Period. If it is necessary to knock off the corner, then it should be done with a clean chamfer (angled surface that breaks the corner) that looks as though it was meant to be.

I don't know why those little pocket handguns come with sights. Surely sights are not needed when you're shooting at the close ranges the little guns are made for. And, provided the little guns will only be used for this purpose, it's a smart idea to have the hammer spur removed, although it means you can shoot the gun only double-action.

Custom work on auto pistols is also limited, but for different reasons. The auto pistol is carefully balanced to work with the load for which it was chambered, and any drastic changes may render the gun inoperative. There is considerable work being done with the big .45 Colt in terms of accurizing, but I'm not talking about that. I'm talking about the average shooter and his needs. The average guy can't shoot close enough to realize any benefit from custom accurizing work.

Almost all of the custom work being done seems to be in the area of single-shot pistols, where operational systems are simple and relatively uncomplicated and where the actions are strong enough to contain almost anything anyone would reasonably want to shoot in them. And, of course, there are those who are actually manufacturing gun actions from scratch. This is far more complicated than it sounds and should be attempted only by the skilled and knowledgeable. The "remanufacture" of anything old such as a Very pistol (used for signal flares) or any other ancient single-shots should be avoided like the flu.

HOLSTERS

Shooters are gadgeteers. I'm not sure they're worse than fishermen, but it's likely a close tie. Show me the guy who buys a handgun and then doesn't want a holster for it and I'll be surprised. Once he gets shooting, he's going to want a dozen—or a hundred—other things too.

A Western-type revolver looks best in a Western holster complete with cartridge belt. There are also shoulder holsters, ankle holsters, pocket holsters, and tiny holsters that tuck inside your belt. If you can't find what you want as a standard item there are a dozen holster makers who will make a custom holster for you. Illustrated here are a variety of available holsters; there are others and you ought to review what's available before making a purchase.

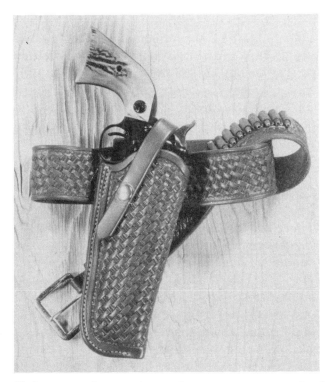

Holsters are the most convenient way to carry a pistol or revolver, and they have been used for many years. One of the oldest and most highly regarded makers is the George Lawrence Co., which made this basket-weave model for a single-action revolver. Sometimes, usually with Western-style holsters, a belt is provided from the same source, as is the case in this example.

Holsters are essential for carrying a pistol or revolver of almost every type except pocket pistols. Shown are a number of typical holsters. At top, Smith & Wesson Model 39 in a small belt holster by George Lawrence Co., and the same pistol in another belt model by Safariland. At far left, a Colt Single Action Army in a typical Western model by George Lawrence Co. and at near left, Smith & Wesson Model 66 stainless .357 with Herret grips in Safariland belt holster.

Law-enforcement officers who tote an auto pistol have need for reserve firepower. This belt-type magazine holder from George Lawrence Co. holds a pair of magazines ready for quick use.

GUN BOXES AND CASES

Target shooters use boxes to carry their guns and range gear and, when opened, to provide a place for their spotting scope. These boxes are generally made to hold the three major target guns owned and used by most shooters: .22, .38, and .45 caliber.

There also are hard cases made for handguns which are about the size of an attaché case and are lined with foam just like rifle and shotgun cases. You simply lay as many handguns in these cases as will fit and close the case; the guns stay put. These are very handy for transporting scoped guns for varmint shooting.

SPEED LOADERS

It's unhandy to reload a revolver when the loose cartridges are in your pocket, or when they're in belt loops. So several firms make "speed loaders" which hold the full complement of six fresh cartridges and are simply positioned, whereupon you push a button and the cartridges fall into the charge holes. These are especially valuable for combat-course shooting and, naturally, for the police officer. Other cartridge holders are made that hold extra ammunition nice and flat like a cigar case and keep the cartridges from rattling.

GUN LOCKS

There are any number of devices to put on the trigger guard of a loaded gun so kids can't operate it. One of these which works on the pressure principle is illustrated. It takes an adult's finger pressure to release the lock. The theory is that a child hasn't got the strength to open it. I don't know about that. Kids sometimes have a way of getting into things they shouldn't despite the best efforts. A case in point is all those bottles aspirin and prescription drugs come in these days. I have hell's own time getting the damned things open (maybe one reason is that I can't see the alignment marks unless I put on my glasses), but kids can open them with ease. If you can't figure out how to operate one of these things, just ask a kid to show you how.

This is a "gun pressure lock" from Safariland. It works by an adjustable pressure that you can set too tight for small hands to work. As you can see, it prevents the gun from being fired. I do not believe in these devices, because a gun is meant to be used, and when you have it inoperative, it's time-consuming to get into action. When you need a gun you need it now—fast and quietly.

These trigger locks leave me with mixed emotions. They are based on an excellent principle: Keep guns so kids can't work them accidentally.But it's also a fact that if a gun is to be of any use to you, you have to be able to grab it quickly, noiselessly, and surely. These locking devices don't permit that in most instances, and to a degree they defeat the purpose of having a loaded gun. I've always felt it best to control your kids the old-fashioned way and educate them about guns as soon as they're old enough to comprehend, in which event guns are most unlikely to be a problem. But this is something each parent must decide for himself.

MISCELLANEOUS EQUIPMENT

Screwdrivers ruin more guns than any other single item. Used wrongly, a screwdriver will mar screw heads and make them look terrible. Used as a pry, they will ruin a revolver sideplate if you take it off that way. (The right way is to remove the screws with a fitted screwdriver, then tap the frame with the handle of the screwdriver or some other object that won't mar the steel. This will make the sideplate pop off.) There are many good screwdrivers on the market, such as those sold by Bonanza.

Auto-pistol magazines should be classed as accessories, because there are some on the market with greater capacity than those supplied with the gun. Just why anyone needs a twenty-shot magazine is a question I can't answer, but some think it necessary. Years ago there was a curled-up Luger magazine that resembled a snail and held thirty-two 9mm cartridges. Sometimes a longer than normal magazine won't work as well as you'd think, because it must have a long spring which is under heavy pressure when fully loaded and far less pressure when feeding the last few cartridges. These sometimes fail to feed properly at either extreme of spring tension.

Auto-pistol magazines most commonly fail to feed because the lips get battered or bent and present cartridges at the wrong angle. It is always a wise idea to buy an extra magazine with a new gun (many models come with an extra) and keep a spare in new, pristine condition. Then if you begin to experience troubles, you can compare the used one with the unused one

and very likely spot the trouble. Magazine lips are usually bent by either dropping them or trying to force a cartridge in when you shouldn't, or forcing it in at the wrong angle.

I will have more to say about it in the next chapter, but the Lee machine rest ought to be considered an accessory. This is a most useful gadget that can be used to check out gun accuracy, to work up loads, to try different brands of ammo, etc. It eliminates most of the human error and still provides as much accuracy as the gun can deliver. It uses a three-point alignment arrangement. You place the handgun, with proper Lee attachment, on the rest and fire. The gun recoils away from the rest, leaving the base exactly as it was before you fired. Then you place the gun back against the alignment stops for the next shot. Very clever. Very accurate. And moreover, very inexpensive.

Ear protection is one of the most important things for every shooter. I've known many old shooters who were pretty hard of hearing (and I've been told I'm getting that way myself). This is pure carelessness. Every shooter ought to have some sort of kit box, kit bag, or whatever to hold his range equipment, and it must include some ear protectors. The handgunner is better off than any shoulder-gun shooter because he can wear muffs, which offer the best protection. Muffs are used by some long-gun shooters, but others find they get in the way. There also are many other ear devices, including the Lee Sonic Ear Valve made by a division of the Norton Company. This device is calculated to allow conversation but is activated by a sharp, loud noise such as a gun report.

It has been my own experience that a clean cleaning patch or wad of clean cotton works just about as well as most of the complicated kinds of ear protectors.

Next in importance, or perhaps of most importance, is eye protection. It's just as important in handguns as long guns, even though all the action is at arm's length. Shooting glasses are made of a tempered glass and are to be preferred to ordinary spectacles, although the latter are far better than nothing. Moreover, shooting glasses can be fitted with a small device, which you can buy or make yourself, that covers the aiming eye, leaving a pinhole through which to sight. As in a camera lens, this tiny hole sharpens your sighting eye and is a great boost to achieving better scores.

But the main reason for glasses is to protect your eyes. You're issued only one set during your lifetime; it just makes sense to protect them. While it happens rarely, guns do blow up and primers do get pierced, which moves tiny chunks of metal rapidly in many directions. Moreover, a revolver sometimes spits a bit of shaved lead through that gap between cylinder and barrel when charge hole and barrel are not perfectly aligned.

Target hammers and target triggers are classed as accessories, and are often available on factory guns on special order. These are usually much wider than standard and often checkered more deeply for a better grip. You also can buy trigger "shoes" for most revolvers which serve the same purpose. Costing very little, these are simply placed over the trigger and fastened by a pair of tiny set screws. A wide trigger permits a better pull because it distributes the trigger pull over a wider area and that makes the pull *seem* lighter. Trigger shoes are offered by Pachmayr, Pacific, and others.

Cleaning equipment, stands for holding muzzleloading revolvers, and dozens of other gadgets could be classed as accessories. The list has no end. Buy good equipment and take good care of your gun. If you do, it will serve you a long time. You'll find the use of a number of accessories will aid your shooting and in addition, make it more enjoyable.

CHAPTER TWENTY-ONE

ACCURACY

The word "accuracy" requires some defining. The obvious ultimate in accuracy would be the gun that puts every shot through the same hole, regardless of range. This is impossible, although it has been virtually accomplished in rifles (see *The Accurate Rifle*, Warren Page, 1973, Winchester Press). The modern benchrest rifle, with appropriate ammunition and in the hands of a skilled marksman, can *usually* put ten shots into a tiny, ragged hole at 100 yards and often at 200 as well. But not every time.

Pistols and revolvers are much less accurate than rifles, although the finer target models will perform astoundingly well. But we must define what kind of accuracy is needed. The pocket defense revolver or pistol need not be expected to hit a target the size of a mouse at 50 yards. Such a gun is meant to hit a man-sized target at very short range. So there we have one definition of accuracy.

Another definition would be that required for a service sidearm—again, the gun is meant to hit a man-sized target, but this time at longer range. This accuracy definition is finer than that for the pocket gun, but not appreciably so.

Target and sporting accuracy, while there are distinctions between the two, are of a far finer sort than the foregoing. We can then define "accuracy" according to need—or the purpose for which the gun was made or will be used. While the sighting equipment and skill of the shooter play a major role in delivering accuracy, we are here concerned only with the inherent accuracy built into the gun.

Two views of the Ransom machine rest, with different pistols, showing both sides of this fine rest which is used by many serious handgunners. The principle advantage to using such a machine rest is to remove the human element so you know the gun's capability. Unless you know that, there is no way you can judge your performance with any degree of reliability. Moreover, different ammunition provides different accuracy. A machine rest is the only reliable way to test that as well.

Why should one gun be more accurate than another? Is an autoloader more accurate than a revolver? Or the other way around? Why should one be more accurate than another? Won't the simple addition of decent sights make a service gun just as accurate as one made specifically for target shooting?

And what about ammunition—the fact that one gun might shoot well with one brand of ammunition and not another? Why are there variations from lot to lot of ammunition from the same maker? And so on. The point is that most pistol and revolver shooters don't know how to shoot well enough even to know if they're getting decent accuracy, so they have to settle for what they have.

A good pistol or revolver is capable of astonishing accuracy—sometimes it will put the average "deer rifle" to shame. This five-shot group with a .41 Magnum proves my point. Cartridges were loaded in five charge holes (some revolvers shoot best if you use the same charge hole for each shot, but a good one will perform equally with all holes). This same revolver has shot groups as small as 3 inches at 100 yards over sandbags.

This need not be so at all. There are a number of rests on the market designed to remove the human element as much as possible, which will allow almost anyone to test a pistol or revolver with various makes of ammo, or handloads, and determine just how well his own gun can shoot.

An inexpensive shooting rest is very handy for testing pistol or revolver accuracy. This model is by Lee Custom Engineering and is adaptable to most guns by changing grip adaptors. It is shown with a Dan Wesson revolver. In use, you fire the gun by hand, allowing it to recoil up and away from the base. Then simply place the gun back on the base for following shots. There are three points of contact for correct alignment.

Of course, the armrest method in a sort of benchrest technique will also help significantly but is no substitute for a rest, since it requires you to sight.

The least expensive rest of all those on the market to my knowledge is the Lee. It's a marvel of simplicity and retails for $26 in 1977 (you also have to buy a holder for your specific gun for an added $15.98). This simple rest can be bolted or clamped to a solid table or bench. You hand-hold the gun when fired, and the gun is allowed to recoil freely away from the rest's base. To fire the next shot you simply replace the unit on the base and position it against the three stops. This is quite slick and I've made enough tests with a sample Lee rest, using Dan Wesson .357, Colt .45, and Smith & Wesson large frame revolvers in .357, .41, and .44 Magnum, to know that this is a perfectly adequate tool for the hobbyist. The perfectionist will be better satisfied with a more elaborate rest like those made by Ransom, Potter, and others.

You and you alone can determine what degree of accuracy you want or require from a gun. I will tell you what sort of accuracy can be obtained and how to go about getting and testing a gun that will perform. But don't ever expect to get top accuracy from a gun that wasn't made for the purpose.

Most target shooting in the United States is based on three calibers: .22, .38, and .45. I'm not sure anyone today can remember why it's so, but I suspect it's because the .22 is such a joy to bang at paper targets and it's so easy (relatively) to hit the 10-ring with it. The .38, of course, is the most popular and widely used police service caliber, so it quite naturally falls into place. And the big .45 is the U.S. service pistol, which accounts for its presence. As a result, most of the accuracy work on target guns is in these calibers, and that's especially true with the .45 auto.

.22 CALIBER

There are .22-caliber pistols and revolvers available all the way from cheap, imported derringers which are no bargain at any price to exquisite free pistols such as the Swiss Hammerli costing the better part of a thousand dollars. The accuracy potential of these guns varies as widely as the cost. Generally speaking, you will get about what you pay for in terms of accuracy, but you might be surprised and find exceptional accuracy with a gun you don't expect to perform that well.

Most target shooters use autos in preference to revolvers. There are several reasons. A revolver poses more problems in target shooting because it must be cocked for each shot, has a longer hammer fall and thus longer lock time, and, many shooters claim, is not as well balanced for target work. These are not factors for any sporting use. The point is that if your interest is purely target shooting, your choice ought to be an autoloader; but if it's a sporting gun you have in mind, then you may choose either one according to your personal likes. Keep in mind also that top target shooters are always experimenting, always trying to wring out whatever little extra advantage they can find. Their preferences do not necessarily parallel those of the sportsman. You might consider as a parallel the fact that a target rifleman uses an entirely different rifle for target shooting and for hunting.

The big advantage autoloaders have over revolvers would seem to be that there is only one chamber rather than the revolver's cylinder with six to nine charge holes. This doesn't necessarily mean better accuracy, but it does mean that it costs more to machine all the parts necessary to perfect alignment in a revolver. This means that dollar for dollar you have a better chance of getting a more accurate gun at a lower price with the auto simply because there's less manufacturing time involved.

Autoloaders do not require you to recock the gun each time it's fired, which is a big advantage for the target shooter, because he doesn't have to change his grip, nor does he have to take the time to cock, but gets back on target quicker. More or less in the same breath it should be mentioned that the longer hammer fall of the revolver produces slightly slower lock time. On the other hand, it also provides a heavier and more consistent hammer fall with corresponding better ignition. I suspect these two might cancel each other out.

Which gun provides the better grip is purely subjective and need not be a consideration except that it is frequently given as a "reason" by

Swiss Hammerli target pistols come high. The Model 150 for International and Olympic shooting is called a free pistol, which means that no restrictions are imposed on the type of gun used. A single-shot, this model listed at $795 in 1977; it's a .22 Long Rifle especially designed for 50-meter targets.

many top target pistoleers and so cannot be ignored completely.

On the other hand, many .22 autoloaders mount their rear sights on a movable slide, front sights on the fixed barrel. This has to be listed as a disadvantage, although it's a slight one indeed. The modern *target* .22 auto, however, does not have this combination but has the rear sight on a fixed rib, extension rib or bar, or whatever you wish to call it so that the sights are both on fixed pieces with the slide free to recoil underneath. And at least one model, the Ruger, contains the movable bolt within its receiver, so this problem is nonexistent.

It is interesting to note too that it is normal to test several guns of the same make and model and average their performance. That's really the only fair way to run any test. But that's not what you do when you buy a gun. You don't take ten samples home and run each through its paces to pick the best one. You lay down your money and take what the store has. So it's not unfair practice to do the same thing when you're testing guns.

Another vital element in accuracy in any gun is the trigger pull. I have elsewhere commented on the pull, but a few words in regard to its contribution to accuracy are in order here. The pull must be correct in order to shoot with any degree of accuracy. It is a fact that some shooters have proved in competition that they can shoot better scores with a gun with less inherent accuracy but with a better trigger pull than another gun. I am speaking here of trifling differences,

but the point remains the same regardless of the degree. You may accept it as a rule that a good trigger pull is essential for accurate shooting. Most guns on today's market have decent triggers, but not all have excellent triggers (these remarks apply to .22 autoloaders).

If you have decided to take up target shooting you will require one of the better target pistols, and you might or might not be satisfied with it as it comes from the factory. If not you will want it "accurized" by one of the top pistolsmiths and/or you will want special sights to increase your advantage (real or imagined).

Most of us, however, are far more interested in just buying a gun and having fun shooting it. We'll use it for target shooting because that sport offers the most activity and the practice will pay off in better marksmanship. We'll also use it for field work in any one of a thousand legitimate ways, but we'll always want to hit what we aim at. For such uses any of the modern .22 pistols or revolvers from a reliable maker will perform sufficiently well. The two factors most essential to any such gun are a good trigger pull and decent sighting equipment.

Sights were covered in Chapter Ten and there is little point on elaborating on them here except to point out one little-known fact: Sight radius enables you to sight more closely (with a longer radius), but it also emphasizes wobble! The result is that some shooters are better off with a shorter radius. Closely allied with sighting radius is barrel length, which does not noticeably affect accuracy and need not be a consideration in that department. (However, see Chapter Eighteen regarding barrel length and velocity, which is another subject entirely.)

What about inherent accuracy? And what is it? Inherent accuracy is the accuracy of which a particular gun is capable when the human element is removed. The only variable in a pistol or revolver's inherent accuracy will be the brand and/or lot of ammunition, because, unlike the rifle, there are no such things as bedding problems. The fit of wood to metal in the one-hand gun is no factor.

You can check inherent accuracy only by the use of a machine rest as previously mentioned, and you will note that nearly all pistols and revolvers are capable of far finer accuracy than you may have imagined.

The acid test of accuracy is the ten-shot group, and it's generally fired at 50 yards with .22 target guns. Most of these will average around 1 inch. There will be a few tight clusters plunking their ten shots into as small a group as .700 inch (less than ¾ inch). Groups are measured from center to center of the widest shots. But there will be an occasional group as large as 2 inches. For further clarification, the 10-ring of the 50-yard target measures 3.39 inches in diameter and the X-ring is 1.695 inch. (The X-ring is used to break ties when two or more shooters have fired perfect scores; the shooter with the largest number of Xs wins.)

You can see from these dimensions that today's better target guns are inherently accurate enough to put all their shots into the 10-ring, and some can put them all into the X-ring. That's without the human element. Of course, any competent shooter is going to shoot better with a gun that has such inherent accuracy than with a gun that has poorer accuracy. You must add the human error to the gun's error. There are times when a poor hold will offset a poor shot, but the law of averages will not permit that to happen very often, and it's far more usual for a 3-inch human error to be added to a 3-inch gun error to produce a 6-inch group.

To put this sort of accuracy in perspective, consider that it is a fine *rifle* indeed that will put all its shots into 1 inch at 100 yards. That we have some .22 auto pistols, as well as some fine free pistols, that will put ten shots into less than 1 inch at 50 yards is extraordinary. (It is not strictly legitimate to double 50-yard performance and expect it to be 100-yard performance; it's always more than double. However, it may be doubled for purposes of this discussion and will be close enough for a comparison.)

Of course, there are many target rifles that will shoot a good deal tighter than 1 inch, so we're really comparing apples and oranges, but the important thing to keep in mind is that we are talking about *pistol* accuracy. It's a hell of a lot better than most people think. Especially when you realize that it was only about twenty-five years ago that any rifle that kept its shots in a 3-inch cluster at 100 yards was considered pretty good. The rare "1-inch rifle" in those days earned the distinction of being called "gilt-edge" and was highly prized by its owner. That's old hat today, since I have several rifles in my rack that shoot less than 1 inch and some much less. One, a Winchester Model 70 in .338 Winchester Magnum, shoots groups as small as ⅝ inch. And the .338 is a heavy hunting rifle.

What about the cheaper .22s? How do they stack up, and are they really suitable for sporting use? The answer is usually yes. You will not expect to find the same degree of consistency from gun to gun when you pay less, so there will be an occasional hot gun and there also will be some that will spray their shots to some degree. This brings up the question of cheapness. What is cheap? For our discussion of accuracy it is safe to assume that you will not achieve the same sort of accuracy from a pistol or revolver in the $50 range that you will get from one of the target-grade autos from High Standard, Smith & Wesson, or Ruger ranging from $112 for the Ruger to about $200 for the rest of them. Then there are models of the Swiss Hammerli that run over $800. All prices are 1977 list.

.38 SPECIAL

Capable of fine accuracy, the .38 Special has seen a recent trend toward autoloading pistols that has gradually begun to phase the revolvers out of their former role with this caliber. Smith & Wesson offers a fine target pistol in .38 Special that handles the wadcutter ammo so favored by

This Swiss Hammerli is a special autoloading model in .38 Special caliber. A conversion unit for .22 Long Rifle may be ordered as an extra. The combination may be used for target shooting under International and NRA rules for both calibers. Listed in 1977 at $750 for the .38 alone plus an added $375 for the conversion unit.

target shooters. These flatnosed bullets cut such clean holes in targets you'd think a paper punch did the work. Yet such a cartridge is a perfect abomination to feed, because it must be raised level; it will not tolerate angled feeding. The S&W has won world championships when taken right out of the box with no further attention, which is quite an achievement. Another interesting .38 Special pistol is the Swiss Hammerli, which has a .22 conversion unit to provide "low-cost practice" (hardly an important factor, since the gun with conversion unit runs over $1,100).

As with .22 and .45 ACP ammunition, those who manufacture cartridges spend an uncommon amount of research and development time and dollars on the .38 Special. The result is that target-grade ammunition in these three loadings is exceptionally accurate. Ammunition accuracy proved to be the lacking ingredient in rifle accuracy, as was learned by the benchrest shooters during the past twenty-five years, and the advances have rubbed off on the handgun world. The leading offender was the bullet. Bullets must be absolutely concentric to deliver top accuracy, and while imbalance is not as noticeable over typical pistol ranges as it is at rifle distances, the same attention to detail is necessary for top accuracy from any firearm.

The finer .38 Special revolvers are capable of extremely good accuracy when equipped with suitable sights. Indeed, they have been the choice until the comparatively recent perfection of the autoloaders. The latter are preferred for the same reasons that .22 autos are preferred over revolvers.

.45 ACP

The .45 Auto has been our service pistol since 1911. It has been used for target shooting since that time. The big .45 is often condemned by many because they tried to shoot the gun in the service and found that better accuracy could often be had by throwing the gun at the target. It's true that many service .45s have awful accuracy, generally because they were made during wartime and because they were "gunsmithed" by service armorers with skimpy ability. Service pistols also have poor sights. Many, admittedly not pistol shooters, believe the big gun kicks like the proverbial mule and they find it hard to handle. Hence it has a somewhat tarnished reputation among those who know little about guns.

Actually, the .45 doesn't kick hard (those who think it does have never fired a .44 Magnum), and, given a properly "accurized" gun and good ammunition, it will shoot exceptionally well.

There are two routes to getting a good-shooting .45: Buy the Colt Gold Cup model or have a good auto "accurized" by one of the better pistolsmiths. Among the latter are Clark, Pachmayr, Behlert, and others. This work is not undertaken lightly; a complete accuracy job can

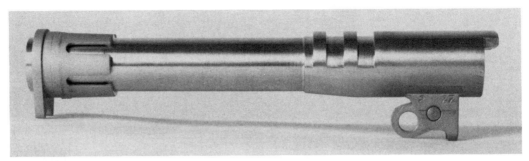

A stainless-steel replacement barrel for the .45 Colt Auto by Bar-Sto Precision Machine. In most cases you can install the barrel yourself, although some require custom fitting. These barrels greatly improve the accuracy of the standard .45 pistol with no other changes; Bar-Sto barrels are also available for other auto pistols.

run to about $500. When completed these jobs will shoot 1-inch-or-better groups at 25 yards from a machine rest.

Accurizing is a very sophisticated procedure. The gunsmith will test-fire your gun when he gets it to determine if its original barrel is suitable. If not you will be advised and he will supply a new barrel. The following is what happens to your .45 when you send it to Pachmayr and order its "signature" system, which is claimed to be the most sophisticated and boasts nine patents. The Pachmayr people polish all internal surfaces to eliminate interferences to assure reliable functioning. They precision-fit slide to frame and special barrel bushing to slide and barrel. They rebuild and custom-fit the barrel hood, removing all side and end play. They match and polish ramps for improved feeding. They fit a custom-made wide link and patented slide stop and pin to the barrel locking lugs and frame to eliminate play and looseness. They precision-bevel the slide's bottom to match the beveled surface of the patented "slide tightener unit." (When adjusted correctly, this unit removes all up-and-down play between the slide and frame.) They install a patented barrel bushing assembly, which consists of a precision self-aligning bearing that allows the rear end of the barrel to move up and down without binding while precisely controlling the barrel.

Pachmayr tested all makes of .45 Auto pistols (many were made by various contractors during wartime) and ammunition to learn that headspace sometimes accumulated variations up to .047 inch. When the firing pin must drive the car-

tridge into a too-deep chamber, varied or weak ignition will result. So a patented "zero headspace" unit is also installed. It firmly seats every cartridge in firing position and eliminates all headspace problems. Finally, the whole job is fitted with a special trigger and target grips, and polished and blued.

While that outlines the Pachmayr accuracy job, other gunsmiths perform essentially the same sort of alterations to the .45. This pistol needs a lot of help, because it is primarily a service pistol made to be reliable rather than accurate. For a gun to operate consistently under varied conditions you must have ample tolerances—which aid function but do not contribute to target accuracy. Service .45s generally have an inherent accuracy of from 5-inch to 14-inch groups at 50 yards. Some drastic action is necessary to tighten those groups enough to be of target quality. This might well be termed making a silk purse out of a sow's ear, because even the junkiest .45, as long as the frame is in good condition, can be made to shoot along with the finest. In the same fashion, a battlefield relic Mauser can be made to deliver benchrest accuracy with extensive gunsmithing. Such work is costly because any precision product is worth a lot of money today.

As you might expect, .45 ACP ammunition runs the full range from excellent in terms of accuracy to awful. Military ammo is known among shooters as "hardball," which loosely means a full-jacketed roundnosed bullet. Military ammo is sometimes capable of decent accuracy, but other lots or batches are not. If storage has been suitable, old ammunition doesn't pose problems for the shooter except that very old ammunition (military cartridges are always dated) has corrosive primers and the gun must be cleaned with hot water or a water-based cleaner.

Modern target .45 ammunition is loaded to very high standards of accuracy and will perform brilliantly in any good .45 pistol or revolver. Depending on the gun (and the shooter), some of this ammunition will group inside 1 inch or less at 25 yards.

OTHER CALIBERS AND CARTRIDGES

By no means is pistol/revolver accuracy limited to the .22, .38, and .45. These were mentioned first because nearly all formal target shooting is done with them. One of the better and more popular revolver cartridges is the .22 WMR (Winchester Magnum Rimfire), which is described elsewhere in this book. In terms of revolver accuracy this is a fine cartridge giving a good muzzle velocity (Winchester states 1600 fps from the 8⅜-inch barrel which is available in the Smith & Wesson Model 48).

Revolvers chambered for the .22 WMR are very popular. Quite frankly, this cartridge met with considerable skepticism when it was first announced. Nobody really could see much need for it, and early ammunition was loaded to very high pressures. The ammunition problem was licked and the cartridge became fairly popular after overcoming the adverse publicity. One of the outstanding attributes of the .22 WMR is its adaptability to revolvers with an extra cylinder for the .22 Long Rifle. There is little doubt in my mind that this is the most logical and practical use for the cartridge. As a rifle cartridge it isn't very popular and isn't much needed. But it sure does pep up the revolver world and provides excellent shooting. The good shooting comes from basic excellent accuracy plus a flat trajectory.

A fine "golden oldie," if you can find one, is the ancient .32/20, which not only provides good accuracy but also stops with considerable authority when the bullet hits the target.

The magnums are a case by themselves. The first, the .357, is the most popular of all, and since a .38 Special can be fired in any .357, it makes a very sensible choice. Excellent accuracy, good speed, and flat trajectory make the .357 an ideal gun for the sportsman. Indeed, it would be difficult to choose a more useful revolver.

Revolvers in .41 and .44 Magnum also possess astounding accuracy for guns of such power. And their speed allows one to sight about an inch high at 25 yards, with the bullet 1½ inches high at 50 yards and only 1¼ low at 100 yards. These figures are approximate for both cartridges. But note how effective they are for any sporting use. At any range up to about 115 yards you need not hold off the target at all.

The world's most popular military cartridge, the 9mm Parabellum or Luger, is not among the most accurate by any means. Moreover, it is not much of a sporting proposition. There would appear to be several reasons for this. The cartridge has been manufactured for military use, and service ammunition is far from target grade. Most pistols for which it is chambered are service guns, and like the .45 Auto service pistol they are made for reliability rather than accuracy. But there has been no great surge of interest in shooting this cartridge at targets, so there's been no interest in accurizing 9mm pistols. It's possible the situation might change, since Ruger now chambers a revolver for this cartridge and since good bullets are available for the handloader. Should the Ruger revolver prove popular and should enough shooters begin loading accurate ammunition and doing some good shooting with this gun, it's possible that it may be elevated in accuracy ratings. I'd have to guess the odds are not in its favor, largely because it's scarcely needed. The .38 Special is as accurate as any centerfire cartridge for pistol/revolver use is likely to be, and the .357 is a better shooter than the 9mm any day. Since both cartridges can be fired in the same revolver and since they bracket the 9mm's performance, of what use is the 9mm to American sportsmen?

The 9mm will continue to be a fine service sidearm; it has suitable accuracy for that. But it's hardly a gun for any sporting purpose unless you handload, and even then the gun would be suspect unless accurized or unless it is the Ruger revolver.

A much-ignored cartridge which really deserves more attention from shooters and manufacturers alike is the .38 Colt, which is available in the Colt Auto pistol. It needs more guns made for the cartridge and more shooters using it. The cartridge itself is a good one.

One of the old-timers that has retained its popularity well over the years is the .44 Special. A good reason for this continuing popularity is the fact that it can be fired in .44 Magnum guns. Nevertheless, all on its own the .44 Special is a fine cartridge that delivers very good accuracy and substantial whack on the hitting end. It does require handloading for best results, however, because there are too many older-model guns still in use and factory ammunition must be loaded to standards that are safe in the old guns. New guns can safely handle a lot more pressure.

The old .45 Colt is in the same category, in that many old guns abound and must not be shot with hot handloads. But guns of recent manufacture in this caliber respond with remarkable accuracy and authority when handloaded.

When choosing a cartridge you can see that your best accuracy will come from a good gun, preferably one that has been accurized by a top pistolsmith, chambered for the .22 Long Rifle, .38 Special, or .45 ACP. A few others will also give exceptionally good accuracy, perfectly suitable for most sporting use.

CONCENTRIC BULLETS

Bullet balance is not as big a factor in handgunnery as it is in riflery, because the ranges are shorter, but the principles remain the same. Only concentric bullets can be depended upon to deliver top accuracy, for reasons fully explained in earlier chapters.

Bullet balance is important to some degree for handgunners. If your forte is long-range varmint popping with a scope-sighted pistol like the .221 Fire Ball, you have to be aware of it. If you're a 25- and 50-yard target shooter, you can forget about it, and if you're only going to use a pistol or revolver for plinking or beheading a snake on a fishing trip it is no factor at all.

"COMBAT" GUNS

There is a target-shooting trend today toward a type of competition known as combat shooting. It calls for special guns, which are drawn from

A .45 Colt Auto pistol altered by Austin Behlert for "combat" shooting. This alteration consists of shortening and reducing the depth of the gun to make it easier to get on target quickly. Other accurizing features are also incorporated.

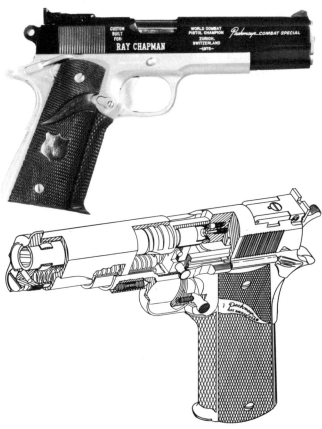

The .45 auto pistol custom-made by Pachmayr for World Combat Pistol Champion Ray Chapman. This gun has every possible refinement. The cutaway shows the internal working of the Pachmayr accurizing job. The treatment can render a service .45 meant to work in the tropics and the Arctic, the mud and desert, into a capable performer guaranteed to put its shots into 1 inch or better at 25 yards.

the holster and fired at a silhouette target with a very fast time limit. A number of guns are considered good for this purpose, and many of them are customized quite extensively for the purpose.

Combat shooting is mostly practiced by law-enforcement officers, although a number of civilian shooters have taken it up. This kind of shooting calls for accuracy, but accuracy of a far different type than we've been talking about, because the range is short. What counts here is getting the gun clear of the holster and firing it fast. An inch or so of error in the gun is of little consequence, so these guns are selected or customized to make them faster to get into operation and faster to reload. Austin Behlert of Union, N.J., claims to be the only pistolsmith in the country currently shortening the "Big Three": .45 Auto, Browning P-35, and Smith & Wesson 39. The operation consists of cutting these guns shorter and shallower while retaining the basic function and disassembly. The result is a faster-handling gun. And such a gun costs more than $500 in 1977.

PRACTICAL ACCURACY

The foregoing discussion has primarily concerned pure accuracy. The basic accuracy built into the gun, and the gun/ammo combination, is its inherent accuracy. But many types of shooting do not demand top accuracy. If your objective, say as a law-enforcement officer, is to hit a man-sized target at a distance no more than about 25 feet, you have no need for an accurized .45 Auto that will keep ten shots inside an inch at three times that distance.

We will define "practical accuracy" as that required to hit our target, regardless what that target might be. While the capability of the shooter should be involved in that buying decision to a degree, it ought not to get in the way too much, because it's an imprecise factor and because it can generally be improved by practice.

For example, if you plan to use a handgun for long-range shooting at woodchucks or crows or other varmints, then your choice will be some special-purpose gun like the Thompson/Center in one of its appropriate chamberings, or the .221 Remington Fire Ball or something of that sort with a scope mounted. If your planned use will be big-game hunting—and I don't recommend this use for a pistol or revolver—then your gun must have the necessary power and accuracy to hit the beast you'll be hunting in a vital spot over the ranges you are likely to shoot. Only you can make that determination.

If your use is for home defense or pocket use, then almost any decent gun will have sufficient accuracy. So practical accuracy is impossible to define categorically; only you are in a position to make the judgment.

Hand in hand with any consideration of practical accuracy goes a study of trajectory. That's the flight of the bullet, and it's important here because the high arcing flight of a .45 Auto is useless at long range even if the gun is scoped. Trajectory is a function of bullet shape, diameter, weight, and velocity, and flatness of trajectory helps because it minimizes errors of aim and misjudgment of range.

Generally speaking, today's well-made pistol or revolver will deliver far better accuracy than 99 percent of the shooters will ever be able to handle. Nevertheless, it is well to keep in mind the fact, true with any firearm, that you can never shoot better than the gun is capable of delivering. Other things being the same, it is wise to choose a gun and ammunition that possess good accuracy, because that will reduce your inaccuracy to that caused by your aiming and holding errors.

CHAPTER TWENTY-TWO

USES

The uses of pistols and revolvers are many and varied. This chapter is not an attempt to advise anyone what is legal or illegal, but rather suggests what I feel are proper uses of the handgun along with advice concerning the type of gun to use and caliber selection.

SPORT SHOOTING

Sport shooting includes almost everything—it depends upon the person doing the defining. I shall try to hew the line and keep my definitions accurate, and I suggest you do the same by following the rules of common sense and decency in your shooting habits.

Target shooting generally covers everything from the formal variety on a legitimate range to the guy who bops pop bottles and tin cans in a dump or quarry or gravel bank or whatever. Target shooting need not be formal, but it ought to be done on a proper range. There are usually local gun clubs within the reach of everyone, and most clubs have a number of persons with an interest in pistol shooting (as opposed to rifle shooters, skeet shooters, and trap shooters, who, while they usually speak to each other, have not much more than that in common). You'll find these folks are almost invariably helpful.

It isn't necessary for you to become an expert pistol shooter, but it is necessary for you to become proficient enough to put your shots all on the paper and close enough to accomplish what you want.

And that might be anything from game shooting to home defense. Should there be no local range available, then you should seek a place with a safe backstop, such as a gravel pit or a suitable hillside. Then of course you ought to get the permission of the landowner.

Punching holes in paper is regarded as boring by many and they often turn to bottles and cans. This is a rotten habit and should be discouraged. Nothing gives shooting a worse name than this sort of irresponsible littering and messing up the landscape. If you must pop a tin can, at least have the decency to bury the remains. There is no excuse whatever for shooting glass objects.

The sort of target shooting I'm recommending here can be done with a rest to start, because then you'll learn how well the gun can perform and how it should be sighted. A stepladder makes a fine rest for the two-hand hold and will be found very handy. Once you have determined what the gun can do, then you can practice to achieve similar results with the one-hand hold. There are many books on target shooting with pistols and revolvers.

Plinking is the most loosely defined word in all gundom; if you ask ten shooters I think you'd get the same number of definitions. Basically it covers banging away at almost any object that is not a formal target on a formal range. Thus plinking might well be considered what I've just described as informal target shooting. Campers and fishermen often tote a small handgun for snakes, then sometimes pop away at nearby objects while taking a lunch break. There's nothing wrong with this kind of plinking so long as it doesn't disturb others and you don't leave any mess behind you.

SMALL GAME AND VARMINTS

It's a bit difficult to separate these two, for the requirements are very similar. For example, you can shoot red, gray, and fox squirrels with a .22 pistol; but red squirrels are varmints and gray and fox squirrels are small game. Squirrel shooting with a .22 pistol is an exciting sport that calls for excellent marksmanship. If you haven't tried it it might seem an impossible thing to accomplish, but it's really not that difficult if you can handle your gun.

Edible small game should be shot with solid nonexpanding bullets to reduce the damage to edible meat. If your gun is a .22 Long Rifle, for example, the solid lead bullet ought to be used. The .22 WMR is loaded with a metal-cased bullet that's ideal for small game and is also a fine turkey load (where you hold for the wing butts).

Recently there has been increased activity in shooting varmints at long range. This is usually done with special handguns capable of handling big cartridges and performing well at long range — for example, the .221 Remington Fire Ball pistol and the Thompson/Center Contender chambered for one of the mighty cartridges available. The ordinary revolver can be used in some cases but is not especially suited for such long-range precision shooting. However, a good .357 Magnum, fitted with a scope and with enough testing, could be used.

As a youngster in the 1930s I used to have a lot of fun popping red squirrels with a Colt .22 Woodsman auto. These were more innocent days and I got to the point where I could hit quite a few of them. While I only participated once because I found it distasteful, some folks I know regularly shoot rats in a dump. I suspect the rat is one step below a varmint, but he does afford excellent practice and is an ammo maker's delight because a fearful amount of ammo is burned up. The rat-per-box ratio is worse than in dove shooting during a high wind. But shooting in a dump is hardly conducive to sporting shooting and extreme care must be taken about the direction of fire.

Shooting a woodchuck at long range with a scoped handgun is a challenge and, given a good gun, can be a very sporting proposition.

BIG-GAME HUNTING

This is a sport that I don't care to recommend to the handgunner, but it is practiced by a number of very capable marksmen. I must emphasize the word "capable" — not only capable shots but shooters with the capability of taking only a sure shot with a gun and load that are up to the job.

I have in my possession a dramatic photo of Robert E. "Pete" Petersen, chairman of the board of Petersen Publishing (*Guns & Ammo, Hunting,* and other magazines), with a trophy polar bear taken with a .44 Magnum revolver. Pete shot this bear shortly after the .44 was first announced, when polar-bear hunting was legal. The photo proves that such game may be and has been taken with the handgun. Mr. Petersen is an excellent shot and a lover of fine guns; he knows what he's doing (and he was backed up by a companion with a powerful rifle).

The .44 Magnum can take such game. So can the .41 Magnum, and so can several of the cartridges for which the Thompson/Center Contender is built. The Contender is a single-shot pistol, however, something of a disadvantage, especially if you're tackling dangerous game. Another development, the Auto-Mag, is designed purely for hunting and is an autoloading gun that lends itself beautifully to powerful handloaded wildcat cartridges.

Should your interest lie in the direction of big-game hunting, you should check out the big handguns, make your selection, and learn how to use the gun. And you should use a scope on the gun.

A number of professional guides pack a big gun on their hip when afield with their clients because the gun offers ample power if needed and leaves the guide's hands free for other tasks. I hunted boar on a Vermont preserve a few years ago and noted that the guide carried a .44 Smith & Wesson Magnum slung on his hip. When you understand what a boar can do to you and will do if he gets a chance, it's evidence why such a handgun is comforting.

CALIBER CHOICE AND LOAD SELECTION

The first handgun anyone should buy is a .22. It's the most useful of all guns and can be used all the way from home defense (the .22 Long Rifle high-speed hollowpoint is very effective) to small-game and varmint shooting at close range. If a bit more power is needed you can choose a revolver with extra cylinder for the .22 WMR (only available in revolvers).

Shooting a .22 produces no recoil problems, and the ammunition is cheap. It's the best gun to use when learning how to shoot a handgun. The .22 is capable of the finest accuracy, as is evidenced by the fact that it's the caliber used in free-pistol shooting at Olympic and International matches.

Just about the only danger of a .22 handgun is that some think it is a toy. It most certainly is not, and this should be made clear at the earliest possible moment if you are teaching a youngster, or *anyone*, to use it.

Beyond the .22, caliber choice and load selection depends upon the intended use. The two cannot be separated. If your choice is a revolver, then the next most logical step is the .38 Special or .357 Magnum. The Magnum is a better choice, because it will also shoot .38 Special ammunition, but if the gun is to be used for undercover work a smaller .38 would be the choice. Both these cartridges are available in a wide variety of bullet styles. Another noteworthy point is

One of the most useful .22 pistols on the market is the Ruger Standard, available in 4¾-inch barrel as shown as well as in heavy-barrel target versions. This little pistol is superb for plinking and informal target shooting and may be used for some defense and as a trail sidearm on a camping or fishing trip.

that there is a more potent .38 Special load suitable for use in certain revolvers, designated +P and so stamped on the head of the cartridge. These cartridges must be used only in guns designated by the manufacturer as suitable for their extra pressure.

The next step up from the .357 is the .41 Magnum and, above that, the .44 Magnum. Both are excellent guns, and they are fairly similar in versatility (the .41 is factory-loaded with a lighter lead-bullet load for police work and practice shooting; the .44 Magnum may be used with lighter .44 Special ammunition). Properly used, either of these guns will drop any game animal in North America; but don't think I am recommending that you try it.

I think the most useless gun ever produced is the little .25 Auto, which is very puny. The next step up is the .380, available only in pocket autoloaders. The .380 has no other use and should be considered only for pocket (or bedside-table) use. Among the .38 calibers you can choose the 9mm or the Colt Super .38. The latter is a good cartridge, though it has never achieved the popularity of the 9mm because the latter is a military cartridge and has long been used by many major nations around the globe.

A 9mm has little sporting use aside from target shooting. It remains a great military cartridge and is available in a wide variety of guns, nearly all of them autoloaders (Ruger has a revolver in this caliber).

A very early, and well-used, sample of the .25 Colt Auto pocket pistol invented by John Browning. Shown in my hand, it can easily be palmed out of sight.

Colt's big .45 Auto is useful only for target shooting and defense. It has no application in the hunting world. There is a tremendous interest in this fine cartridge, and today there are a couple of new smaller and lighter guns on the market that handle it. A good, fairly light target load is available in .45 ACP that is easy to shoot.

The above are the most common handguns. Beyond them are the special-purpose numbers like the wide variety of chamberings offered by Thompson/Center for their single-shot Contender pistol, which range from .22 to the mighty Herrett wildcats and include a dying cartridge that's always been a favorite of mine, the .25/35. That was always a great cartridge for deer shooting when the hunter could take his time and carefully place his shot.

And you have such oddities as the Auto-Mag, a stainless-steel autoloader in some whopping calibers. Doubtless there will be others as time goes by, and there have been some real weirdos developed, including a handgun for the .45/70 that would require more than normal stamina to handle.

SHOCKING POWER OF GAME LOADS

If you expect a precise list of numbers indicating the shocking power of each load, you're in for a disappointment. This can't be done with any degree of reliability.

In any discussion of shocking power of game loads you must first define what you're talking about, for it's obvious that a load suitable for popping a woodchuck at 100 yards will be something vastly different from a genuine stopper for a wounded Alaskan bear. And there is also a vast difference between handloaded ammunition and that available over the counter. For an example of that extreme, take note that the .30 Herrett cartridge is often used with the 124 Sierra bullet, which it drives at about 2300 fps out of the Contender pistol. That is a suitable load for antelope, deer, and game of similar size. That is, assuming you can place the bullet where you want to; otherwise all bets are off.

Of course, the shooter who buys one of these special-purpose guns and knows how to use it needs no advice from me on what his loads will do. He knows which bullet to use for what purpose as well as I do. You will find useful information in Chapters Sixteen and Seventeen on this subject.

"Shocking power" means the ability of a bullet to transmit its energy to the game. This is accomplished by a combination of bullet weight, construction, and speed (at point of impact). The placement of the shot is also of vital importance, for it affects the expansion of the bullet and thus the energy transmitted as well as the amount of shock that will be utilized (meaning that a hit in the flank of an animal might transmit the same energy but will not be as meaningful as a hit in the vital organs of the rib cage).

John Taylor in his book *African Rifles and Cartridges* stated it wisely when he said your bullet should be placed at the shoulder and should have the capability of *breaking both shoulders.* While he was talking about dangerous game, the same reasoning applies to any game for two important reasons: The shot that breaks both shoulders will anchor any four-legged beast on the spot. He can go nowhere on just his hind legs, so this shot is very important, assuming a broadside opportunity, with dangerous game. The other reason is that a bullet which can plow through and break both shoulders is also going to pass through the lung/heart area and will be a fast-killing shot as well.

This sort of penetration is a function of bullet construction and velocity as well as the particular game involved. I find it very questionable that any handgun bullet can be depended upon to break both shoulders of a grizzly bear, for example. Certainly it would not be a good bet to depend on it. Packing a .44 Magnum on the hip in bear country is sensible; taking a shot at a bear unless it's attacking or already wounded is not especially smart.

Under this subject it should be noted that Remington is now doing a very smart thing on its ammunition boxes. For example, the back of a box of .221 Remington Fire Ball cartridges has an illustration of the "pointed softpoint" bullet loaded in this box. The copy tells what the bullet is designed for (rapid penetration and high shocking power without deep penetration) and adds: "Remington recommends these bullets for varmints and light, thin-skinned game."

That tells the story pretty well, and Remington should be credited with giving the consumer some good advice that the gun industry in general doesn't bother to give. Of course I can quarrel with part of their recommendation too. "Light thin-skinned game" would probably include squirrels and rabbits, and there's no question that a hit with one of these high-speed thunderbolts would decimate one of these small animals. Unless you like to eat the hide you're advised to aim for the head if using a Fire Ball on such game. But for varmints this bullet will be found superb.

The hunter who shoots squirrels, rabbits, and other edible small game with handguns using solid or jacketed bullets—say in .22 caliber, which would include the .22 Long Rifle and WMR—is well advised to try to hit the head. I acknowledge this calls for some damned close shooting, but you shouldn't hunt with a handgun unless you can hit that small a mark. A head shot has big advantages: It's either a total miss or an instant kill and it destroys no meat.

I read not long ago the story of a fellow who was watching through a high-power scope when his wife slammed a deer with a .243 Winchester slug at about 100 yards. The bullet reportedly took the animal in the neck, and he reported that the whole animal was so shocked by the impact of that fast slug that its eyes popped and a sort of wave swept through the length of the animal, which was dead before it hit the ground. The point of the story is that it was a shock effect, which is a frequent by-product of high velocity, that killed the animal. During the early days of high-velocity rifles this hydraulic shock effect was credited with enormous and mysterious qualities. Most of them were false, but there is something to the phenomenon; it does exist and does work under certain conditions. However, not that many handguns develop such a shocking speed; hydraulic shock is far less of a factor with handgun hunters unless you are smashing a woodchuck at 100 yards with the .221 Fire Ball.

The shocking power of most handgun bullets lies in their sheer mass, with a boost from sheer speed. By which I mean that the .44 Magnum (like the .41 Magnum) is a massive bullet that rides at good speed. That's what does the killing —sheer impact. The .357 Magnum, on the other hand, is a relatively small bore by comparison and it has excellent velocity. Its killing power is more a function of penetration than is the case of the fatter .44.

A fatter cartridge yet, the .45 ACP, or the .45 Colt, which is available for single-action revolvers, doesn't have the speed of the .44 Magnum and doesn't have the killing power. Using a .45 Auto on game would be a mistake, because the combination of slow speed with jacketed bullet would not have enough penetration to be effective. The .45 Colt, on the other hand, while a slow-moving slug, has a lead bullet which will transmit more energy to the target than will the ACP.

No matter how you slice it, no matter how you justify or excuse it, the hunting of game animals with a handgun should be undertaken only by experts. Frankly, I think such shooting is done mostly for its stunt value and that most hunters ought to stick to the rifle and leave handguns to their intended purpose. The handgun is a *sidearm*.

DEFENSE USE

The role of a handgun is defensive. While it is used offensively on occasion, a handgun was always intended to be something with which a man could defend himself at close quarters. Handguns are still primarily defensive arms; one of their most important roles is to defend oneself or one's family. The law-enforcement use of a handgun is purely defensive—even to a larger degree than usual, because a cop almost always has to give the crook the first shot. Mili-

tary use of the handgun is also defensive, and aside from sporting use, the civilian use of a handgun is to defend.

There are several ways in which the gun is used defensively: carrying the gun on your person, storing the gun in a handy place in the home, and carrying it in a vehicle. When a gun is kept for defense purposes it is important to note that it *should be kept loaded*. Should the gun be needed it will be needed quickly or quietly or both. Fumbling around in the dark to bring gun and its ammunition together completely defeats the purpose.

Naturally, a loaded handgun should be kept out of the reach of children and should be kept out of sight. The choice of a pistol or revolver is left up to individual preference. I would suggest that the caliber be either .22 or .38, because such a gun will have other uses and its owner should become familiar with his gun and should have fun with it in addition to owning it for its defensive role.

A gun to be carried on the person must be small and compact, which rules out the brutes like the .44 Magnum or the .45 Auto. Still, my old friend Elmer Keith used to carry his "social .44" (a .44 Special) everywhere he went. Most such guns are slim pocket autos like the .380s, and they fit into a neat holster without being obvious. Some prefer a small revolver in .38 Special. This is an individual choice.

The Colt Agent pocket revolver is typical of the modern double-action revolver used for undercover work. Chambered for the .38 Special cartridge, this is a popular style for police use. At one time it was popular to grind off the hammer spur and remove the front of the trigger guard for pocket use.

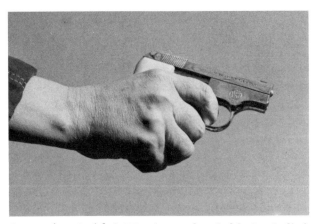

At one time Smith & Wesson marketed this dandy little .22 Long Rifle Escort model; it has been withdrawn from the line. Shown here in a woman's hand, the Escort was an ideal defensive sidearm.

If a gun is to be carried in a vehicle it must be out of sight but readily accessible. You can obviously carry a heavy handgun this way, and the choice should be as heavy as you want it for the possible use to which it might be put.

You should not get the idea that I'm advising you to carry a handgun either on your person or in your vehicle. These are legitimate uses of guns in some places by some people and should be considered in that light.

CHOICE OF A GUN

The choice of a handgun boils down to pistol or revolver, caliber, and make.

Some claim a revolver is safer than an autoloader, an argument I can't accept because you should first know how to handle a gun before you own one, in which event either is as safe as the other. The reason it's often claimed that an auto pistol is less safe is that when you remove the magazine there may still be a cartridge in the chamber. Some guns provide for this by having an extractor that protrudes when a round is chambered and you can see or feel it. Others have a magazine safety which means the gun can't fire while the magazine is removed. But others can be fired, and that's why you must know your own specific gun.

Pistols are often more accurate than revolvers, but this is not infallible either because a well-designed and well-made revolver will deliver extraordinary accuracy. Blowback autos like the .22s are usually quite accurate because their barrels don't move as those of a recoil-operated gun do, but in the latter case an "accuracy job" will

Single-action revolvers are very popular and very useful. They usually are priced lower than comparable double-actions of equal quality. This is Ruger's new model Super Blackhawk, .44 Magnum with 7½-inch barrel.

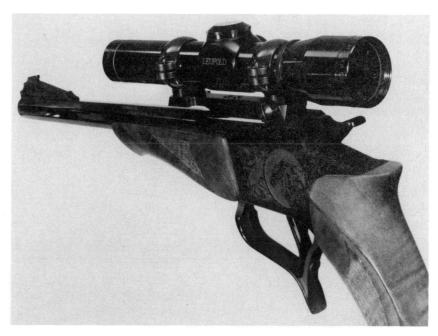

The Thompson/Center Contender is quite possibly the most versatile pistol ever produced. Barrels are quickly interchangeable and available in dozens of calibers. A unique choke device provides astonishing performance with .44 Magnum (equals .410 gauge payload and velocity) and .357. Shown here mounted with Leupold M8 scope.

be able to bring them up to a very high standard of accuracy.

The first gun you buy ought to be a .22, as I've said before, because you can use it for nearly everything. You can go on from there to any other caliber you wish. There are so many good .22s to choose from that personal preference ought to rule its selection.

Brand and price are two subjects I will avoid except to say that there are more good brands on the market today than ever before; some are American-made, others are imported. The trend here is to more and more American-made products, because the cost advantage of overseas production is quickly disappearing.

Today there are a number of single-shot pistols available also, and the most important one of these is the Thompson/Center Contender, which is available in a wide range of calibers. The T/C is strictly a sportsman's gun—it could perhaps more accurately be called a short-barreled, one-handed rifle than anything else. It definitely fills in a gap in the market, especially for the handgun hunter.

CHAPTER TWENTY-THREE

EXPERIENCES AND OPINIONS

Some years ago my friend Jack O'Connor wrote a column in *Outdoor Life* which he titled "The Quick and the Dead." It was about cartridges that have lasted and those that have gone. Often the reasons for the development of a cartridge are difficult to plumb, and at other times excellent cartridges never make the grade for reasons that are equally difficult to plumb.

Jack's title was only partly right: some of the hottest cartridges have fallen. But in general he's on the button. Back in 1965 I wrote a book called *The Anatomy of Firearms* and made some forecasts. How did I do now that twelve years have passed? If I could guess the football scores as well I'd break Jimmy the Greek. At least in the rifle-cartridge world, where I had only predicted one wrong.

I didn't do as well in the handgun forecast, since I predicted that the .22 Jet, .221 Fire Ball, and .256 would all disappear. The .221 hasn't gone, which indicates that Remington is selling enough of these pistols to keep it in the line—unless the firm has some other reason for keeping a pistol in production which they haven't talked about. I consider the .256 a dead duck, even though the Thompson/Center is chambered for it.

But then I pulled a real bomb by predicting that the .41 Magnum would slowly outdistance the .44 Magnum. That was a bad guess. I still think I'm right about what *should* happen with the .41; that it hasn't caught fire is a mystery.

Now for some new forecasts.

The .32 Smith & Wesson Long continues in the S&W and H&R lines for reasons that defy any common sense. A 98-grain bullet at 705 fps is not worth building a fine revolver for, and this number ought to be dropped right now. The .25 ACP ought to be dropped, but it won't be. This is a weak cartridge by any measurement (it's at least equaled if not exceeded by the .22 Long Rifle in similar-sized pocket pistols) and there is no excuse for its continuation.

The .380 ACP was gone for a brief period but is back again, bigger than ever. There are now more pistols made for the .380 than at any time in history—that's a big statement but I believe it's true. For years and years the only gun on the American market was the old Colt pocket pistol, aside from an occasional Browning and Walther in this chambering. Today there are many models of .380, by many new companies unheard of a couple of years ago, and I think this trend will continue. It would be smart of the Colt people if they dusted off the old tooling and put their pocket model back in production. Colt has a strange habit of dropping the wrong models at the wrong time. They dropped their old Model P Single Action Army in the 1940s only to have Ruger come along with a single-action revolver and show them the way. And, in 1977, Colt has dropped their .22 Auto pistol—the classic old Woodsman.

The 9mm and .45 ACP will continue to grow and expand. Efforts to tame the .30 U.S. Carbine in handguns will probably continue, but it's a case of trying to make a silk purse out of a sow's ear. Among the current crop of handgun wildcats I see some steady popularity, on a small scale, for the two Herrett chamberings in the T/C gun. But these can't ever achieve real volume because they are not adaptable to revolvers or autos. The Auto-Mag event will continue to have some mild attraction for its followers, but that's about the extent of it.

An excellent cartridge that I'd like to see brought back in a good revolver is the old .32/20. According to Winchester ballistics, this number fires a 100-grain bullet at a respectable 1030 fps muzzle velocity. Compare that with the .32 S&W Long and you'll quickly see what I mean about the two. S&W would do well to simply drop their Model 31 and add a new model to the K frame series chambered for .32/20 and with good, adjustable sights. I think they'd have a winner.

Now let's consider the strange case of the .41 Magnum. It has been said that one of the problems this gun has encountered in the market is the word "Magnum," because the word itself contains mystical, and mythical, connotations. It is meant for the law-enforcement business, but cops are leery of its power and don't want to try it. The fact that the lead bullet load is a tame one has been lost on the market.

I helped the company introduce the gun in 1964 as its advertising agent. However, I was involved only with the very first series of advertisements, because a competitive situation reared its head and I was forced to resign the Smith & Wesson advertising account (advertising agencies usually do not handle competitive accounts). At that point I know that the .41 was pushed by a number of gun writers, notably Elmer Keith, although there were others. It was their claim that there were too many cops being outgunned by crooks and that the standard .38 Special was inadequate. It was they who more or less dictated the .41 caliber and the two loads for this gun. The ammunition was developed by Remington in a cooperative venture with Smith & Wesson.

So the gun was launched. It ran into a storm of criticism among gun writers for reasons which are obscure. Maybe some of them were miffed because they hadn't been consulted. Maybe they just changed their minds. The reasons are not easy to understand. And even those who had been pushing for the .41 failed to respond with enough enthusiasm to help carry the gun over the top. Criticism by the pack has certainly hurt the .41, for gun writers, despite their ability or lack of ability, do have a certain following. *Somebody* believes them no matter what they say.

I think the writers were far off base in their critique of the .41. It's a fine cartridge, and if I had to choose between the .41 and .44 I'd choose the .41. It will do just about as much and with less fuss, muss, recoil, and boom.

It is somewhat gratifying to note that some of the more knowledgeable scribes are belatedly coming along to this conclusion and they are now boosting the .41. Given a decent chance, this cartridge ought to "slowly outdistance the .44" as I prophesied in 1965. But it will be a long time before that happens. I will cover the .41 in more detail in Chapter Twenty-four as it applies to law-enforcement use.

STAINLESS STEEL

I had, I believe, the very first stainless-steel revolver to leave the Smith & Wesson plant in 1965, the Model 60 Chief's Special. This was a .38 Special with 2-inch barrel. The only things on that gun that weren't stainless steel were the walnut grips. After shooting the gun for a few weeks I thought it would be a good exercise to subject it to something of a torture test to see what would happen. So I buried the uncleaned gun in the fall in our rose garden. Next spring I dug it out. It had been buried from November until the following April and subjected to the usual rigors of a southern New England winter, which included rain, snow, and frozen ground.

When I dug it up I just washed it off with the garden hose (see photos), loaded it, and fired it. From that day on, as long as I had the gun, it was never cleaned or even oiled. And it never failed to work properly. There was a slight discolor-

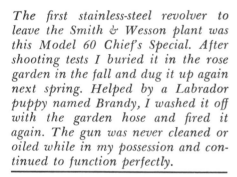

The first stainless-steel revolver to leave the Smith & Wesson plant was this Model 60 Chief's Special. After shooting tests I buried it in the rose garden in the fall and dug it up again next spring. Helped by a Labrador puppy named Brandy, I washed it off with the garden hose and fired it again. The gun was never cleaned or oiled while in my possession and continued to function perfectly.

ation on the hammer and trigger, which was the result of a heat treatment of these parts which added carbon to make the parts harder. Otherwise the gun looked just as it did when it was buried. Even the grips stood the treatment well.

Since that first model in stainless, S&W has added a number of models, Ruger has gone all out to produce stainless revolvers, and a batch of new companies and imports are using the metal as though they just discovered it.

Stainless steel is made by adding chromium to steel. It is important to know that there are as many kinds of stainless as there are grains of sand. Generally speaking, stainless costs more to buy than other steels and it is more difficult to machine. The more chromium (and thus the more rust resistance) in the alloy, the harder it is to machine, and this is especially true with a difficult operation like barrel drilling. Some manufacturers use stainless bar stock, others use stainless forgings, and others, especially Ruger, use stainless investment castings.

Ruger's investment-casting method is probably the least costly of all because parts made by this process require very little machining, a great advantage with stainless. This procedure, which is quite common today, is roughly as follows. The part to be made is carefully crafted in an exact wax mold of the part. Intricate surfaces can be made as an integral part of the wax mold. The wax is then coated with several layers of a ceramic material, which is cured and then heated to allow the wax to melt away. The cavity is then filled with molten steel (stainless or any other alloy desired), and the result is a part which is an exact replica of the wax model. In production many parts are made at once, and the investment casting process, often called the lost-wax process, is revolutionizing industry and has been applied by a number of gun makers.

I applaud the introduction of stainless steels to handgun manufacture. It's important for the sportsman because it helps protect the gun from neglect or abuse on hunting, fishing, or camping trips. But it really shines for the law-enforcement officer, especially game wardens in coastal areas where their arms are constantly exposed to salt water and salt spray. The only criticism I have of stainless steels is the finish, which I commented on in Chapter Twenty.

THE POCKET-AUTO SHORTAGE: ALTRUISTIC MOTIVES?

In 1950, the late Gen. Julian S. Hatcher wrote in his *Official Gun Book* (Crown, 1950, p. 46), referring to small pocket automatic pistols: "They are looked on with disfavor by law-enforcement agencies and by such forward-looking organizations as the National Rifle Association. The leading firearms makers of this country have taken the same view and, in spite of the loss of revenue involved, they have discontinued the manufacture of .25-, .32-, and .380-cal. pocket-sized semiautomatic pistols."

That refers to Colt, which did not resume production of these models after World War II, although the company briefly imported a .25 auto which was branded Colt. For a short period Smith & Wesson manufactured the little .22 Escort, which was introduced in 1970 and later removed from the market for the very reason stated by Hatcher.

If indeed this is the reason for removal from the market of these products, the companies have their corporate heads in the sand. Other makers are filling the gap. There isn't a damned thing wrong with a pocket auto, any more than there is anything wrong with any reasonable type of firearm. It's the *use* to which a gun is put that can be good or bad, and that bears no relation to the gun itself.

Whether or not law-enforcement agencies look upon such guns with favor or disfavor is none of their damned business and bears no relationship to the question. In 1950 Gen. Hatcher might have considered the NRA a "forward-looking" outfit, but I think the good general would think otherwise today.

If the big gun makers—and the big ones today are Smith & Wesson, Ruger, and Colt, in that order—are not making pocket autos, why are they not?

I think S&W has enough trouble trying to fill revolver orders; the company isn't much concerned with new models at this time. Ruger—and I'm strictly guessing—has always pointed its products to the civilian sportsman market, with a couple of notable recent exceptions (the double-action revolver obviously was intended for the law-enforcement market and the Mini-14 rifle for a military market). But the time might well come when Ruger turns its talents toward the market for a good pocket pistol in .380 and/or .22 Long Rifle.

I think Colt is missing a bet by not getting back in the market with its great line of Browning-designed pocket autos. Why they are not making such models today is more than I know. Interestingly, both Colt and S&W are making short-barrel revolvers for off-duty or pocket use. So what's the difference between this particular gun and a similar auto?

Browning, for many years, marketed pocket autos in .25 and .380 calibers. These guns have always been manufactured in Belgium, and with passage of the "1968 Gun Control Law," certain guns could no longer be imported, though parts could be imported and assembled here. So Browning now lists the 9mm auto and its new .22 Challenger II, which is manufactured in the U.S. As far as I know, nobody considered Browning sinister because the company imported these pocket auto pistols. And nobody considers these new companies sinister because they've begun the manufacture of neat pocket autos in .380, 9mm, and even .45 caliber.

PREWAR AND POSTWAR

"They don't make 'em like they used to" is a popular phrase indeed. I suspect it's been used in other generations as well. Probably one of the most frequent applications of this phrase in all gundom was in reference to the pre-'64 vs. post-'64 Winchester line. Massive changes were made in product in 1964, which were unappreciated by the public (and which Winchester has had to abandon).

But the handgun market is totally different. In the first place, the prewar handgun manufacturers consisted only of Colt and Smith & Wesson, with a small boost from Harrington & Richardson, Iver Johnson, and High Standard. There were a few imports—the most important were the Walther, Browning, Luger, and Mauser. But there were very few.

Prewar Colt autoloading pistols are much sought after, as they should be. They consisted of the popular .45 plus the pocket pistols which we've already mentioned and the neat Woods-man .22 pistol. Many claim that revolver production before the war was better than it is today, and in some respects they may be right. But they are not right when it comes to general usefulness, newer cartridges, better grips, better sights, and so on.

Before World War II there was no Ruger and none of the rest of a score or more of the new manufacturers. Some things don't change, though, and I think you'll find the current production of Colt Model P revolvers and the Colt .45 Auto still about the same as it has always been. Still, if you locate one of the older models, one of those prewar gems, pick it up if the price is right and treat it gently. It's a collector's item and will only increase in value. It won't shoot any better and chances are not as well. To put this another way, there isn't as much difference between prewar and postwar handguns as there is between prewar and postwar long guns. But take note that prewar handguns are rare, because there wasn't much handgun production in the '20s and '30s, and so they are valuable.

WHY ARE REVOLVERS MORE POPULAR?

Good question. We've had revolvers in America since Sam Colt's first in 1836 out of the old Paterson, N.J., factory. And we've had autoloaders since around 1900, when John Browning first turned his attention to them. Smith & Wesson has been a revolver maker and still is a revolver maker even though the company makes a couple of autoloading pistols. No matter how you slice it, S&W is not really an autoloading-pistol company. It seems they just don't believe in them.

Bill Ruger started his company with an automatic .22 pistol which is still in the line. But that's the only autoloading pistol Ruger has ever made—and his company has been in business since 1949. During that period Ruger has introduced many new models, all of them with innovative features, including rifles and shotguns. But no more automatic pistols.

Colt, long the nation's leading producer of auto pistols, used to make a fine line of pocket autos and the finest .22 autoloader made. But today that company is down only to autoloaders in big service models—the .45 Government Model and models which can only be called adaptations of that model in Super .38 and 9mm calibers.

On the other hand, we now have a host of new companies making auto pistols, and only time will tell if they are going to succeed. Meanwhile there are as many imported revolvers as there are auto guns, which is a switch, since most imports used to be autos. Browning continues to offer a couple of models of automatics, still made in accordance with the original Browning patents, and this company has not begun to make or import revolvers.

Why are revolvers more popular in America? I'm not sure the question can be answered. It's no secret that Smith & Wesson is a stronger company than Colt, so maybe it's a better idea to copy S&W. Maybe it's because Bill Ruger showed the way with his many models of successful revolvers. Maybe it's because revolvers are built around more powerful and more imaginative cartridges. And maybe revolvers have greater sporting application.

These reasons are pure speculation, but they have some validity. Yet the recent interest in this country in protecting one's family and self has apparently spurred a rash of new pocket autos. Is this only the result of crime and the need for protection? Or is it in relation to the activities of the anti-gun crowd? I suspect it may be a combination of the two. Every time there's a new law proposed it seems more people go out and buy guns in order to get them "while they still can."

SOME EXTINCT MODELS

A number of guns have come along and failed to make it. Some of them were excellent, some were awful, and some were purely and simply ahead of their time.

One of the first of these was the elegant Tompkins .22 single-shot pistol, which resembled a nineteenth-century dueling pistol with its one-piece walnut stock. This was a truly fine target pistol with one of the sweetest trigger pulls of all time. Introduced in 1947, it was gone in only about two years.

In 1953, Sheridan introduced its Knockabout, also a single-shot .22 rimfire. I have described it in another chapter; it retailed for around $17 and was riveted together. Nonetheless it was a fine little gun, just the ticket to have in your pack for emergency use. But the Sheridan marketing thrust was entirely air-gun-oriented and the pistol was withdrawn from the line.

Even Savage Arms got into the handgun field briefly (again, the company made some fine pocket auto pistols in the years between the wars) in 1959 with a single-shot revolver patterned after the single-action sixguns. But this didn't last either, and, as I remember, the market didn't get very excited about this one.

Several derringers have come and gone in the years since World War II, and this is no big loss. Most of these were imports and some were of dubious quality. "Derringer," as I have explained elsewhere, is a corruption of Deringer, after the original pistol by Henry Deringer of Philadelphia. Several years ago I met, and fished with, Henry Deringer's great-grandson, army Lt. Col. Cliff Deringer, who spends some of his time excusing the fact that one of his ancestor's pistols killed Lincoln.

THE FUTURE OF THE PISTOL AND REVOLVER

Despite all the laws, despite all the efforts of a liberal, anti-gun media, handguns seem to be selling in larger volume than ever. Or maybe because of their efforts. Nonetheless:

I should like to see the .32/20 come back in a good, modern strong revolver that will stand a modern load in this fine old handgun cartridge.

I'd like to see a better ejection sytem in revolvers. Perhaps a return to the old top-break systems used by Smith & Wesson a hundred years ago in some pretty heavy calibers and still used by Harrington & Richardson in several .22 models. I can't be convinced that American know-how can't overcome the problem of a strong lock in such a revolver system, or, alternatively, a system of primary extraction as a swingout cylinder is opened. Either one of these would be of great benefit because it would offer much easier and faster extraction and ejection, and an argument could be made that it would provide a stronger lockup between cylinder and frame. The present double-action-revolver system of locking the cylinder leaves something to be desired in my opinion, since it only holds the rear of the cylinder with a small, short pin. Some models fasten the front of the ejector rod with another very small pin. This is hardly very secure and is subject to damage, as, for example, by a bent ejector rod.

I'd like to see the .41 Magnum get the attention it deserves, because it's a far finer cartridge than most people realize. Maybe the boys should pull in their horns, withdraw the ".41 Magnum," and reissue the same gun with a new name—say the ".410 RSW" (for Remington, Smith & Wesson) or some other name. A few years ago when Remington goofed with their .244 rifle by making it with a too-heavy barrel and with a too-slow rifling twist, they withdrew the whole thing and reissued the identical cartridge and called it the 6mm Remington. At the same time they lightened the barrel and corrected the rifling twist, they also changed the bullet weight of their factory loads, and the rifle is now successful. Sometimes you have to pause and regroup, as they say in the military. Hell, they could even give the .41 a metric name—a complete switch.

I'd like to see a nice, cheap single-shot .22 Long Rifle pistol not unlike the old Sheridan Knockabout back on the market—a little gun suitable for camping, fishing, and hunting trips that didn't cost enough to be a factor if you lost it out of a canoe. Such a pistol could save your life and ought to be a part of every emergency kit, along with fishing tackle, so a man can survive in the wilderness. Such a gun should not cost more than $25.

I'd like to see Colt bring back their .380 pocket auto and the Woodsman .22. The latter was dropped in 1977, and I found myself shocked silly by this news. This was the king of the .22 autos for so many years, including all the years of my youth. It was copied by the original Hi-Standard in 1932, but nobody seriously considered the Hi-Standard quite as good (the HS was a damned fine gun, but the Colt simply was a cut above everything else). Now it's gone, but I think Colt could sell this gun provided it followed the lines of the old prewar model. Even if listed at a premium price this model would sell. Colt seems to move the Colt-Sauer bolt-action high-powered rifle at a whale of a premium price, so I'd think a reintroduced Woodsman would sell.

And I'd like to see Colt tackle the .41 and .44 Magnums. They have steadfastly ignored many of the hottest developments that occur in Springfield, only some 25 miles up the river.

Finally, though I don't know if this can be done, I'd like to see a slimmer, less bulky optical sight for handgun use. The little Insta-Sight distributed by Thompson/Center is a step in the right direction, but it's hellishly expensive. If a small optical sight could be added to that cheap, little single-shot emergency pistol I spoke about earlier it would certainly help, and when you need an emergency kit in the wilds you may well be disabled, in which case you need every bit of help you can get.

CHAPTER TWENTY-FOUR

LAW ENFORCEMENT

The police officer's sidearm is the basic tool of his trade. It backs up his authority. It helps him extend the long arm of the law. The handgun is to a policeman what the rifle is to a soldier.

It's a pity that more police officers are not trained to shoot better than they do. The average policeman hardly ever fires his gun and probably couldn't be depended upon to hit a man if he had to. This isn't true universally, of course, because some police forces provide excellent marksmanship training. But too many have no provision for such training. The result often is guns that don't work right because of neglect or abuse, or policemen who can't shoot.

Nearly all policemen carry a 4-inch-barreled .38 Special revolver. A few carry .357s, .44s, and .45s, but these are the exception. There have been several forces that have adopted the .41-caliber revolver which was introduced especially for police work in 1964.

The .38 Special cartridge was originally developed in 1902. It has significantly more power and performance than the old .38 Long which it replaced. A number of experienced people think the .38 Special has outlived its usefulness; other experienced people think it's just as good as ever. The question may not be resolved for a long time (after all, some policemen are still armed with .32-caliber revolvers!). In any event, law-enforcement handgun requirements differ considerably from those of the sportsman's handgun.

The world's most popular police revolver is the Smith & Wesson Model 10 .38 Special held in the man's right hand. In the other hand is the .41 Magnum Model 58, which is slightly heavier but basically the same. Many experienced and knowledgeable officers regard the .41 as a far superior sidearm for police use.

First of all, a sportsman is a gun hobbyist if he's interested in owning a handgun. This means he doesn't much care if his gun develops a lot of recoil. He expects it, and I believe many sportsmen actually like recoil. The average policeman carries a gun because the regulations say he must. It's a weight on his hip, something he must care for, and, in general it's a nuisance.

Recoil also bothers the average officer. He doesn't like it and, truth is, he's afraid of it. This appears to be one reason the word "Magnum" doesn't appeal to cops. Yet many police officers want more power. The laws of motion are just as unrepealable as the laws of gravity—when you have more power at the business end you must expect more recoil at the back end as well. Recoil bothers some people more than others and is present to a more noticeable degree in some guns than others. Manufacturers, for example, build more weight into a gun for a heavy-recoil caliber to help soak up recoil. Correctly shaped grips will help distribute recoil over a wider area so no one part of the hand is required to take all the punishment. The way a man holds the gun is also important.

But I believe the major police problem with heavier handguns is that the police don't have that much interest in handguns. A few departments have apparently coped with the problem by offering incentives—such as extra pay for marksmanship ratings and so forth.

While police forces usually have other arms, such as tear-gas guns, .30/30 carbines (a short rifle, usually with 20-inch barrel), Thompson submachine guns, riot shotguns (loaded with buckshot and guaranteed to clear an alley or frighten a criminal into submission), and other devices, the handgun remains the policeman's individual weapon. It's the gun that can save his life. He ought to learn to use it well.

SPECIAL REQUIREMENTS

A fear of any police officer is that he may have to fire his gun in a crowd and run the risk of killing or wounding an innocent bystander. This can happen in one of several ways, the most common being that he may miss his man and hit another person or that his bullet may go right through the criminal and fly on with enough remaining energy to hit the inevitable little old lady with shopping bag and umbrella. The answer to the first is improving the shooting ability of the cop. The partial answer to the second is in the gun and, especially, the ammunition he uses.

The cop's shot must knock his adversary off his feet, must flatten him so he can't shoot back. Whether it kills him or not is entirely secondary. What is important—indeed, vital—is that this shot must prevent the armed criminal from firing back (which would place more innocent people as well as the officer in jeopardy).

Your aim must be true to place the bullet where desired. The gun must be capable of helping deliver the bullet where you want it, and the cartridge must be powerful enough to give the bullet enough energy to do the job it's asked to perform. But once the trigger has been pressed and the bullet is on its way, man has lost control of the situation and it's up to the bullet to finish the mission. Bullets behave in many ways and their behavior is so important that it is necessary to thoroughly explore their construction and behavior (see Chapter Sixteen).

A serious question is raised from time to time along these lines: "Suppose you were responsible for crippling the man at whom you shoot?" Experienced lawmen regard such a question as ridiculous. They counter that a cop uses his gun only when he is legally justified in doing so, and consequently the question is academic. If a criminal shoots at a police officer, he means to cripple, wound, or kill the cop. The cop is trained to

know when he must resort to the use of his gun, and his attitude must be that he'd better damned well stop the criminal. It's a clear case of kill or be killed.

There has been considerable publicity given the fact that police officers have been killed in gunfights when the cops were armed with .38 Special revolvers. In spite of several .38 hits, the criminals have continued to shoot back and, too many times, have killed cops. These incidents support the opinion that police officers today need more power in their sidearms than the .38 Special offers.

The trouble with a .38 Special is that, as with the older .38 Long, a man can absorb one or more shots and still be able to shoot back. Clearly, this does not contribute to the longevity

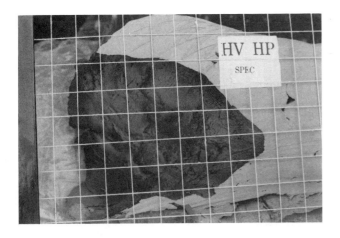

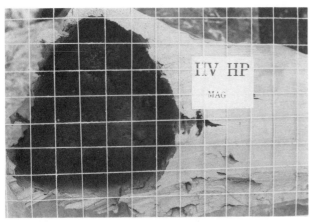
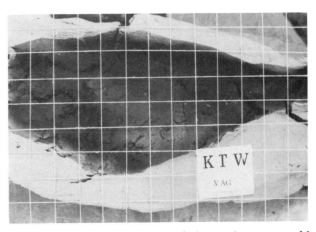

There are several companies manufacturing special ammunition for law enforcement. Their products are sold only to law-enforcement groups. These photos graphically show how superior such products are. On the left is shown the cavitation produced in 40-pound blocks of sculptor's clay by conventional high velocity .38 Special (top) and .357 Magnum (below). To the right of each is an example of the destruction wrought by a special brand known as KTW.

of police officers. Some departments have answered by switching to the .357 Magnum, a cartridge with considerably more power. But knowledgeable officers don't approve the choice of the .357. In spite of their different names, both cartridges are of the same diameter. (You can shoot .38 Special ammo in a .357 revolver, but not conversely.) What gives the .357 more power is its greater powder charge, which, in turn, simply adds velocity. And greater velocity gives the .357 Magnum more penetration than the .38 Special. The added speed permits the bullet to go through a criminal and travel for blocks, with the great danger that some innocent citizen might stop the slug.

What the police need is more "stopping power" rather than more sheer power as it's defined on ballistics charts.

If you read police-department files involving gunfights you will agree that there have been too many times that the .38 Special has proved inadequate. A New York officer stabbed to death by a man in whose stomach he'd placed six .38's. Another in New York also stabbed to death with six .38s in his assailant's chest. A Los Angeles officer shot a man eleven times and still had to overpower him by hand. A Kansas City hoodlum killed an officer and shot two citizens after he'd absorbed nine .38s and sixty buckshot!

Another of today's problems is that the criminal can hop in a car and get away. His car becomes a tank as far as the .38 Special is concerned, for many tests have proved the .38 inadequate in penetrating auto bodies. About the only chance an officer has is the remote possibility of knocking out a tire. A more practical solution is the roadblock if it can be set up quickly enough. The cop must stay a few jumps ahead of the crook, and outmoded firepower hardly lets them do it.

THE .41 MAGNUM

At the request of a good many law-enforcement officers, Smith & Wesson and Remington cooperated in a joint development to help answer this problem. Their solution was a new cartridge and a gun to handle it. The cartridge is the .41 Magnum, and it's available in two loadings, one with 210-grain soft lead bullet with a muzzle velocity of 1000 fps, meant for city street use. To the surprise of nearly everyone who fires the .41 for the first time, the .41 is as easy to fire as, if not easier than, the .38. The gun is a 4-inch-barreled S&W Military & Police Model 58 which scales a trifle heavier than the .38 of the same model.

Another load is available for the .41 and is called a Magnum load. It also uses a 210-grain bullet but a softpoint jacketed slug at a muzzle

The first police officer to fire a .41 Magnum was George Carello of the Cranston, R.I., police department. He is shown here firing my .41 in 1964. This is the Model 57 for sporting use, not the police model.

The .41 Magnum "police" load at left features a Keith-style sharp-shoulder lead bullet at a muzzle velocity of 1050 fps. The Magnum load at right features a soft-point jacketed bullet at a muzzle velocity of 1500 fps. (Both figures are from an 8⅜-inch "conventional" barrel without the revolver's cylinder/barrel gap.) The respective figures for a vented barrel are 965 fps and 1300 fps.

velocity of 1500 fps. For police use, this load would be the one for open-country use and against automobile bodies. The load has also been found excellent for sportsmen, since it develops nearly as much killing power as the bigger .44 Magnum with less recoil. Either cartridge may be fired in the same gun.

Interestingly, the first police department to standardize on the .41-caliber sidearm was Amarillo, Texas. Chief Wiley Alexander of that department wanted its adoption widely publicized "to impress upon criminals that Amarillo was going to be an unhealthy place to practice their trade."

The .41 does point up some of the issues involved in introducing something new to police. For example, many forces make their officers buy their own sidearms. New York City is one (all the cop is given in New York is his badge), another is San Antonio, and there are many more. But other towns and cities provide guns—which remain city property. In the case of municipalities where cops buy their own sidearms it's a simple matter to convert to a new caliber. You can tell the men they have a certain time period in which to purchase a new gun, let attrition do the job by only making new officers buy

the new model, or issue orders to make the change immediately.

If the situation is one where the guns are town- or city-owned, however, you have another problem: that of raising the money. And that can be a stumbling block, not only because it's hard to raise money but because the whole issue then becomes a public one in more ways than one and there is stiff resistance at several levels.

It naturally follows that any town or city that switches from the old .38 Special to something like the .41 *Magnum* provides a news item for the local press, which often leads to some citizens and groups asking why the change. And other people and groups begin to talk about how Magnums are for killing poor innocent crooks who really should be slapped on the wrist and certainly shouldn't be shot. They might be hurt that way. Then someone brings up the Geneva Convention (which has nothing whatever to do with law enforcement) and its regulations about "civilized" warfare.

Some of these resistances did pop up when police forces wanted to change to the .41 Magnum. An added factor was that the .41 cost about $20 more (to police) than the .38 Special. But perhaps the biggest single source of resistance was the word "Magnum."

It's a simple enough word. It means large, as in champagne bottles. Its usage in firearms has been imprecise. I believe the first legitimate use of the word was in England and related to rifle cartridges. Holland & Holland, Ltd., of London were surely among the first to popularize the word with their excellent cartridges known as the .300 H&H and .357 H&H Magnums. In revolvers, the .357 Magnum of 1935 was the first, and it was a Smith & Wesson development. This cartridge was highly touted and was claimed capable of driving a bullet through the block of an automobile engine. I never knew anybody who actually tried that stunt, but I guess it was done. It surely was talked about with considerable awe. So the word "Magnum" began to have meaning—power. (It means much less today, since the word has been used to embrace all manner of cartridges, some of which are of enormous power and some of which are not.)

Then came the .44 Magnum, and it also stormed the pistol/revolver world. Here was a gun so mighty it could flatten any of the biggest bears in North America. And it did just that. It also belched fire, smoke, and lead and hit the shooting hand a wallop. It became known that it took a man to handle the .44 Maggie, all of which aided and abetted the mystique of the word "Magnum."

So when the .41 Magnum was introduced in 1964 it carried the Magnum label. Translated to the unknowing that meant the damned gun would rupture your ears and split your hand when fired. It's interesting to read the surprise recorded by police officers—not run-of-the-mill cops but cops with substantial sidearm knowledge—the first time they fire a .41 Magnum. "It's not as bad as I thought." "It doesn't kick much more than a .38." "I can shoot it better than I can my .38." And so on. The point is that there is a myth about the word that seems to unglue anyone unless and until he learns otherwise by actual experience.

My own experience is that the .41 Magnum isn't that bad to shoot. Compared to the .44 it weighs a little more, and that helps soak up recoil. It also has a bit less bark and bite in its own right and is much more pleasant to shoot than the .44. And it is fairly easy to compare the two, since they are available in virtually identical Smith & Wesson revolvers.

I think Smith & Wesson failed to do its marketing homework on this gun if they were after the law-enforcement market, which they were. The gun should not have been called a Magnum. The references to power should have been minimized and the gun's attributes for police use played up instead.

In 1947—ten years after the gun's introduction, the city of San Antonio, Texas, also switched to the .41. A very interesting report has been submitted by Detective Bill McLennan, member of the committee that chose the Smith & Wesson Model 58 and made the recommendation. In a few weeks the city had 400 guns and a supply of ammunition from Remington. According to McLennan, it has been just as easy to train new recruits with the .41 as with the .38, and a number of policewomen were also trained in its use with no problems.

As a matter of fact, I have trained my own daughter in the use of the .41, and, with mild handloads, she has had no trouble. She doesn't like the hot loads, but few police officers would have use for them either.

Most police forces who have investigated the .41 and turned it down have either gone back to the .38 Special or adopted the .357 Magnum. There are several reasons this is a mistake. They have not realized that you train differently for the big-bore than with the .357. They have placed emphasis on scores in combat courses of fire (which are most unlike the usual situations in which a cop has to use his gun). And they offer a variety of reasons, or excuses, why the .41 is not for them: The gun is too heavy, the cost of ammunition is too high, the gun is too bulky, women can't handle it, and so forth. These reasons can be shot down quite easily.

I was interested in the reports of several officers, including San Antonio's Bill McLennan, all of whom appear to be very knowledgeable about guns. They were unanimous in their recommendation and enthusiasm for the .41 revolver. It is equally interesting to note that there is a lot of condemnation from other sources.

RELATIVE STOPPING POWER

One of the main areas of chatter is over what the law enforcement really needs in a sidearm. All agree it is something called "stopping power." This isn't killing power, it is the power to *stop* an assailant. Consider that the cop is usually required to give the assailant the first shot. This means the assailant is in position to fire again if necessary. The cop, assuming he's still operative, must respond with a telling blow that will render his assailant incapable of firing another shot, wielding a knife, or whatever. To define the differences between stopping and killing power, you can kill a man with a .22 Short. If he dies, the gun had killing power by simple definition. On the other hand, you would never expect the .22 Short to stop a man bent on killing you. At the other end of the range, the .45 Automatic is an excellent stopper because a hit almost anywhere in the body will slap a man to the ground.

The late Gen. Julian Hatcher, one of the most astute pistol and revolver experts I've ever known, devised a formula many years ago for evaluating what he called "relative stopping power." Note that the term is "relative"—which simply means that a factor of 50 has half the stopping power of a factor of 100. It doesn't say that a given factor will stop a man under certain conditions. No chart or set of rules could ever do that. There are vast variations in the effect of a shot on a person. If an assailant is hopped up on dope, or even adrenalin, his reaction will be different from that of a person who is relatively relaxed.

Hatcher's formula was first proposed in the mid-1930s in his *Textbook of Pistols and Revolvers* (Small Arms Technical Publishing Co., 1935). In it he refers to tests made in 1904 by two army colonels, John T. Thompson (also the inventor of the Thompson submachine gun) and Louis A. La Garde.

Hatcher used a rather complicated method of arriving at his figures, and the significant factor in his computations is that he used "momentum" (obtained by dividing the energy by the velocity), which was then multiplied by the sectional area of the bullet in square inches and by the "shape factor," which is arbitrary. The result is a decimal with three places, and this is converted to a whole number with no change in comparative results.

Interestingly, Hatcher's figures not only agreed with those found in 1904 by Thompson and La Garde but they are still as close to right as we can get. Remember, we're talking about "relative" stopping power, and remember that it's not going to work the same way on every assailant but that it will work on an average.

There have been tests of all kinds to try to fit pistol and revolver performance into one niche or another, but none have come any closer than Hatcher's.

The following chart is taken from McLennan's report and is based on actual velocities obtained at the San Antonio Police Laboratory. Except for the Charter Arms Bulldog, all guns used were Smith & Wesson; model numbers are given. These figures were obtained by using the Hatcher formula for relative stopping power. You may see or may have seen similar charts giving different RSP numbers, but if they were compiled from the Hatcher formula, the numbers will be relative and should conform.

| CALIBER | REVOLVER | | | BULLET | | | | | |
	MODEL	BARREL LENGTH (in.)	WEIGHT (oz.)	TYPE	WEIGHT (gr.)	MUZZLE VELOCITY (fps)	RELATIVE STOPPING POWER (RSP)	RECOIL ENERGY
.38 Special	36	3	21	JSP	90	1052	22.4	2.1
.38 Special	36	3	21	JSP	110	1102	28.7	3.5
.38 Special	36	3	21	JSP	158	818	30.5	4.0
.38 Special	60	2	19	JSP	158	763	28.5	3.4
.38 Special	10	4	34	JSP	110	1195	31.1	2.6
.38 Special	10	4	34	JSP	125	980	28.9	2.2
.38 Special	10	4	34	JSP	158	850	31.8	2.7
.38 Special	19	4	35	JSP	158	799	29.8	2.4
.38 Special	10	4	34	LdRN	158	855	31.9	2.9
.38 Hi-Velocity	10	4	34	Lub.	158	1090	48.5	4.7
.38 Special	10	4	34	LdRN	200	730	32.9	3.0
.357 Magnum	19	4	35	JSP	110	1375	35.8	3.4
.357 Magnum	66	4	35	Lub.	158	1146	51.0	4.9
.41 Police	58	4	41	LdSW	210	947	72.5	5.0
.41 Magnum	58	4	41	JSP	210	1247	84.0	8.6
.44 Special	29	4	43	LdRN	246	657	51.4	3.3
.44 Special	Bulldog	3	19	LdRN	246	658	51.5	7.5
.44 Magnum	29	4	43	JSP	240	1267	120.9	11.7

(Case history shows that a caliber must develop an RSP of 60.0 plus to give 90% effect.)

JSP—Jacketed Soft-Point   LdRN—Lead roundnose   Bulldog—Charter Arms
Lub—Lubaloy   LdSW—Lead semi-wadcutter   Bulldog .44 Special

A very interesting set of figures, but don't go away. We have more figures to show that may dispute some of what you've just read.

The December 1974 FBI Law Enforcement Bulletin contained some information that completely refutes what I've related above. Information used to compile this report was based on ongoing tests made at the Southwestern Institute of Forensic Sciences in Dallas, Texas. The tests consisted of firing bullets into gelatin blocks and measuring the velocity before entering the block and upon exiting the block. Then the figures were used to calculate the kinetic energy transmitted to the block (lost in the block). The theory on which these tests were made was that it was ki-

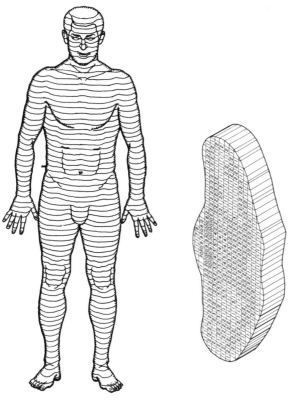

Your tax dollars at work. These sketches are from the U.S. Department of Justice, Law Enforcement Assistance Administration, National Institute of Law Enforcement and Criminal Justice. The object of this detailed study was to evaluate police-handgun ammunition. Shown is their version of "The Computer Man" (which really exists in the computer only) and another sketch indicating the varied values of different target areas. In my opinion, the results of this test, as published in the summary report, are ridiculous and are typical of research in gun matters by theorists with no practical knowledge whatever.

netic energy lost in the target that could be equated with the wounding effect of ammunition. A special gelatin used in such ballistic tests is supposed to roughly approximate flesh.

The results are interesting. And I would quarrel with them. For example, they indicate that the .45 ACP is no more effective than the 9mm, using similar bullets. Then they concluded that the .44 Special is less effective than the .38 Special, and they completely plastered the .41 Magnum with these words: "The semiwadcutter (police) load is inferior in wounding effectiveness to almost all the .357 cartridges, most of the .38 Special hollowpoints, and all the 9mm hollowpoint loadings."

I believe there was something seriously wrong with these tests—whether with the methodology or with the conclusions it is hard to say. But certainly the conclusions are suspect.

After spending many years in the advertising business I know that "research" often starts off with the desired result, then sets up a method to produce that result. This is often done in promotional work—yes, in the firearms field as well as others—for the sake of proving a favorable point for a product. This is not to suggest the above information was obtained in this manner, but rather to advise you that such practices exist.

Another series of tests was made by the National Bureau of Standards for the National Institute of Law Enforcement and Criminal Justice. It is entitled "An Evaluation of Police Handgun Ammunition." In 1973 this division of the Law Enforcement Assistance Administration approved and funded a project to conduct a series of tests of the terminal effects of police handgun ammunition. The study was conducted at Aberdeen Proving Ground, Md., by the U.S. Army Ballistic Research Laboratories.

This group of feds assigned relative values to those parts of the body which, when wounded, would result in "instantaneous incapacitation" (their term for stopping power). These values were encoded in a computer for use in a computerized model of the human anatomy known as "The Computer Man"—the result of several years' work. This "man" consists of brick-shaped sections .2 × .2 × 1 inch in size. Within each of these "volume elements" all tissue types have been identified and encoded.

In this study it was determined that the single feature of the bullet's action most important to relative stopping power was the temporary cavity the bullet generates as it penetrates. Thus the bullet that produces the biggest hole will have the highest RSP. (Had it been known in advance what was to be the most important criterion in this series of tests it would have been simple to design a bullet that would win the tests—in almost any caliber.)

Other factors measured, and factored into the methodology, were velocity, mass, shape, caliber, deformation and construction, shooter accuracy, point of aim, and "hazard to bystanders."

As you might expect, the results vary widely from those obtained by the Hatcher method—though they do run closer to the previously mentioned FBI bulletin than anything else I've seen.

Both reports rate the .45 ACP very low in RSP. One says it's no better than the 9mm, and the other shows the 9mm higher in its rating. And both rate the .41 with lead bullet extremely low on the scale.

I simply cannot accept these findings, either set of them. They fly in the face of all we've known for years about bullet behavior, as well as that learned over the years by experienced police officers. There are legitimate uses for good research, but I think these studies exceed the limits of common sense. One must not forget that if the basic premise is wrong, then the results will also be wrong. It follows the old saying often quoted with regard to computers: "Garbage in, garbage out." You have to program the machines right or they won't give you a responsive answer.

In my opinion, these results are foolish. Their conception and execution and the printing of results by the U.S. Government Printing Office were one hell of a waste of taxpayers' money.

TARGET SHOOTING

Ordinary target shooting is great practice, and it wins lots of medals. But the man who can draw and shoot with reasonable accuracy in the dead dark of night stands a better chance of staying alive than the department's champ on the range. A law-enforcement officer should use the regular range for beginning shooting, but then graduate to the tough combat course—and stay with it. This is the only way he will get confidence in his gun. And the only way he can carry out his duties to the full is by having this confidence.

A man who intends to become a police officer should expect to live with and by his gun for the rest of his life, and learning how to use it should be part of the obligation. If the department won't issue ammunition for training, then it should be the officer's obligation to learn anyway, by lots of dry firing and wax-bullet shooting and as much actual shooting as he can afford. By the same token, I believe the department that is too niggardly to provide ammunition ought to be reorganized.

UNDERCOVER GUNS

The undercover gun is meant for concealment, pure and simple. It should be a combination of as much power as can be contained in the largest package one can conceal. That can vary considerably. A man can carry a pretty big gun concealed in the wintertime with heavy clothes, and a woman can carry anything up to a .44 Magnum in an ordinary purse.

A scaled-down version of the big .45 Colt (top) is known as the Detonics .45. Made by a Seattle firm, the smaller gun can be hidden in a large palm and is meant for pocket use. It also fires seven .45 Auto cartridges without reloading, making it one of the most potent pocket guns going. The gun is also popular for combat-course shooting.

A new cartridge featuring a hollowpoint bullet has been added to the CCI-Speer Lawman line of pistol ammunition. This load, known as the .380 ACP Reserve, is intended to provide expansion with its 88-grain bullet at the 1000 fps produced in most pocket autos.

But change the specifications to a golfing outfit, or an evening gown, and you have to shave the gun down accordingly. Many police officers are required to carry their sidearms at all times, while others are not permitted to do so except while on duty. Generally speaking, an off-duty sidearm is a pocket pistol or revolver carried in a belt, shoulder, ankle, brassiere, or other holster.

Regardless of the type of gun, it is basic that the law-enforcement officer, man or woman,

become completely proficient and completely comfortable with his sidearm or sidearms. He must be ready at any time, just like the bird hunter, to go into action from whatever position he may be in or from whatever direction the assailant may appear. Such action must be entirely a reflex. Ask any bird hunter: He doesn't stop to think but goes into action with a smooth, fluid motion the minute a bird rises. Ask him later what he did and you'll find he wasn't conscious of his action, yet he did everything correctly. It was all done by reflex born of constant practice and familiarity.

The cop must live with his gun, because proper training and familiarity can save his life. Police officers who regard their sidearms as a hindrance, as "too heavy" or "hard to shoot," and who shun practice are the cops who have such minor accidents as shooting themselves in the leg, whose guns get stolen, and whose guns may be inoperative when needed most. Such officers are not doing their job. Departments that tolerate such actions need a housecleaning, and local governments that tolerate such departments may also need a change.

INDEX

Aberdeen Proving Ground, 226
Accuracy, 191-201
  "combat" guns, 200-201
  concentric bullets, 200
  definition of, 191
  .45 ACP and, 197-199
  other calibers and cartridges, 199-200
  Pachmayr "signature" system for, 198
  practical accuracy, 201
  .38 Special handgun and, 196-197
  .22 caliber handguns and, 194-196
Accurate Rifle, The (Page), 191
African Rifles and Cartridges (Taylor), 147, 207
Alexander, Chief Wiley, 223
Aluminum, 76
American Rifleman, The, vii, 129, 170, 173, 174
Ammunition, 105-109
  caseless, 109
  Colt and, 119
  European vs. American equivalent, 122
  experimental, 109
  fixed, 4, 6, 106
  history of development, 105-107
  interchangeability of handgun cartridges, 121-122
  KTW, 221
  for law enforcement, 221
  Magnums, 107-108, 212, 220, 222
   definition of, 104
  rifle vs. handgun, 106-107
  shot cartridges, 108-109
  types of, 105
  types for handguns, 112-121
  See also Bullets; Cartridges
Anatomy of Firearms, The (Wallack), 211
Antimony, 143
Appel, Dr. Gerhardt, 75-76
Appel process, 75-76
Autoloader feeding systems, 51-53
Autoloader locking systems, 46-47
  barrel-lug locks, 46-47
  inertia locks, 46
  toggle locks, 47

Autoloading pistols, *see* Pistols, autoloading
Auto-Mag recoil-operated pistol, 36, 44, 46, 124, 129

Bain & Davis, 124
Bakelite, 82
Ball Powder, 136
Ballistic coefficient, 167
Ballistics, *see* Bullets, the flight of
Bangor Punta (conglomerate), 9
Barlow, John H., 177
Barrel, the gun, 71-80
  Bar-Sto, 198
  chambers and headspace, 77
  early methods of making, 71-72
  fastening barrels, 78-79
  Damascus, 71, 72
  laminated, 71-72
  leading, 76-77
  length of, 79-80
  length and velocity, 169-176
   gap, 170, 172
   revolver gas loss, 170-172
   short barrels, 172-174
   Sperbeck's table of comparative ballistics, 175-176
  proofing, 77-78
  recoil compensators, 80
  rifled, 73-74
  rifling systems, 74-76
  steel for, 72
  stub, 71-72
  twist, 71-72
Barrel-lug locks, 46-47
Bar-Sto barrels, 198
Bar-Sto precision machine, 198
Behlert, Austin, 89, 197, 200, 201
Belgium, 215
Benchrest shooter, 151, 158
Berdan primer, 130
Beryllium copper alloy, 63
Biesen (gunsmith), 152
Big-game hunting, 204-205
Black powder, 97-101, 105, 134, 135

Black-powder guns, 8, 13, 97-101
Blank powder, 138
Blowback, 5, 31-32, 38-41
Blue pills, 77
Bluing, 15, 184
Boer War, 117
Bo-Mar, 89
Bonanza screwdrivers, 189
Booth, John Wilkes, 12
Borchardt, Hugo, 5, 34, 119
Bore
  diameter, 152
  sealing of, 153-154
Box magazines, 52
Boxer Rebellion, 41
Boxes, gun, 188
Brass, 127-128
Breech action locking systems, *see* Locking systems, breech action
Breechloading firearms, 4
Broach, 74
Browning, John, 5, 32, 38, 40, 41, 46, 70, 125, 146, 206, 215
Browning, 34, 152, 170, 216
  Auto-5, 31, 64
  Automatic Rifle (BAR), 5
  recoil-operated machine gun (1917), 41
Buehler, Maynard, 94, 95
Bullet's Flight from Powder to Target, The (Mann), 150-151
Bullets, 141-147
  Core-Lokt, 142, 155
  definition of, 141
  diameter of, 143-144
  disintegrating, 142
  dumdum, 104
  the flight of, 149-167
   air resistance, 162-164
   alignment of bullet and bore, 151-152
   balanced bullet, 154-155
   barrel time and total time, 157
   bearing area, 153
   bullet size and bore, 152-153
   cartridge shape, 157
   deformation in the bore, 160-161
   drift, 165

Bullets (*Continued*)
  efficiency, 161-162
  external ballistics, 162
  flight characteristics, 163
  gravity, 164
  loading density, 158
  muzzle blast, 161
  other factors affecting trajectory, 164-167
  recoil, jump and vibration, 158-160
  tip, 166
  twist, 155-156
  velocity and energy, 167
  velocity vs. twist, 157-158
  wind deflection, 166
  yaw, 166
  gas checks, 144
  ignition, 156-157
  jacketed, 142
  Keith-style, 155
  lead, 142-144
  metal-cased, 145-146
  miscellaneous, 146-147
  Omark/Speer, 160, 161
  roundnose solid-jacket, 146
  shapes of, 142
  spherical, 144-145
  three common styles, 142
  .22 bullets, 144
  wadcutter, 155
Buntline, Ned, 14, 79
Buntline Special, 14, 79
Bushnell, Dave, 90
Bushnell Phantom scope, 90, 92
Button trigger, 63

Caliber, definition of, 104
Caliber choice, 205-206
Carbide, 152
Carbines, 36, 117
Carello, George, 222
Cartridge brass, 127
Cartridges
  ammunition types, 112-121
  cases, 127-130
  centerfire, 106, 111-112, 130
  comments on, 125-126
  definition of, 103
  hot Magnum, 15
  interchangeability among, 121-122
    European designations, 122
  names and numbers of, 123
  primers, 130-131
  rimfire, 111-112
  shot, 108-109
  .22 short rimfire, 4
  wildcats, 123-125, 146
  World War II and, 125-126
Case-hardening, 184
Cases, 127-130, 188
  improved, 129
  metallic, 127-129
  shotgun, 129-130
Center, Warren, 27-28
Centerfire ammunition, 104
Centerfire cartridge, 106, 111-112, 130
Centerfire pins, 64
CETME rifle, 48
Champlin, 152

Chapman, Ray, 200
Charcoal, 134
Charter Arms, 15, 120, 225
  firing pin, 63
Checkering, 84
Chronographs, 167
Churchill, Winston, 117
Civil War, 5, 6, 13
Clark (gunsmith), 197
Classic Arms International, 100, 101
Cleaning equipment, 190
Clip magazines, 51-53
Cocking, 7, 16, 33
Coil springs, 67-68
Cold-formed rifling, 75-76
Colt, Sam, 12, 50, 215
Colt Industries, viii, 5, 8-9, 15, 18, 23, 50, 152, 173, 214-217
  Agent pocket revolver, 208
  ammunition, types of, 119
  black-powder revolvers, 98, 99
  Browning machine gun, 40
  Browning's autoloading pistol, 41
  Buntline Special, 14, 79
  commemorative guns, 181-183
  conversion kit, 36, 37
  double-action revolver design, 20-22
  .45 ACP, 50, 64, 77, 125, 146, 197-199, 206
  .45 autoloading revolver, 5, 46-47, 58, 59, 64, 78, 121, 206
  Government Model .45 auto, 32-35
  gun finish, 184
  invention of the revolver, 3-4
  Model 1895 machine gun, 41
  Model P (Peacemaker), 9, 13, 14, 85
  Paterson revolver, 70
  pocket .25 auto pistol, 39
  revolving cylinder, 16
  sights on service revolvers, 88
  single-action revolver design, 17
  single-shot pistol, 25
  .38 Super Colt Auto, 36
  .380 pocket auto, 58, 59
  .25 auto, 59, 67
  value of early models, 5
  World War I and, 125
Colt's Patent Fire Arms Co., 12
Computer Man, The, 226
Connecticut Valley Arms, 99
Copper units of pressure (cup), 156
Cordite, 104, 135, 136, 139
Creep, in a trigger, 62-63
Crimp, 179
Crossman, Captain Edward, 182
Cupro-nickel alloy, 145, 146

Daisy (air-rifle company), 109
  V/L system, 68-69
Damascus barrels, 71, 72
Dan Wesson Company, 152
  custom work, 186
  design, 20-22, 50
  double-action revolver, 66
  revolver barrel, 78, 170
  revolver grip shape, 82-84
Dardick gun, 109, 129
Defense handguns, 8, 208-209
Delayed-blowback locking system, 47-48

Delayed-blowback toggle-type action rifle, 47
Deringer, Cliff, 216
Deringer, Henry, 11-12, 99, 216
Deringer handgun, 4
Derringers, 11, 12, 99, 216
Dervishes, 104
Detonics .45, 227
Deutsche Waffen und Munitionsfabriken (DWM), 5, 178
Dillinger, John, 108
Direct-hammer firing system, 61-62
Disconnectors, 69
Disintegrating bullets, 142
Dixie Gun Works, 97, 98
Double-action autoloading pistol, 37-38, 70
Double-action locking, 44
Double-action revolvers, 4, 13
Double-base powder, 136
Drop test, 30
Dum-Dum (arsenal), 104
Dumdum bullets, 104
DuPont, 27, 43, 134
  IMR powders, 135, 136
  SP 7625 powder, 137
Dynamite, 134

Ear protectors, 189
Earp, Wyatt, 14
Egypt, 28
Ejection, 7, 16, 33, 55-59
Enfield System, 74
England, 78, 104, 125, 139, 223
Engraving, 181-183
Ethan Allen Pepperbox, 100, 101
European ammunition vs. American equivalent, 122
"Evaluation of Police Handgun Ammunition, An," 226-227
Extraction, 7, 16, 33, 55-59

Fabrique Nationale (FN) plant, 5
Fairbanks Morse Company, 9
FBI Law Enforcement Bulletin (December 1974), 226
Federal, 151, 152, 178
Feeding systems, 7, 16, 34, 49-53
  autoloader, 51-53
  definition of, 49
  by hand for single-shot firearms, 49
  revolver, 50-51
Field & Stream, 151
Finishes, 184-185
Firing, 6, 15, 32
Firing pins, 61, 63-65
  fixed, 64
  and hammer, 64
  inertia, 64
  protrusion, 67
  spring-loaded, 64
  supported, 64
Firing systems, 61-70
  the blow and indentation, 65
  caseless experiment, 68-69
  electric ignition, 68
  disconnectors, 69

firing pins, simple, 63-65
firing-pin protrusion, 67
  lubrication, 67
  modern revolver firing systems, 65-67
  open-bolt system, 68
  safeties, 69-70
  springs, 67-68
  the trigger pull, 62
Fixed ammunition, 4, 6, 106
Fixed firing pins, 64
Flintlock, 100, 105, 106
Floating chambers, 36
Flobert, Louis, 106
Flobert rifles, 116
Floyd, Pretty Boy, 108
Franklin, Benjamin, 68
Frizzen, 105, 106
Fulminate of mercury, 106

G-3 automatic rifle, 48
Game loads, shocking power of, 206-208
Garcia (gunsmith), 46
Geneva Convention, 146
George Lawrence Company, 187, 188
Germany, 27, 47, 67, 70, 75, 119, 178
German silver alloy, 145
Gilding metal, 145
Glasses, shooting, 189-190
Goncalo Alves (wood), 82
Goodstal, L. K., 12
Graphite, powdered, 67
Greener, W. W., 68
Grips, 81-85
  materials for, 82
  safeties, 70
  shape of, 82-85
  stag, 82
Groove diameter, 152
Gun blue, 15, 184
Gun Control Law (1968), 215
Gun Digest, 170, 174, 185
Gun Digest Company, 175-176
Gun and Its Development, The
  (Greener), 68
Guncotton, 134
Gunn, William, 19, 120
Guns & Ammo, 204
Gyrojet Rocket, 109

H. P. White Company, 29, 119, 170
Hammer, firing pins and, 64
Hammerli (gunsmith), 46
  target pistols, 27, 68, 195
  .38 Special caliber, 197
Handguns
  custom work for, 185-186
  defense, 8, 208-209
  definition of, vii
  feeding systems for, 49-53
  for law enforcement, 220-222
  makers of, 8-9
  manually operated breech action,
    11-30
  selection of, 209-210
  semiautomatic breech action, 31-41

service, 7
  seven steps of operation, 6-7
  sporting, 7-8, 203-204
  stainless steel for, 15, 184-185, 213-214
  testing, 28-30
  types of, 7-8
  undercover, 227-228
  uses of, 7-8
    defense, 8, 208-209
    sporting, 7-8, 203-204
    target, 7
  World War II and, 8-9, 215
  See also Pistols; Revolvers
Handloading, 177-180
  major equipment for, 179-180
Hangfire, 131
Harbour, Loren, 178
Harrington & Richardson (gunsmith), 8,
    14, 15, 28, 152
  Model 676 revolver, 79, 115
  Model 999 revolver, 88
  revolver barrels, 78
  revolvers, extraction and ejection in,
    57
  top-break guns, 57
Harris, Clint, 178
Harris Machine Company, 178
Hatcher, General Julian S., vii, 147, 170,
    173, 174, 214, 224
Hatcher's formula, 225, 227
Hawken plains rifle, 28, 97
Headspace, 129
Hebard, Gil, 27
Hechler & Koch (firm), 47-48, 75
Hellstrom, Carl, 19
Hercules powder, 136
Herrett, Steve, 83, 84, 124, 147
Herrett handgun stock company, 124
Herrett wildcat, 157
High Standard (gunsmith), 8, 9, 217
  the Crusader revolver, 23, 67
  double-action revolver design, 22-23,
    25
  electric ignition development, 68
  gun finishes, 185
Hills, Fred, 21
Hodgdon, Bruce, 134, 178
Holland & Holland, Ltd., 223
Holsters, 186-187
Home Guard, 78
Hornady, Joyce, 100, 101, 145, 147, 151,
    152, 178, 180
Hornet standard rifle, 157
Horse pistols, 6
Hot Magnum cartridges, 15
Hunting, 204
Huntington, Fred, 178

Ideal Manufacturing Company, 177
India, 104
Inertia firing pins, 64
Inertia locks, 46
Interarms (gun importers), 27, 33, 34, 70,
    125
International Shooting Union (ISU), 7,
    27, 40-41, 68, 205
Investment-casting, 214
Iver Johnson fail-safe system, 65

Jacketed bullets, 142
Jaeger rifle, 5
Japan, 92
Johnson, Iver, 8, 24

Keith, Elmer, 142, 147, 155, 208, 212
Keith-style bullets, 155
Kelly, Machine Gun, 108
Kentucky rifle, 6, 97
Kilbourn, Lyle, 124
Kirkland, Turner, 97
KTW ammunition, 221

La Garde, Louis A., 225
Laminated barrels, 71-72
Lapping, 76
Law enforcement, 219-228
  .41 Magnum, 222-224
  relative stopping power, 224-227
    Hatcher's formula for, 225
  special ammunition for, 221
  special handgun requirements for,
    220-222
  target shooting, 227
  undercover guns, 227-228
Lead bullets, 142-144
Lead units of pressure (lup), 156
Leading, 76
Leaf spring, 67
Lee Custom Engineering, 193
Lee machine rest, 189, 193, 194
Lee Sonic Ear Valves, 189
Leisure Group (conglomerate), 178
Lesmok Powder, 138
Leupold scope, 92, 94, 95, 209
Lincoln, Abraham, 216
Lobo scope, 92
Lock time, 65
Locking, 7, 16, 34, 44
Locking systems, autoloader, *see* Auto-
  loader locking systems
Locking systems, breech action, 43-48
  autoloader locking system, 46-47
    barrel-lug locks, 46-47
    inertia locks, 46
    toggle locks, 47
  delayed-blowback locking systems, 47-
    48
  revolver locking system, 44-45
  single-shot locking systems, 45-46
  turning-bolt system, 44
Locks
  barrel-lug, 46-47
  gun, 188-189
Loctite, 18
Long recoil, 32
Lubrication, 67
Luger, Georg, 34, 119
Luger (Parabellum) pistol, 5, 9, 32-36,
    41, 47, 58, 59, 70, 77, 117, 119, 125,
    127
  firing pin, 64
  loading tool, 51
  .380, 50, 52
Lyman, 124, 177, 178, 180
  gunsights, 98, 99

M1 Garand, 64
Machine guns, 9, 31, 41, 47, 49
McLennan, Detective Bill, 224, 225
Magazines, 51-53, 189
    rotary, 52
    safety, 70
    tubular, 52
Mag-na-porting, 80
Magnums, 107-108, 212, 220, 222
    definition of, 104
Mann, Dr. Franklin W., 150-152, 154, 155, 161, 165-166
Marlin, 26, 152, 177
    Micro-Groove system, 152-153, 160-161
    Model 336 rifle, 62, 70
Marlin-Rockwell machine gun, 9
Martini falling-block action, 46
Mauser, Peter Paul, 44
Mauser Works, 5, 9, 33, 125
    autoloading pistol, 117
    military pistol, 52
    military rifle, 38, 51
Mercury, 143
    fulminate of, 106
Metal-cased bullets, 145-146
Micro (gunsight makers), 89
Miniature Machine Company, 89
Moros, 118, 146
Mother-of-pearl, 82
Muzzleloading, 105

National Bureau of Standards for the National Institute of Law Enforcement and Criminal Justice, 226
National Muzzle Loading Rifle Association, 97
National Rifle Association, 40, 214
Navy Arms, 11, 45, 46, 80
    Rolling-block single-shot pistol, 28
Nelson, Baby Face, 108
Newton, Charles, 75
Nipple, 106
Nitrocellulose, 134-136
Nitroglycerin, 134-136, 139
Nobel, Alfred, 136
Nobel Prizes, 136
Norma (bullet maker), 152
North, Fulton, 147
Norton Company, 189
Nosler (bullet maker), 178
    Partition bullet, 155

Obturation, 153-154
O'Connor, Jack, 211
Oerlikon 20mm automatic cannon, 40
Official Gun Book (Hatcher), 214
Ohio National Guard, 25
Olympic shooters, 27, 40, 46, 68, 92, 205
Omark Industries, 108, 113, 130, 178
Omark/Speer bullets, 160, 161
Ortgies pistols, 59, 67
Outdoor Life, 211

Pachmayr, Frank, 82
Pachmayr Company, 89, 190, 197, 200

"signature" system for accurizing, 198
Pacific Tool Company, 178, 190
Page, Warren, 151, 191
Paris Exposition (1851), 106
Pelouze, Théophile Jules, 134
Pepperboxes, 4, 11, 12
    Ethan Allen, 100, 101
Percussion-cap guns, 106, 131
Petersen, Robert E., 204-205
Petersen Publishing, 204
Philippine Insurrection, 118, 146
Pistols
    autoloader feeding systems, 51-53
    autoloading, 5, 23-24, 31
        barrels, 78
        extraction and ejection in, 58-59
    double-action autoloading, 37-38, 70
    future of, 216-217
    horse, 6
    Ortgies, 59, 67
    single-shot, 25-28
    small pocket automatic, 214-215
    star, 46
    starter's, 14
    See also Handguns
Plains rifle, 6
    Hawken, 28, 97
Plinking, 8, 204, 205
Pocket automatic pistol, small, 214-215
Poly-Choke, 80
Polygonal rifling, 75
Pope, Harry, 80
Potter (gunsmith), 194
Powder
    Ball, 136
    black, 97-101, 105, 134, 135
    blank, 138
    definition of, 104
    double-base, 136
    Lesmok, 138
    propellant, pressure curves for, 156
    Pyrodex, 100, 101, 134
    single-base, 136
    smokeless, 120, 128, 134-138
    See also DuPont; Hercules powder
Powdered graphite, 67
Power, shocking, 206-208
Primary extraction, 55
Primers, 65, 130-131
    definition of, 103-104
    hangfire, 131
    staking, 131
Proofing, 77
Propellant powders, pressure curves for, 156
Pyrodex powder, 100, 101, 134

"Quick and the Dead, The" (O'Connor), 211

Ransom (gunsmith), 194
    machine rest, 192, 194
Recoil, 5
    compensators, 80
    operation, 32
Relative stopping power (RSP), 147, 224-227
    Hatcher's formula for, 225

Reloading, *see* Handloading
Remington Arms Company, Inc., 5, 15, 107, 121, 145, 151, 152, 155, 169, 170, 171, 173, 178, 217, 222, 224
    ammunition, 207, 212
    ballistic laboratory, 159
    Core-Lokt bullet, 142, 155
    Fire Ball, 11, 26, 44, 79, 116, 146
    .41-caliber rimfire derringer, 12
    Mohawk Model 600, 44, 80, 116
    Rider, 80
    rolling-block, 45, 46
    single-shot pistol, 26-28
Remington-Rider rolling-block action, 13
Revolvers
    advantages and disadvantages of, 23-24
    alignment of charge hole and barrel, 16-17
    derringers, 11, 12, 99, 216
    development of, 12-15
        TV and, 13, 18
        World War II and, 13
    double-action, 4, 13
    ejection, 56-58
    extraction, 56-58
    feeding systems, 50-51
    the future of, 216-217
    locking system, 44-45
    modern firing systems, 65-67
    new safety feature for, 24-25
    pepperbox, 4, 11, 12
    popularity of, 215-216
    Schofield, 57
    seven steps of operation, 15-16
    single-action design, 17-19
    See also Handguns
Rider, Joseph, 13, 45
Rifles, 97
    Browning Automatic, 5
    G-3 automatic, 48
    Hornet standard, 157
    Jaeger, 5
    Kentucky, 6, 97
    plains, 6
        Hawken, 28, 97
    Springfield military, 51
Rifling, 73-74, 77
    cold-formed, 75-76
    polygonal, 75
Rimfire ammunition, 105, 130
Rimfire cartridge, 106, 111-112
Rimfire brass, 127
Rimfire firing pins, 63-64
Rock Chuck Bullet Swage (RCBS), 178
Rodman, Colonel, 136
Rotary magazines, 52
Roundnose solid-jacket bullets, 146
Rowe, C. Edward, Jr., 28
Ruger, Bill, viii, 9, 13, 24, 26, 215
Russia, 17, 57, 120
Russian AK 47 Assault Rifle, 48

SAAMI, *see* Sporting Arms and Ammunition Manufacturers' Institute
S. D. Myres Saddle Company, 90
Safariland, 187, 188
Safeties, 69-70
    grip, 70

magazine, 70
  thumb, 70
Saltpeter, 134
San Antonio Police Laboratory, 225
Saturday-night special, 27, 29, 79
Savage Arms, 152, 216
Schofield revolver, 57
Scopes, 90-95
  Bushnell Phantom, 90, 92
  Leupold, 92, 94, 95, 209
  Lobo, 92
  manufacturers of, 92
  recoil problems, 94-95
  terms used, 91-92
Scotland, 134
Screwdrivers, 189
Sealants, 18
Sears, Robert N., 40
Sectional density, 167
Semiautomatic breech actions, 31-41
  blowback operation, 38-41
  gas operation, 41
  short-recoil autos, 32-38
    seven steps of operation, 32-34
Service handguns, 7
Sheep dip, 184
Sheridan, 27
  Knockabout, 217
Shocking power, 206-208
Shooting glasses, 189-190
Short-recoil autos, 32-38
  Colt Government Model .45 auto, 32-37
    seven steps of operation, 32-34
  Luger, 32-36
  Smith & Wesson's Model 39, 36
  variations of, 36-38
Shot cartridges, 108-109
Sierra (bullet maker), 151, 152, 178
Sights, 87-95
  custom-made, 89-90
  scopes, 90-95
    Bushnell Phantom, 90, 92
    Leupold, 92, 94, 95, 209
    Lobo, 92
    manufacturers of, 92
    recoil problems, 94-95
    terms used, 91-92
  on service revolvers, 87-88
  slide-mounted, 88-89
Silencers, 185
Single-action locking, 44
Single-action revolvers, 17-19
Single-base powder, 136
Single-shot locking systems, 45-46
Single-shot pistols, 25-28
Skeet shooting, 203
Small-game hunting, 204
Smith, Horace, 106
Smith & Wesson Company, 4, 8-9, 15, 23, 50, 104, 152, 173, 212, 214-216, 217, 223-225
  ammunition development, 106, 117, 118, 212
  "button" triggers, 63
  double-action revolvers, 19-22, 24-25
  firing pins, 63
  .44 double-action revolver, 19
  .44 Russian cartridge, 17, 57, 120
  gun finish, 184
  heavy-calibered revolver, 14
  machining operations at, 17

Military & Police Model 58, 222
Model 10 .38 Special revolver, 7, 88, 220
Model 29 revolver, 56
Model 39 auto, 36, 51, 58, 59
Model 41 auto pistol, 40-41, 47
Model 52 Master auto pistol, 34
Model 52 revolver, 78
Model 60 Chief's Special, 213-214
Model 66, 82
No. 1 revolver, 12
proof-testing at, 29
revolver barrels, 78
revolver grips, 83
revolvers, extraction and ejection in, 56-57
sights on service revolvers, 88
single-action revolver design, 17-19
single-shot pistol, 26
stainless-steel revolvers, 15, 213-214
Texas Ranger gun, 181, 182
3-shot (half-moon) clips, 50, 125
Triple Lock model, 44
.22 Escort, 79
.22 Jet, 56, 116
.22 Long Rifle Escort, 39, 208
White patent and, 12-13
World War I and, 125
Smokeless powder, 120, 128, 134-138
Snow, Frank, 178
Southwestern Institute of Forensic Sciences, 226
Spanish-American War, 41
Speed loaders, 188
Speer, Ray, 178
Speer, Vernon, 178
Speer (bullet makers), 151, 152, 178, 180, 228
Sperbeck, Warren, 176
Sperbeck's table of comparative ballistics, 175-176
Spherical bullets, 144-145
Spivey, Jim, 178
Sport shooting, 203-204
Sporting Arms and Ammunition Manufacturers' Institute (SAAMI), 73
Sporting handguns, 7-8, 203-204
Springfield military rifle, 51
Spring-loaded firing pins, 64
Stag grips, 82
Stainless steel, 72, 76, 100
Stainless-steel handguns, 15, 184-185, 213-214
Staking, 131
Stands for holding muzzleloading revolvers, 190
Star pistol, 46
Starter's pistol, 14
Stoeger, A. F., 8, 9, 34
Stub barrels, 71-72
Sturm, Ruger & Co., viii, 9, 13, 15, 21-22, 45, 64, 115, 119, 214-216
  double-action revolver, 21-22, 51
  extractor system, 56
  Old Army percussion revolver, 100
  revolver grips, 83
  sights on service revolvers, 88
  single-action revolver, 19, 25, 66
  single-shot pistol, 26
  stainless-steel revolvers, 214
  standard auto pistol magazine, 52
  Standard Model .22 auto pistol, 39

Super Blackhawk, 209
.22 Standard, 205
Sulfur, 134
Supported firing pins, 64
Swebilius, A. W., 9
Switzerland, 40, 68, 195, 197
Swivel, 68

Target guns, 7
Target hammers, 190
Target shooting, 203
Target triggers, 190
Taylor, John, 147, 207
Television, 13, 18, 121
Textbook of Pistols and Revolvers (Hatcher), vii, 225
Thompson, John T., 225
Thompson, Ken, 28
Thompson/Center, 26
  Contender, 11, 27-28, 43, 45-46, 56, 77, 80, 129, 157, 209, 210
  Hot Shots, 108, 109
  Insta-Sight, 93-94, 217
  revolver barrel, 79
Thumb safety, 70
Tin, 143
Toggle locks, 47
Top-break guns, 57
Townsend, Colonel, 152
Transfer-bar system, 25, 65-67
Trap shooting, 203
Trigger shoes, 190
Trounds, 109, 129
Tubular magazines, 52
Turning-bolt system, 44
.22 short rimfire cartridge, 4
Twist, 74, 155-156
  velocity vs., 157-158
Twist barrels, 71-72

Undercover handguns, 227-228
Union Metallic Cartridge Company, 145
U.S. Army, 17
U.S. Army Ballistic Research Laboratories, 226
U.S. Cavalry, 17, 57
U.S. Department of Justice, 226
U.S. Navy, 41
U.S. Revolver Association (USRA), 8
Unlocking, 6-7, 15-16, 32-33

Varmint hunting, 204
Velocity, twist vs., 157-158
Vieille, Paul Marie, 135
V-spring, 67

Wadcutter bullet, 155
Walther, 9, 27
  GSP Match Pistol, 39
  P-38 double-action auto pistol, 70
  police model double-action auto pistol, 70
  PP double-action autoloading pistol, 37

Walther (*Continued*)
    PPK double-action autoloading pistol, 37
Warren, John, 181
Weatherby, Roy, 129
Weatherby Magnum, 129
Webley (gunsmith), 9, 125
Webley-Fosbery automatic revolver, 9, 38
Wesson, Major Daniel, 15, 20-21, 24, 106, 108
Western Cartridge Company, 136
Wheellock, 105
White, Alvin, 181
White, Henry P., 29

White, Rollin, 4, 12-13, 106
    patent of, Smith & Wesson and, 12-13
Whitney, Eli, 4-5
Wildcat cartridge, 123-125, 146
Williams, David W., 36-37
Winchester Company, 5, 136, 151, 152, 169, 173, 178, 215
    ammunition, types of, 113-119
    Ball Powder 785, 135
    blowback rifles, 38-39
    cold-forming barrels, 76
    gas-operation rifles, 41
    gun finish, 184
    Magnum Rimfire (WMR), 24
    Model 94 rifle, 62-64, 70, 90, 93

Silvertip bullet, 142, 155
.220 Swift rifle, 15
Winchester-Western, *see* Winchester Company
World War I, 50, 117, 120, 125, 146
    Colt and, 125
    Smith & Wesson and, 125
World War II, 5, 13, 19, 35, 36, 48, 70, 75, 78, 117, 119, 165, 184, 214
    brass and, 128
    cartridges and, 125-126
    handguns and, 8-9, 215
    the revolver and, 13
    sporting ammunition and, 177-178
Wotkyns, Grove, 123